AVENGERS K
THE ADVENT OF ULTRON

Original comics written by SEAN McKEEVER, ROBERTO AGUIRRE-SACASA, and ROY THOMAS;
and illustrated by MIRCO PIERFEDERICI, STEPHANIE HANS, and JOHN BUSCEMA

Editor SARAH BRUNSTAD
Manager, Licensed Publishing JEFF REINGOLD
VP, Brand Management & Development, Asia C.B. CEBULSKI
VP, Production & Special Projects JEFF YOUNGQUIST
SVP Print, Sales & Marketing DAVID GABRIEL
Associate Manager, Digital Assets JOE HOCHSTEIN
Associate Managing Editor ALEX STARBUCK
Senior Editor, Special Projects JENNIFER GRÜNWALD
Editor, Special Projects MARK D. BEAZLEY
Book Designer: ADAM DEL RE

Editor In Chief AXEL ALONSO
Chief Creative Officer JOE QUESADA
Publisher DAN BUCKLEY
Executive Producer ALAN FINE

AVENGERS K BOOK 2: THE ADVENT OF ULTRON. First printing 2016. ISBN# 978-1-302-90102-8. Published by MARVEL WORLDWIDE, INC., a subsidiary of MARVEL ENTERTAINMENT, LLC. OFFICE OF PUBLICATION: 135 West 50th Street, New York, NY 10020. Copyright © 2016 MARVEL No similarity between any of the names, characters, persons, and/or institutions in this magazine with those of any living or dead person or institution is intended, and any such similarity which may exist is purely coincidental. Printed in the U.S.A. ALAN FINE, President, Marvel Entertainment; DAN BUCKLEY, President, TV, Publishing & Brand Management, JOE QUESADA, Chief Creative Officer; TOM BREVOORT, SVP of Publishing; DAVID BOGART, SVP of Business Affairs & Operations, Publishing & Partnership; C.B. CEBULSKI, VP of Brand Management & Development, Asia; DAVID GABRIEL, SVP of Sales & Marketing, Publishing; JEFF YOUNGQUIST, VP of Production & Special Projects; DAN CARR, Executive Director of Publishing Technology; ALEX MORALES, Director of Publishing Operations; SUSAN CRESPI, Production Manager; STAN LEE, Chairman Emeritus. For information regarding advertising in Marvel Comics or on Marvel.com, please contact Vit DeBellis, Integrated Sales Manager, at vdebellis@marvel.com. For Marvel subscription inquiries, please call 888-511-5480. Manufactured between 6/17/2016 and 7/25/2016 by R.R. Donnelley, INC., SALEM, VA, USA.
10 9 8 7 6 5 4 3 2 1

AVENGERS K
THE ADVENT OF ULTRON

JIM ZUB
SCRIPT

WOO BIN CHOI with **JAE SUNG LEE**
PENCILS

MIN JU LEE
INKS

JAE WOONG LEE
COLORS

VC's CORY PETIT
LETTERS

WOO BIN CHOI with **JAE SUNG LEE,
MIN JU LEE** & **JAE WOONG LEE**
COVER ART

AVENGERS VS. ULTRON is adapted from AVENGERS ORIGINS: SCARLET WITCH & QUICKSILVER #1,
AVENGERS ORIGINS: ANT-MAN & THE WASP #1, and AVENGERS (1963) #57.
Adaptations written by SI YEON PARK and translated by JI EUN PARK

AVENGERS created by STAN LEE & JACK KIRBY

AVENGERS ACTIVE ROSTER

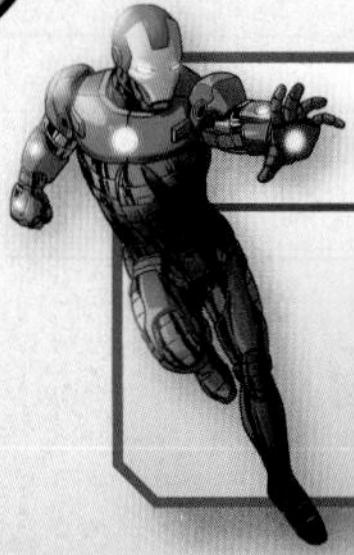

IRON MAN | Real Name: ANTHONY EDWARD STARK

Billionaire playboy and genius industrialist Tony Stark was kidnapped during a routine weapons test. His captors attempted to force him to build a weapon of mass destruction. Instead, he created a powerful suit of armor that saved his life. From that day on, he has used the suit to protect the world as the invincible Avenger Iron Man.

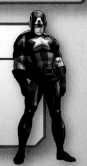

Real Name: STEVEN ROGERS | CAPTAIN AMERICA

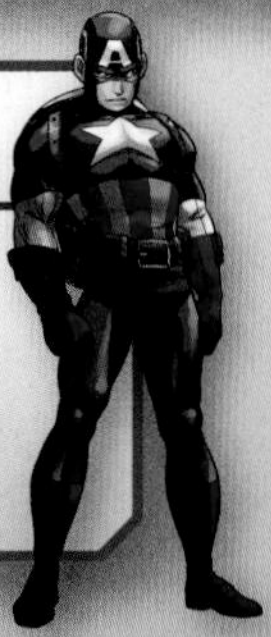

During World War II, a secret military experiment turned scrawny Steve Rogers into America's first Super-Soldier, Captain America. Near the end of the war, Rogers was presumed dead in an explosion over the English Channel. Decades later, Cap was found frozen in ice and was revived. Steve Rogers awakened to a world he never imagined—a man out of time. He again took up the mantle of Captain America, defending the United States and the world from threats of all kinds.

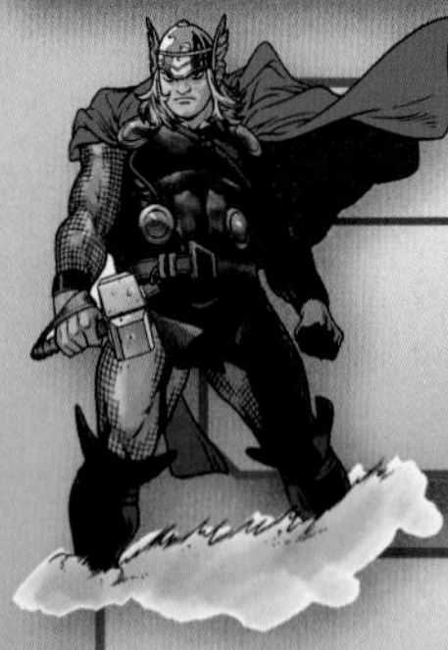

THOR | Real Name: THOR ODINSON

Thor is the Asgardian God of Thunder and an Avenger. Wielding Mjolnir, a mystical uru hammer of immense power, the son of Odin fights to protect Earth and all the Nine Realms.

Real Name: ROBERT BRUCE BANNER | HULK

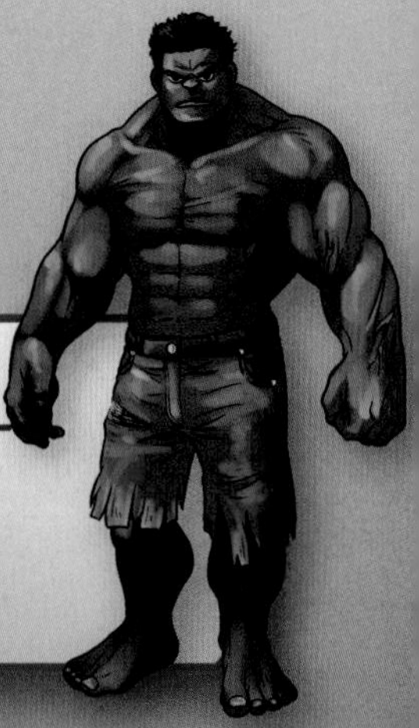

Bruce Banner was a brilliant scientist working for the Army when he was caught in the explosion of a gamma bomb of his own creation and transformed into the nearly indestructible Hulk. Now, Dr. Banner struggles to control his anger and anxiety to keep the Hulk in check while he fights alongside the Avengers.

HAWKEYE
Real Name: CLINT BARTON

Former criminal Clint Barton used his circus training to become the greatest sharpshooter the world has ever seen. He reformed and joined the Avengers, quickly becoming one of the team's most stalwart members.

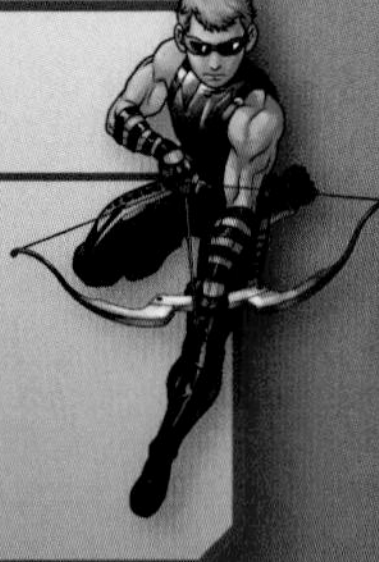

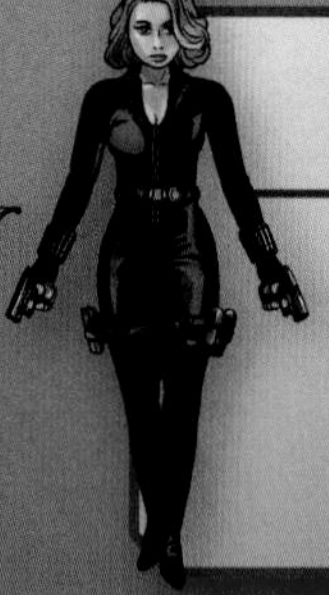

BLACK WIDOW
Real Name: NATASHA ROMANOFF

Natalia Romanoff is a deadly operative equipped with state-of-the-art weaponry and extensive hand-to-hand combat training. Before joining S.H.I.E.L.D. and the Avengers, she was an enemy spy; now, she uses her unique skills to atone for her past.

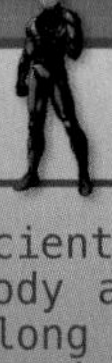

ANT-MAN | Real Name: HANK PYM

Scientific genius Henry "Hank" Pym invented a serum that could change the size of his body at will, and a helmet that allowed him to communicate with and control insects. Along with his partner, the Wasp, he helped found the Avengers and rescue Captain America. But in a stroke of arrogance, he accidentally created his own worst enemy and one of the Avengers' deadliest villains: the artificial intelligence known as Ultron.

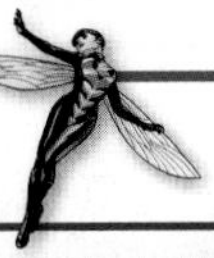

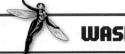

WASP | Real Name: JANET VAN DYNE

Janet Van Dyne was a flighty socialite until she met brilliant biochemist Hank Pym. When Hank shared his size-altering Pym Particles with her, she gained not only the ability to manipulate her size, but also bioelectric stings and wings that manifest when she shrinks to insect-size. Calling herself the Wasp, Janet soon helped form the Avengers.

Real Names: PIETRO & WANDA MAXIMOFF | QUICKSILVER & SCARLET WITCH

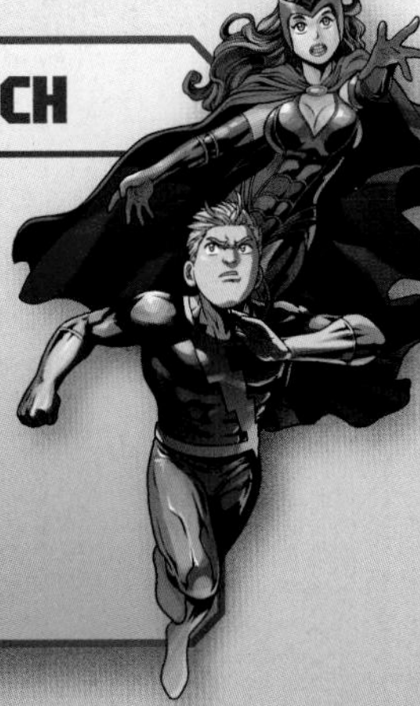

Twins Pietro and Wanda Maximoff were normal children kidnapped by the High Evolutionary, who experimented on them. As a result, Pietro gained the ability to travel at extremely high speeds, able to run across the entire Earth in a matter of minutes; and Wanda gained the ability to manipulate chaos magic. When the twins failed to fulfill his expectations, the High Evolutionary returned them to the Maximoffs, who mistakenly believed they were mutants. When their parents died, Wanda and Pietro came to believe that Magneto was their true father, and had only left them in the Maximoff's charge. After discovering their true parentage, the twins have gone on separate missions: Wanda now travels the globe, helping those in need; and Quicksilver struggles to find a place among the Avengers and X-Men while caring for his teenage daughter, the Inhuman Luna.

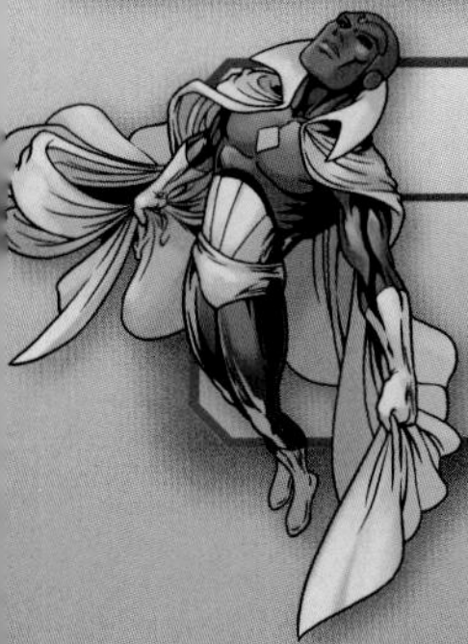

VISION

The Vision is a synthezoid—an android composed of synthetic human blood and organs with the power to control his own density and absorb or emit high-powered heat rays from the gem on his forehead. He was created by Ultron to destroy the Avengers, but instead turned on his "father." He's been a member of the super-hero team ever since.

AVENGERS MOST WANTED:

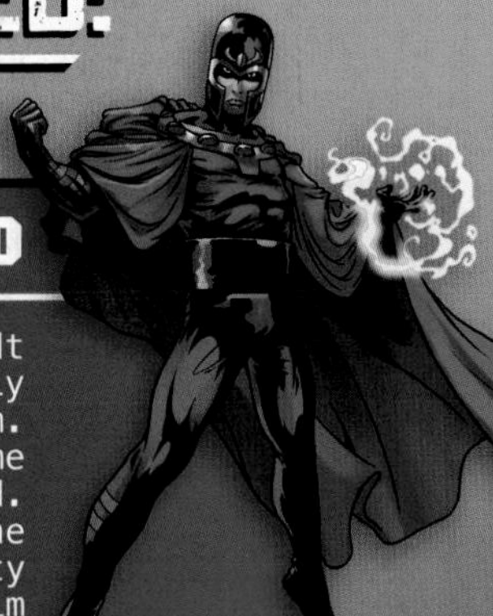

Real Name: MAX EISENHARDT | MAGNETO

Born in Germany during Hitler's persecution of the Jews, Max Eisenhardt witnessed the murder of his parents in an internment camp and barely managed to escape thanks to his mutant ability to control magnetism. Max eventually befriended fellow mutant Charles Xavier, but the two came to disagree on how mutants should fulfill their destiny in the world. Believing that mutants have an inborn right to rule, Magneto formed the Brotherhood of Evil Mutants and devoted his life to punishing humanity for its abuse and neglect of mutants. His iconic helmet protects him from mental invasion, a precaution against Xavier's mutant abilities.

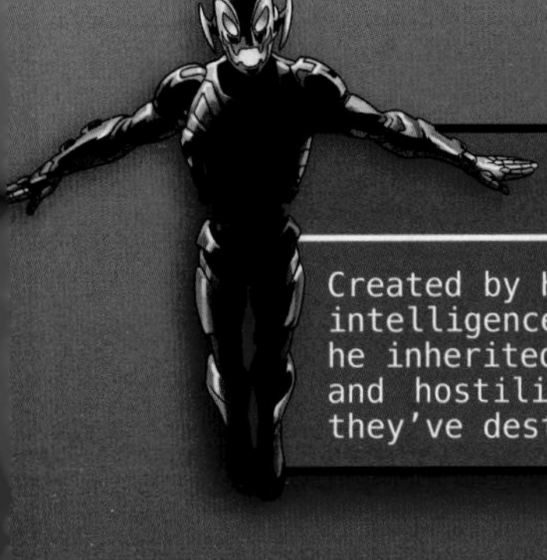

ULTRON

Created by Hank Pym during a period of mental instability, Ultron is an artificial intelligence that has become a powerful foe of the Avengers. During his creation, he inherited Hank's imperfect mental state; that flaw manifested in Ultron as anger and hostility toward human life. No matter how many times the Avengers think they've destroyed him, he always manages to return.

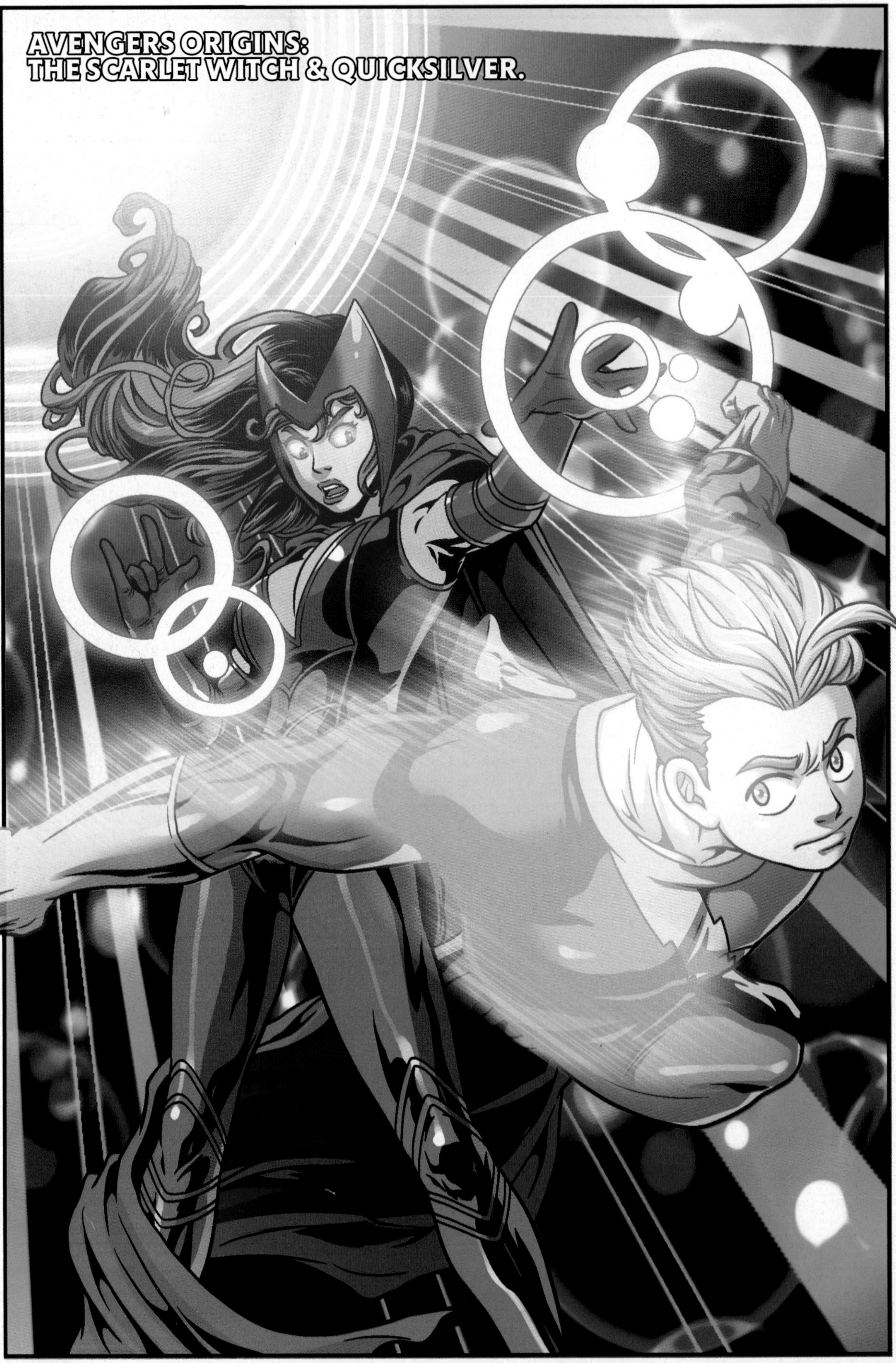
AVENGERS ORIGINS:
THE SCARLET WITCH & QUICKSILVER.

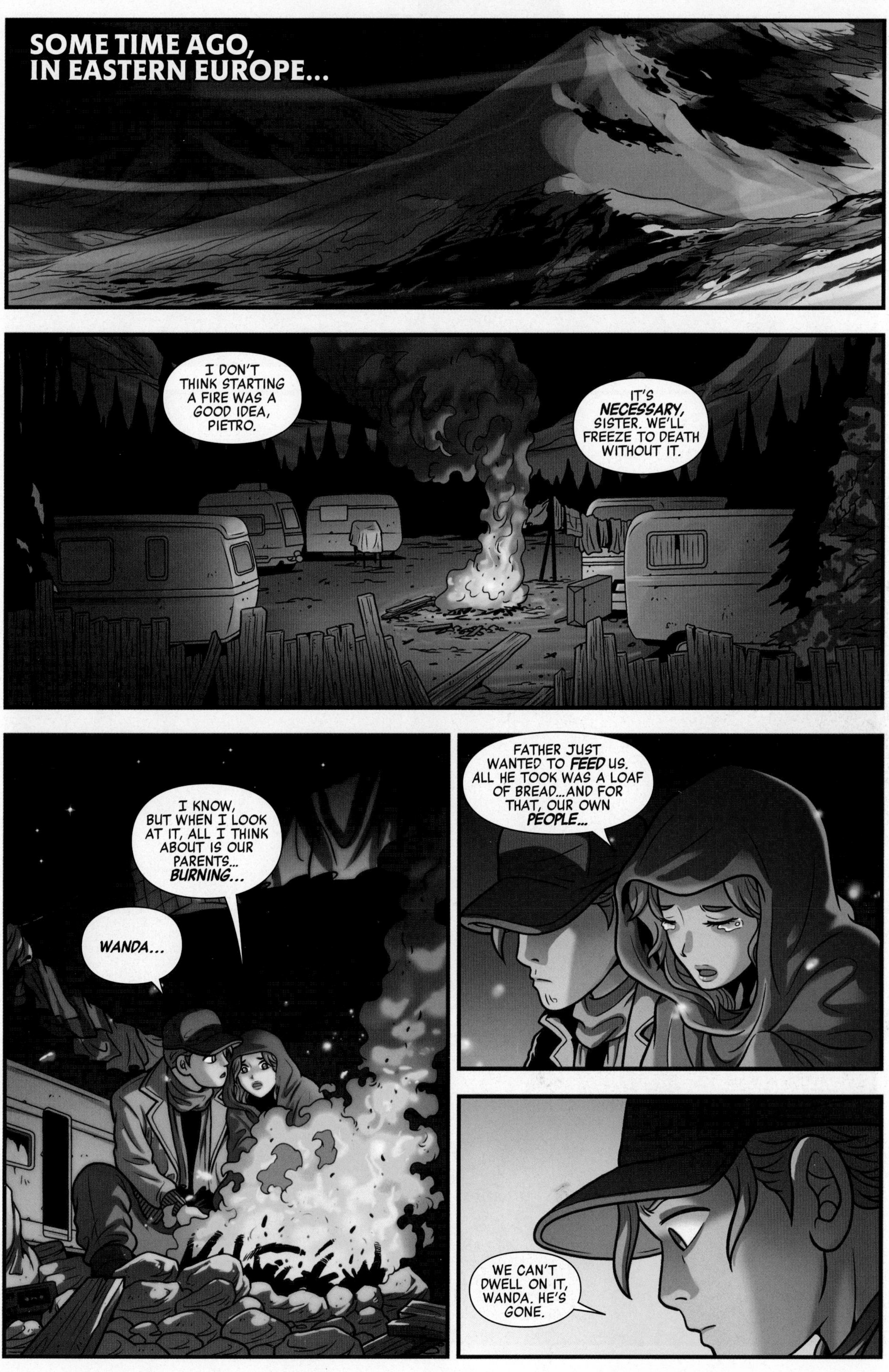
SOME TIME AGO, IN EASTERN EUROPE...
I DON'T THINK STARTING A FIRE WAS A GOOD IDEA, PIETRO.
IT'S NECESSARY, SISTER. WE'LL FREEZE TO DEATH WITHOUT IT.
I KNOW, BUT WHEN I LOOK AT IT, ALL I THINK ABOUT IS OUR PARENTS... BURNING...
WANDA...
FATHER JUST WANTED TO FEED US. ALL HE TOOK WAS A LOAF OF BREAD...AND FOR THAT, OUR OWN PEOPLE...
WE CAN'T DWELL ON IT, WANDA. HE'S GONE.

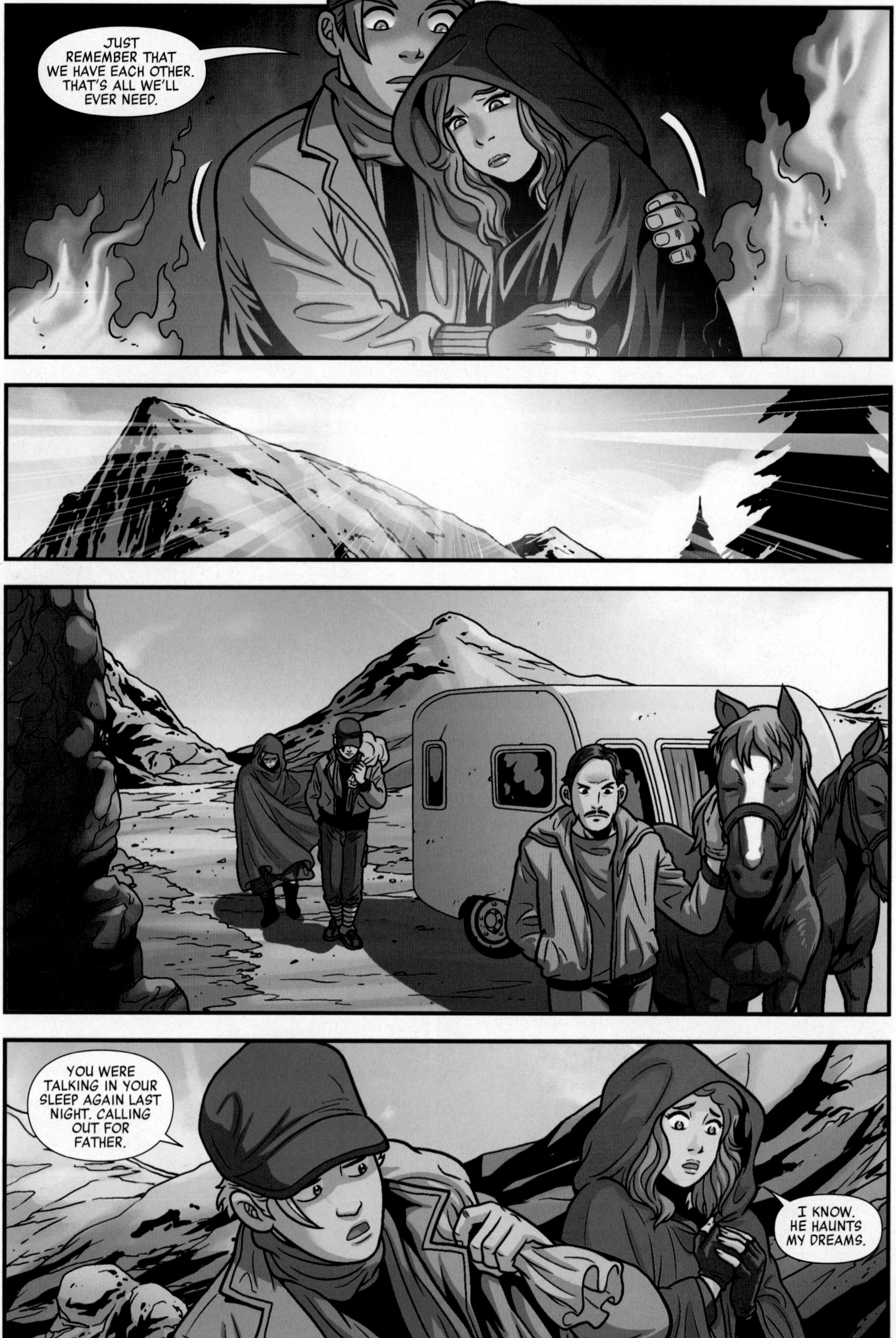
JUST REMEMBER THAT WE HAVE EACH OTHER. THAT'S ALL WE'LL EVER NEED.
YOU WERE TALKING IN YOUR SLEEP AGAIN LAST NIGHT. CALLING OUT FOR FATHER.
I KNOW. HE HAUNTS MY DREAMS.

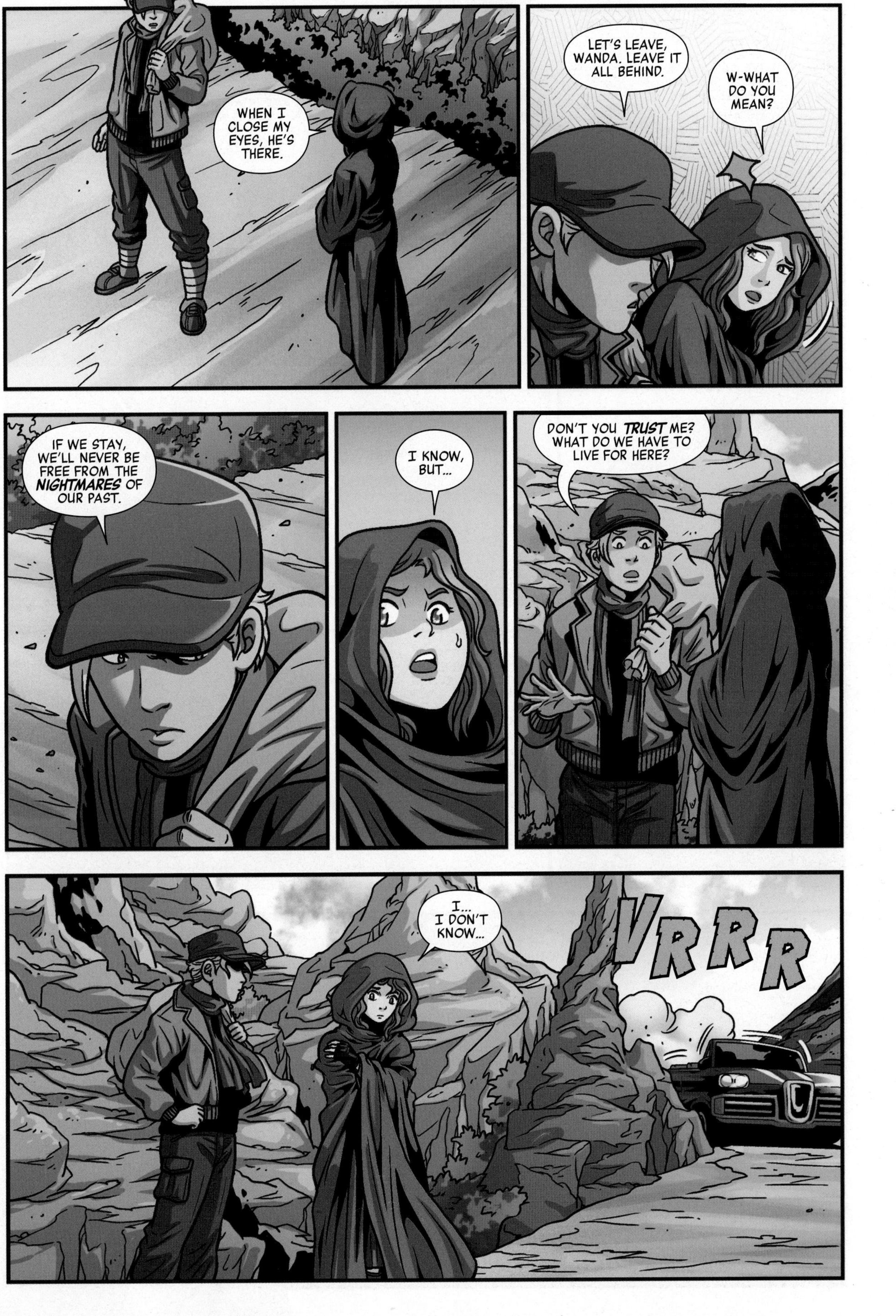
WHEN I CLOSE MY EYES, HE'S THERE.
LET'S LEAVE, WANDA. LEAVE IT ALL BEHIND.
W-WHAT DO YOU MEAN?
IF WE STAY, WE'LL NEVER BE FREE FROM THE NIGHTMARES OF OUR PAST.
I KNOW, BUT...
DON'T YOU TRUST ME? WHAT DO WE HAVE TO LIVE FOR HERE?
I... I DON'T KNOW...
VRRR

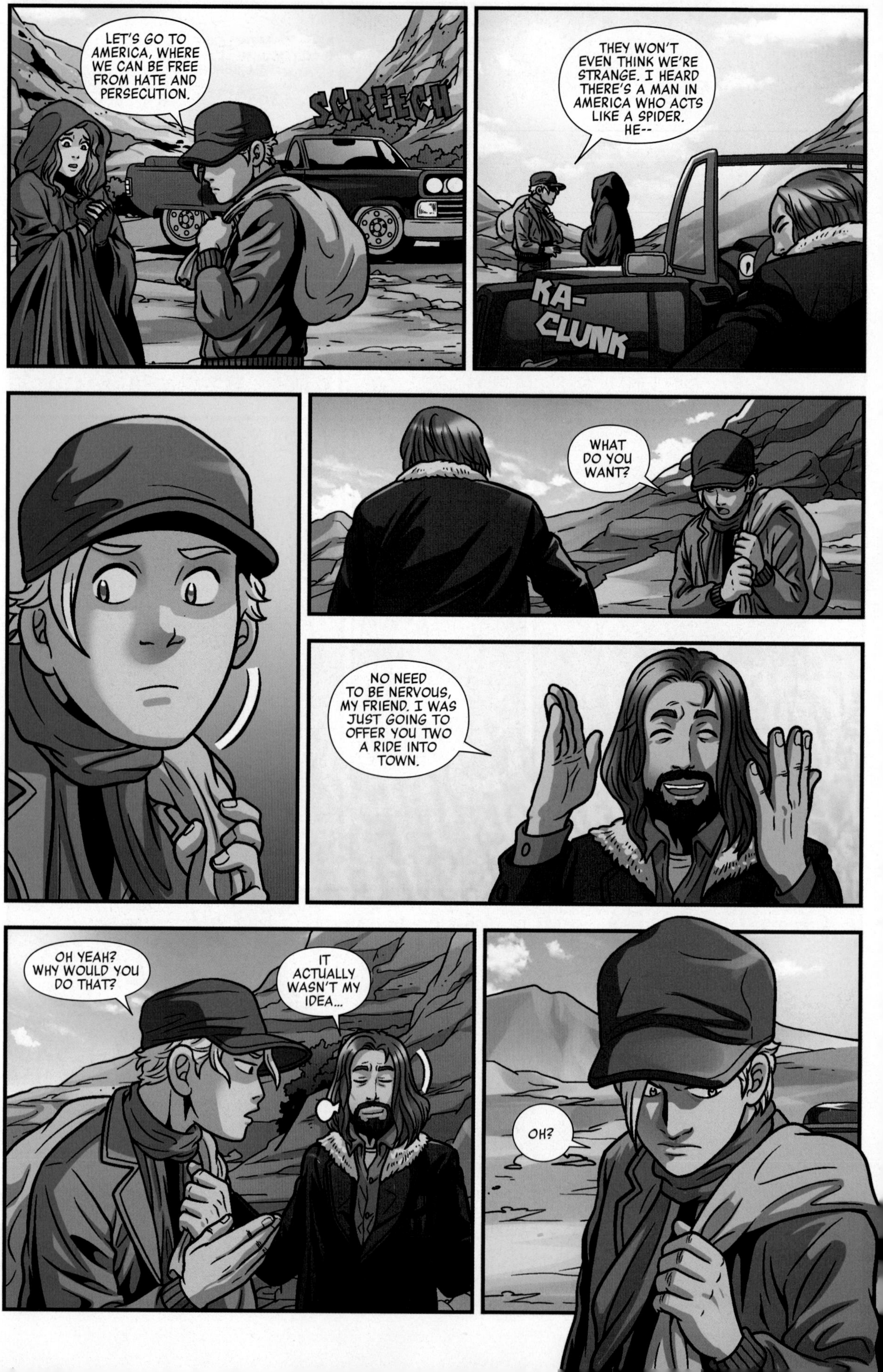

LET'S GO TO AMERICA, WHERE WE CAN BE FREE FROM HATE AND PERSECUTION.
SCREECH
THEY WON'T EVEN THINK WE'RE STRANGE. I HEARD THERE'S A MAN IN AMERICA WHO ACTS LIKE A SPIDER. HE--
KA-CLUNK
WHAT DO YOU WANT?
NO NEED TO BE NERVOUS, MY FRIEND. I WAS JUST GOING TO OFFER YOU TWO A RIDE INTO TOWN.
OH YEAH? WHY WOULD YOU DO THAT?
IT ACTUALLY WASN'T MY IDEA...
OH?

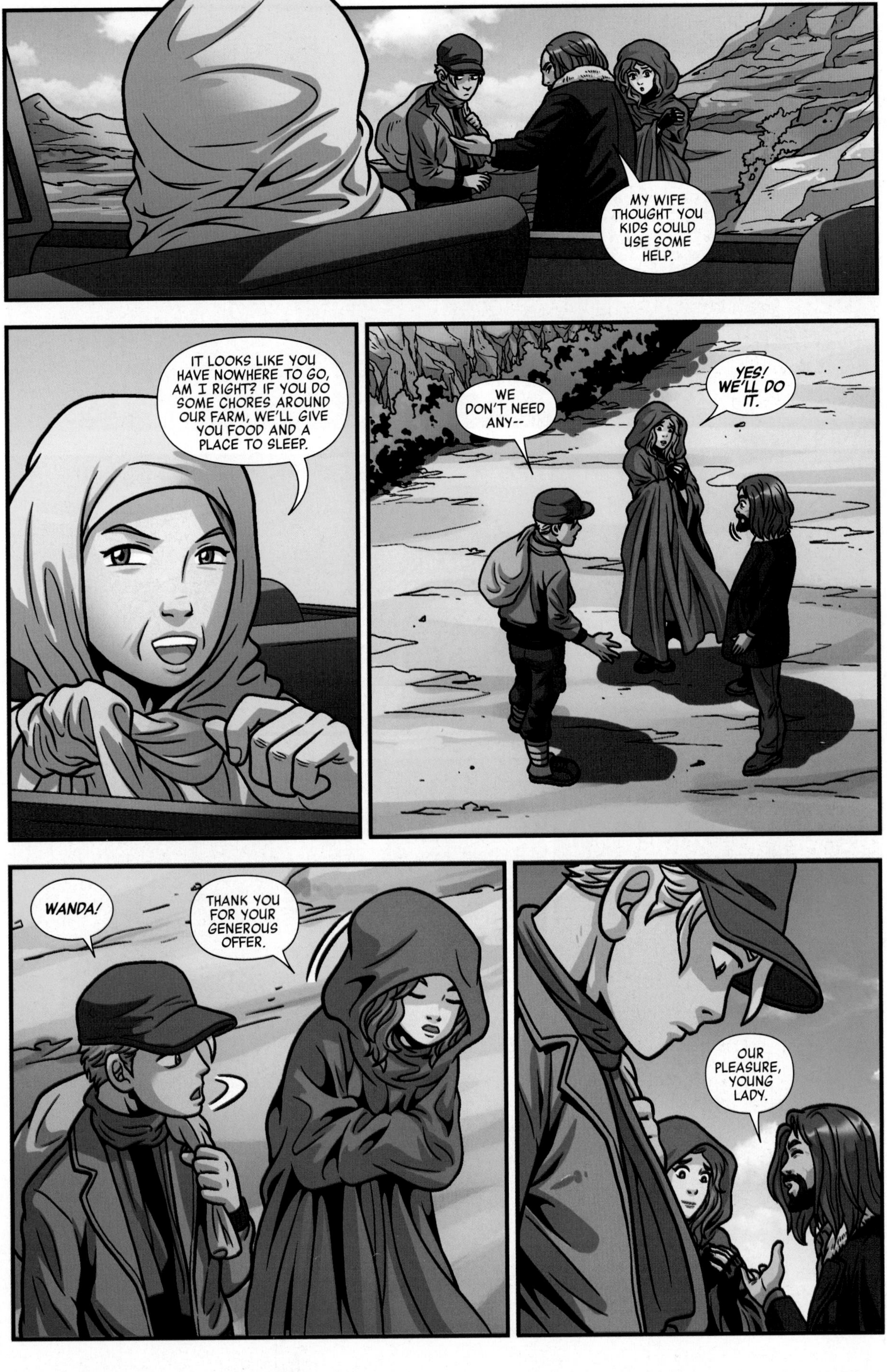
MY WIFE THOUGHT YOU KIDS COULD USE SOME HELP.
IT LOOKS LIKE YOU HAVE NOWHERE TO GO, AM I RIGHT? IF YOU DO SOME CHORES AROUND OUR FARM, WE'LL GIVE YOU FOOD AND A PLACE TO SLEEP.
WE DON'T NEED ANY--
YES! WE'LL DO IT.
WANDA!
THANK YOU FOR YOUR GENEROUS OFFER.
OUR PLEASURE, YOUNG LADY.

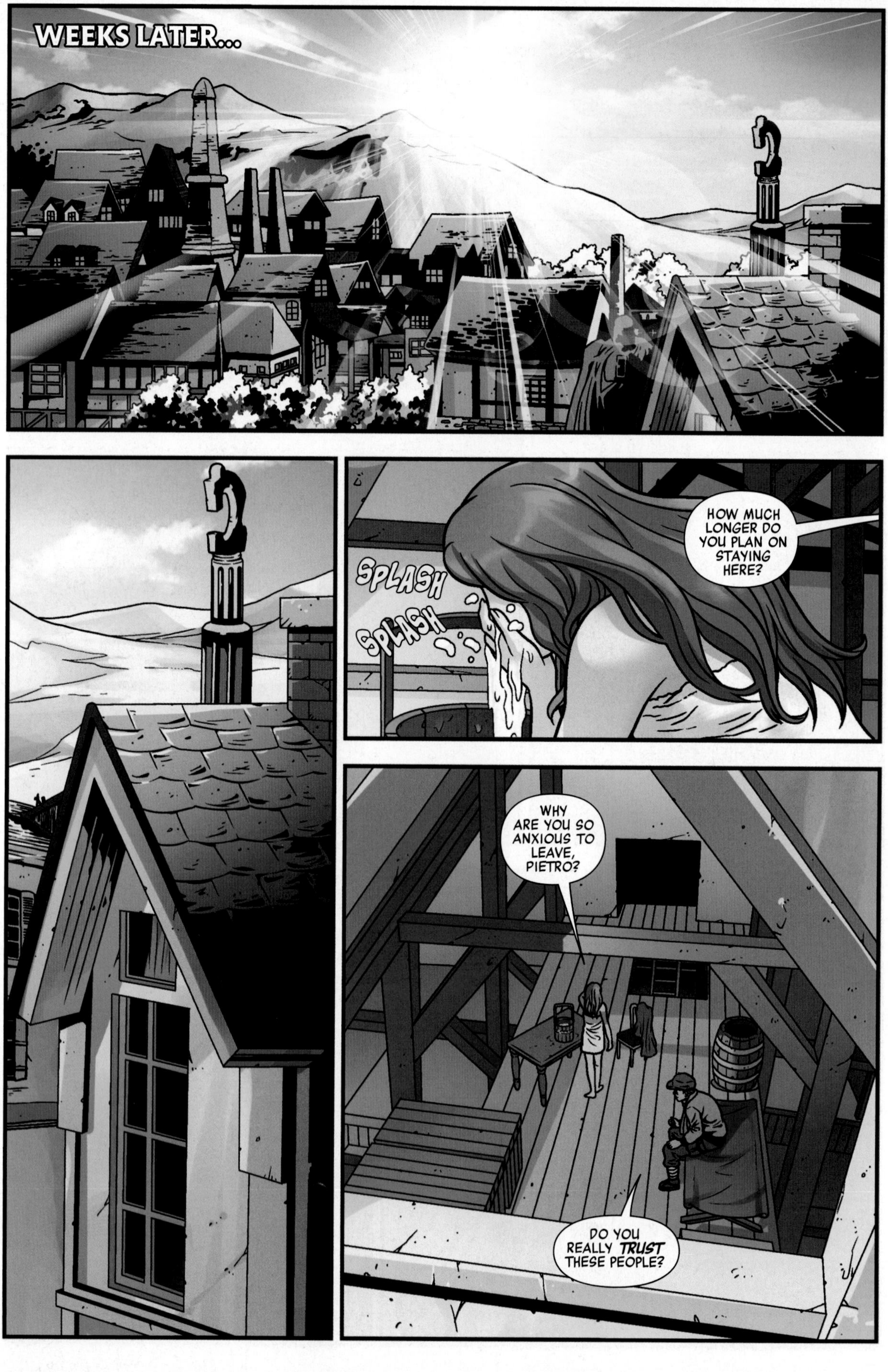
WEEKS LATER...
SPLASH
SPLASH
HOW MUCH LONGER DO YOU PLAN ON STAYING HERE?
WHY ARE YOU SO ANXIOUS TO LEAVE, PIETRO?
DO YOU REALLY TRUST THESE PEOPLE?

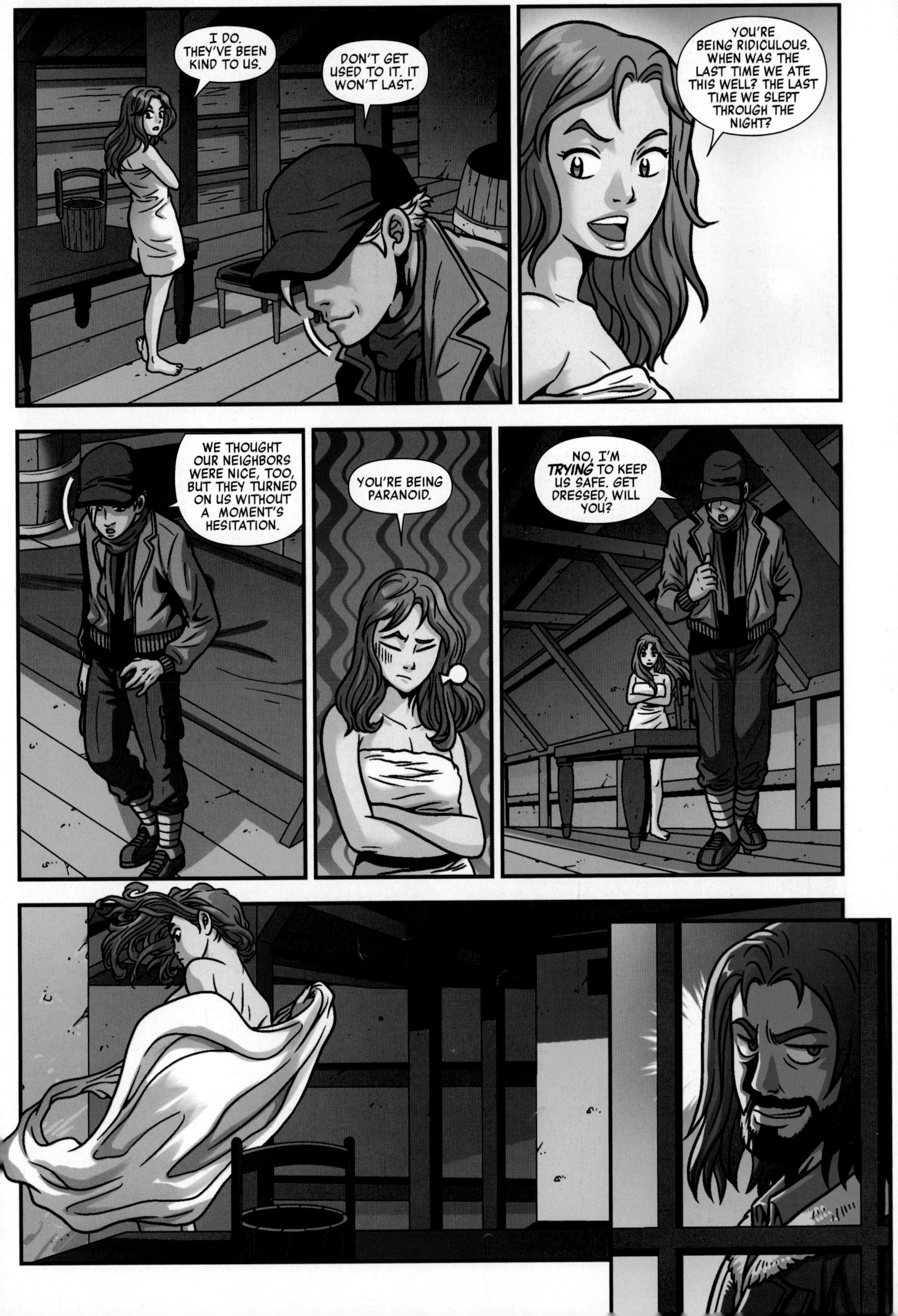
I DO. THEY'VE BEEN KIND TO US.
DON'T GET USED TO IT. IT WON'T LAST.
YOU'RE BEING RIDICULOUS. WHEN WAS THE LAST TIME WE ATE THIS WELL? THE LAST TIME WE SLEPT THROUGH THE NIGHT?
WE THOUGHT OUR NEIGHBORS WERE NICE, TOO, BUT THEY TURNED ON US WITHOUT A MOMENT'S HESITATION.
YOU'RE BEING PARANOID.
NO, I'M *TRYING* TO KEEP US SAFE. GET DRESSED, WILL YOU?

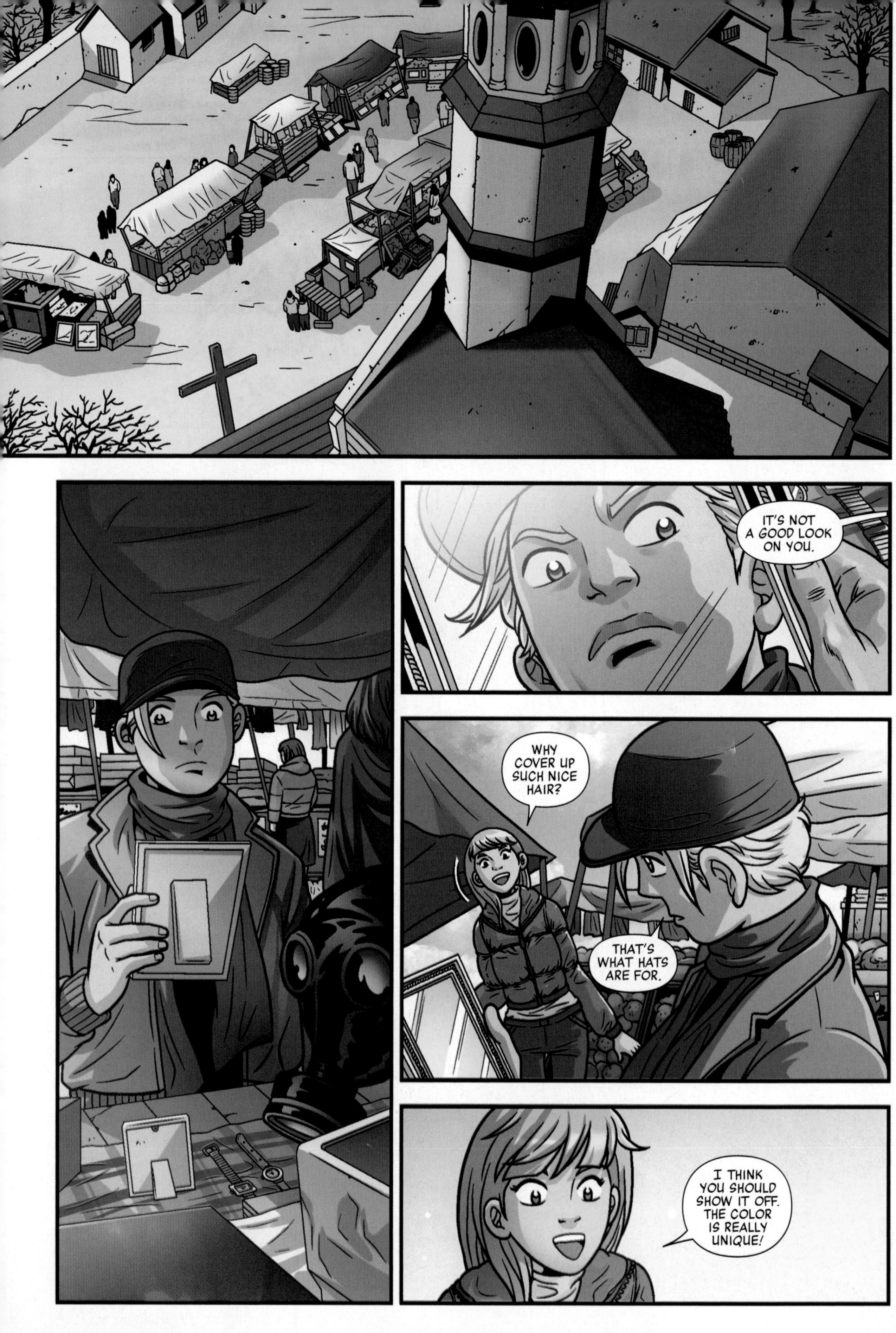
IT'S NOT A GOOD LOOK ON YOU.
WHY COVER UP SUCH NICE HAIR?
THAT'S WHAT HATS ARE FOR.
I THINK YOU SHOULD SHOW IT OFF. THE COLOR IS REALLY UNIQUE!

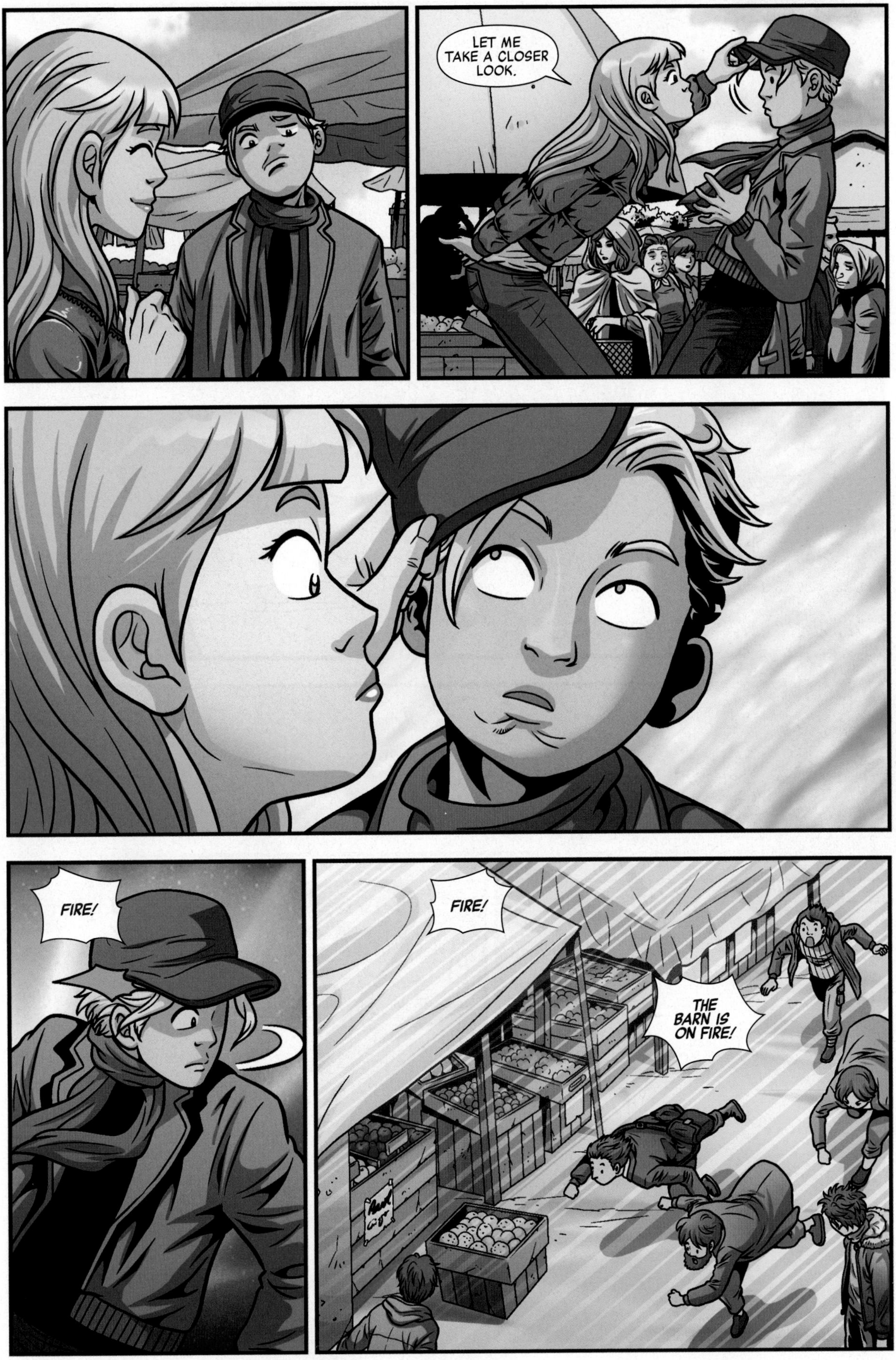
LET ME TAKE A CLOSER LOOK.
FIRE!
FIRE!
THE BARN IS ON FIRE!

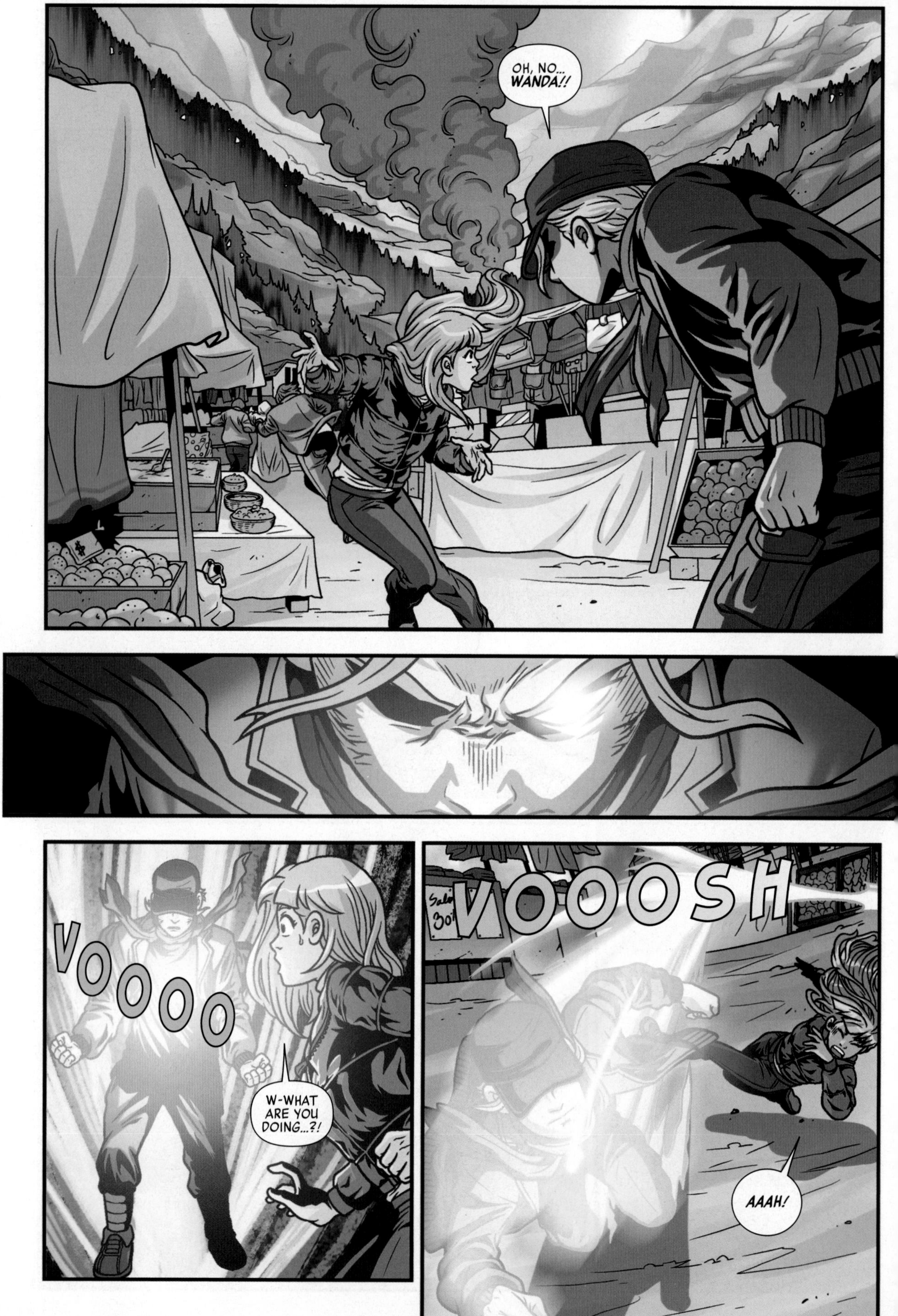
OH, NO... WANDA!!
VOOOO
W-WHAT ARE YOU DOING...?!
VOOOSH
AAAH!

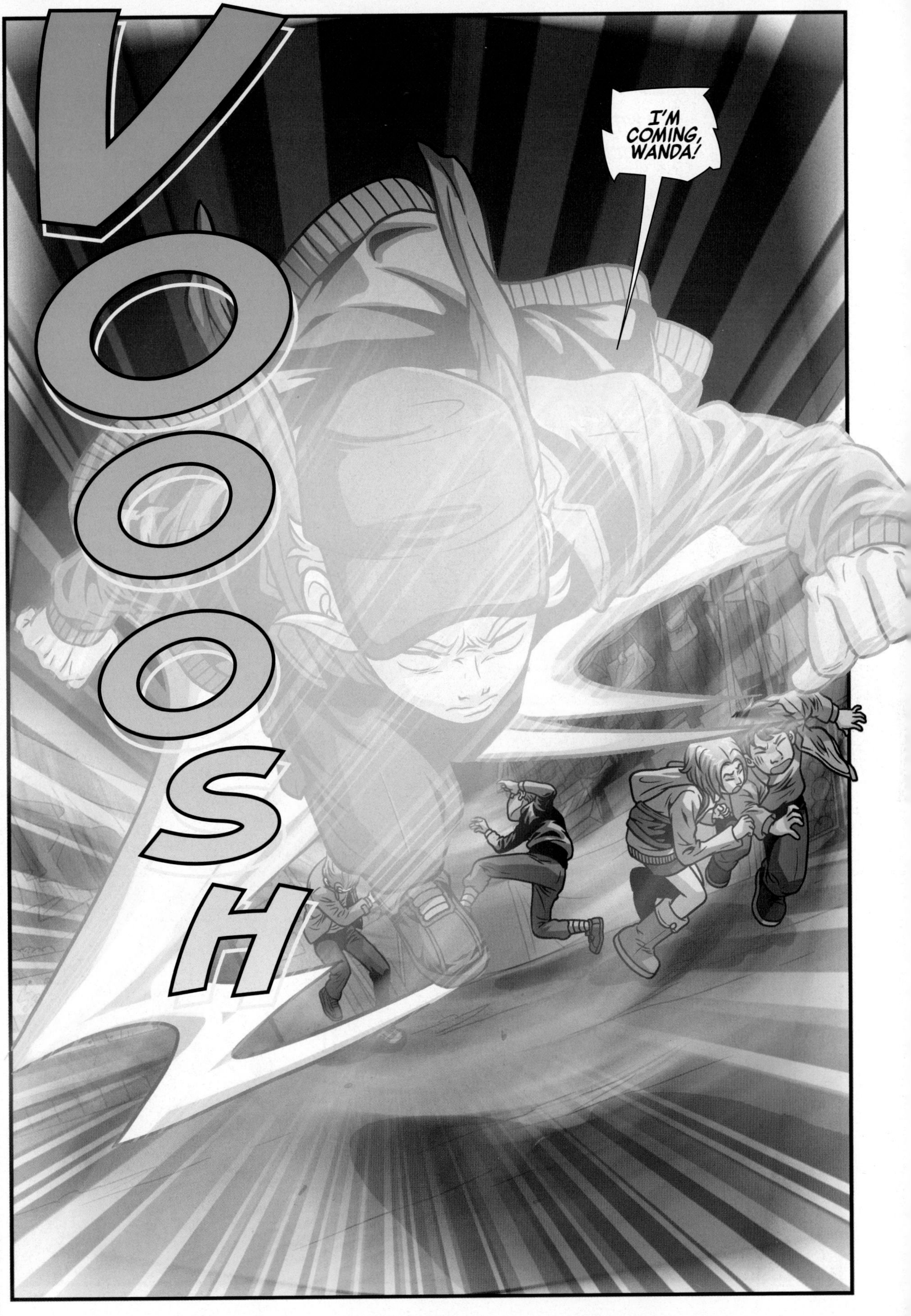
VOOOSH
I'M COMING, WANDA!

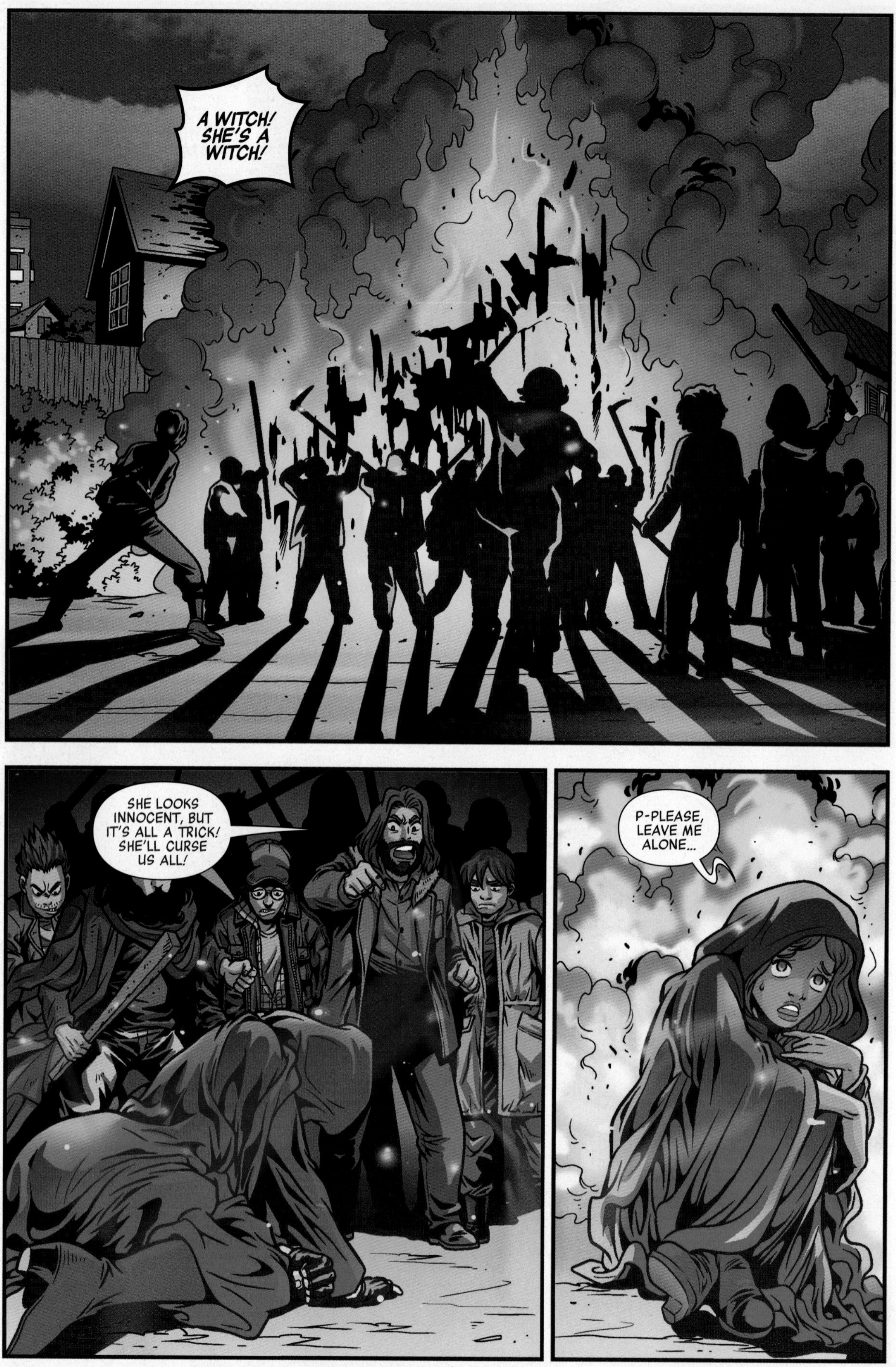
A WITCH! SHE'S A WITCH!
SHE LOOKS INNOCENT, BUT IT'S ALL A TRICK! SHE'LL CURSE US ALL!
P-PLEASE, LEAVE ME ALONE...

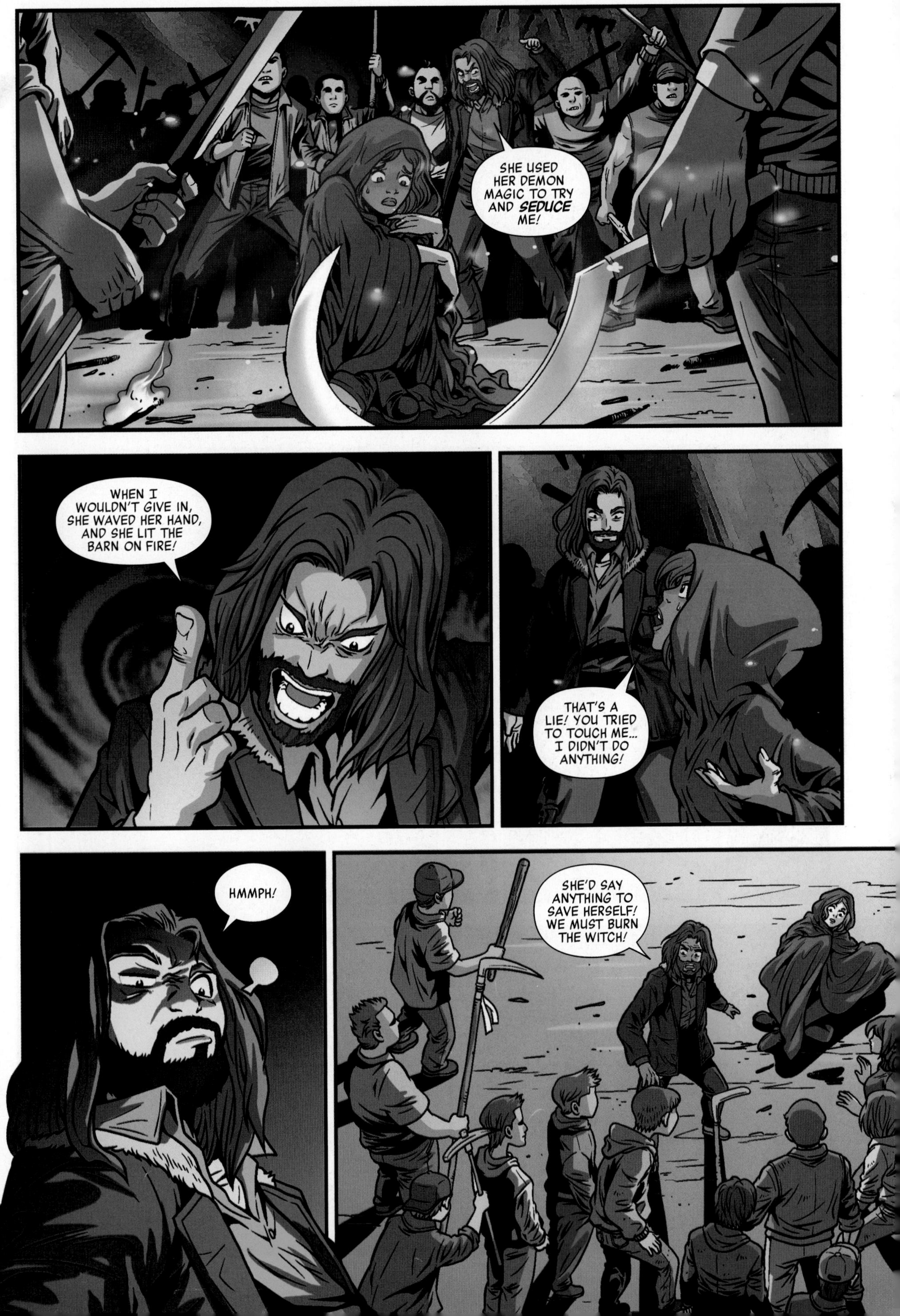

SHE USED HER DEMON MAGIC TO TRY AND SEDUCE ME!
WHEN I WOULDN'T GIVE IN, SHE WAVED HER HAND, AND SHE LIT THE BARN ON FIRE!
THAT'S A LIE! YOU TRIED TO TOUCH ME... I DIDN'T DO ANYTHING!
HMMPH!
SHE'D SAY ANYTHING TO SAVE HERSELF! WE MUST BURN THE WITCH!

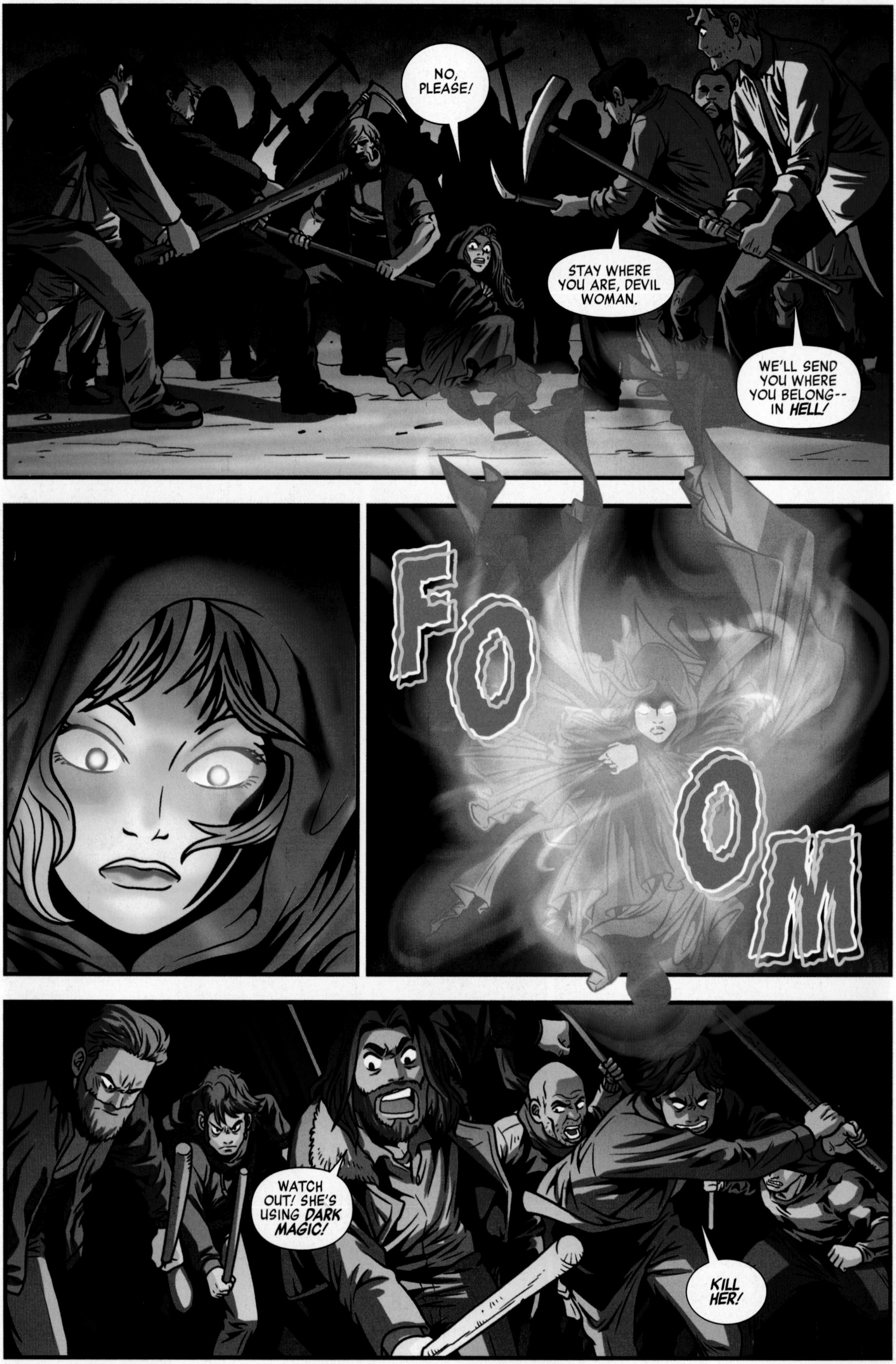
NO, PLEASE!
STAY WHERE YOU ARE, DEVIL WOMAN.
WE'LL SEND YOU WHERE YOU BELONG-- IN HELL!
FOOOM
WATCH OUT! SHE'S USING DARK MAGIC!
KILL HER!

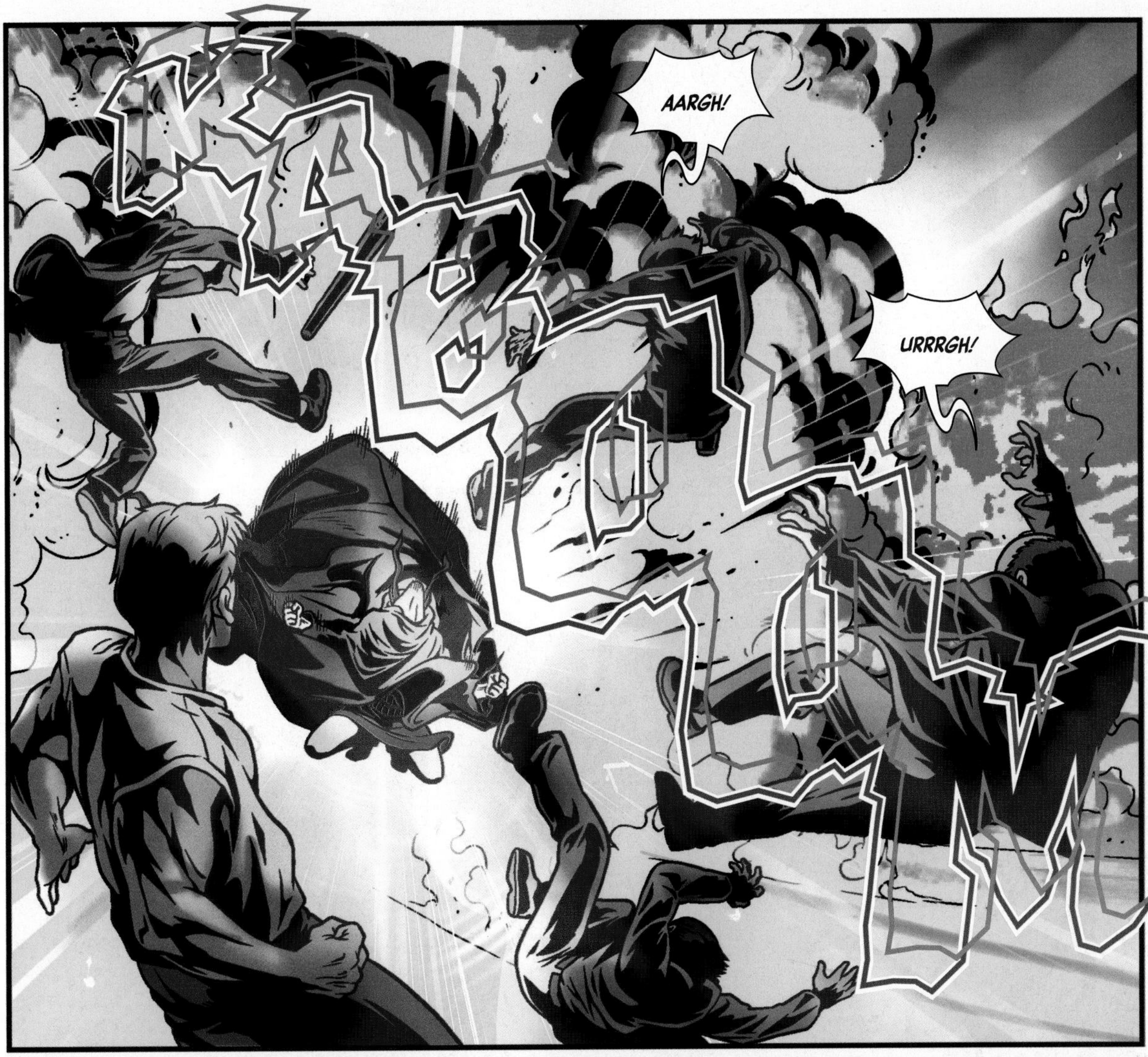
AARGH!
URRRGH!

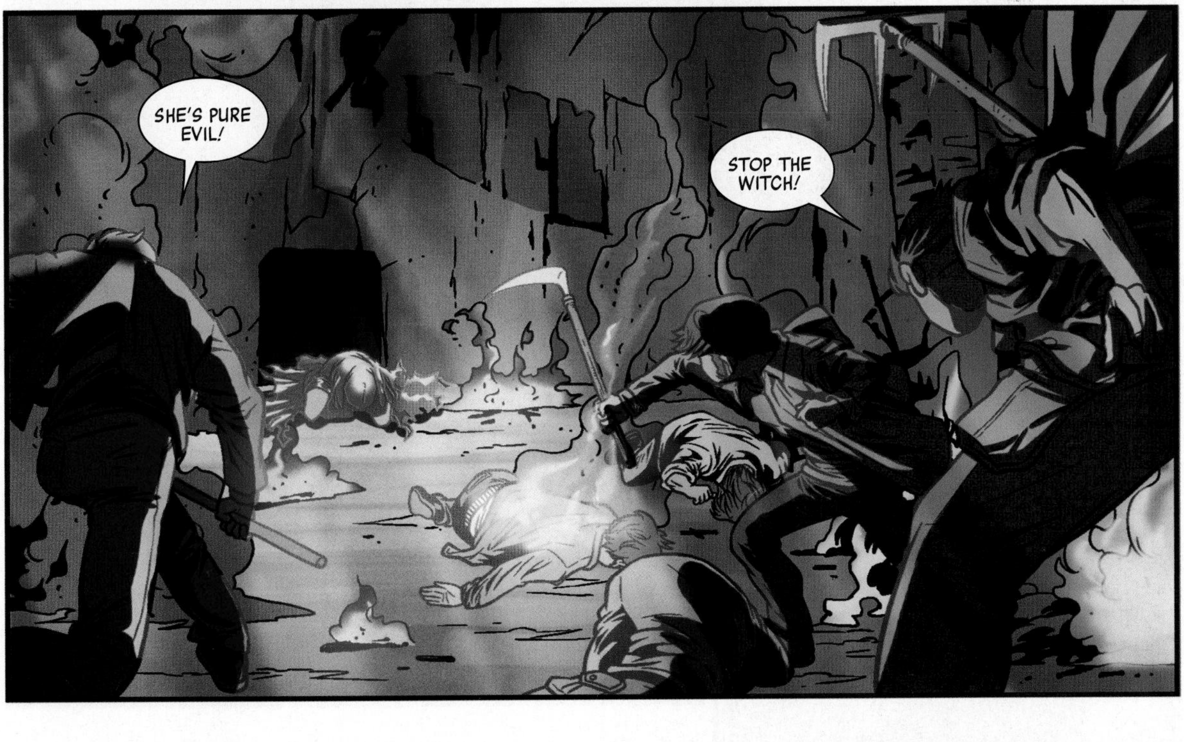
SHE'S PURE EVIL!
STOP THE WITCH!

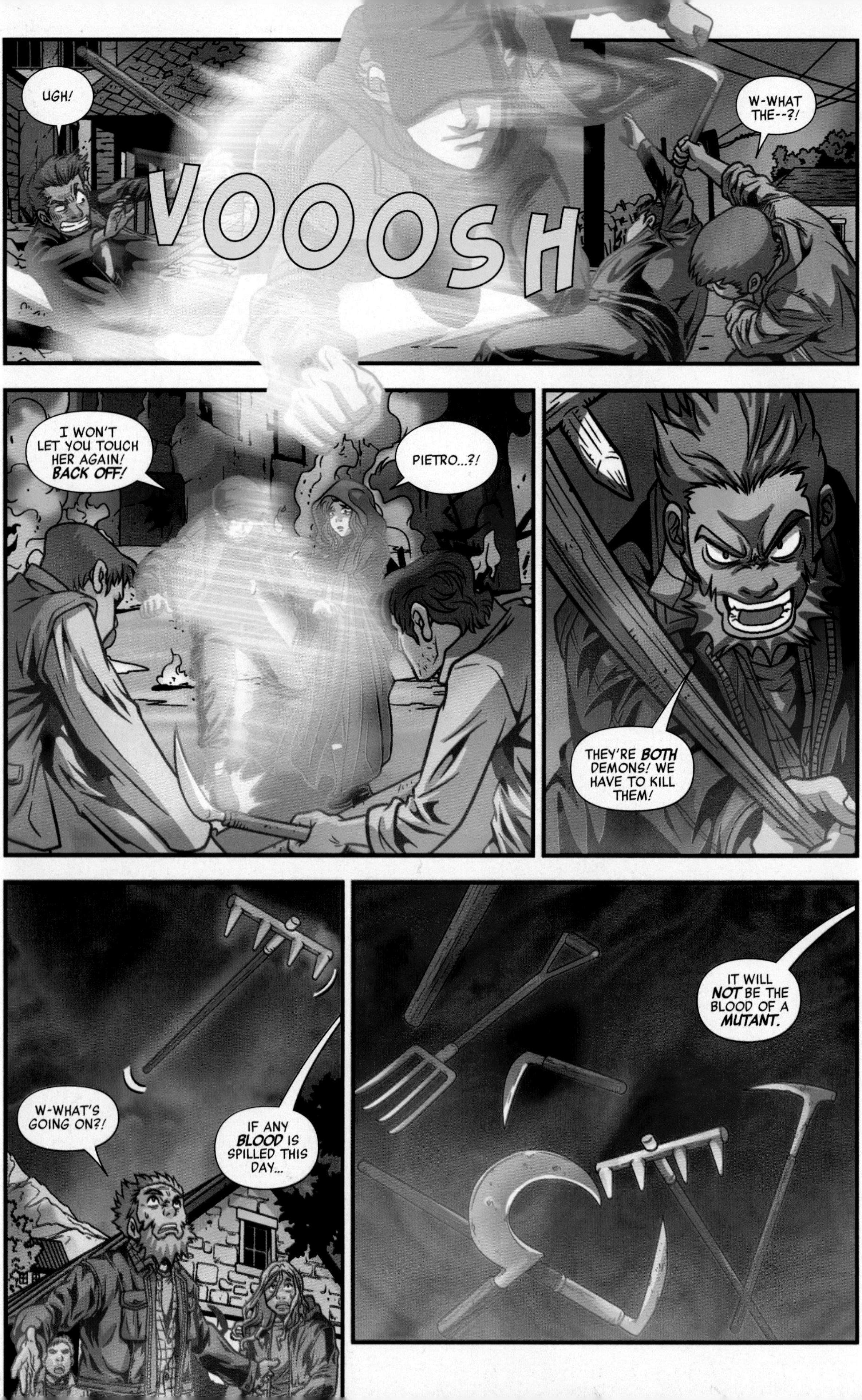

UGH!
W-WHAT THE--?!
VOOOSH
I WON'T LET YOU TOUCH HER AGAIN! BACK OFF!
PIETRO...?!
THEY'RE BOTH DEMONS! WE HAVE TO KILL THEM!
W-WHAT'S GOING ON?!
IF ANY BLOOD IS SPILLED THIS DAY...
IT WILL NOT BE THE BLOOD OF A MUTANT.

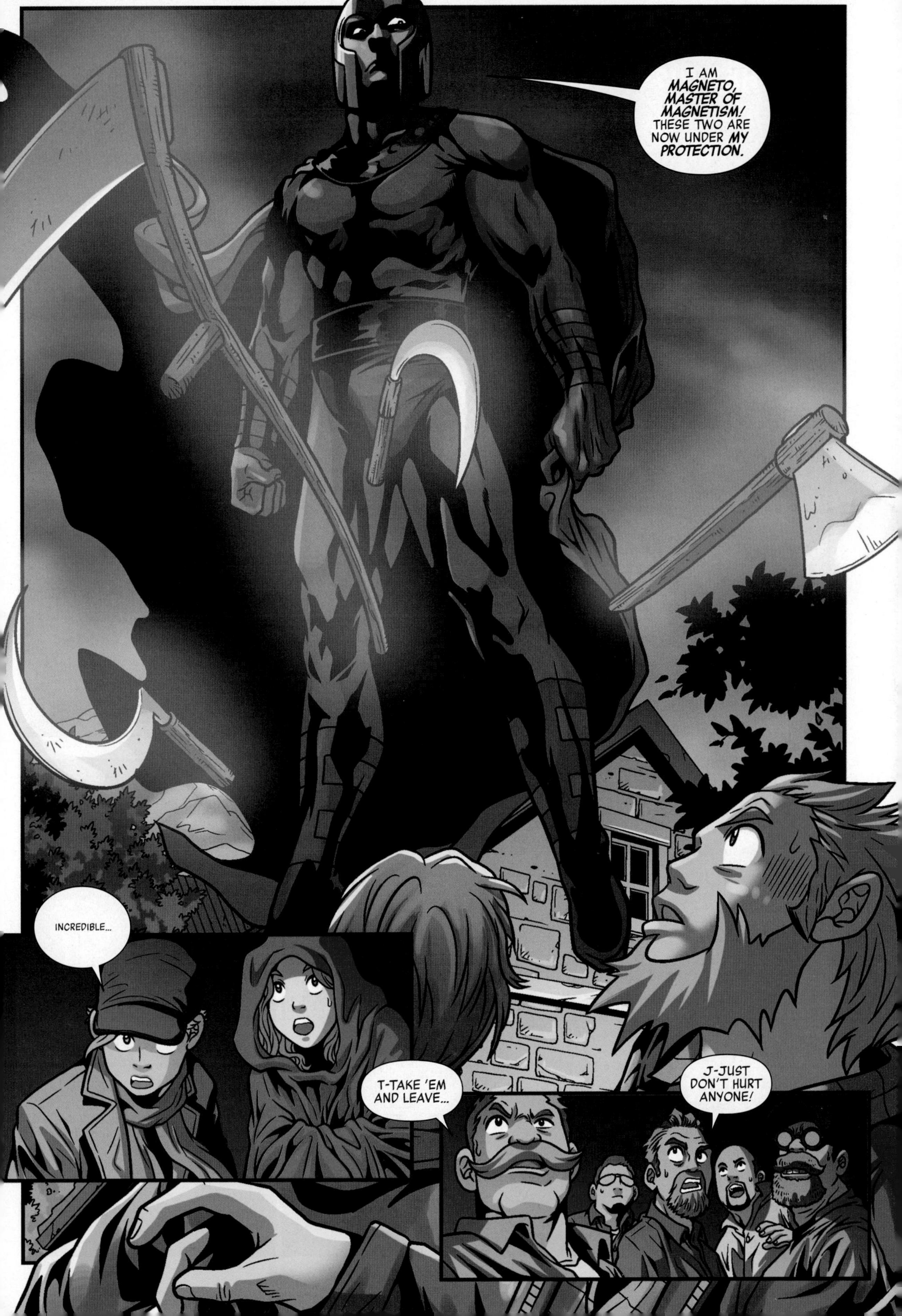
I AM *MAGNETO, MASTER OF MAGNETISM!* THESE TWO ARE NOW UNDER *MY PROTECTION.*
INCREDIBLE...
T-TAKE 'EM AND LEAVE...
J-JUST DON'T HURT ANYONE!

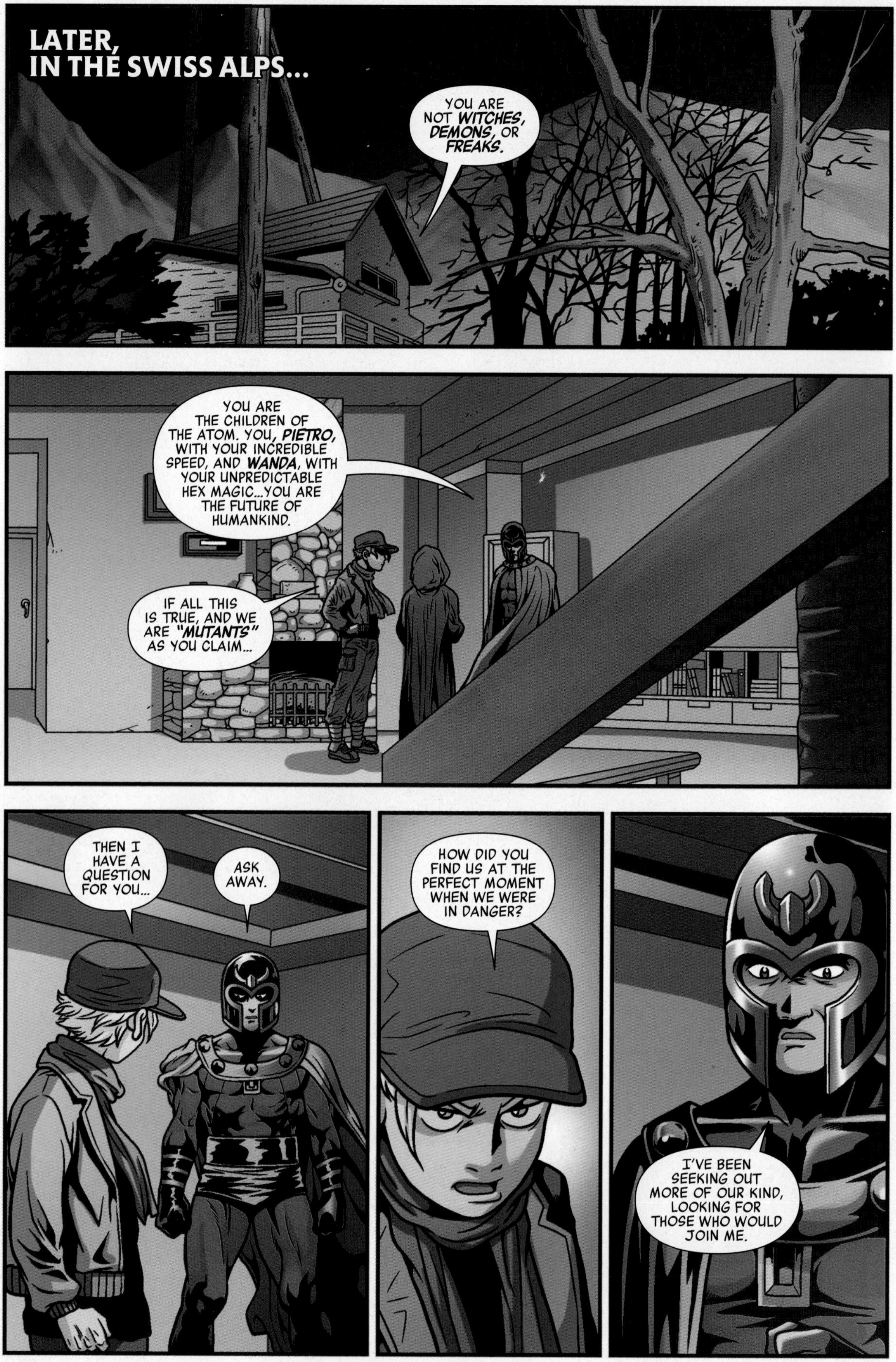
LATER, IN THE SWISS ALPS...
YOU ARE NOT WITCHES, DEMONS, OR FREAKS.
YOU ARE THE CHILDREN OF THE ATOM. YOU, PIETRO, WITH YOUR INCREDIBLE SPEED, AND WANDA, WITH YOUR UNPREDICTABLE HEX MAGIC...YOU ARE THE FUTURE OF HUMANKIND.
IF ALL THIS IS TRUE, AND WE ARE "MUTANTS" AS YOU CLAIM...
THEN I HAVE A QUESTION FOR YOU...
ASK AWAY.
HOW DID YOU FIND US AT THE PERFECT MOMENT WHEN WE WERE IN DANGER?
I'VE BEEN SEEKING OUT MORE OF OUR KIND, LOOKING FOR THOSE WHO WOULD JOIN ME.

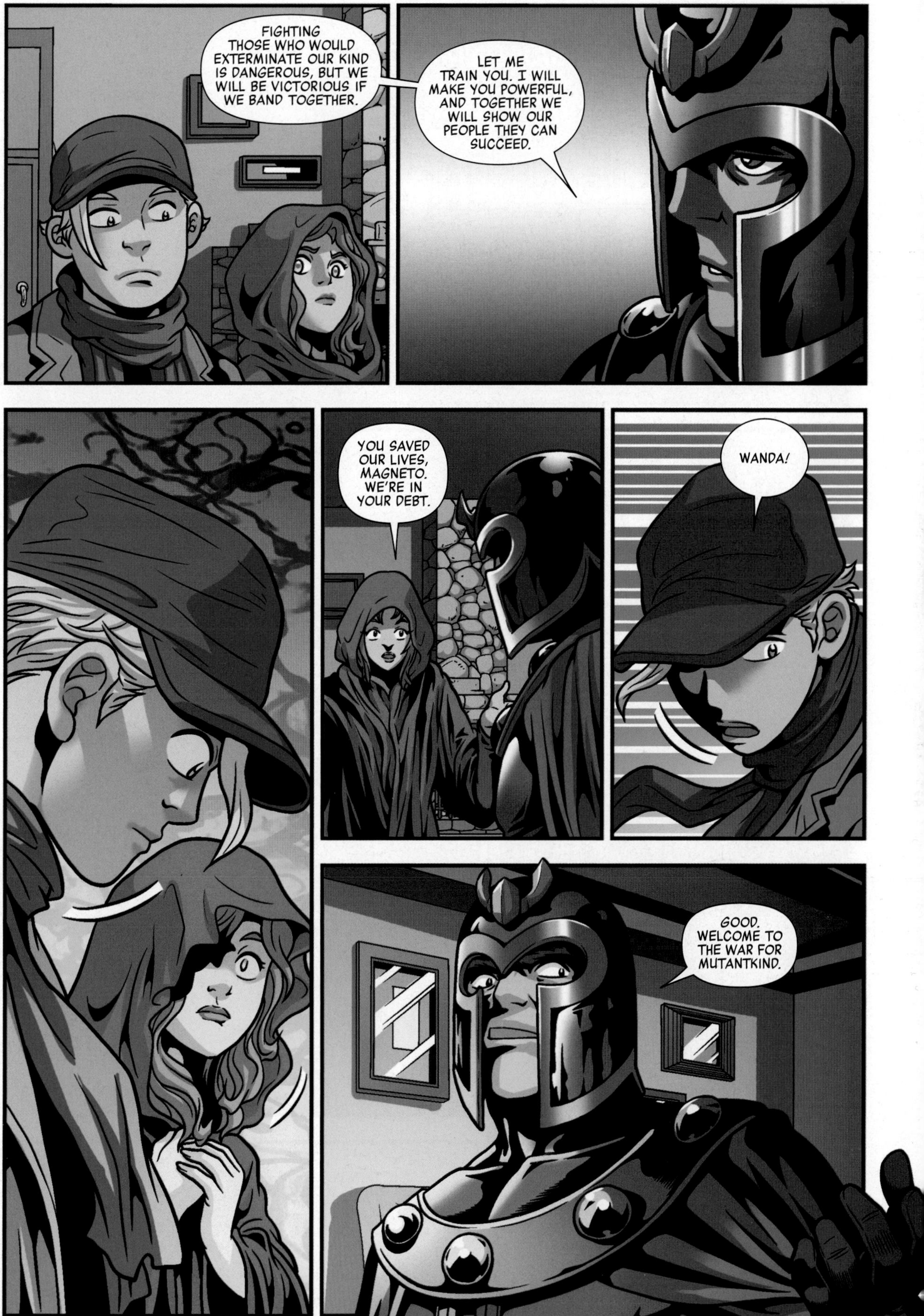
FIGHTING THOSE WHO WOULD EXTERMINATE OUR KIND IS DANGEROUS, BUT WE WILL BE VICTORIOUS IF WE BAND TOGETHER.
LET ME TRAIN YOU. I WILL MAKE YOU POWERFUL, AND TOGETHER WE WILL SHOW OUR PEOPLE THEY CAN SUCCEED.
YOU SAVED OUR LIVES, MAGNETO. WE'RE IN YOUR DEBT.
WANDA!
GOOD. WELCOME TO THE WAR FOR MUTANTKIND.

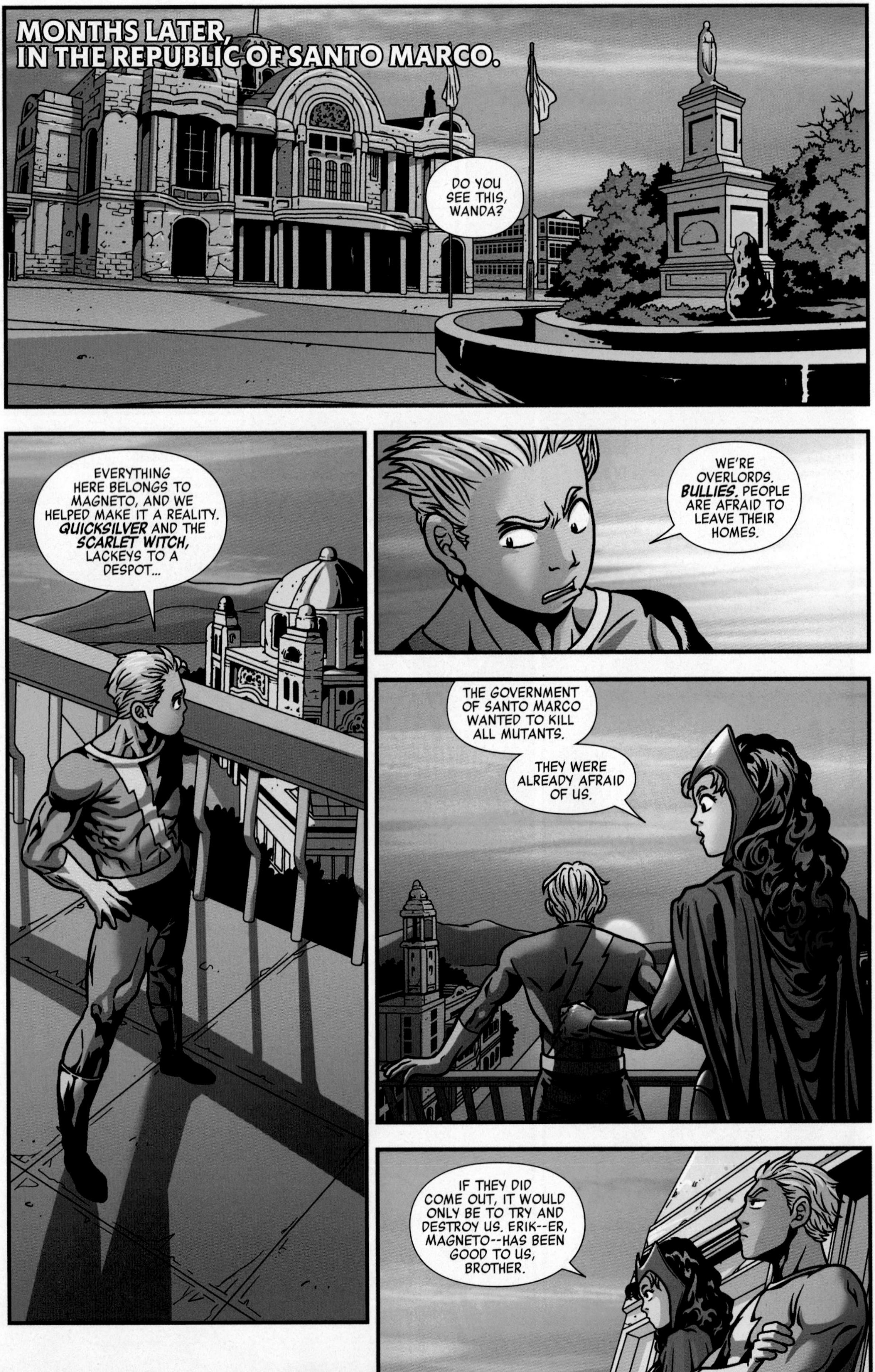
MONTHS LATER, IN THE REPUBLIC OF SANTO MARCO.
DO YOU SEE THIS, WANDA?
EVERYTHING HERE BELONGS TO MAGNETO, AND WE HELPED MAKE IT A REALITY. QUICKSILVER AND THE SCARLET WITCH, LACKEYS TO A DESPOT...
WE'RE OVERLORDS. BULLIES. PEOPLE ARE AFRAID TO LEAVE THEIR HOMES.
THE GOVERNMENT OF SANTO MARCO WANTED TO KILL ALL MUTANTS.
THEY WERE ALREADY AFRAID OF US.
IF THEY DID COME OUT, IT WOULD ONLY BE TO TRY AND DESTROY US. ERIK--ER, MAGNETO--HAS BEEN GOOD TO US, BROTHER.

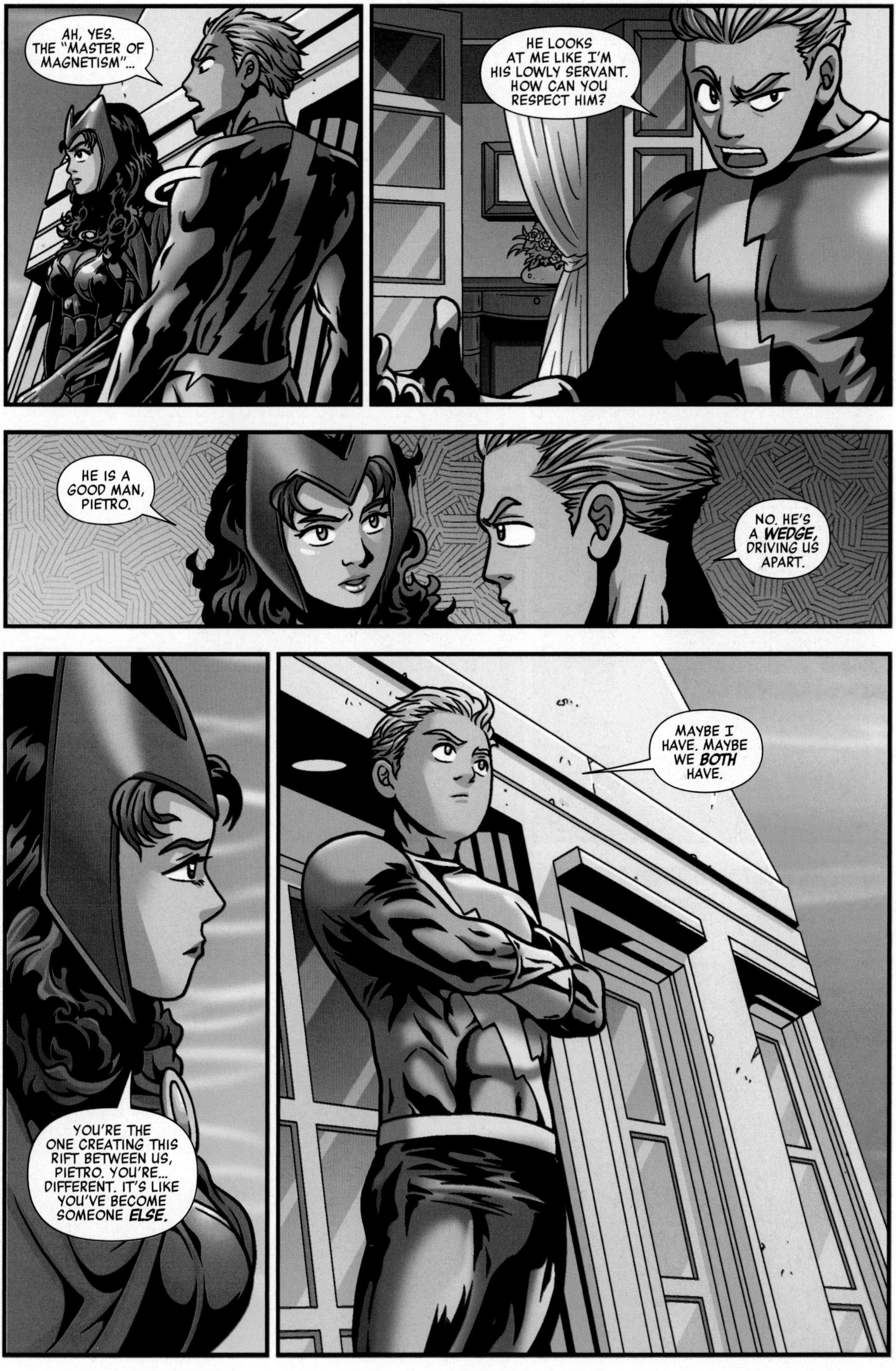

AH, YES. THE "MASTER OF MAGNETISM"...
HE LOOKS AT ME LIKE I'M HIS LOWLY SERVANT. HOW CAN YOU RESPECT HIM?
HE IS A GOOD MAN, PIETRO.
NO. HE'S A WEDGE, DRIVING US APART.
YOU'RE THE ONE CREATING THIS RIFT BETWEEN US, PIETRO. YOU'RE... DIFFERENT. IT'S LIKE YOU'VE BECOME SOMEONE ELSE.
MAYBE I HAVE. MAYBE WE BOTH HAVE.

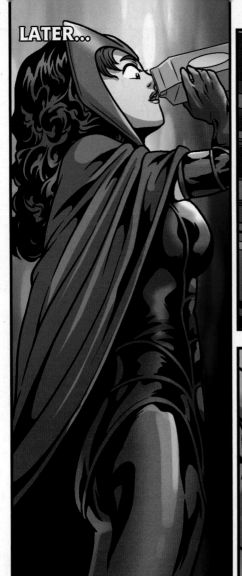

LATER...

THE SCARLET WITCH IS QUITE FETCHING, ISN'T SHE, TOAD?

YEAH, LIKE FETCHING ME A SANDWICH.

VOOOSH

HOW *DARE* YOU TALK ABOUT MY *SISTER LIKE* THAT!

OOF!

COOL *DOWN*, SPEEDSTER, WE'RE ALL ON THE *SAME* TEAM.

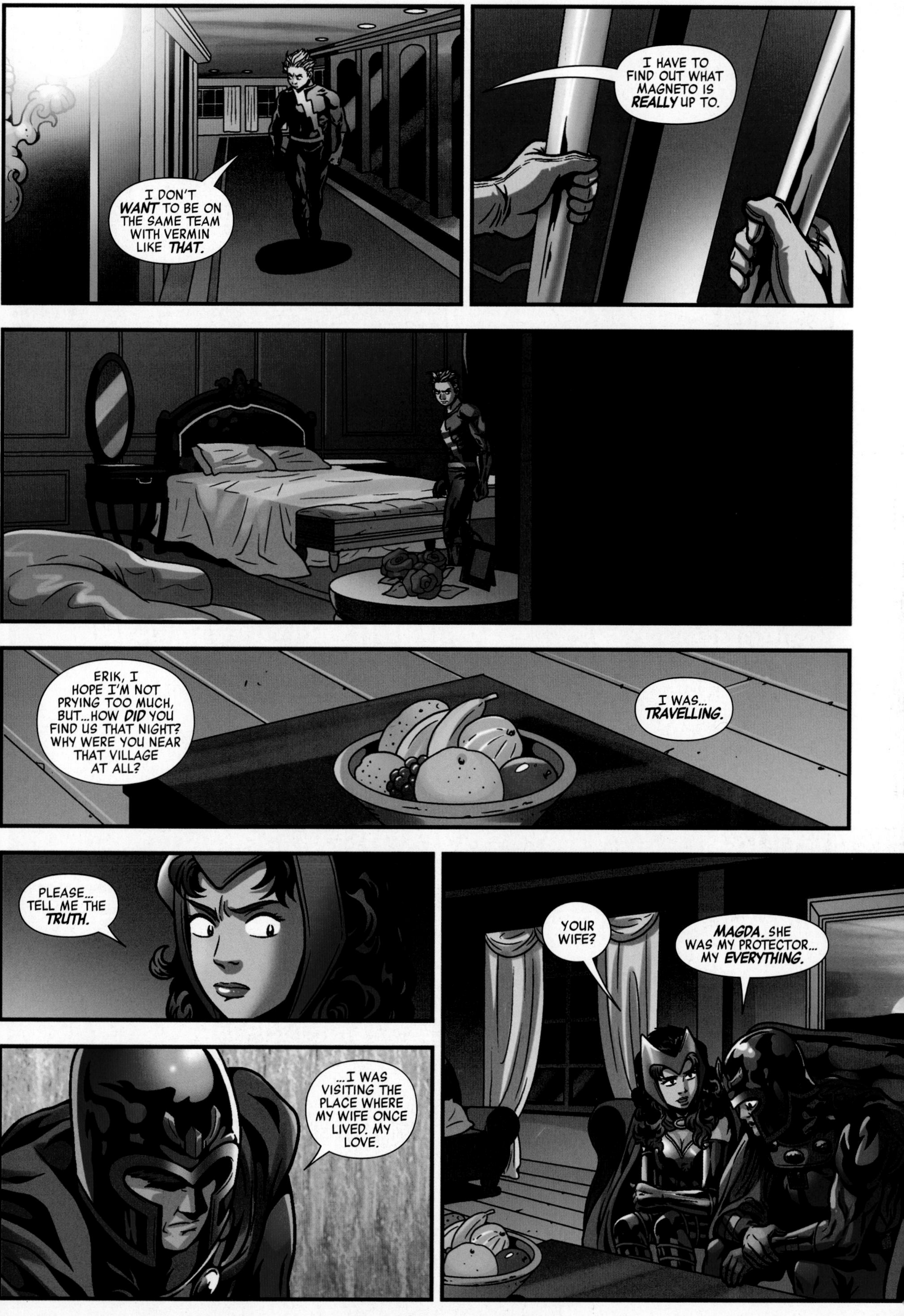
I DON'T WANT TO BE ON THE SAME TEAM WITH VERMIN LIKE THAT.
I HAVE TO FIND OUT WHAT MAGNETO IS REALLY UP TO.
ERIK, I HOPE I'M NOT PRYING TOO MUCH, BUT...HOW DID YOU FIND US THAT NIGHT? WHY WERE YOU NEAR THAT VILLAGE AT ALL?
I WAS... TRAVELLING.
PLEASE... TELL ME THE TRUTH.
...I WAS VISITING THE PLACE WHERE MY WIFE ONCE LIVED. MY LOVE.
YOUR WIFE?
MAGDA. SHE WAS MY PROTECTOR... MY EVERYTHING.

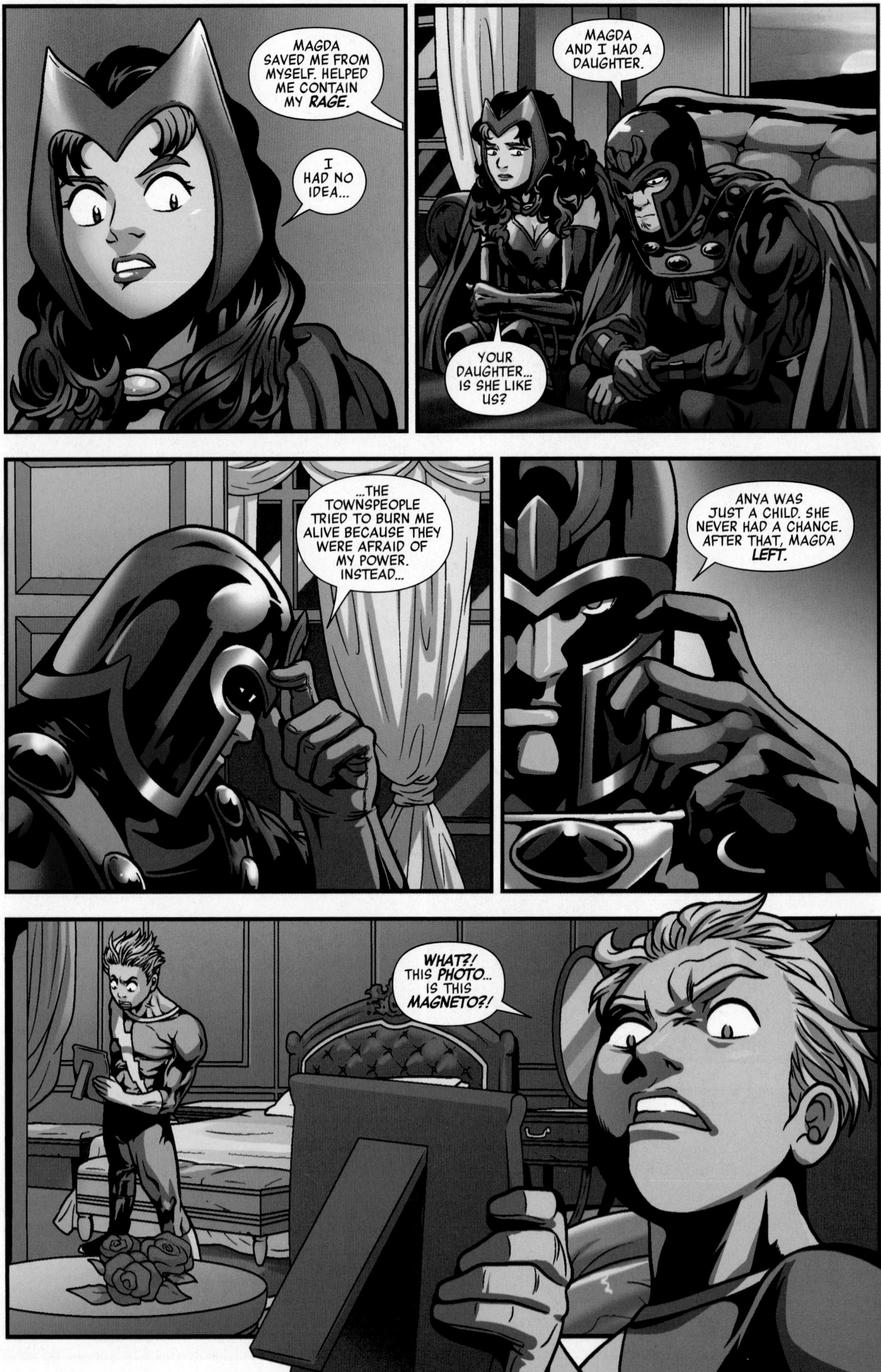
MAGDA SAVED ME FROM MYSELF. HELPED ME CONTAIN MY *RAGE.*
I HAD NO IDEA...
MAGDA AND I HAD A DAUGHTER.
YOUR DAUGHTER... IS SHE LIKE US?
...THE TOWNSPEOPLE TRIED TO BURN ME ALIVE BECAUSE THEY WERE AFRAID OF MY POWER. INSTEAD...
ANYA WAS JUST A CHILD. SHE NEVER HAD A CHANCE. AFTER THAT, MAGDA *LEFT.*
WHAT?! THIS *PHOTO*... IS THIS *MAGNETO?!*

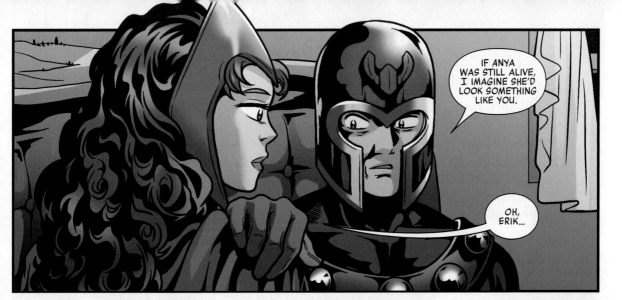

IF ANYA WAS STILL ALIVE, I IMAGINE SHE'D LOOK SOMETHING LIKE YOU.

OH, ERIK...

SLAM

GET AWAY FROM MY SISTER AND EXPLAIN YOURSELF!

TAKE OFF THAT HELMET RIGHT NOW AND SHOW HER!

SHOW ME WHAT, PIETRO?

NO. THIS HELMET PROTECTS ME--IT PROTECTS ALL OF US-- FROM MENTAL MANIPULATION BY CHARLES XAVIER AND HIS X-MEN.

DO IT, OR WE LEAVE RIGHT NOW!

WHAT'S WRONG WITH YOU, PIETRO?

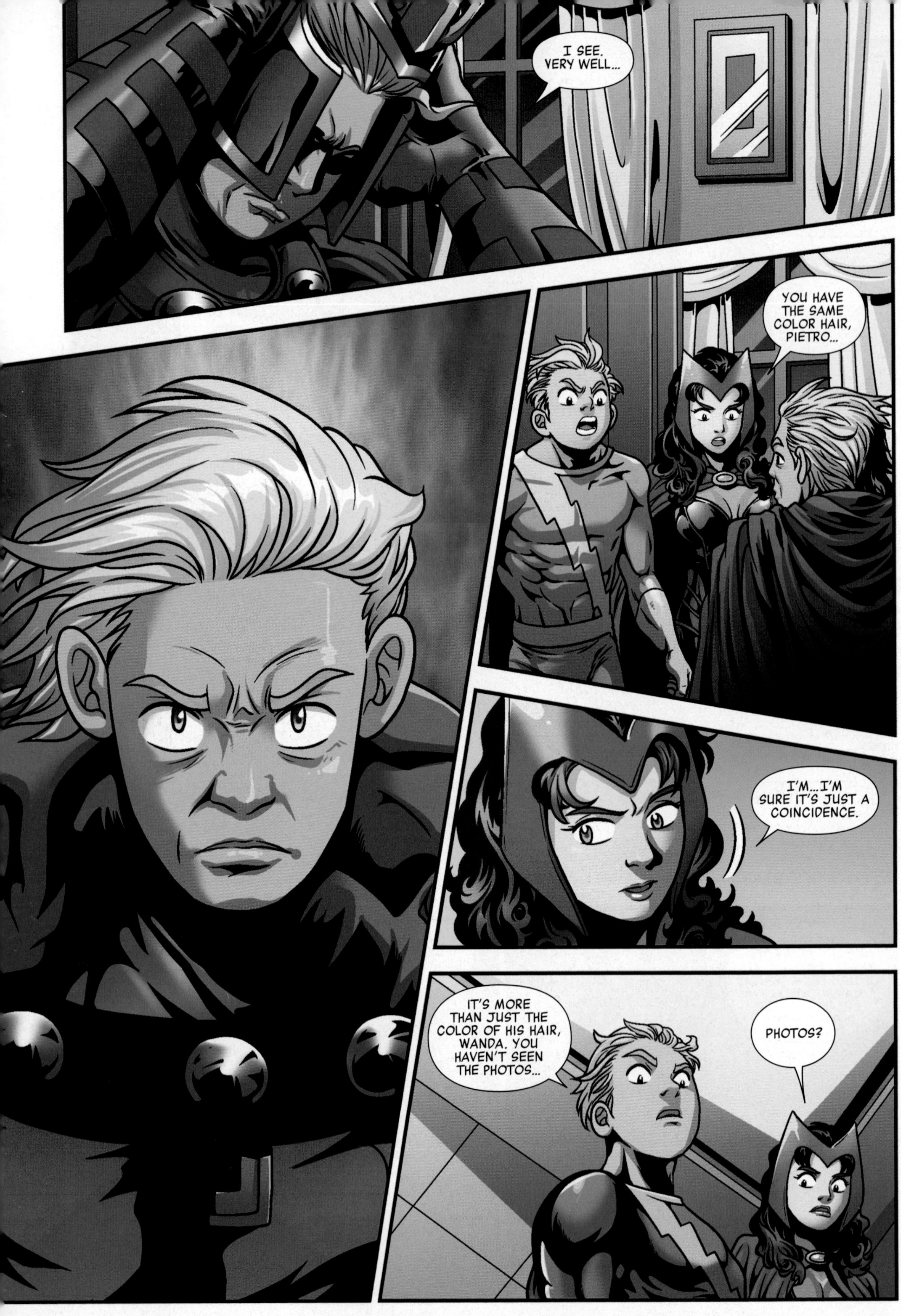
I SEE. VERY WELL...
YOU HAVE THE SAME COLOR HAIR, PIETRO...
I'M...I'M SURE IT'S JUST A COINCIDENCE.
IT'S MORE THAN JUST THE COLOR OF HIS HAIR, WANDA. YOU HAVEN'T SEEN THE PHOTOS...
PHOTOS?

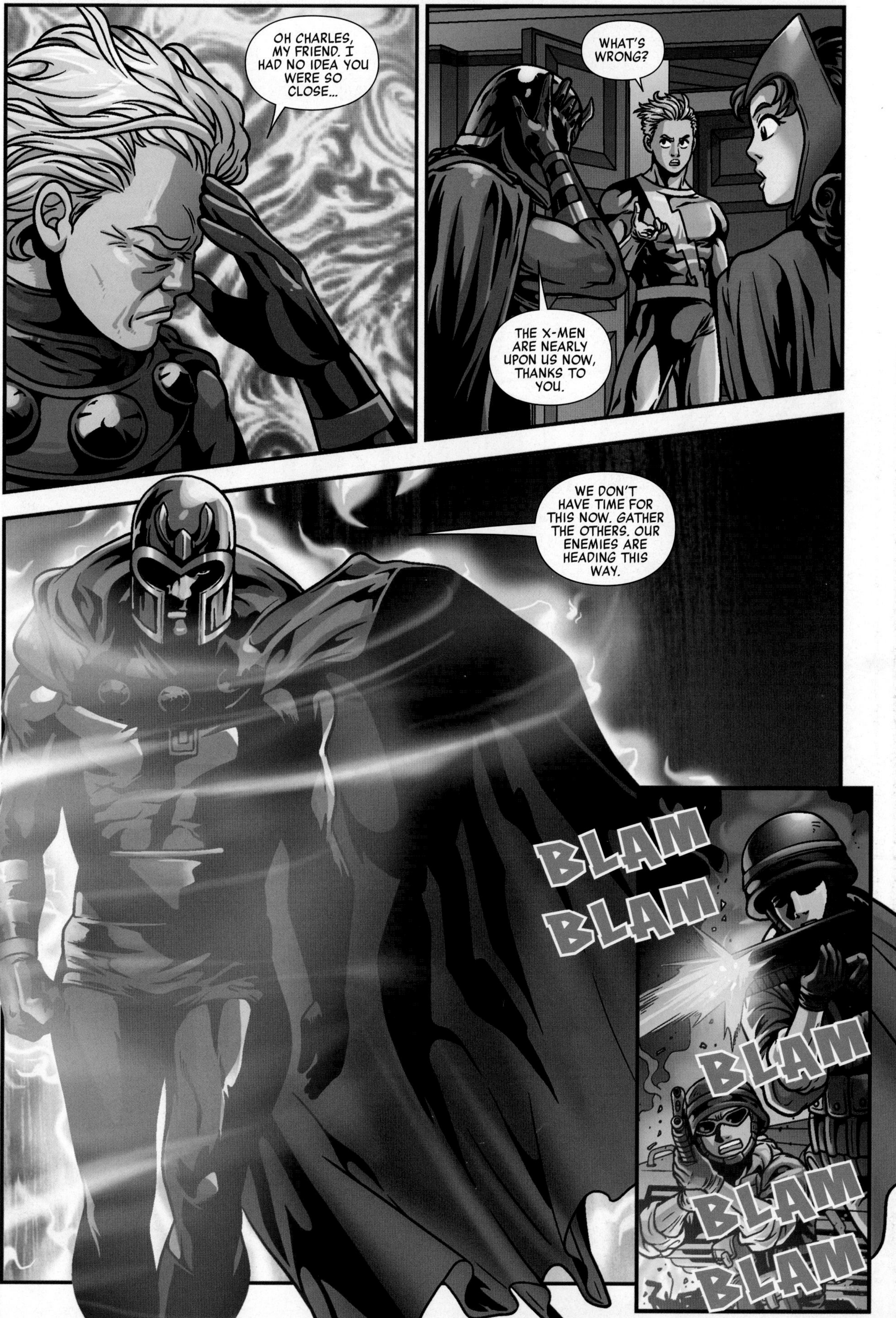
OH CHARLES, MY FRIEND. I HAD NO IDEA YOU WERE SO CLOSE...
WHAT'S WRONG?
THE X-MEN ARE NEARLY UPON US NOW, THANKS TO YOU.
WE DON'T HAVE TIME FOR THIS NOW. GATHER THE OTHERS. OUR ENEMIES ARE HEADING THIS WAY.
BLAM BLAM
BLAM
BLAM BLAM

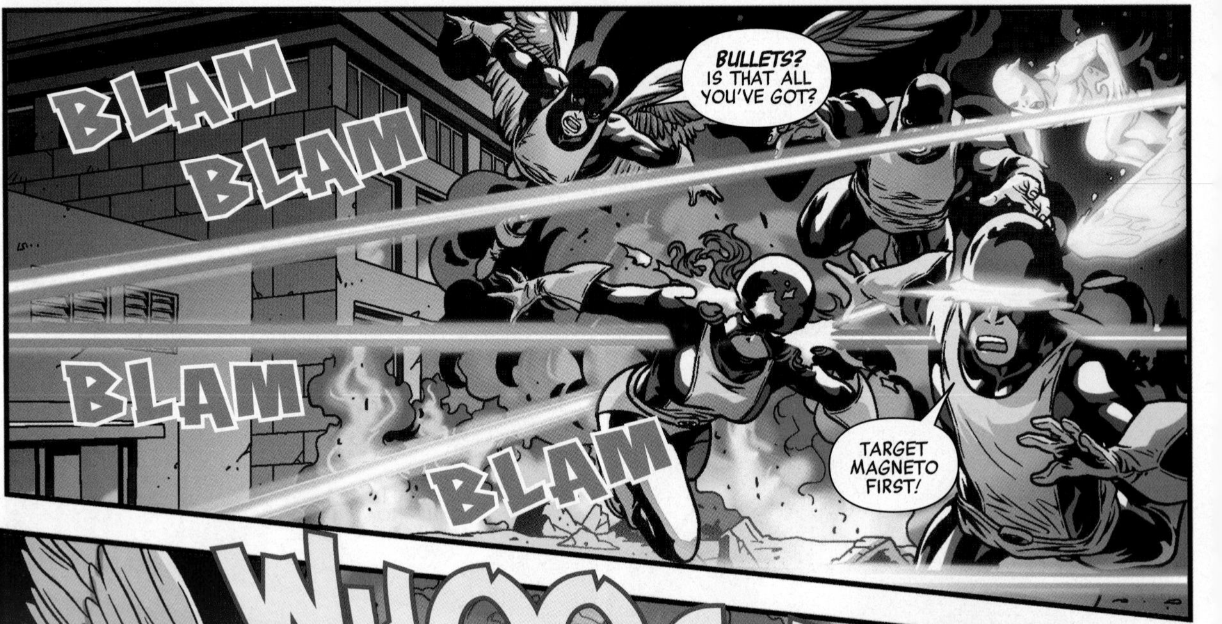
BLAM
BLAM
BULLETS? IS THAT ALL YOU'VE GOT?
BLAM
BLAM
TARGET MAGNETO FIRST!

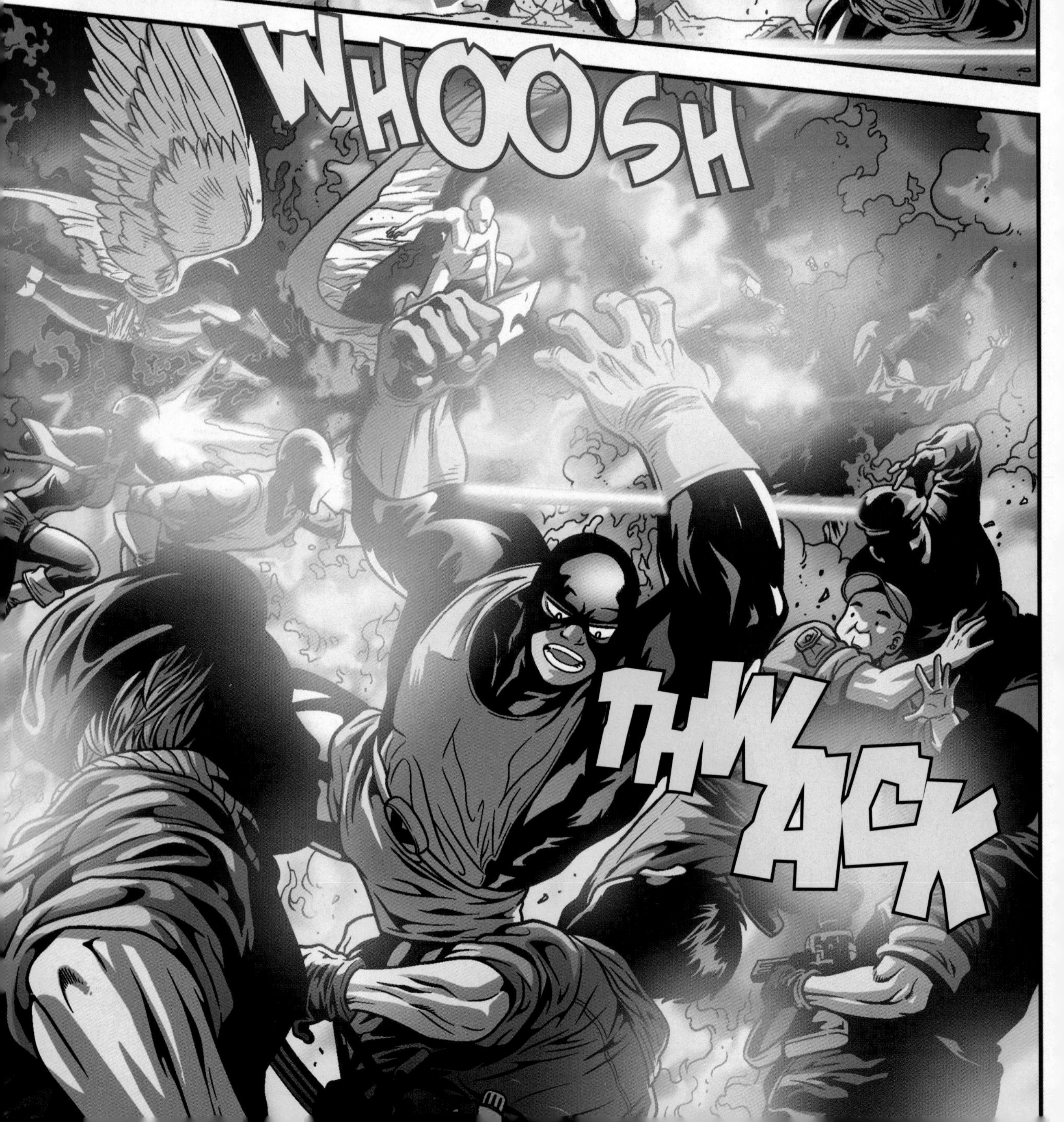
WHOOSH
THWACK

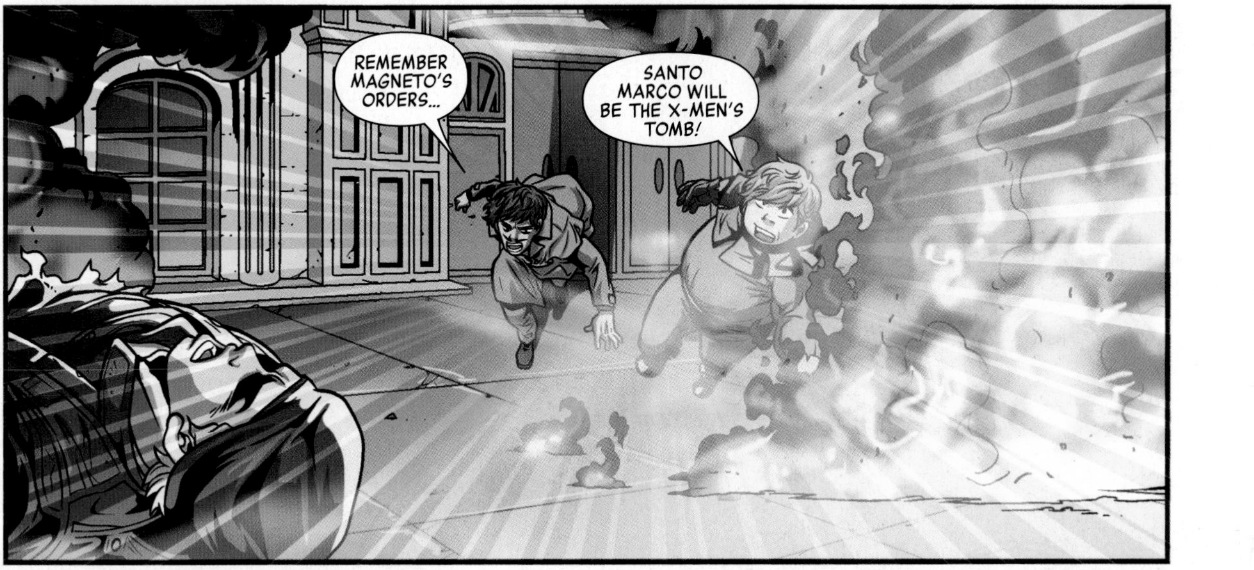
REMEMBER MAGNETO'S ORDERS...
SANTO MARCO WILL BE THE X-MEN'S TOMB!

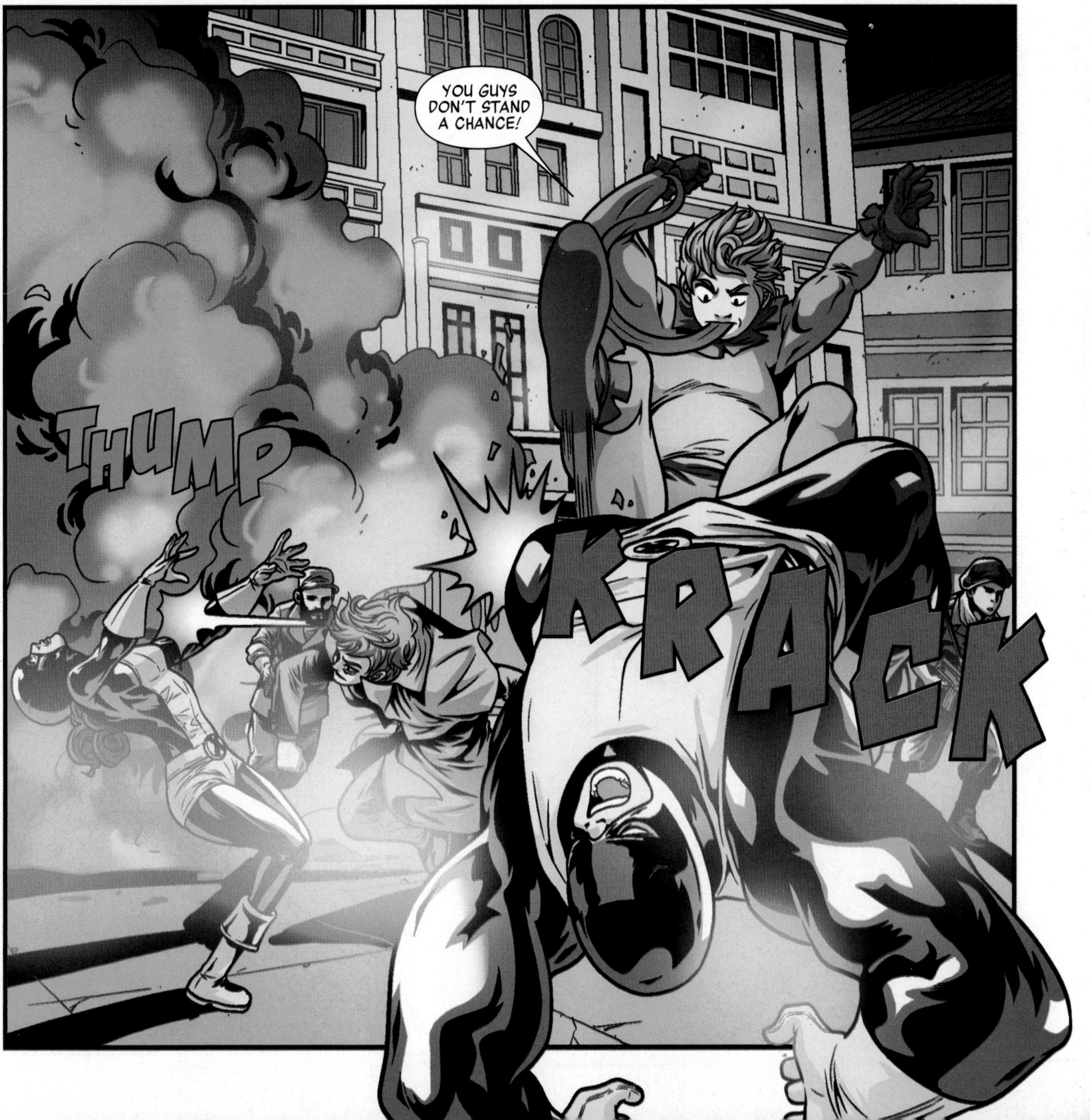
YOU GUYS DON'T STAND A CHANCE!
THUMP
KRACK

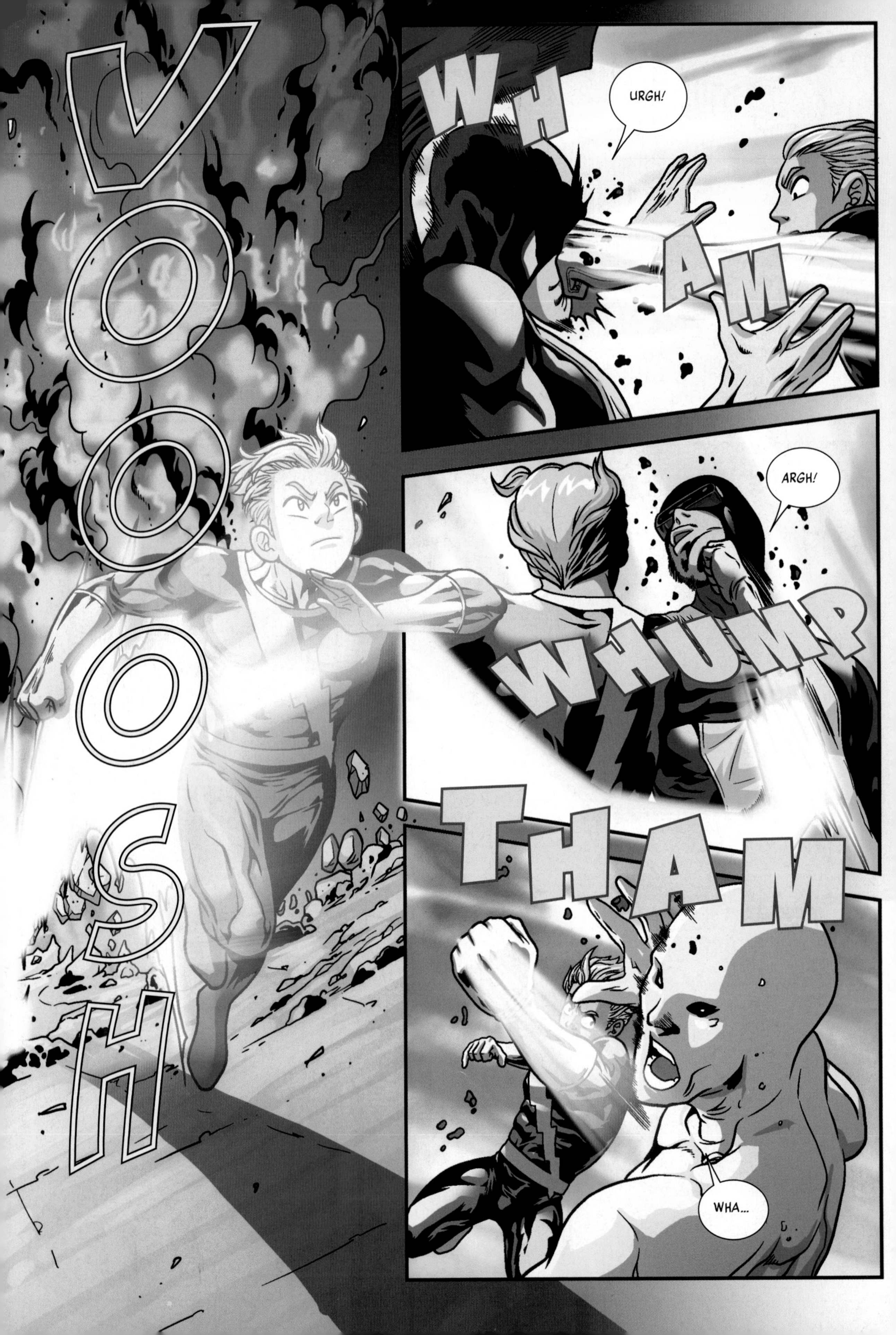
VOOOSH
WHAM
URGH!
ARGH!
WHUMP
THAM
WHA...

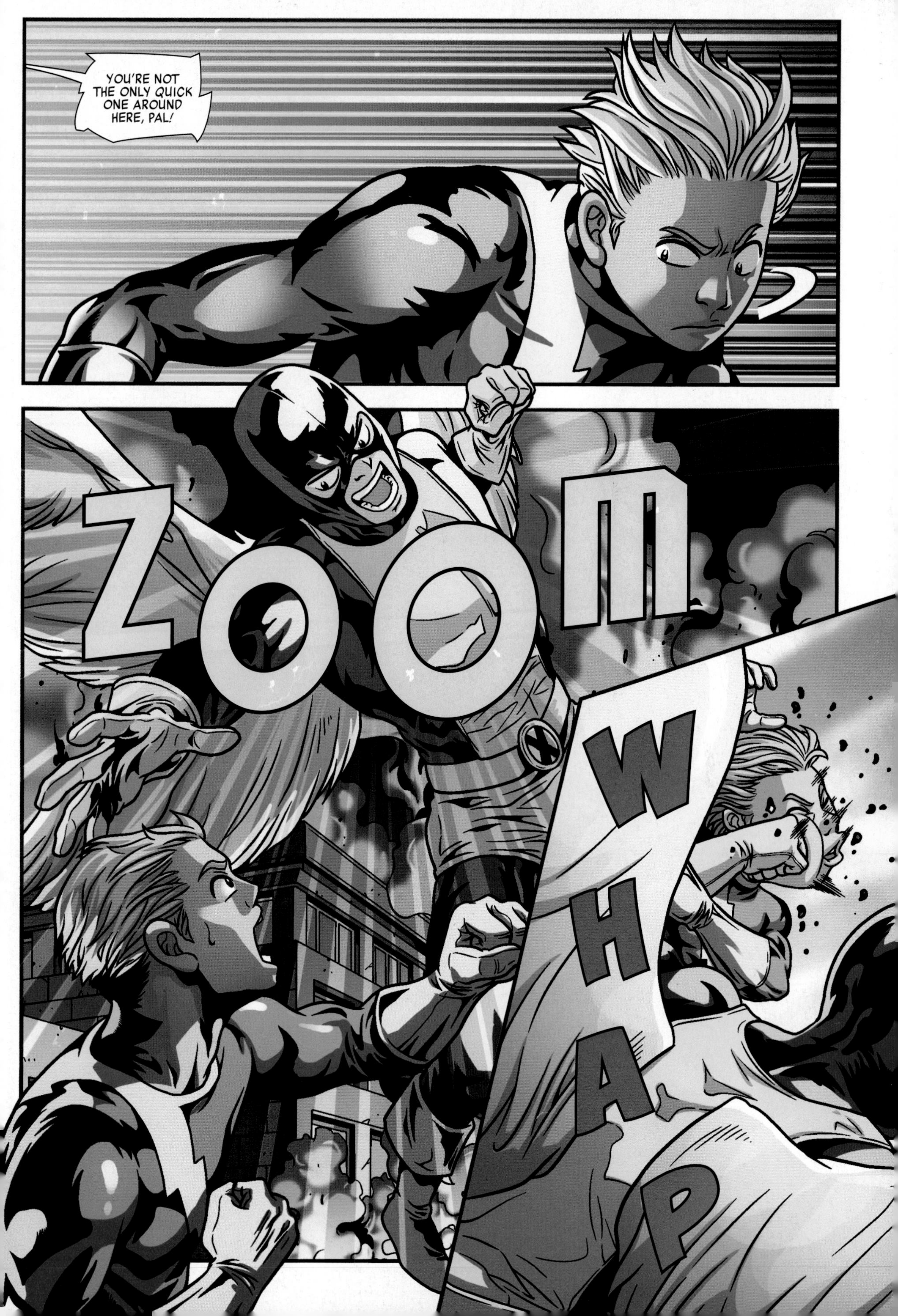

YOU'RE NOT THE ONLY QUICK ONE AROUND HERE, PAL!
ZOOM
WHAP

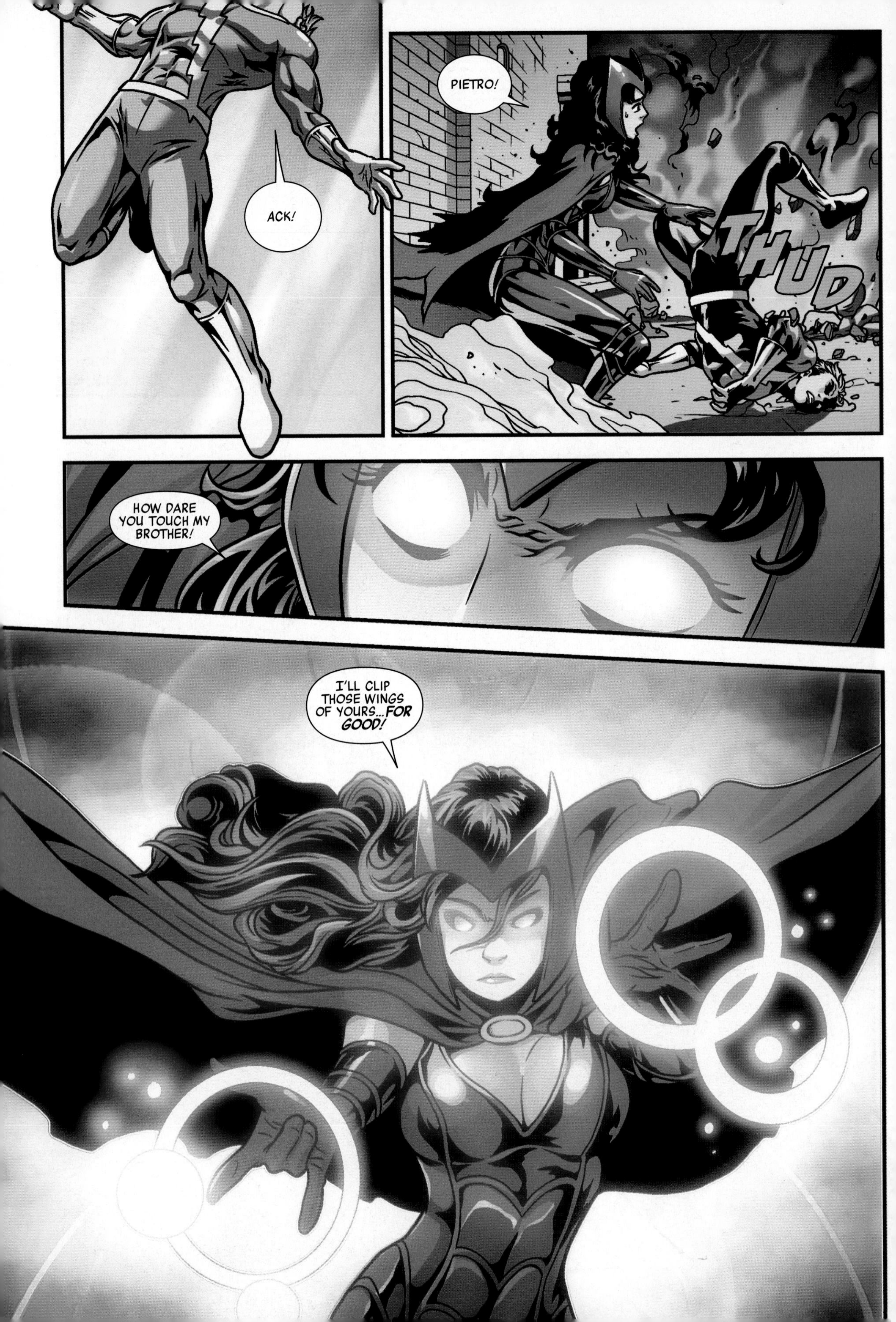
ACK!
PIETRO!
THUD
HOW DARE YOU TOUCH MY BROTHER!
I'LL CLIP THOSE WINGS OF YOURS...**FOR GOOD!**

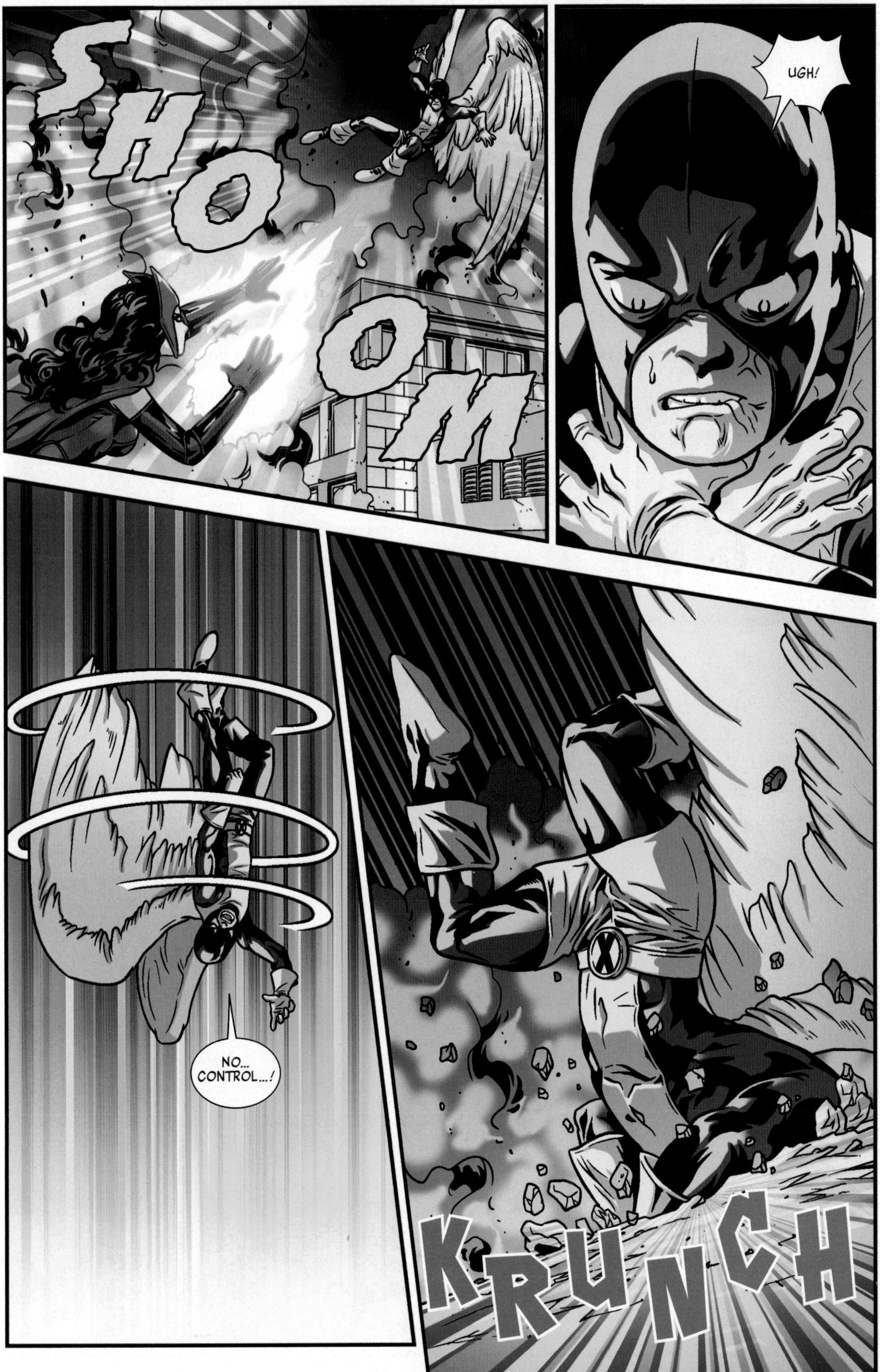
SHOOM
UGH!
NO... CONTROL...!
KRUNCH

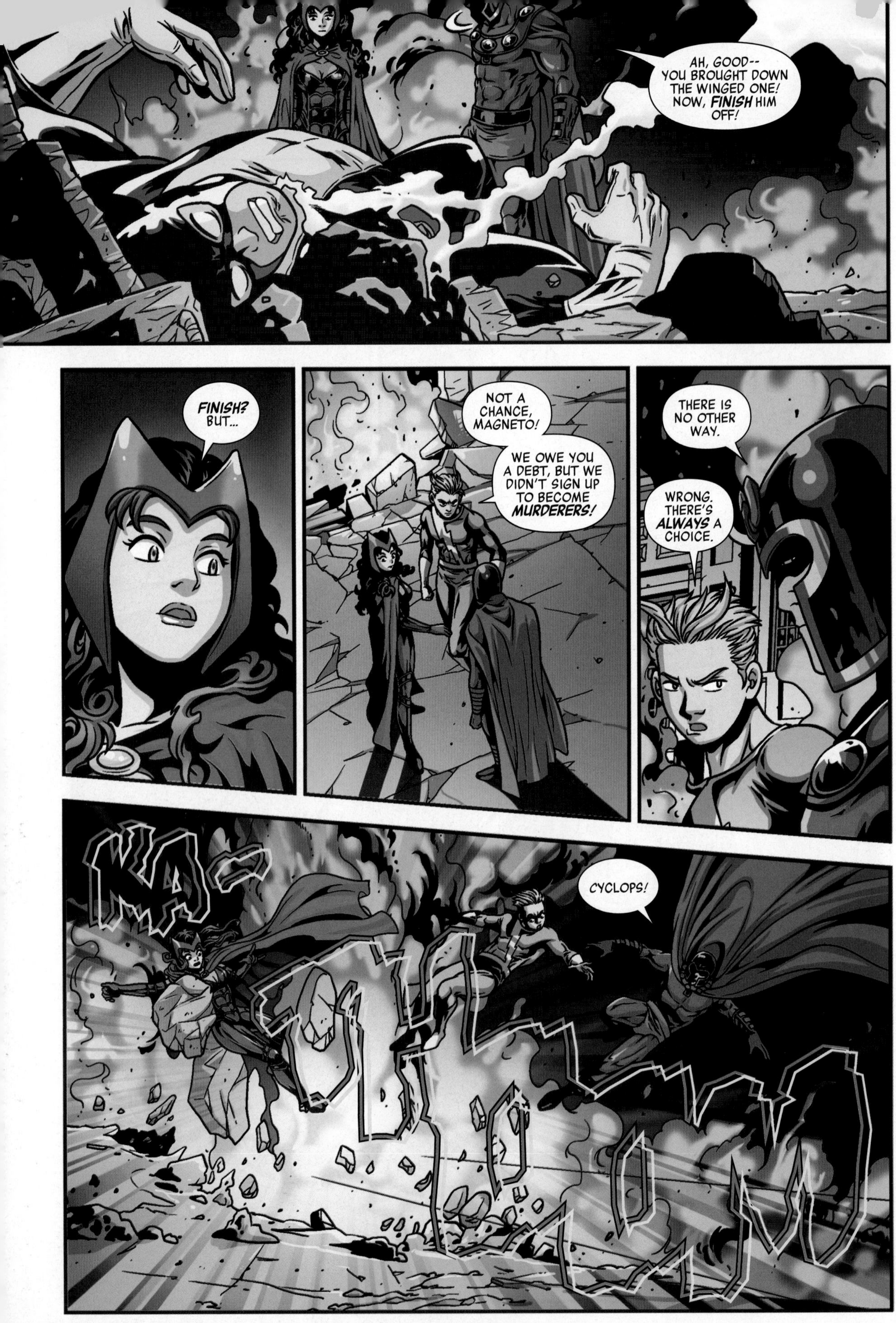
AH, GOOD-- YOU BROUGHT DOWN THE WINGED ONE! NOW, FINISH HIM OFF!
FINISH? BUT...
NOT A CHANCE, MAGNETO!
WE OWE YOU A DEBT, BUT WE DIDN'T SIGN UP TO BECOME MURDERERS!
THERE IS NO OTHER WAY.
WRONG. THERE'S ALWAYS A CHOICE.
KA-
CYCLOPS!
THOOM

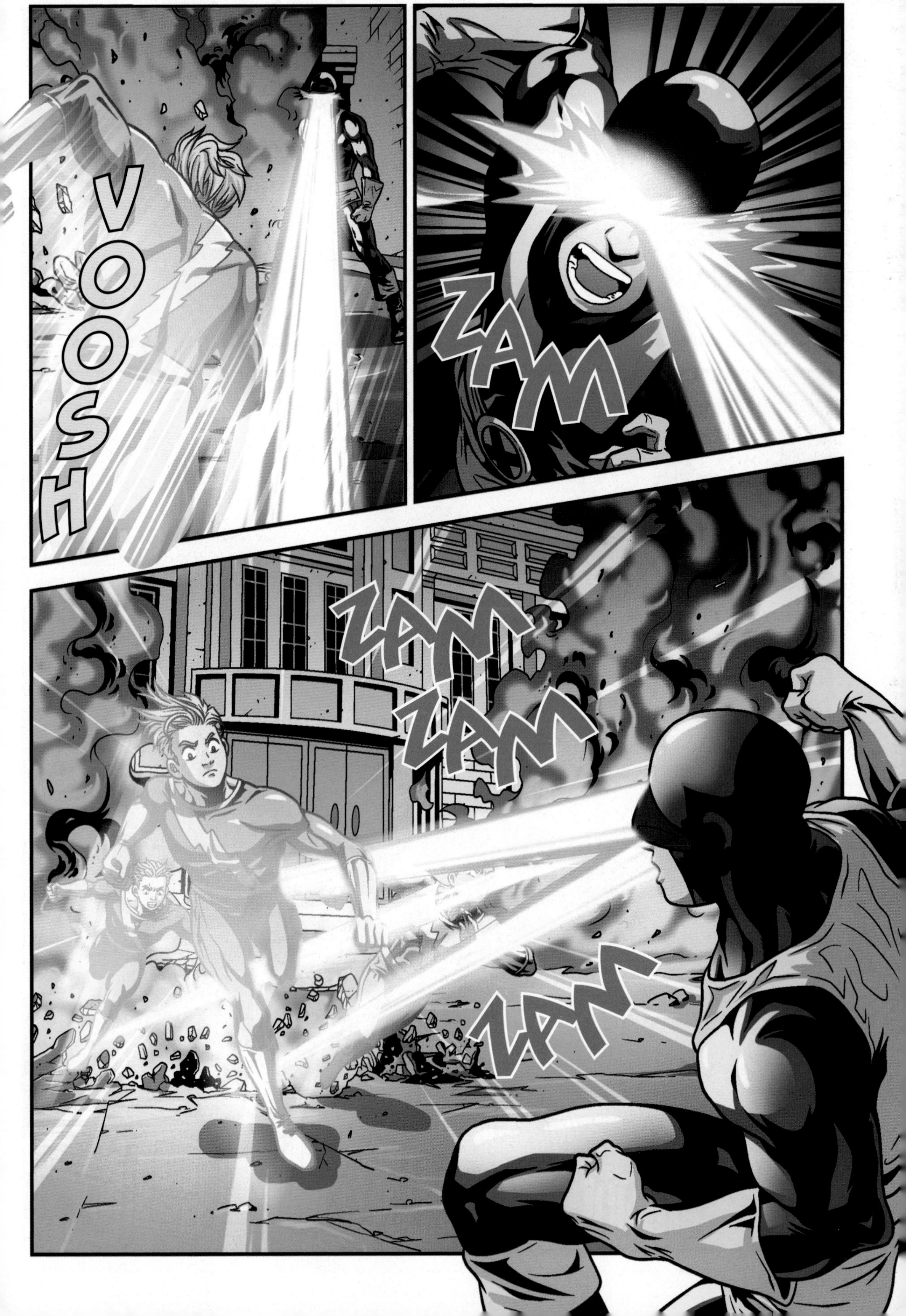
VOOSH
ZAM
ZAM
ZAM
ZAM

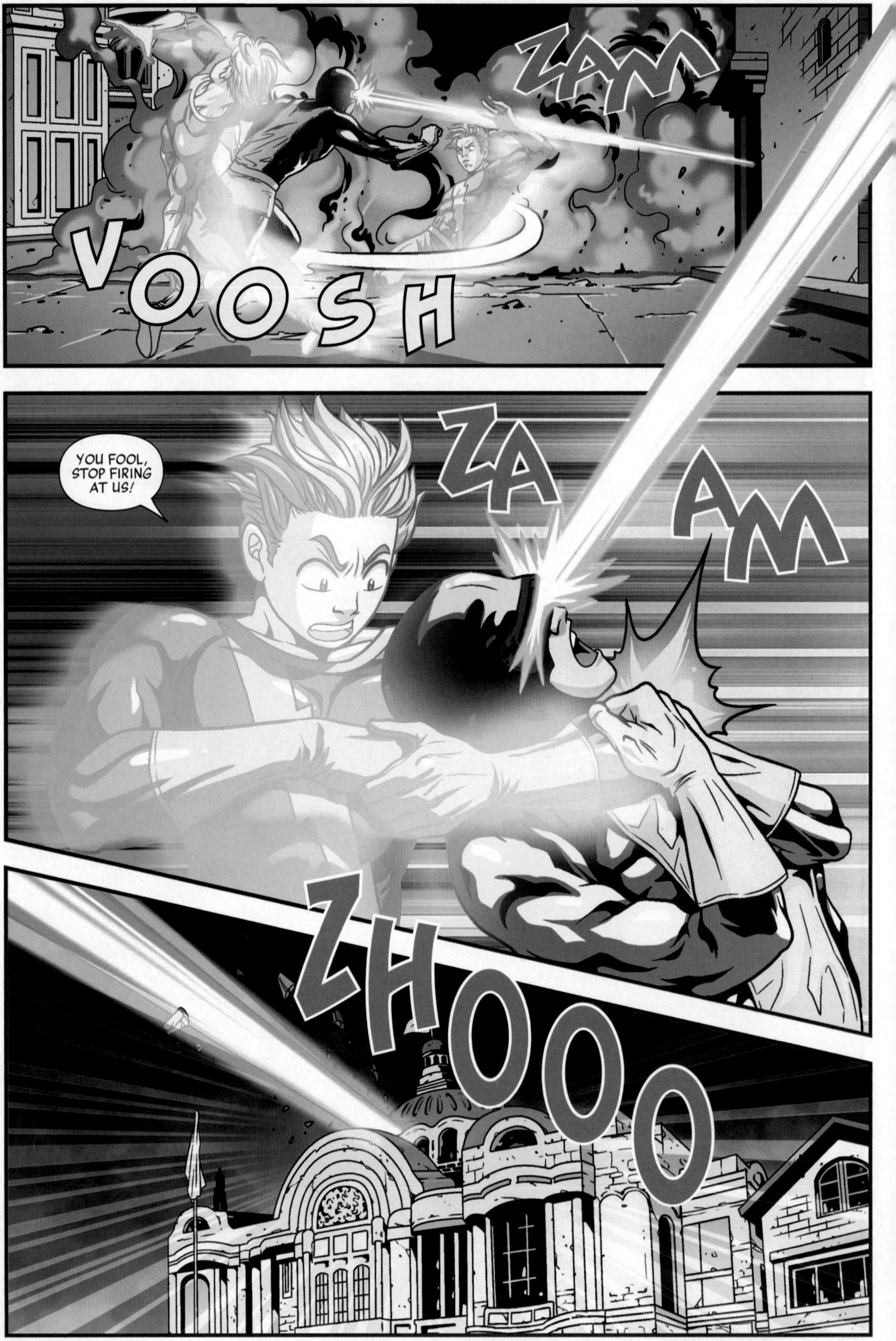
ZAM
VOOSH
YOU FOOL, STOP FIRING AT US!
ZA AM
ZHOOOO

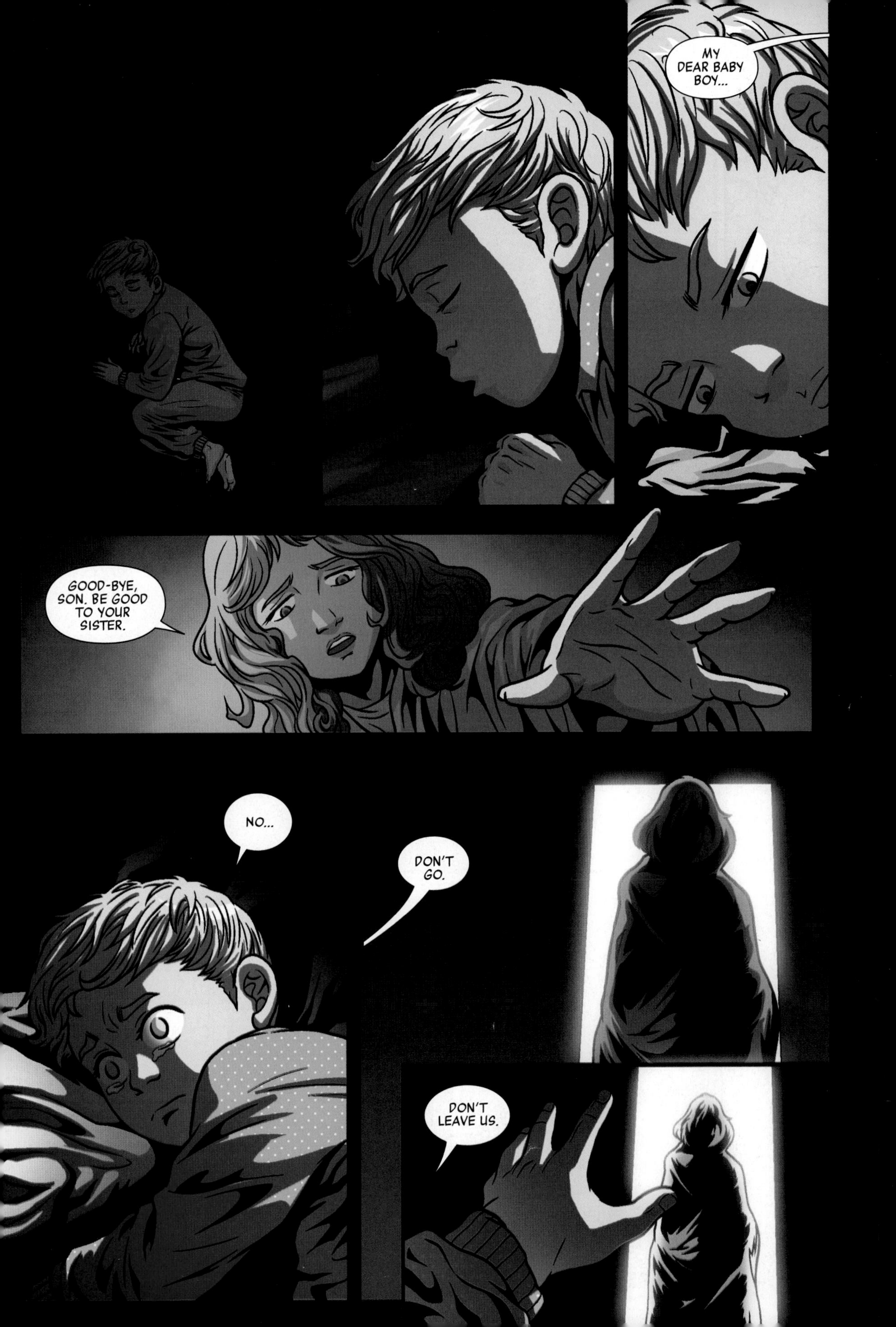
MY DEAR BABY BOY...
GOOD-BYE, SON. BE GOOD TO YOUR SISTER.
NO...
DON'T GO.
DON'T LEAVE US.

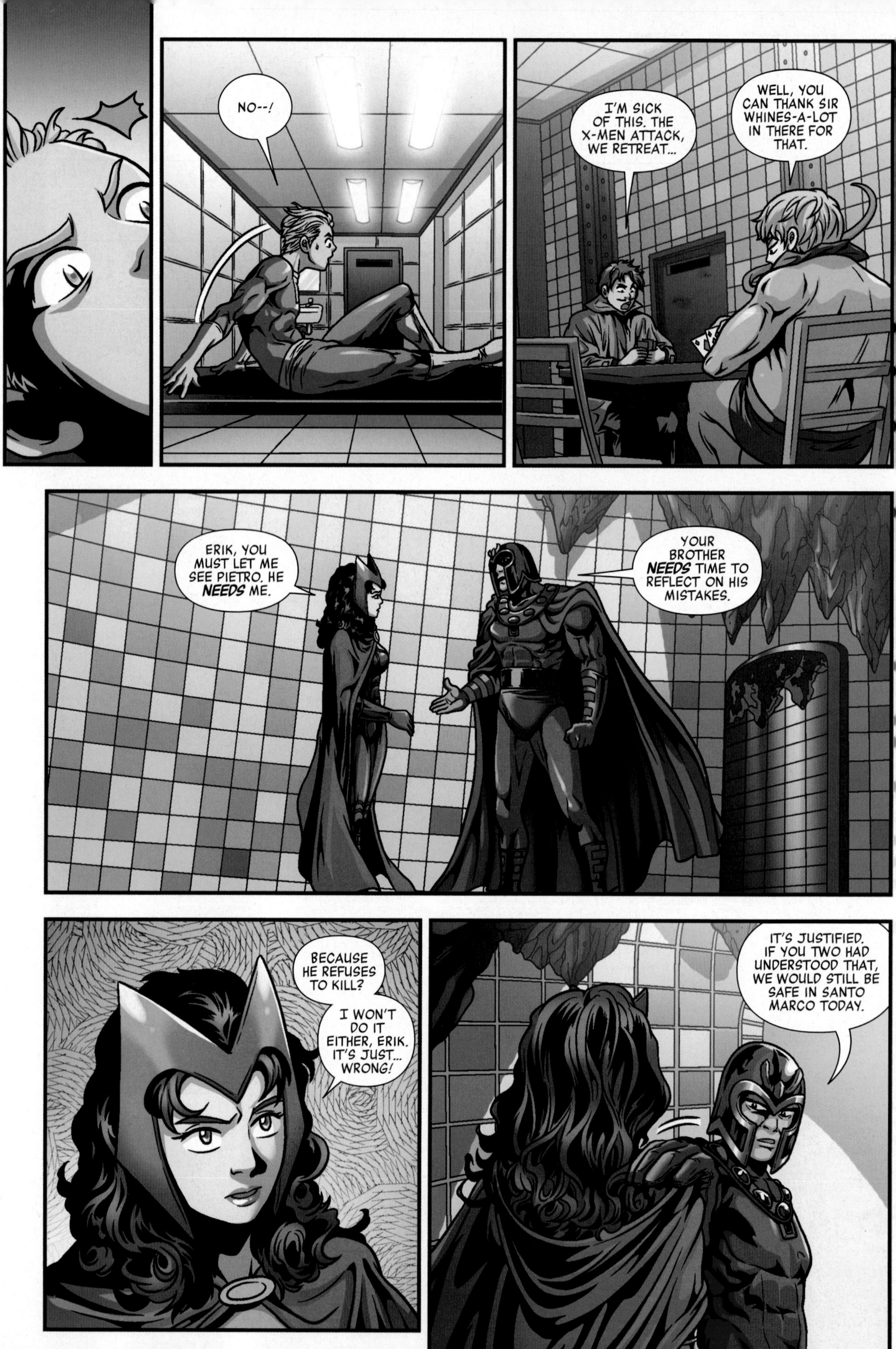
NO--!
I'M SICK OF THIS. THE X-MEN ATTACK, WE RETREAT...
WELL, YOU CAN THANK SIR WHINES-A-LOT IN THERE FOR THAT.
ERIK, YOU MUST LET ME SEE PIETRO. HE *NEEDS* ME.
YOUR BROTHER *NEEDS* TIME TO REFLECT ON HIS MISTAKES.
BECAUSE HE REFUSES TO KILL?
I WON'T DO IT EITHER, ERIK. IT'S JUST... WRONG!
IT'S JUSTIFIED. IF YOU TWO HAD UNDERSTOOD THAT, WE WOULD STILL BE SAFE IN SANTO MARCO TODAY.

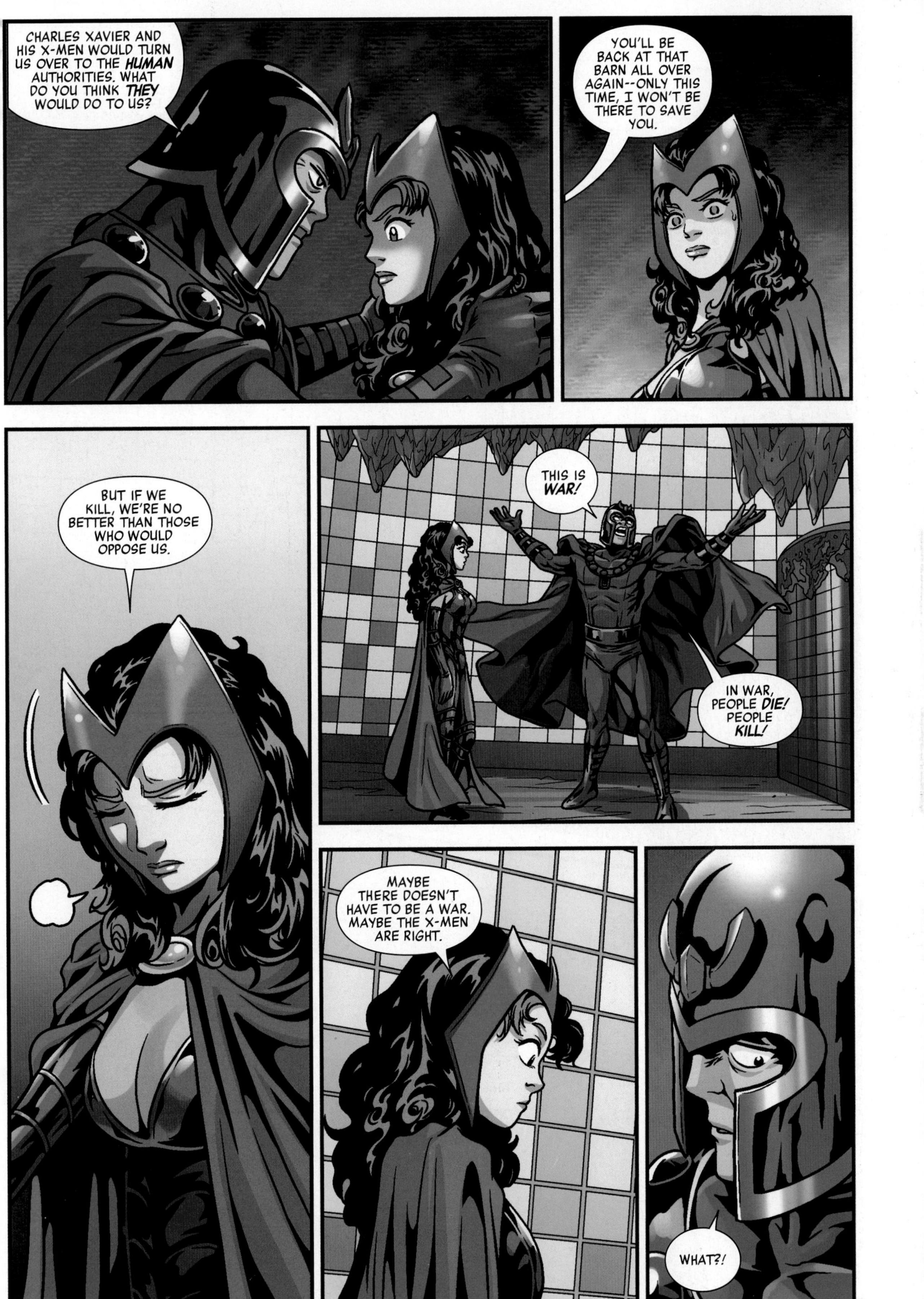
CHARLES XAVIER AND HIS X-MEN WOULD TURN US OVER TO THE HUMAN AUTHORITIES. WHAT DO YOU THINK THEY WOULD DO TO US?
YOU'LL BE BACK AT THAT BARN ALL OVER AGAIN--ONLY THIS TIME, I WON'T BE THERE TO SAVE YOU.
BUT IF WE KILL, WE'RE NO BETTER THAN THOSE WHO WOULD OPPOSE US.
THIS IS WAR!
IN WAR, PEOPLE DIE! PEOPLE KILL!
MAYBE THERE DOESN'T HAVE TO BE A WAR. MAYBE THE X-MEN ARE RIGHT.
WHAT?!

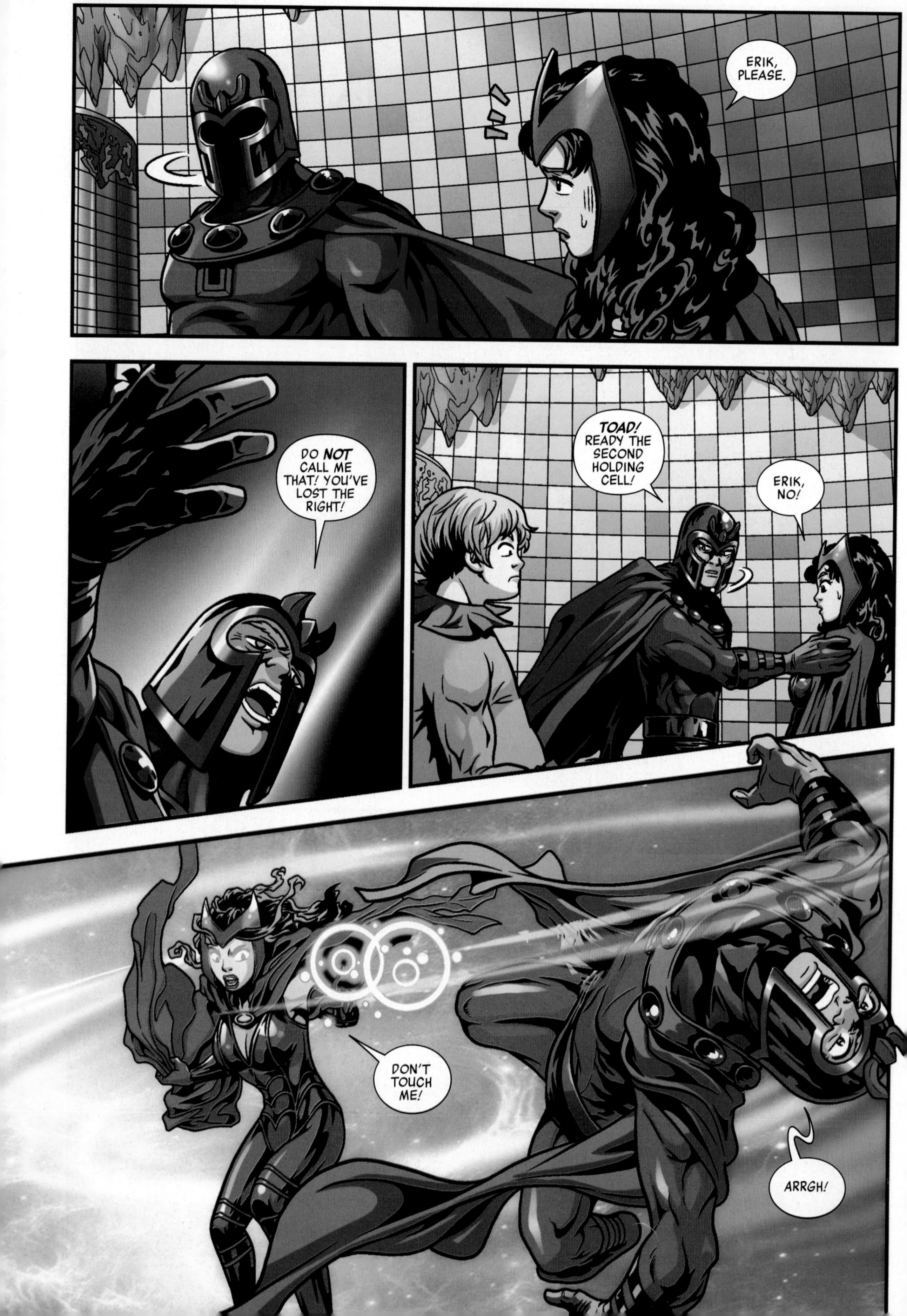
ERIK, PLEASE.
DO NOT CALL ME THAT! YOU'VE LOST THE RIGHT!
TOAD! READY THE SECOND HOLDING CELL!
ERIK, NO!
DON'T TOUCH ME!
ARRGH!

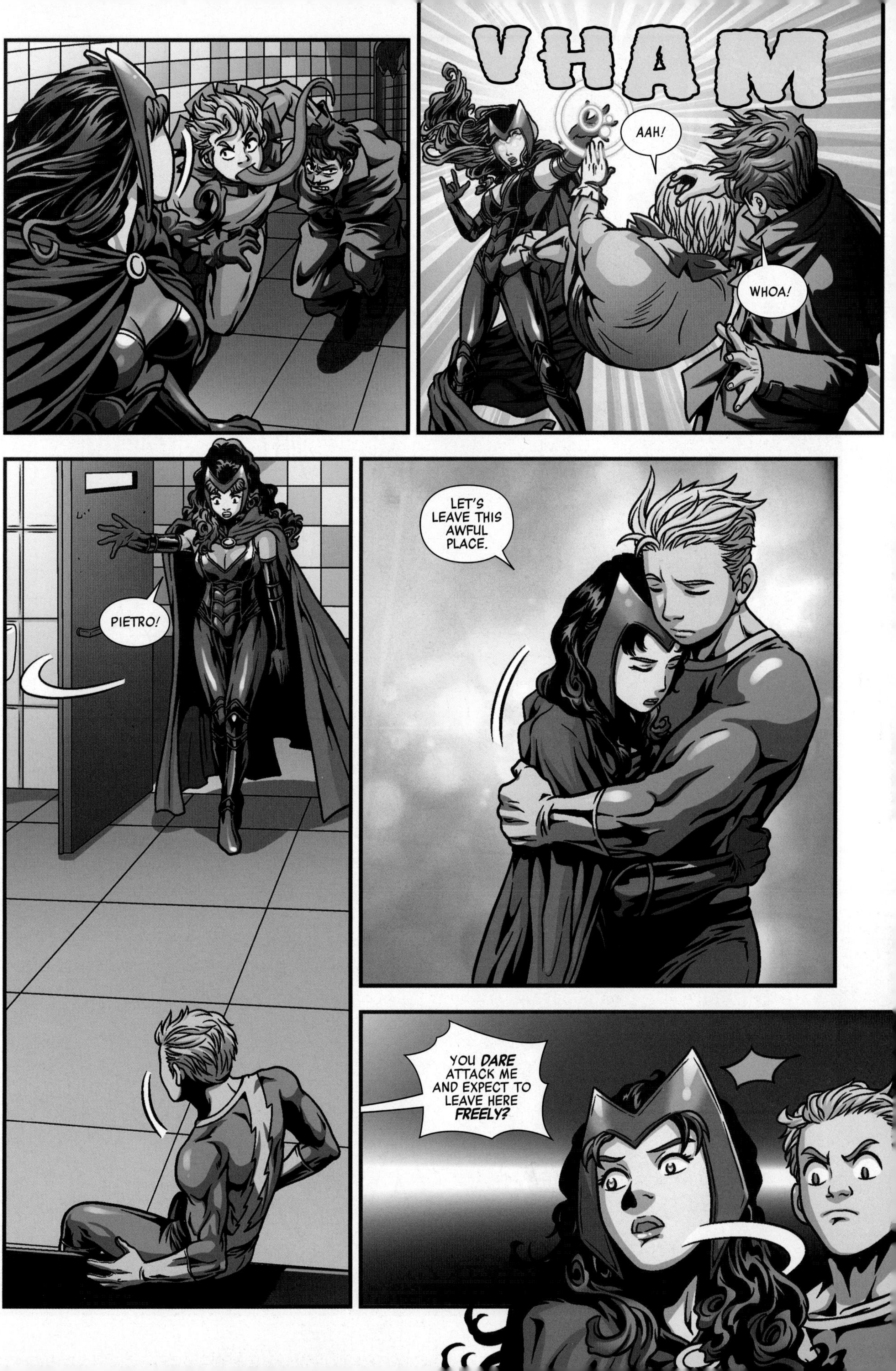
VHAM
AAH!
WHOA!
PIETRO!
LET'S LEAVE THIS AWFUL PLACE.
YOU **DARE** ATTACK ME AND EXPECT TO LEAVE HERE ***FREELY?***

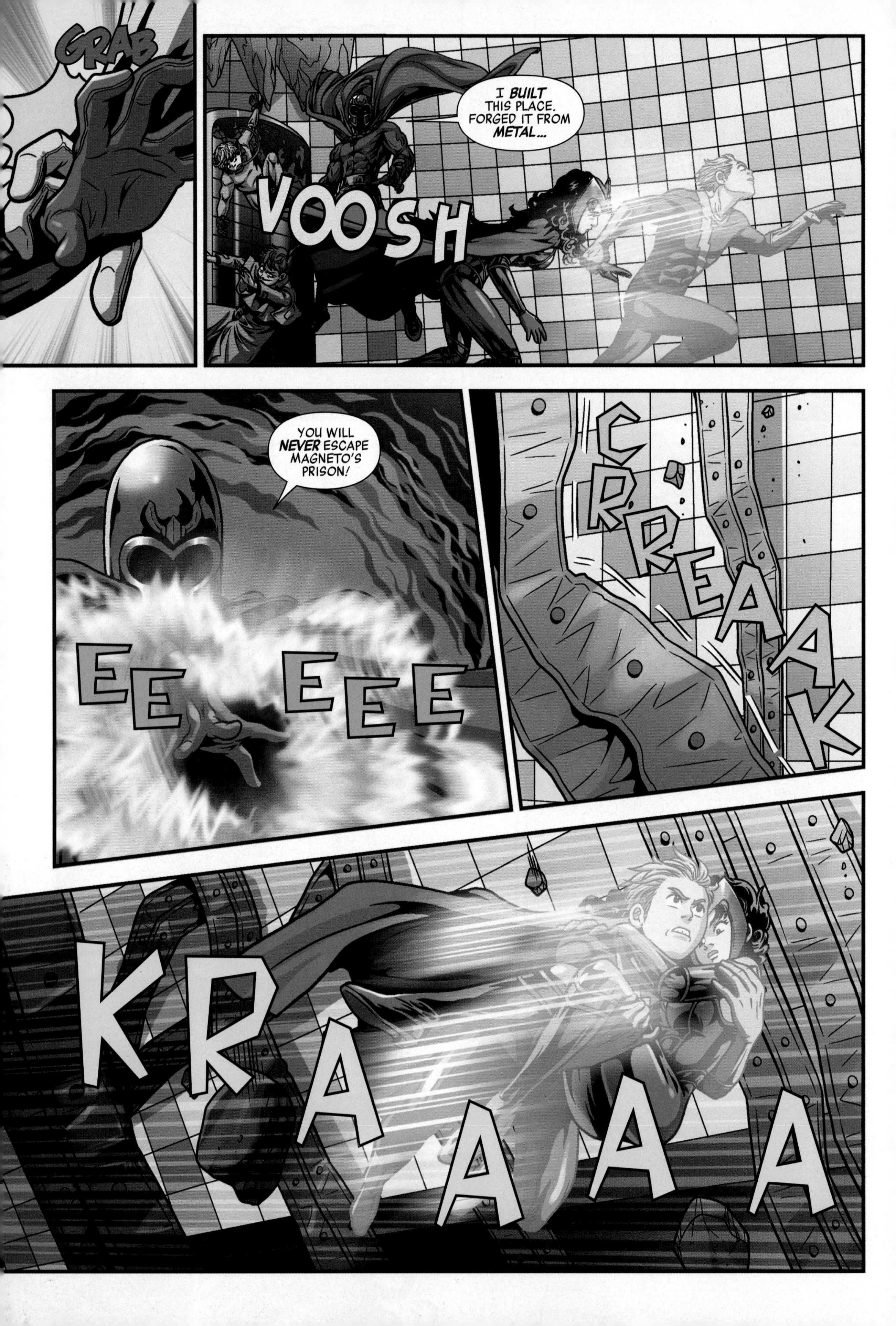
GRAB
I BUILT THIS PLACE. FORGED IT FROM METAL...
VOOSH
YOU WILL NEVER ESCAPE MAGNETO'S PRISON!
EE EEE
CRREAAK
KRAAAA

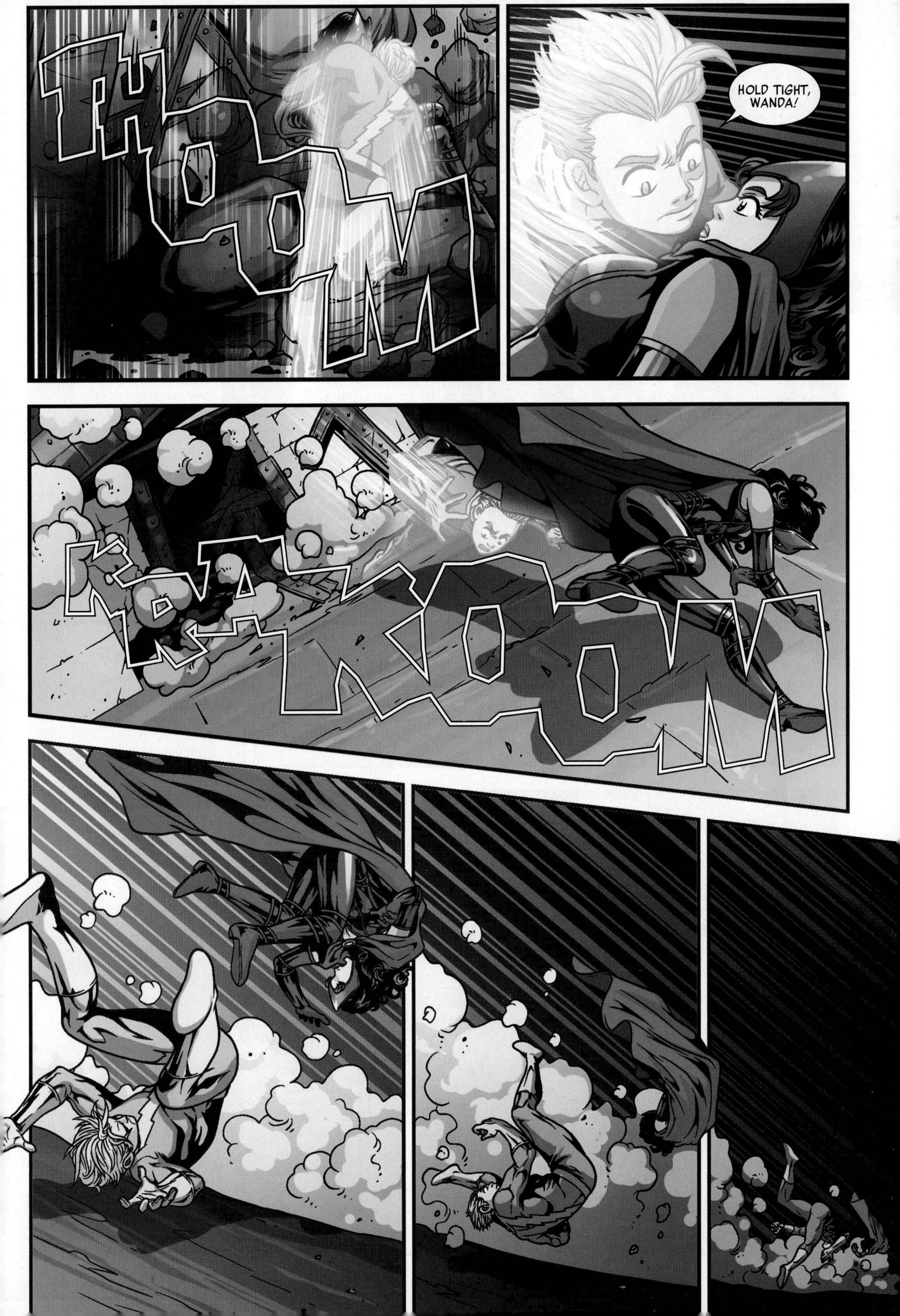
THOOM
HOLD TIGHT, WANDA!
KRAKOOM

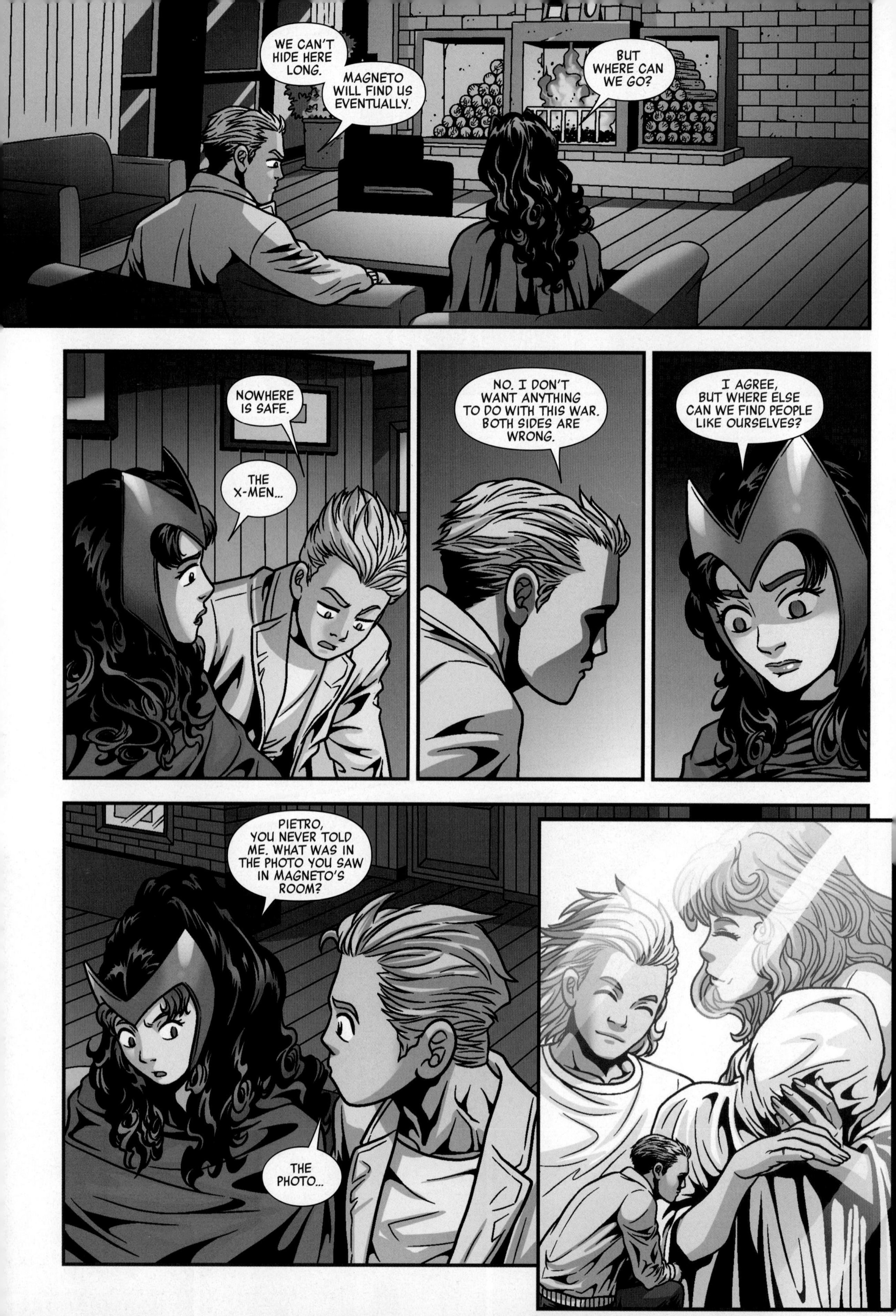
WE CAN'T HIDE HERE LONG.
MAGNETO WILL FIND US EVENTUALLY.
BUT WHERE CAN WE GO?
NOWHERE IS SAFE.
THE X-MEN...
NO. I DON'T WANT ANYTHING TO DO WITH THIS WAR. BOTH SIDES ARE WRONG.
I AGREE, BUT WHERE ELSE CAN WE FIND PEOPLE LIKE OURSELVES?
PIETRO, YOU NEVER TOLD ME. WHAT WAS IN THE PHOTO YOU SAW IN MAGNETO'S ROOM?
THE PHOTO...

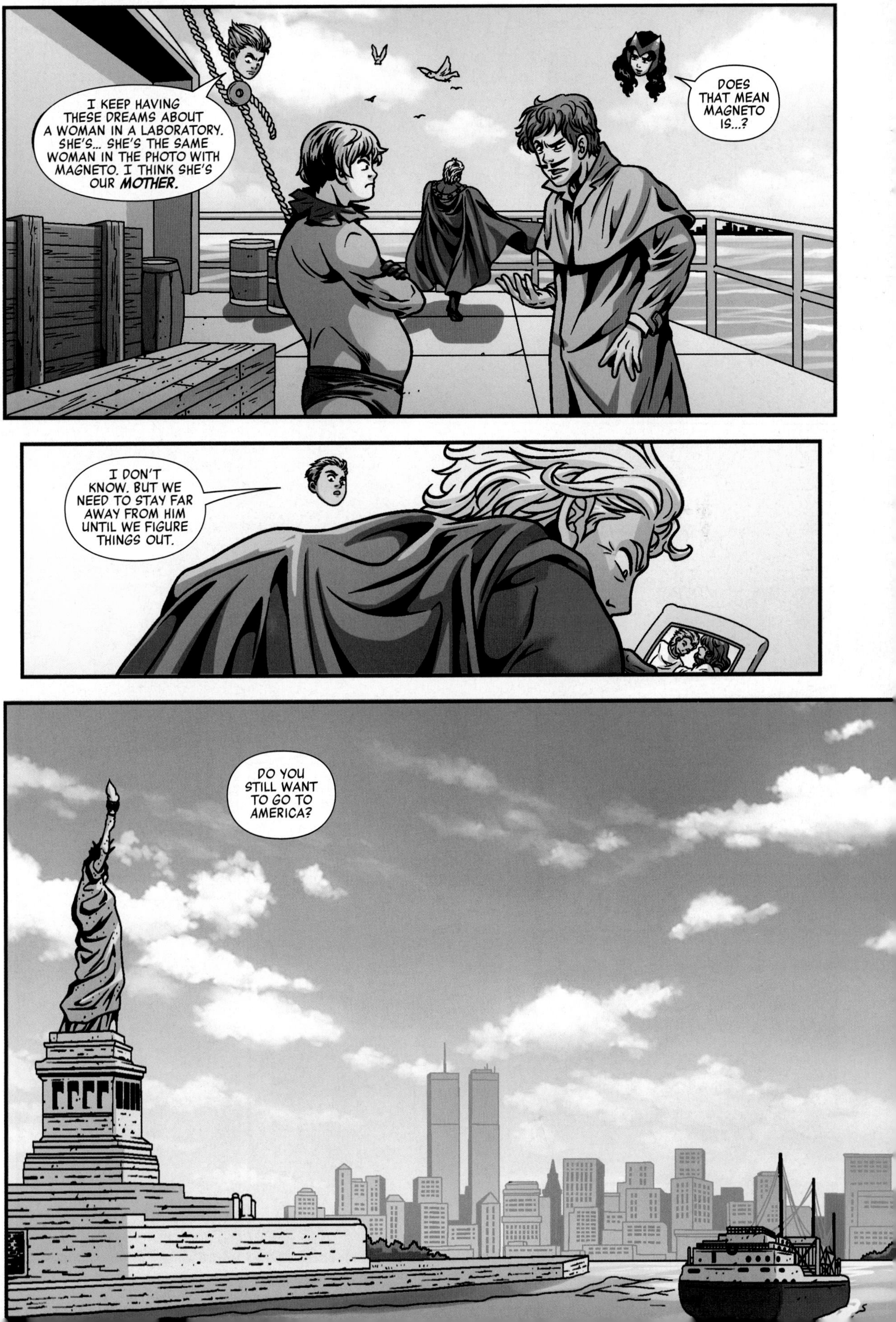
I KEEP HAVING THESE DREAMS ABOUT A WOMAN IN A LABORATORY. SHE'S... SHE'S THE SAME WOMAN IN THE PHOTO WITH MAGNETO. I THINK SHE'S OUR MOTHER.
DOES THAT MEAN MAGNETO IS...?
I DON'T KNOW. BUT WE NEED TO STAY FAR AWAY FROM HIM UNTIL WE FIGURE THINGS OUT.
DO YOU STILL WANT TO GO TO AMERICA?

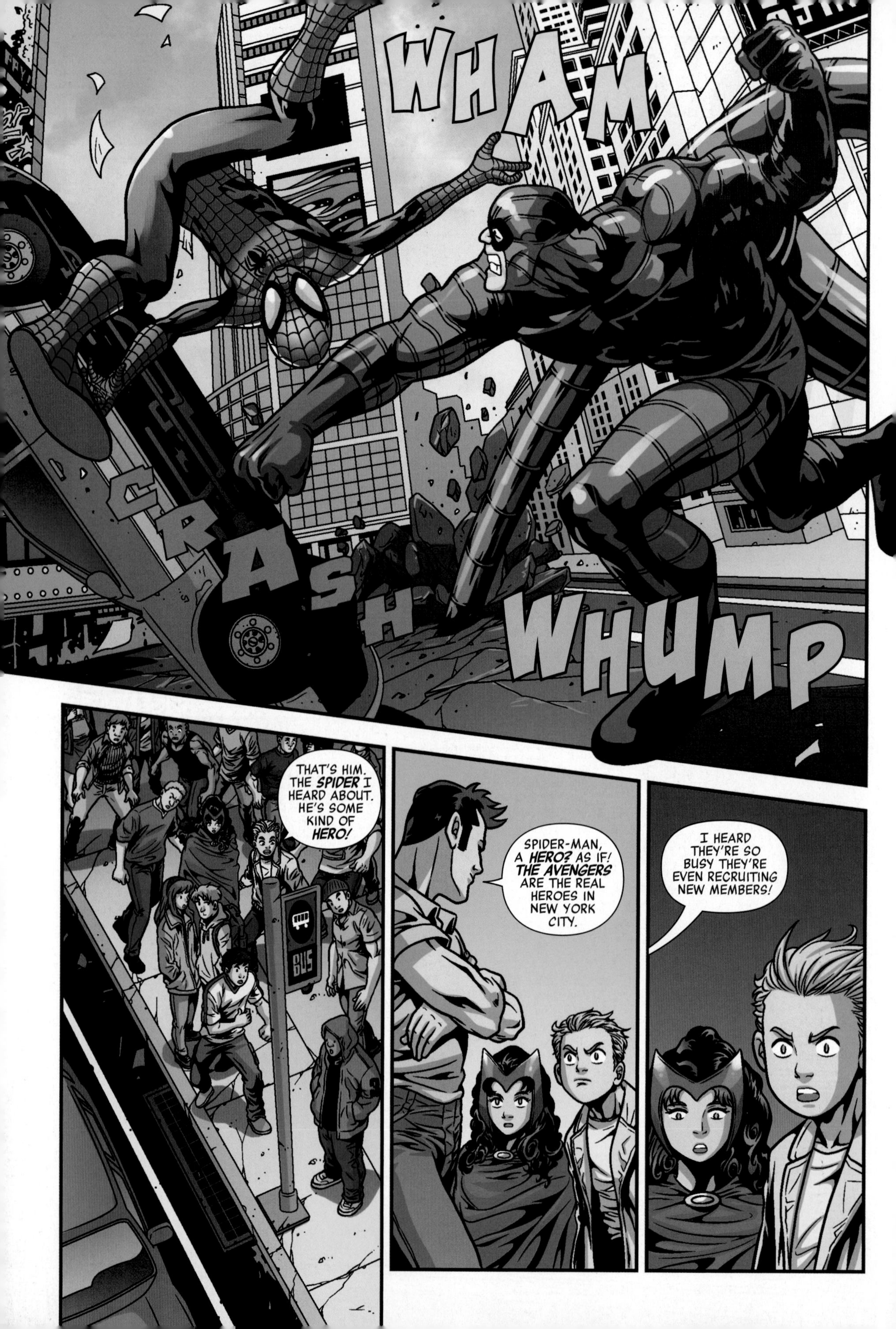
WHAM
CRASH
WHUMP
THAT'S HIM. THE SPIDER I HEARD ABOUT. HE'S SOME KIND OF HERO!
BUS
SPIDER-MAN, A HERO? AS IF! THE AVENGERS ARE THE REAL HEROES IN NEW YORK CITY.
I HEARD THEY'RE SO BUSY THEY'RE EVEN RECRUITING NEW MEMBERS!

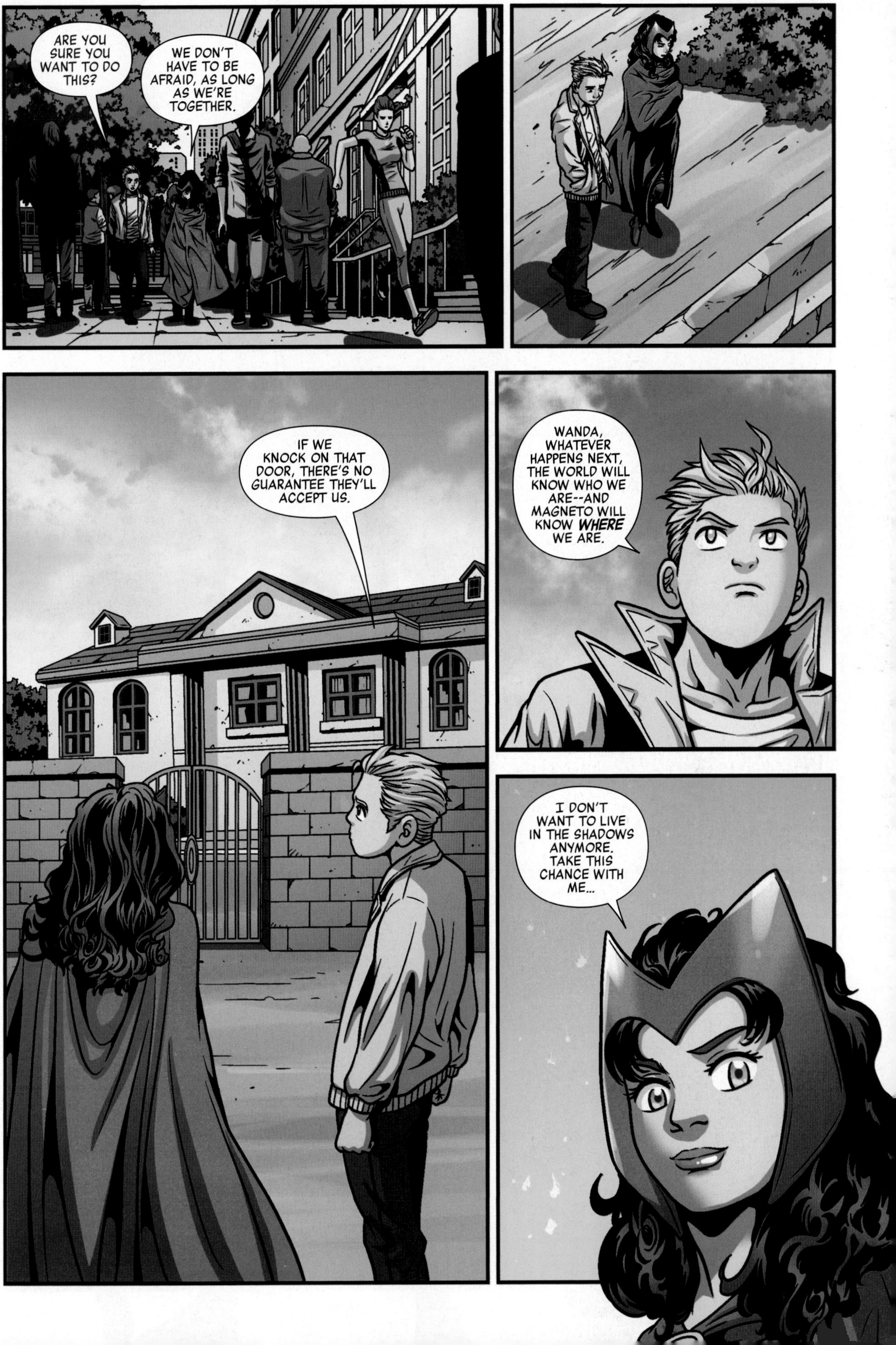
ARE YOU SURE YOU WANT TO DO THIS?
WE DON'T HAVE TO BE AFRAID, AS LONG AS WE'RE TOGETHER.
IF WE KNOCK ON THAT DOOR, THERE'S NO GUARANTEE THEY'LL ACCEPT US.
WANDA, WHATEVER HAPPENS NEXT, THE WORLD WILL KNOW WHO WE ARE--AND MAGNETO WILL KNOW *WHERE* WE ARE.
I DON'T WANT TO LIVE IN THE SHADOWS ANYMORE. TAKE THIS CHANCE WITH ME...

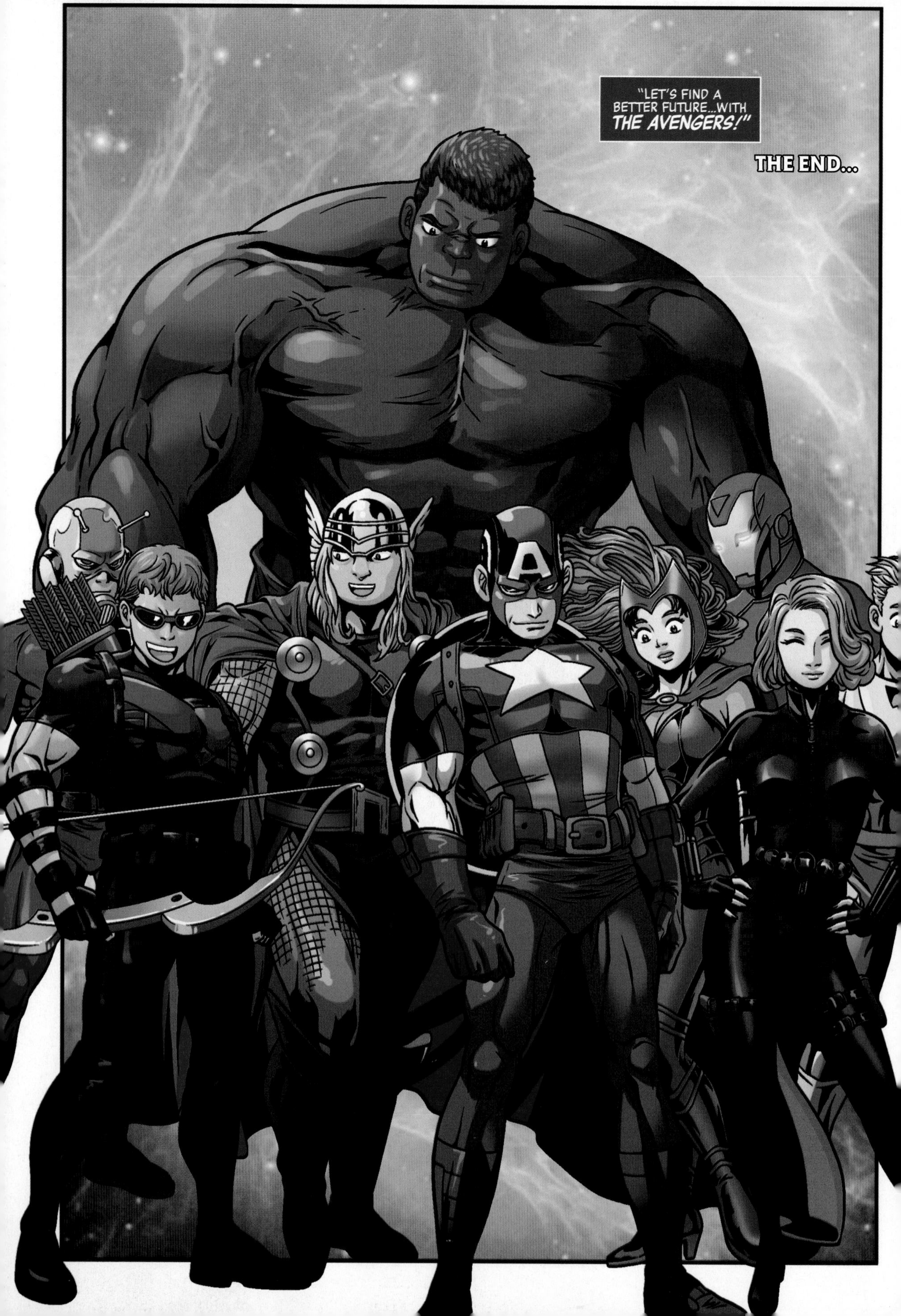
"LET'S FIND A BETTER FUTURE...WITH THE AVENGERS!"
THE END...

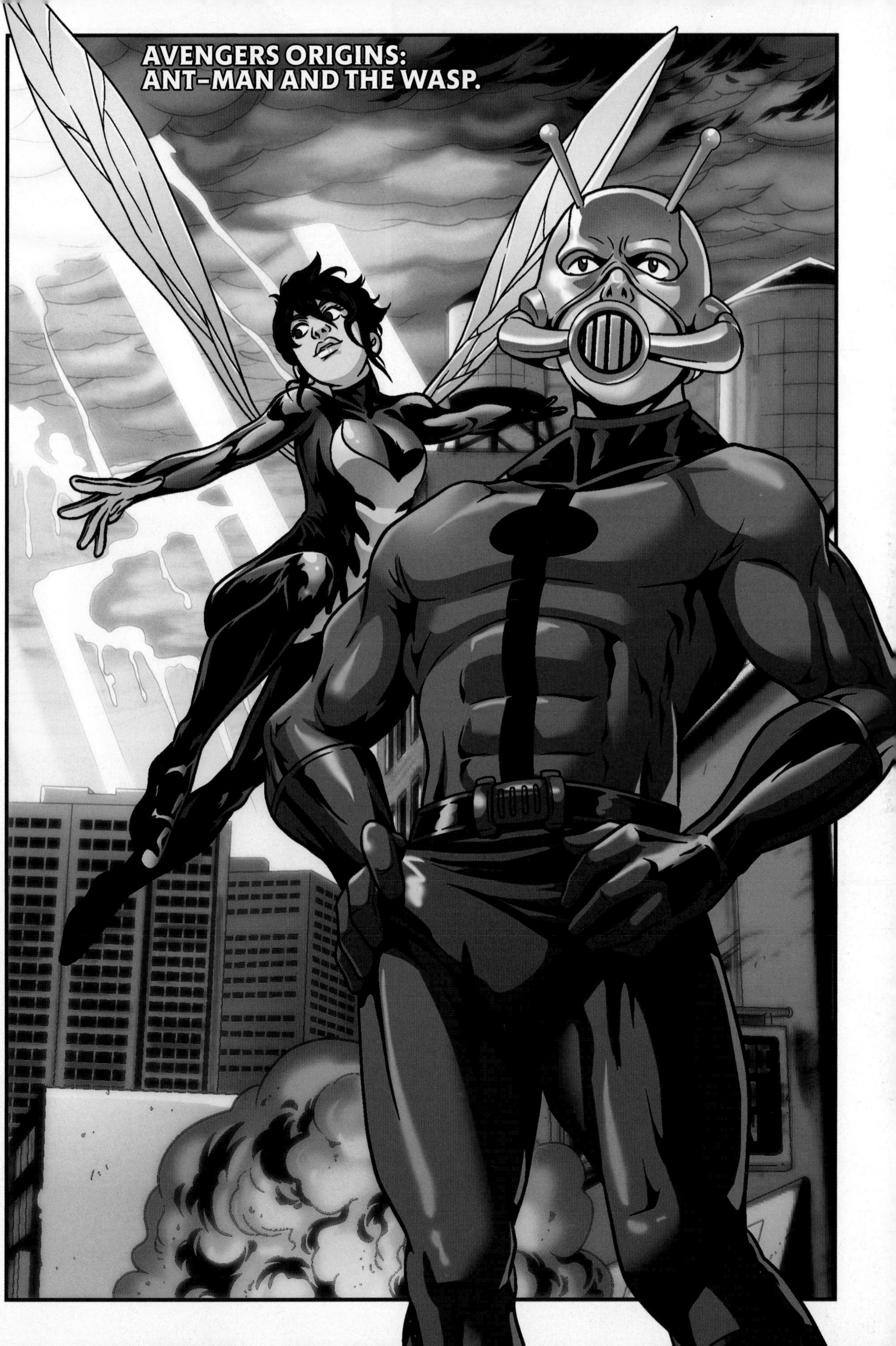
AVENGERS ORIGINS:
ANT-MAN AND THE WASP.

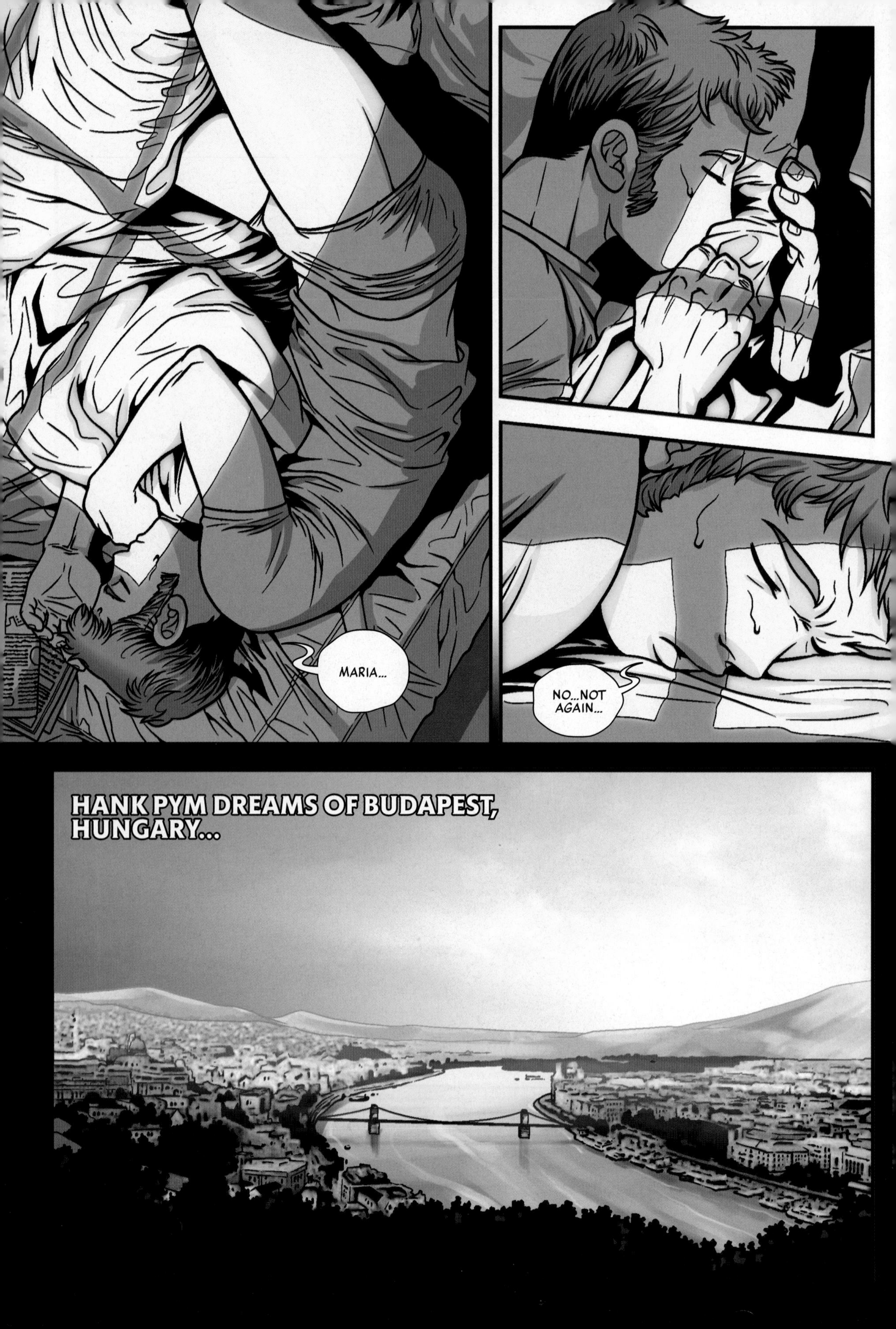
MARIA...
NO...NOT AGAIN...
HANK PYM DREAMS OF BUDAPEST, HUNGARY...

OH, HANK. I'M STILL WORRIED WE MADE A MISTAKE IN COMING HERE FOR OUR HONEYMOON.

I WANTED TO SEE WHERE YOU GREW UP, MARIA.

THE POLITICAL ENEMIES WE MADE, MY FATHER AND I...

...THEY HAVE LONG MEMORIES, AND THEY DON'T FORGIVE.

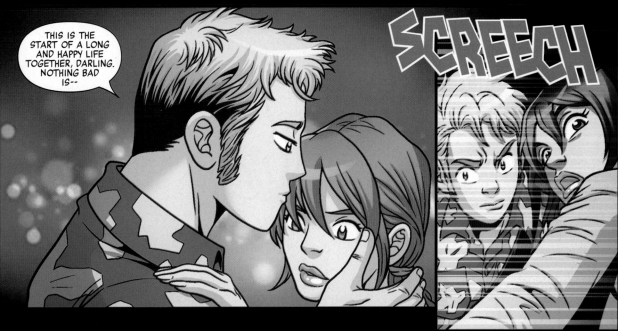

THIS IS THE START OF A LONG AND HAPPY LIFE TOGETHER, DARLING. NOTHING BAD IS--

SCREECH

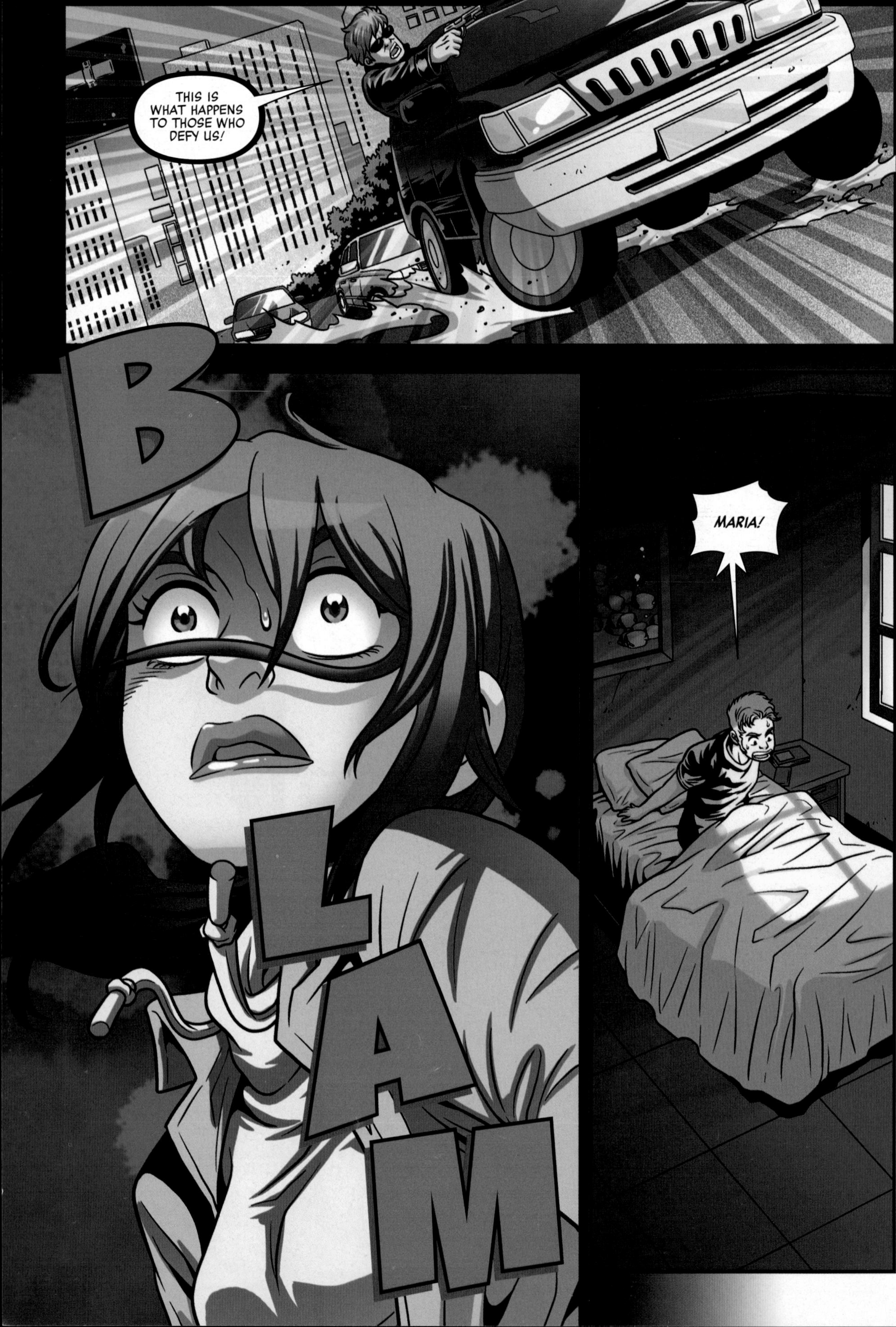
THIS IS WHAT HAPPENS TO THOSE WHO DEFY US!
BLAM
MARIA!

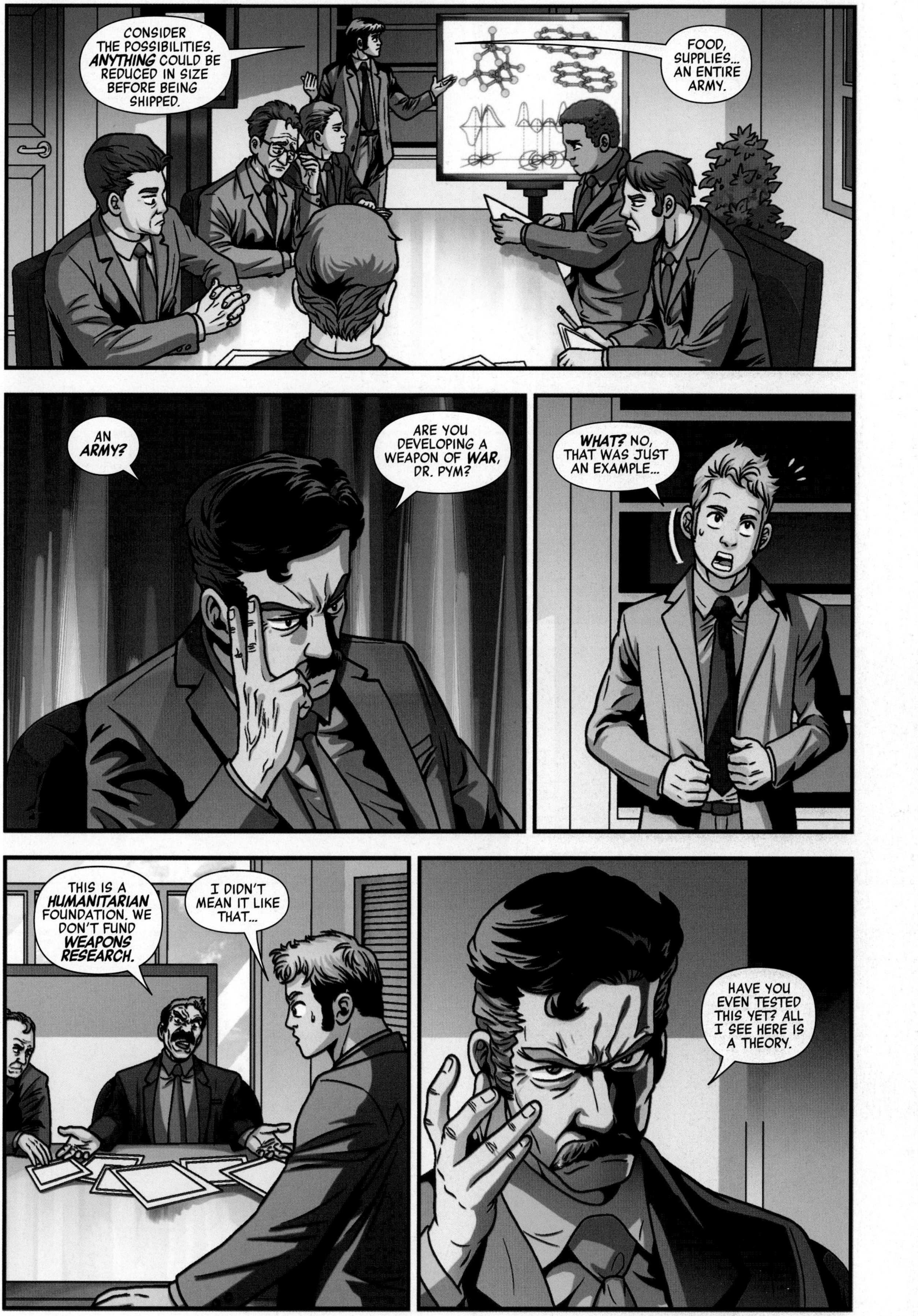
CONSIDER THE POSSIBILITIES. ANYTHING COULD BE REDUCED IN SIZE BEFORE BEING SHIPPED.
FOOD, SUPPLIES... AN ENTIRE ARMY.
AN ARMY?
ARE YOU DEVELOPING A WEAPON OF WAR, DR. PYM?
WHAT? NO, THAT WAS JUST AN EXAMPLE...
THIS IS A HUMANITARIAN FOUNDATION. WE DON'T FUND WEAPONS RESEARCH.
I DIDN'T MEAN IT LIKE THAT...
HAVE YOU EVEN TESTED THIS YET? ALL I SEE HERE IS A THEORY.

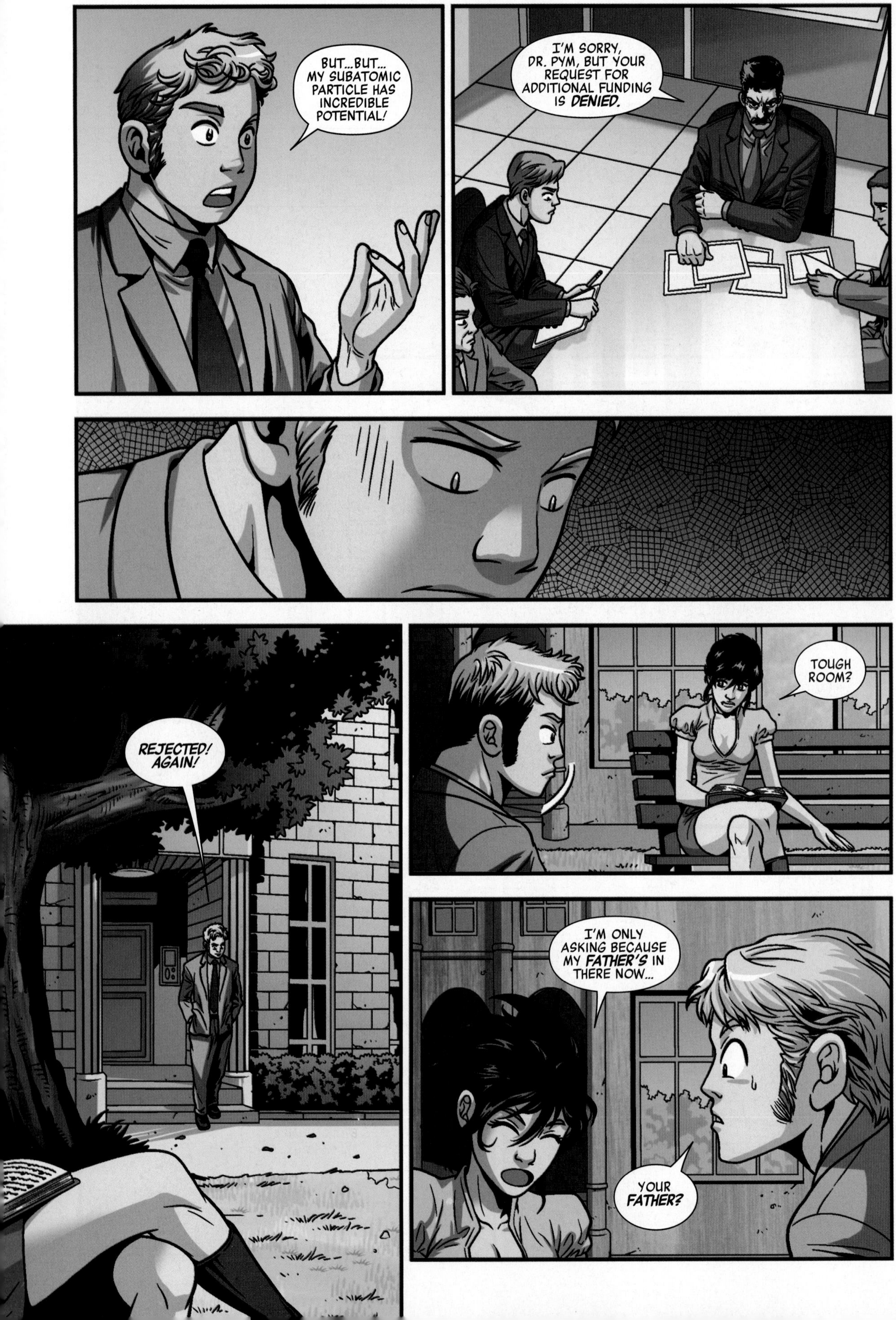
BUT...BUT... MY SUBATOMIC PARTICLE HAS INCREDIBLE POTENTIAL!
I'M SORRY, DR. PYM, BUT YOUR REQUEST FOR ADDITIONAL FUNDING IS DENIED.
REJECTED! AGAIN!
TOUGH ROOM?
I'M ONLY ASKING BECAUSE MY FATHER'S IN THERE NOW...
YOUR FATHER?

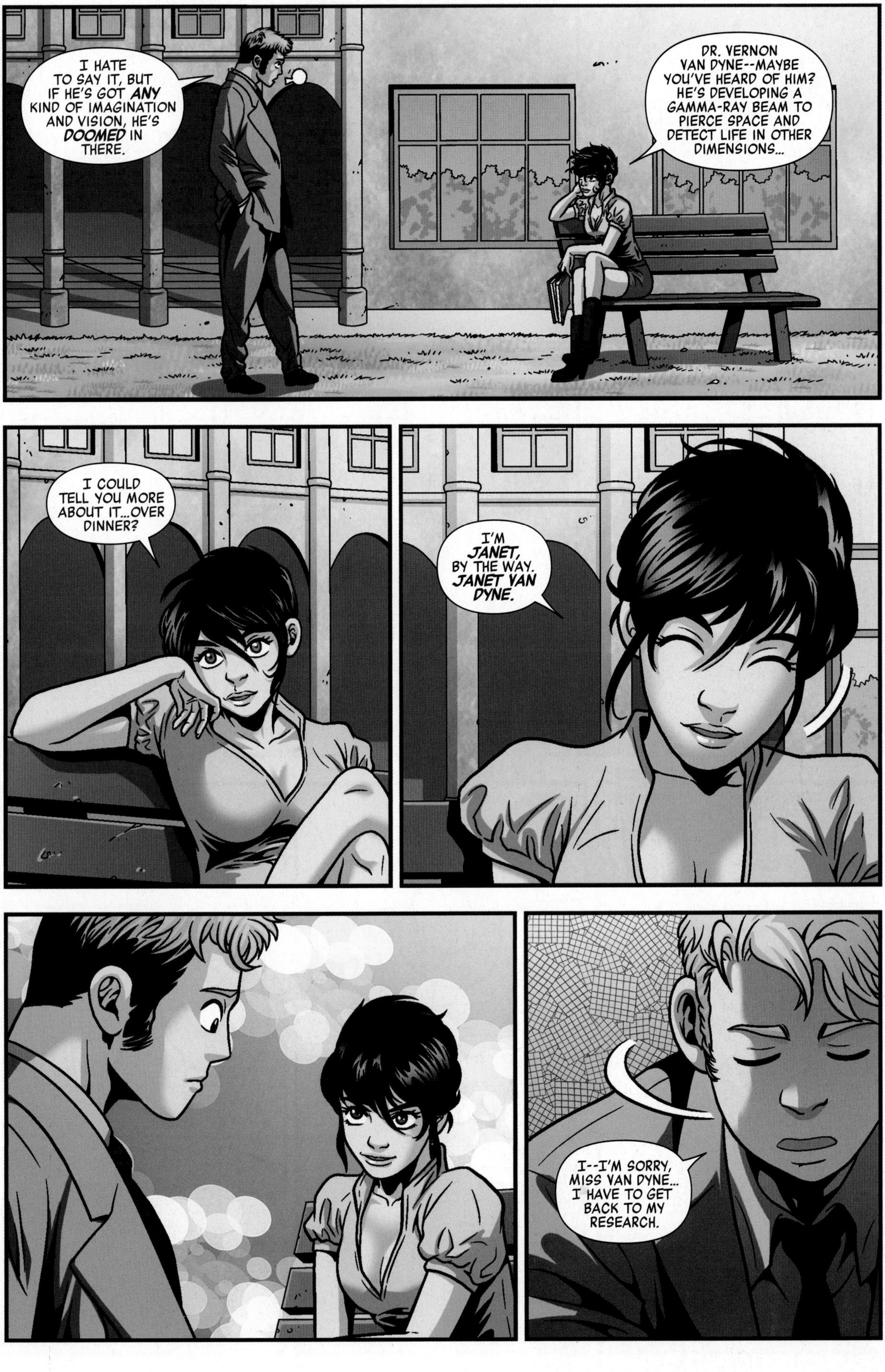
I HATE TO SAY IT, BUT IF HE'S GOT ANY KIND OF IMAGINATION AND VISION, HE'S DOOMED IN THERE.
DR. VERNON VAN DYNE--MAYBE YOU'VE HEARD OF HIM? HE'S DEVELOPING A GAMMA-RAY BEAM TO PIERCE SPACE AND DETECT LIFE IN OTHER DIMENSIONS...
I COULD TELL YOU MORE ABOUT IT...OVER DINNER?
I'M JANET, BY THE WAY. JANET VAN DYNE.
I--I'M SORRY, MISS VAN DYNE... I HAVE TO GET BACK TO MY RESEARCH.

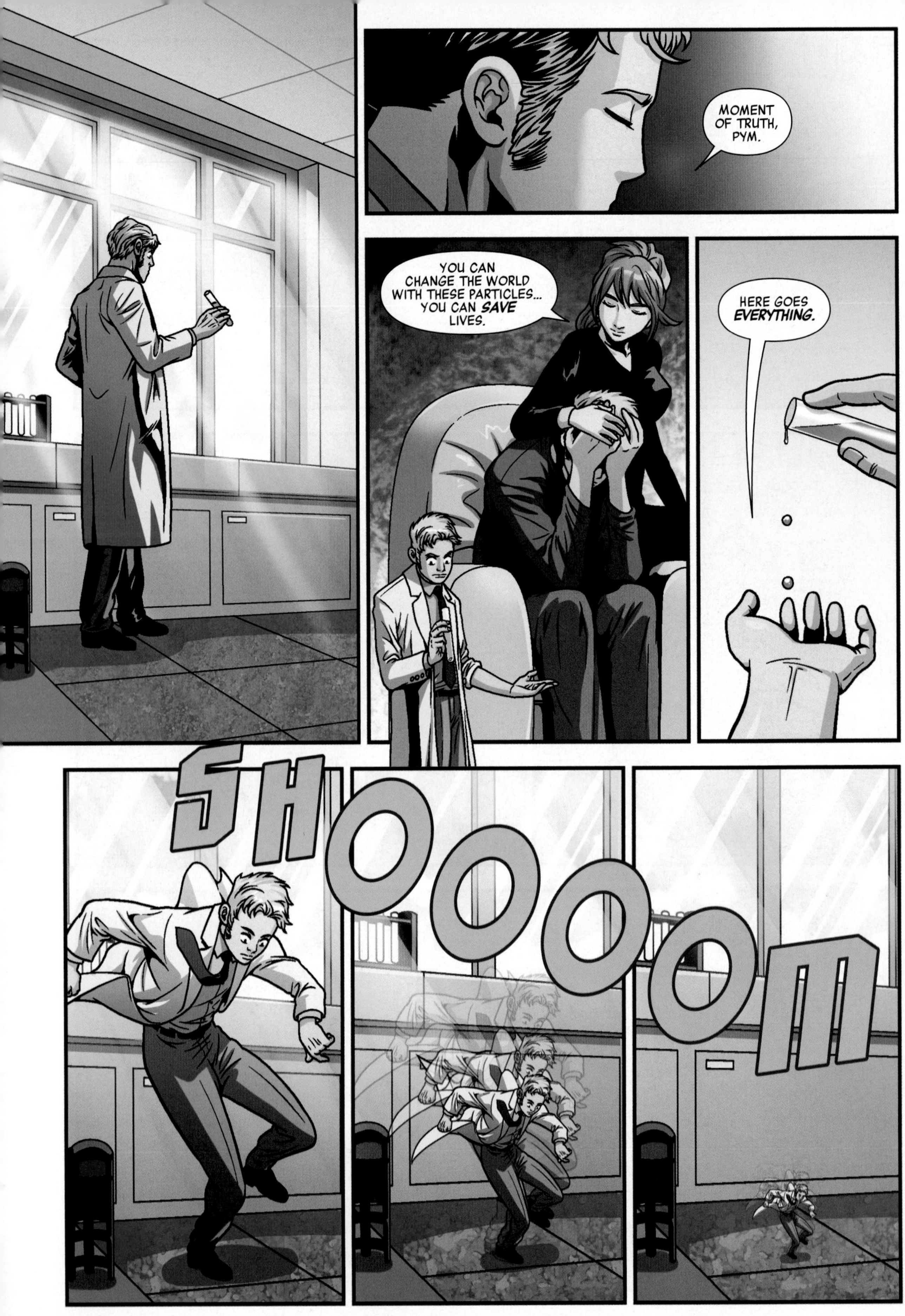
MOMENT OF TRUTH, PYM.
YOU CAN CHANGE THE WORLD WITH THESE PARTICLES... YOU CAN *SAVE* LIVES.
HERE GOES *EVERYTHING.*
SHOOOOOM

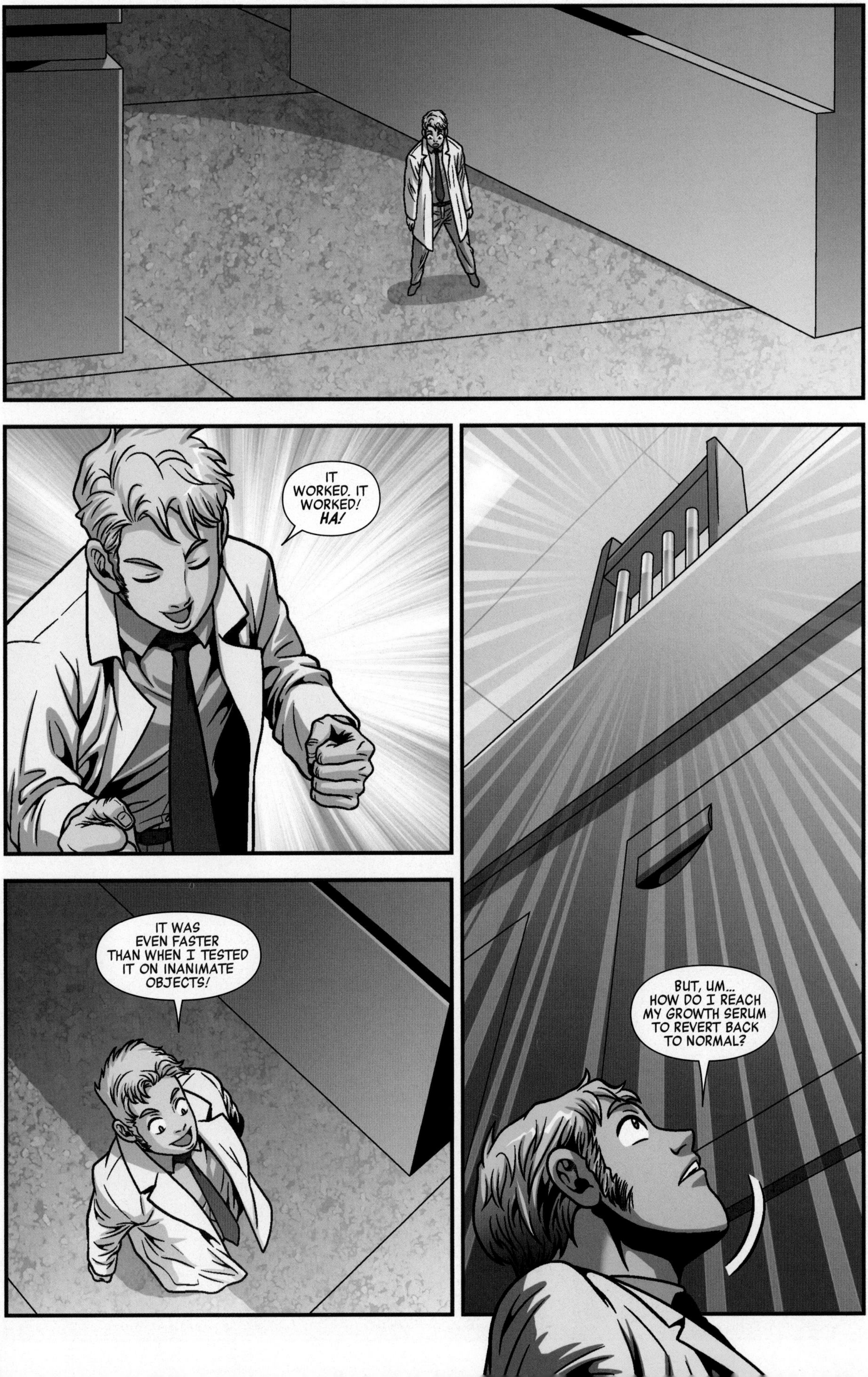
IT WORKED. IT WORKED! HA!
IT WAS EVEN FASTER THAN WHEN I TESTED IT ON INANIMATE OBJECTS!
BUT, UM... HOW DO I REACH MY GROWTH SERUM TO REVERT BACK TO NORMAL?

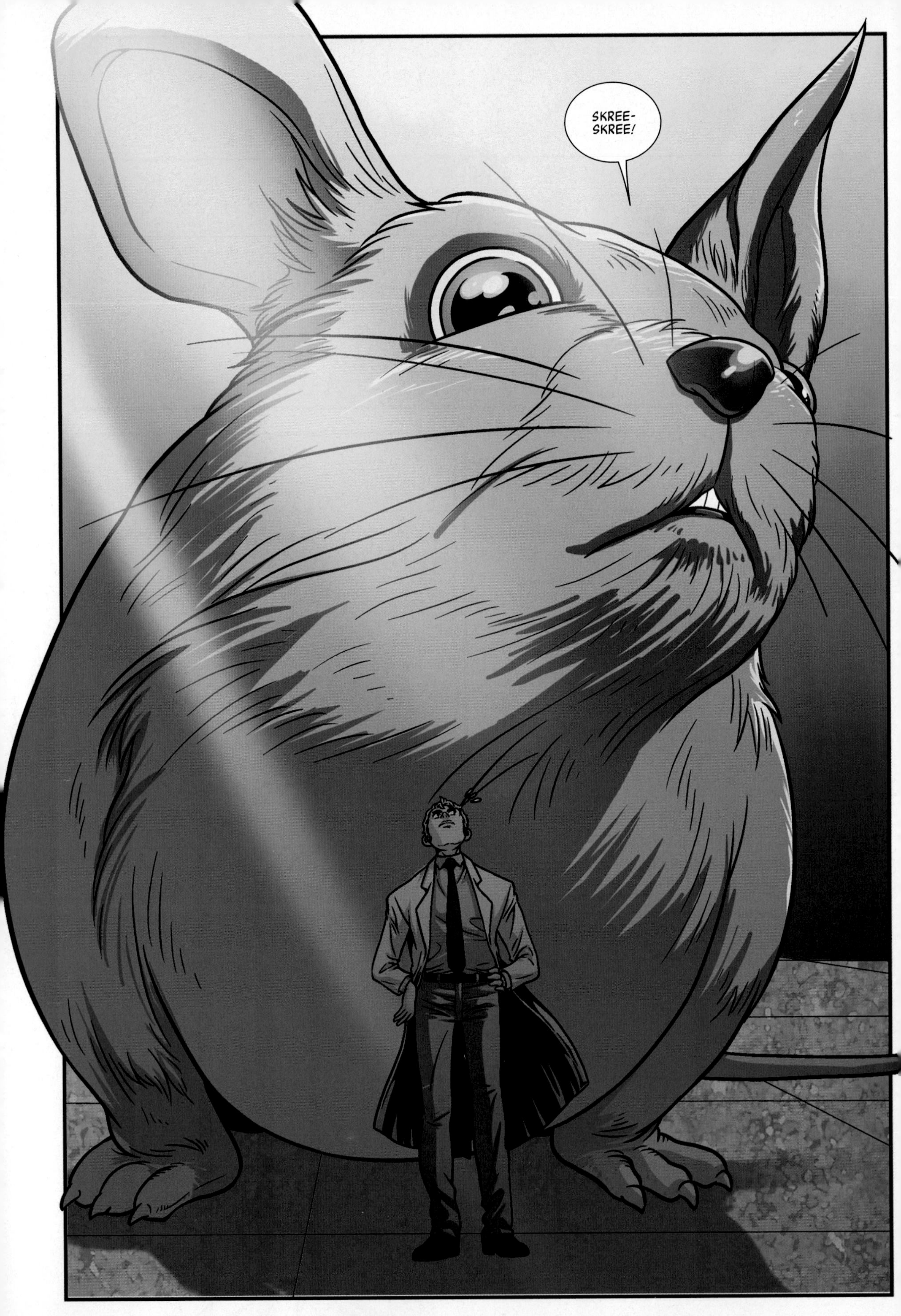
SKREE-
SKREE!

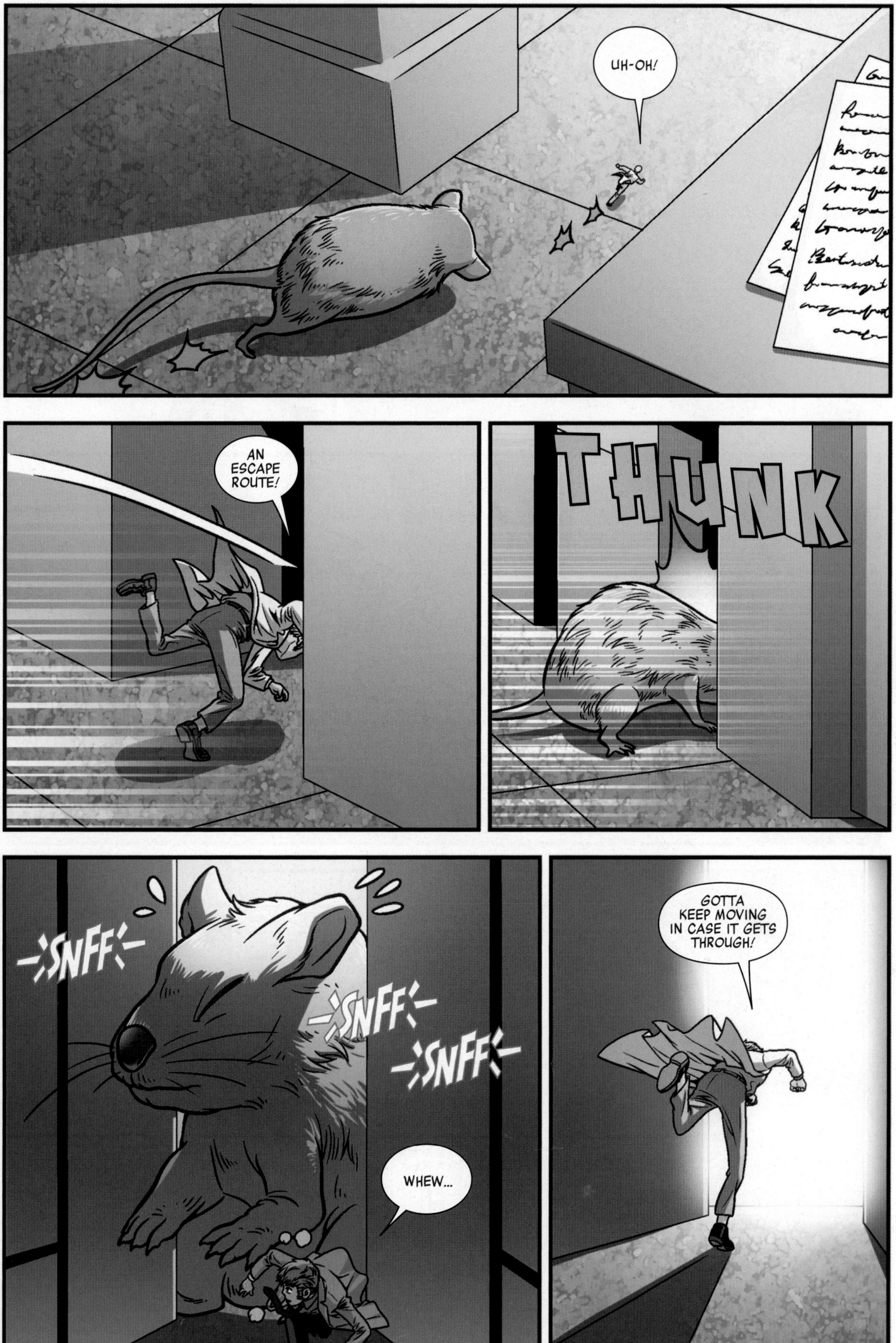
UH-OH!
AN ESCAPE ROUTE!
THUNK
SNFF
SNFF
SNFF
WHEW...
GOTTA KEEP MOVING IN CASE IT GETS THROUGH!

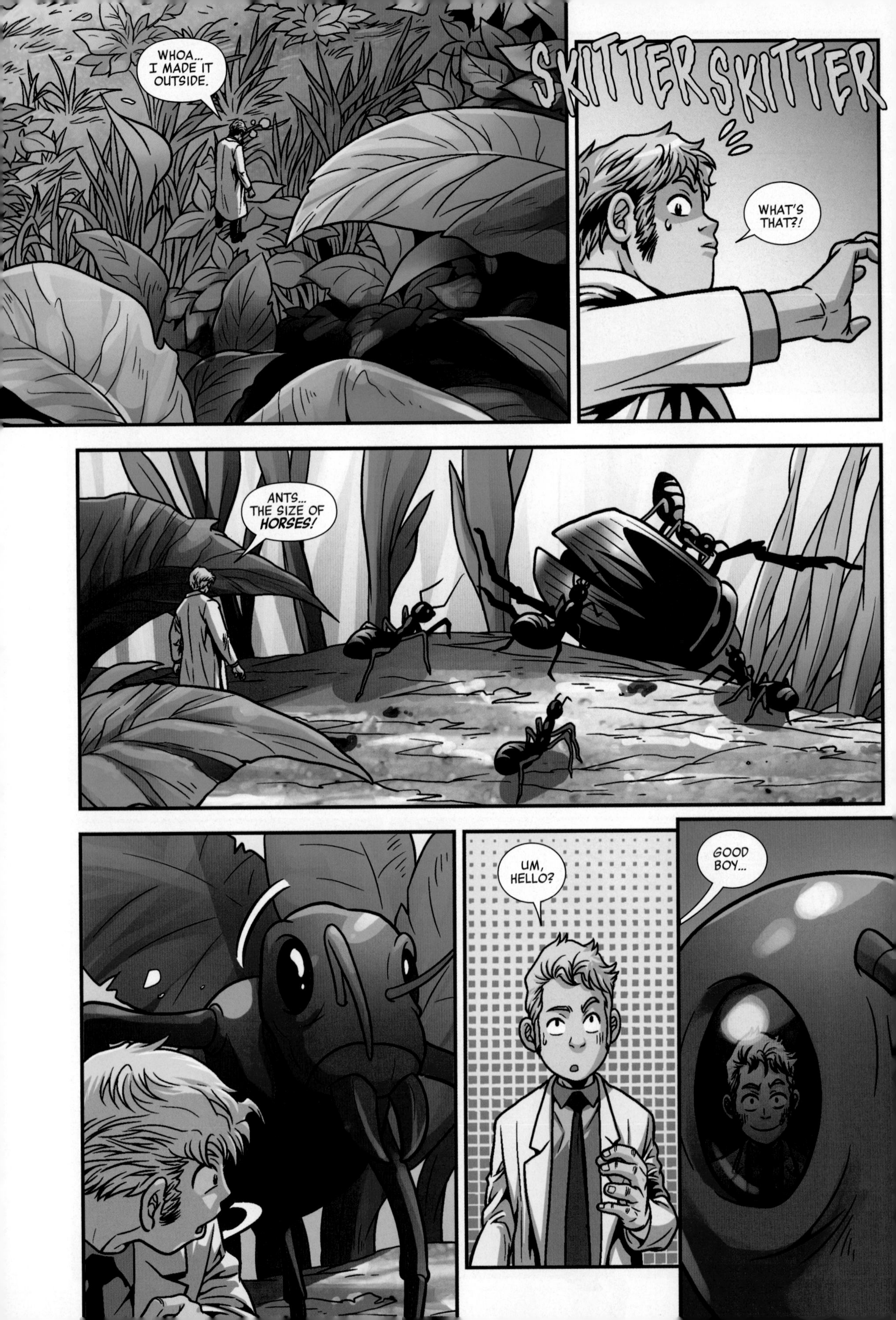
WHOA... I MADE IT OUTSIDE.
SKITTER SKITTER
WHAT'S THAT?!
ANTS... THE SIZE OF HORSES!
UM, HELLO?
GOOD BOY...

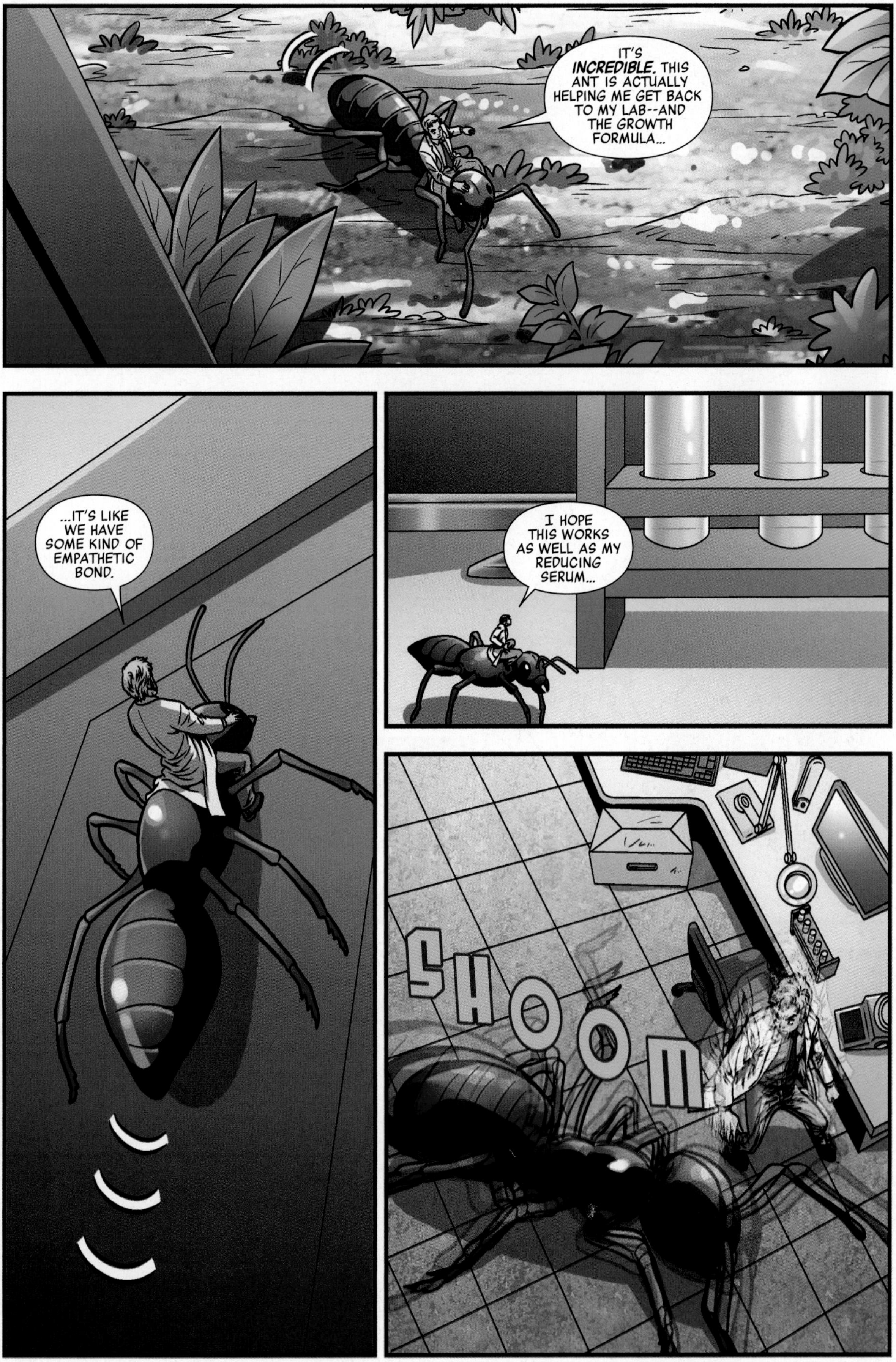
IT'S *INCREDIBLE.* THIS ANT IS ACTUALLY HELPING ME GET BACK TO MY LAB--AND THE GROWTH FORMULA...
...IT'S LIKE WE HAVE SOME KIND OF EMPATHETIC BOND.
I HOPE THIS WORKS AS WELL AS MY REDUCING SERUM...
SHOOM

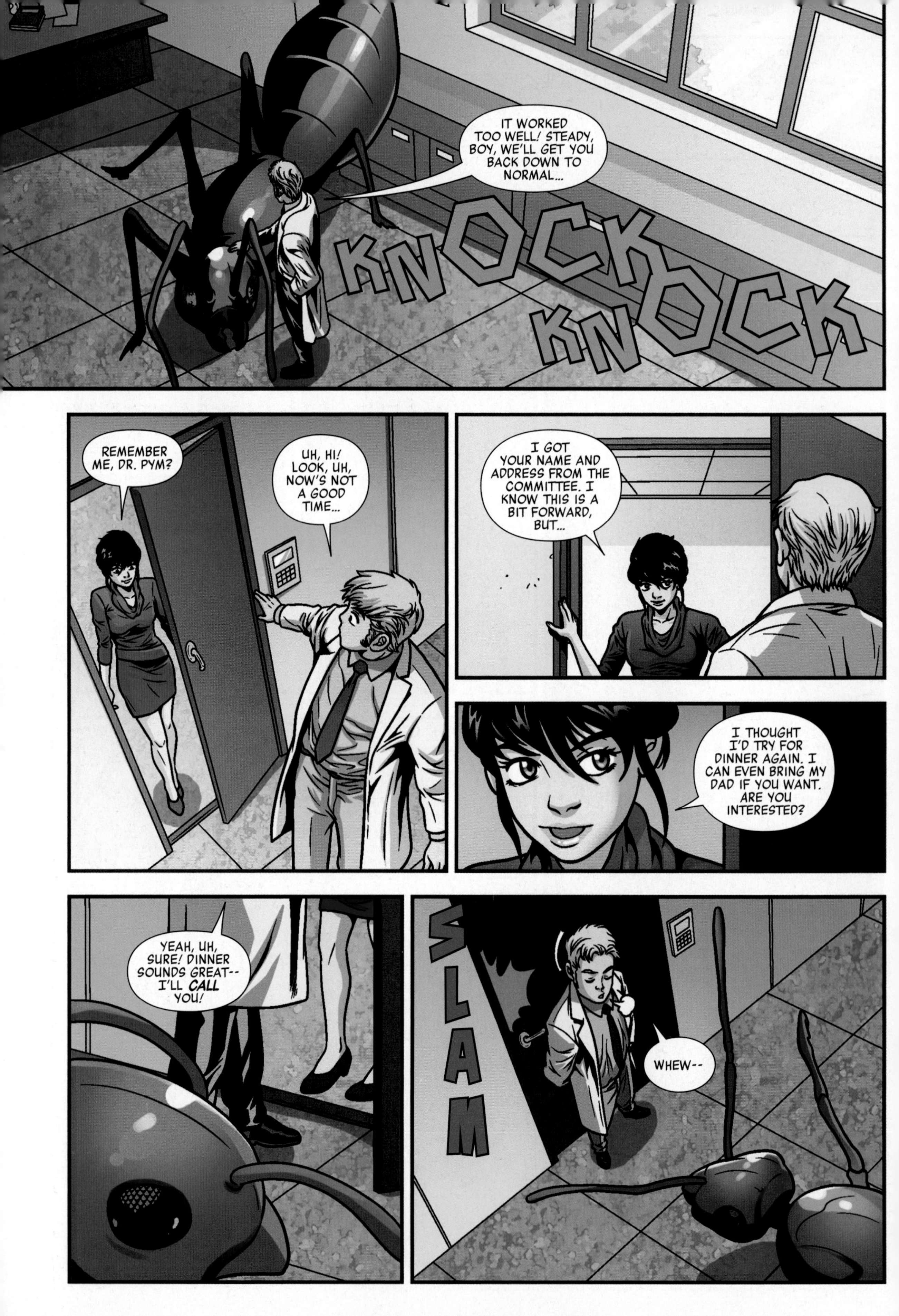
IT WORKED TOO WELL! STEADY, BOY, WE'LL GET YOU BACK DOWN TO NORMAL...
KNOCK KNOCK
REMEMBER ME, DR. PYM?
UH, HI! LOOK, UH, NOW'S NOT A GOOD TIME...
I GOT YOUR NAME AND ADDRESS FROM THE COMMITTEE. I KNOW THIS IS A BIT FORWARD, BUT...
I THOUGHT I'D TRY FOR DINNER AGAIN. I CAN EVEN BRING MY DAD IF YOU WANT. ARE YOU INTERESTED?
YEAH, UH, SURE! DINNER SOUNDS GREAT-- I'LL CALL YOU!
SLAM
WHEW--

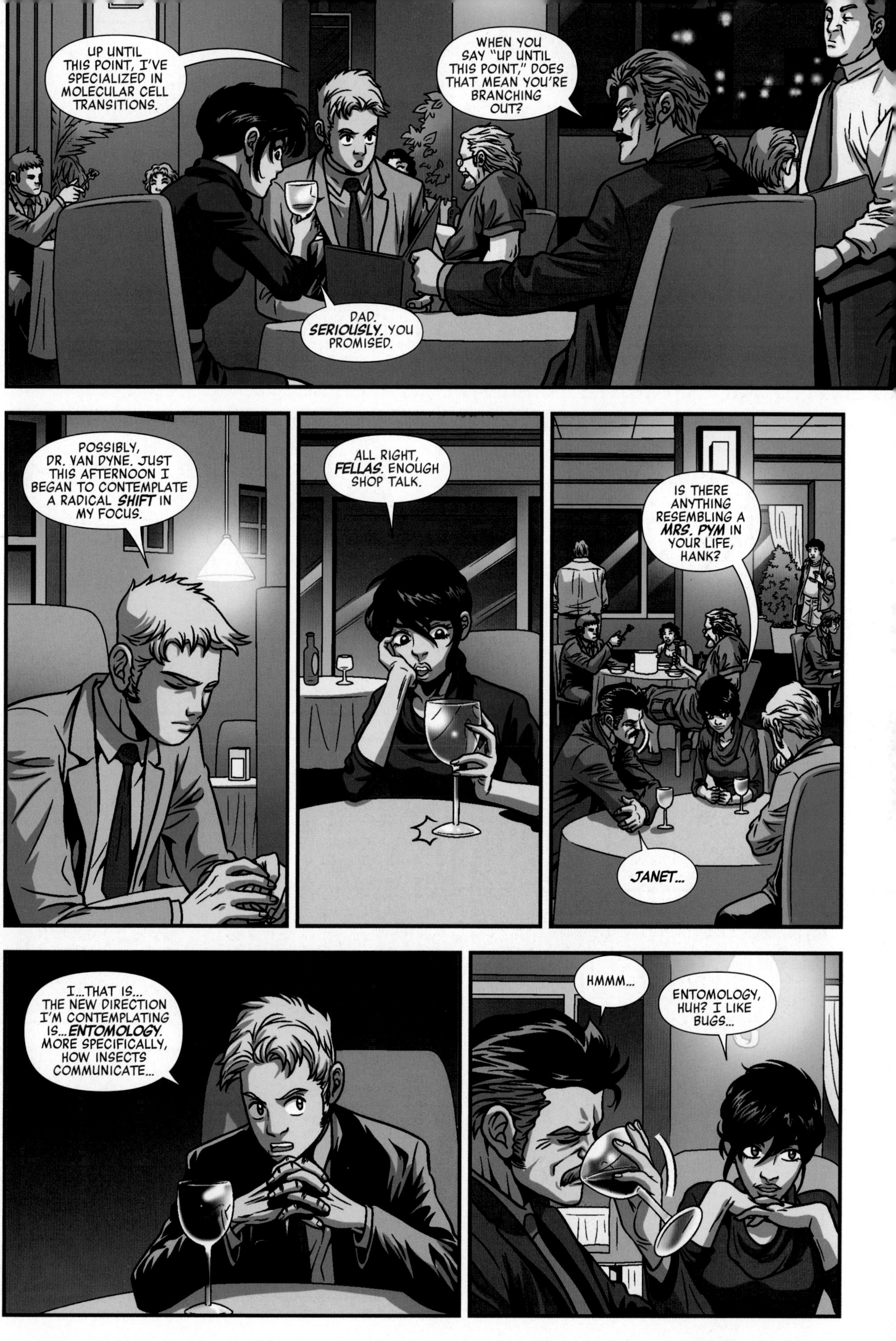
UP UNTIL THIS POINT, I'VE SPECIALIZED IN MOLECULAR CELL TRANSITIONS.
WHEN YOU SAY "UP UNTIL THIS POINT," DOES THAT MEAN YOU'RE BRANCHING OUT?
DAD. SERIOUSLY. YOU PROMISED.
POSSIBLY, DR. VAN DYNE. JUST THIS AFTERNOON I BEGAN TO CONTEMPLATE A RADICAL SHIFT IN MY FOCUS.
ALL RIGHT, FELLAS. ENOUGH SHOP TALK.
IS THERE ANYTHING RESEMBLING A MRS. PYM IN YOUR LIFE, HANK?
JANET...
I...THAT IS... THE NEW DIRECTION I'M CONTEMPLATING IS...ENTOMOLOGY. MORE SPECIFICALLY, HOW INSECTS COMMUNICATE...
HMMM...
ENTOMOLOGY, HUH? I LIKE BUGS...

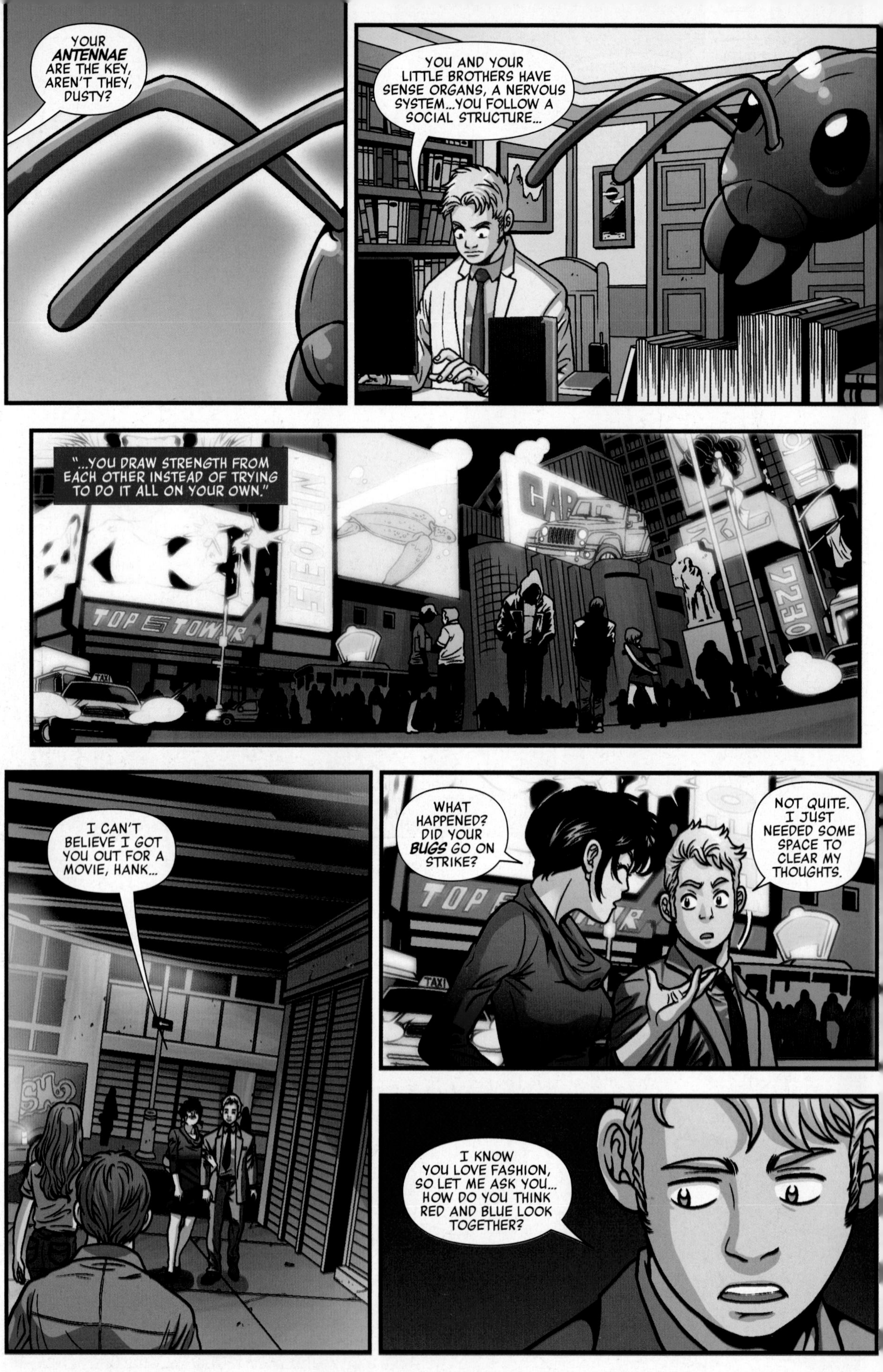
YOUR ANTENNAE ARE THE KEY, AREN'T THEY, DUSTY?
YOU AND YOUR LITTLE BROTHERS HAVE SENSE ORGANS, A NERVOUS SYSTEM...YOU FOLLOW A SOCIAL STRUCTURE...
"...YOU DRAW STRENGTH FROM EACH OTHER INSTEAD OF TRYING TO DO IT ALL ON YOUR OWN."
TOP TOWER
TAXI
I CAN'T BELIEVE I GOT YOU OUT FOR A MOVIE, HANK...
WHAT HAPPENED? DID YOUR BUGS GO ON STRIKE?
NOT QUITE. I JUST NEEDED SOME SPACE TO CLEAR MY THOUGHTS.
I KNOW YOU LOVE FASHION, SO LET ME ASK YOU... HOW DO YOU THINK RED AND BLUE LOOK TOGETHER?

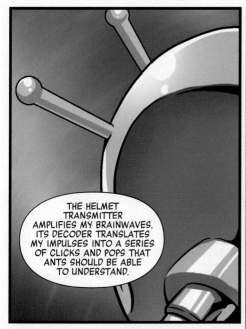

THE HELMET TRANSMITTER AMPLIFIES MY BRAINWAVES. ITS DECODER TRANSLATES MY IMPULSES INTO A SERIES OF CLICKS AND POPS THAT ANTS SHOULD BE ABLE TO UNDERSTAND.

THE RECEIVER ALLOWS ME TO "HEAR" RECIPROCAL EMISSIONS COMING FROM THEM.

THE COSTUME PROTECTS ME FROM ANY RANDOM BUG BITES WHEN I SHRINK DOWN...AND IT LOOKS PRETTY COOL, TOO.

OKAY, HERE GOES. INTO THE RABBIT HOLE AGAIN... ER, MAKE THAT *ANT HOLE*.

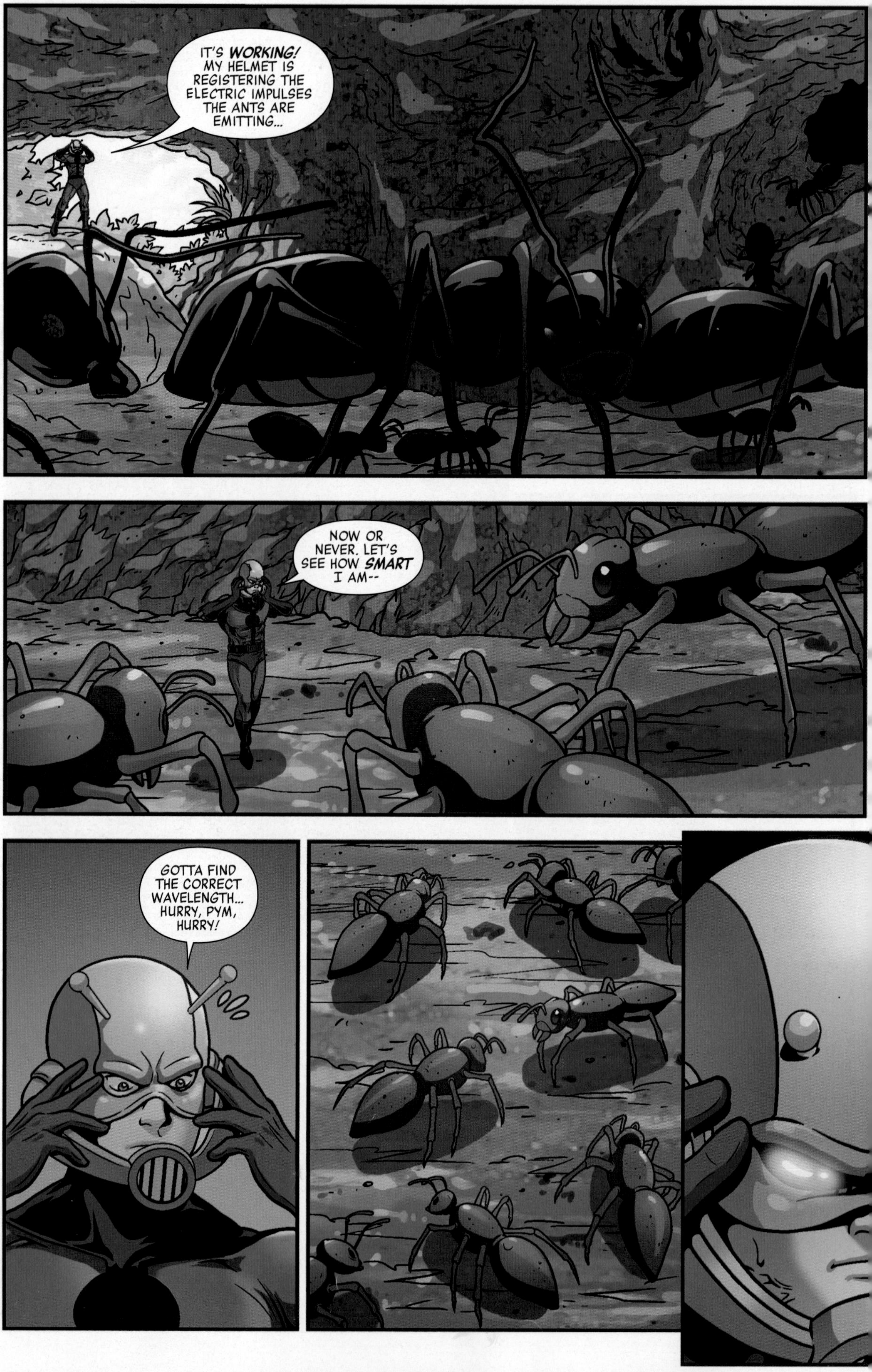
IT'S WORKING! MY HELMET IS REGISTERING THE ELECTRIC IMPULSES THE ANTS ARE EMITTING...
NOW OR NEVER. LET'S SEE HOW SMART I AM--
GOTTA FIND THE CORRECT WAVELENGTH... HURRY, PYM, HURRY!

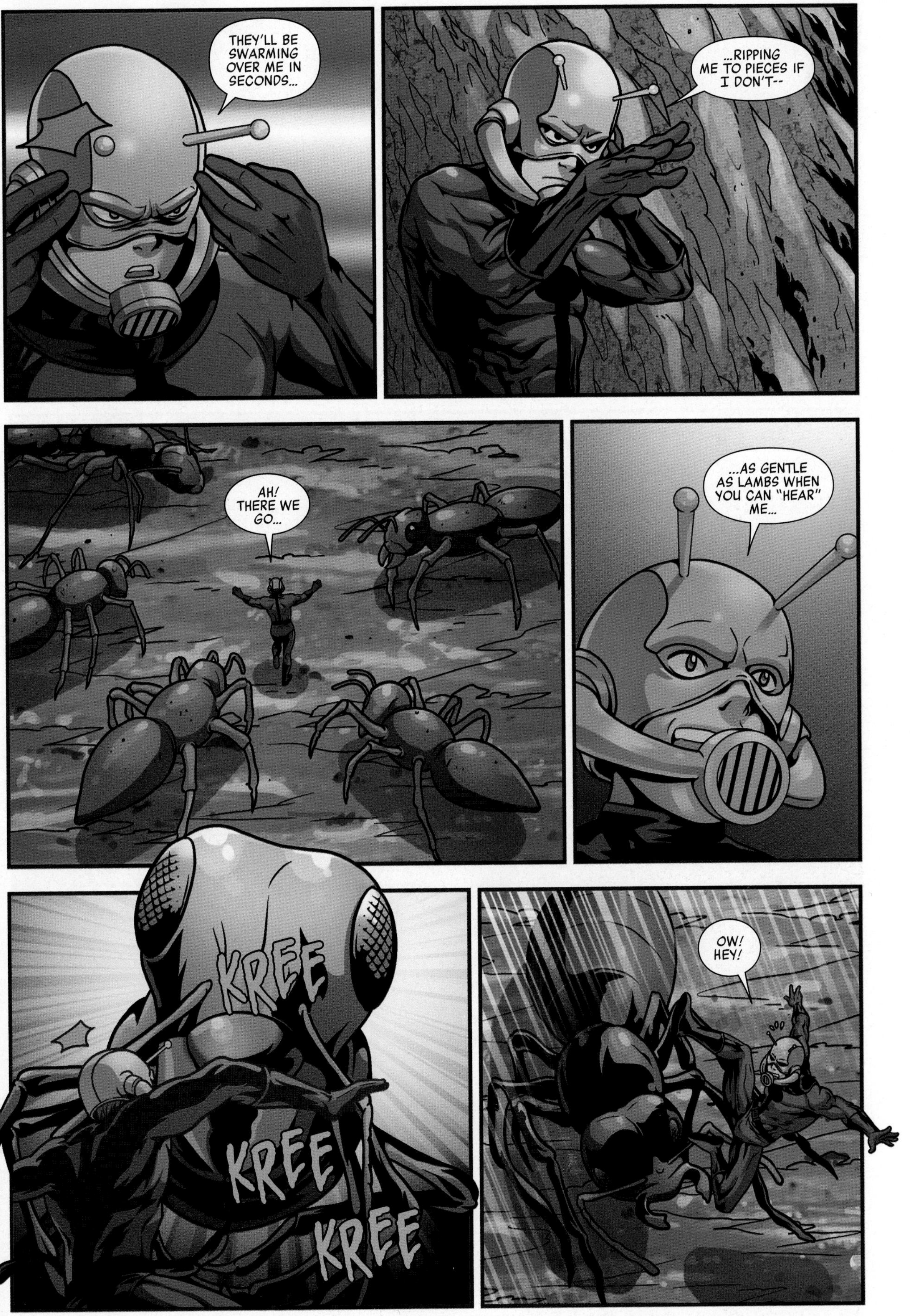
THEY'LL BE SWARMING OVER ME IN SECONDS...
...RIPPING ME TO PIECES IF I DON'T--
AH! THERE WE GO...
...AS GENTLE AS LAMBS WHEN YOU CAN "HEAR" ME...
KREE
KREE
KREE
OW! HEY!

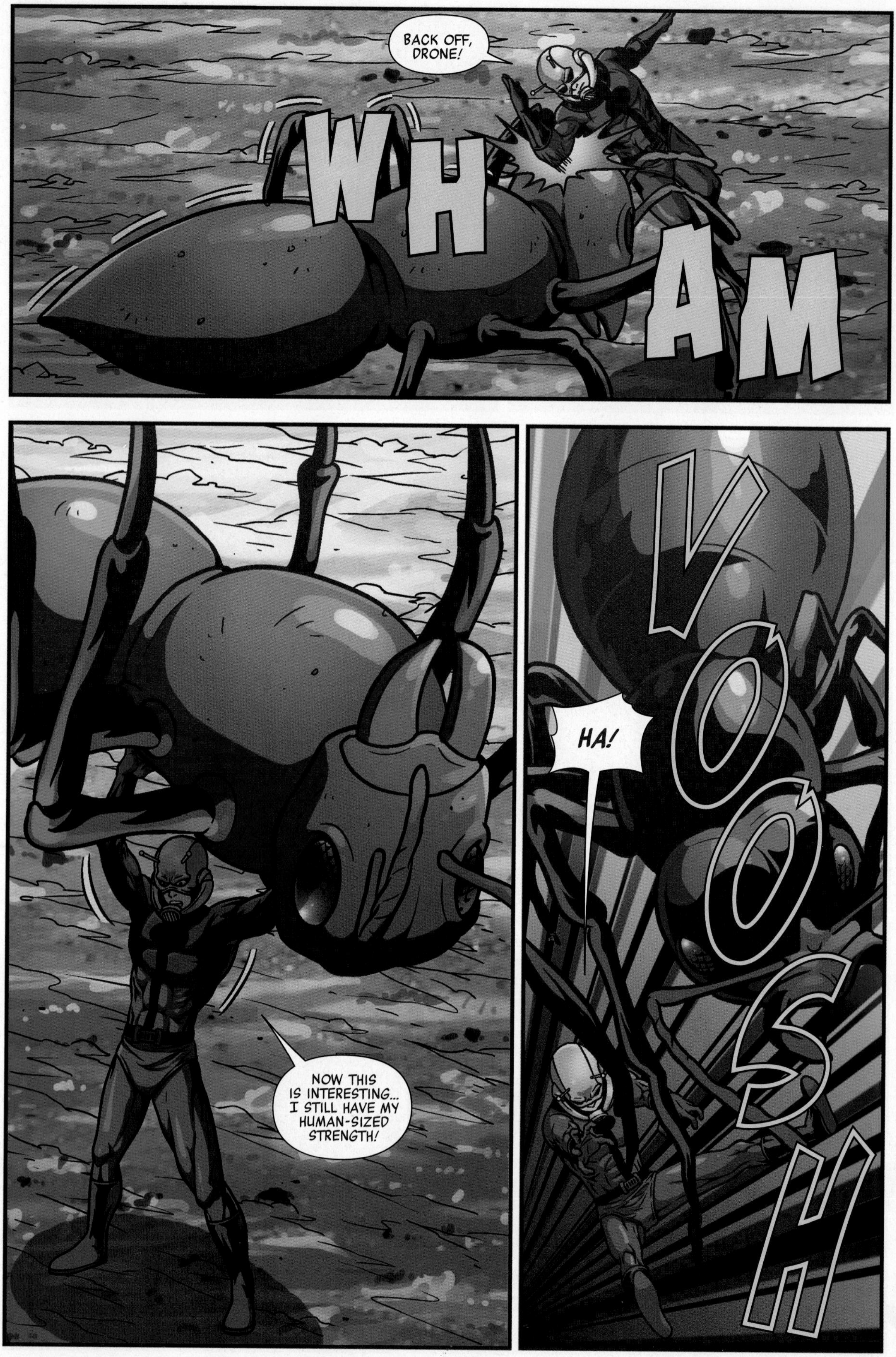
BACK OFF, DRONE!
WHAM
NOW THIS IS INTERESTING... I STILL HAVE MY HUMAN-SIZED STRENGTH!
VOOOSH
HA!

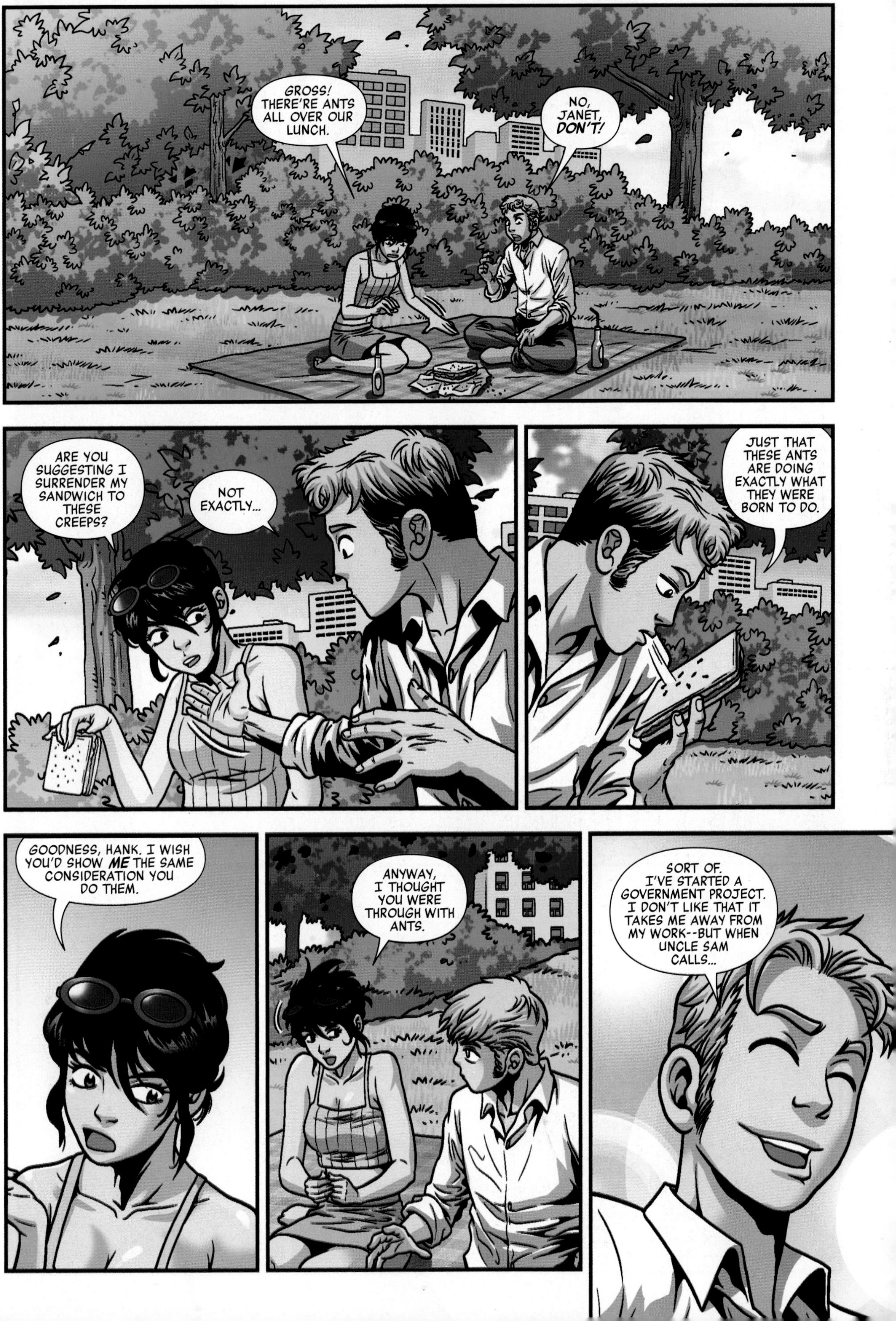
GROSS! THERE'RE ANTS ALL OVER OUR LUNCH.
NO, JANET, DON'T!
ARE YOU SUGGESTING I SURRENDER MY SANDWICH TO THESE CREEPS?
NOT EXACTLY...
JUST THAT THESE ANTS ARE DOING EXACTLY WHAT THEY WERE BORN TO DO.
GOODNESS, HANK. I WISH YOU'D SHOW ME THE SAME CONSIDERATION YOU DO THEM.
ANYWAY, I THOUGHT YOU WERE THROUGH WITH ANTS.
SORT OF. I'VE STARTED A GOVERNMENT PROJECT. I DON'T LIKE THAT IT TAKES ME AWAY FROM MY WORK--BUT WHEN UNCLE SAM CALLS...

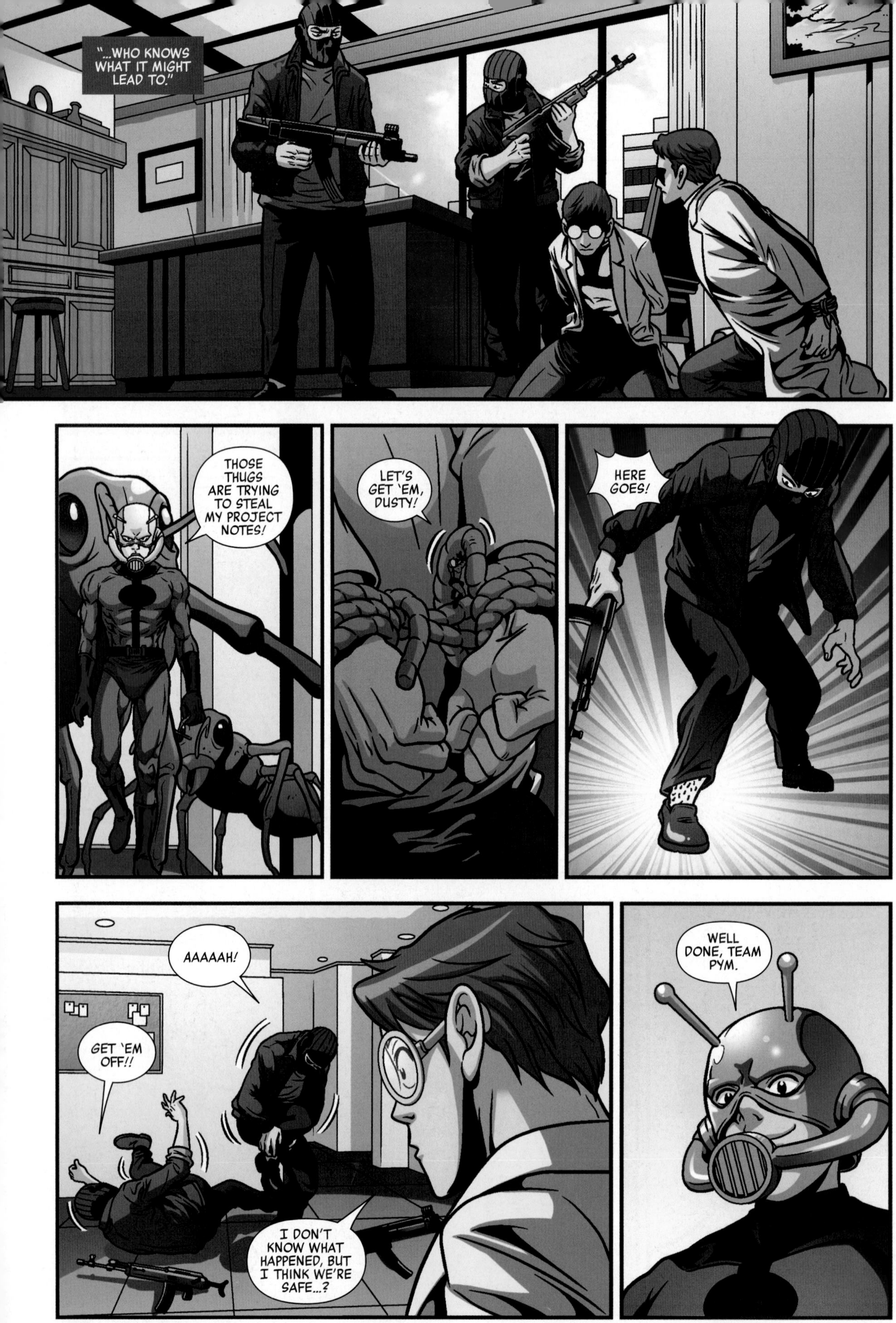
"...WHO KNOWS WHAT IT MIGHT LEAD TO."
THOSE THUGS ARE TRYING TO STEAL MY PROJECT NOTES!
LET'S GET 'EM, DUSTY!
HERE GOES!
AAAAAH!
GET 'EM OFF!!
I DON'T KNOW WHAT HAPPENED, BUT I THINK WE'RE SAFE...?
WELL DONE, TEAM PYM.

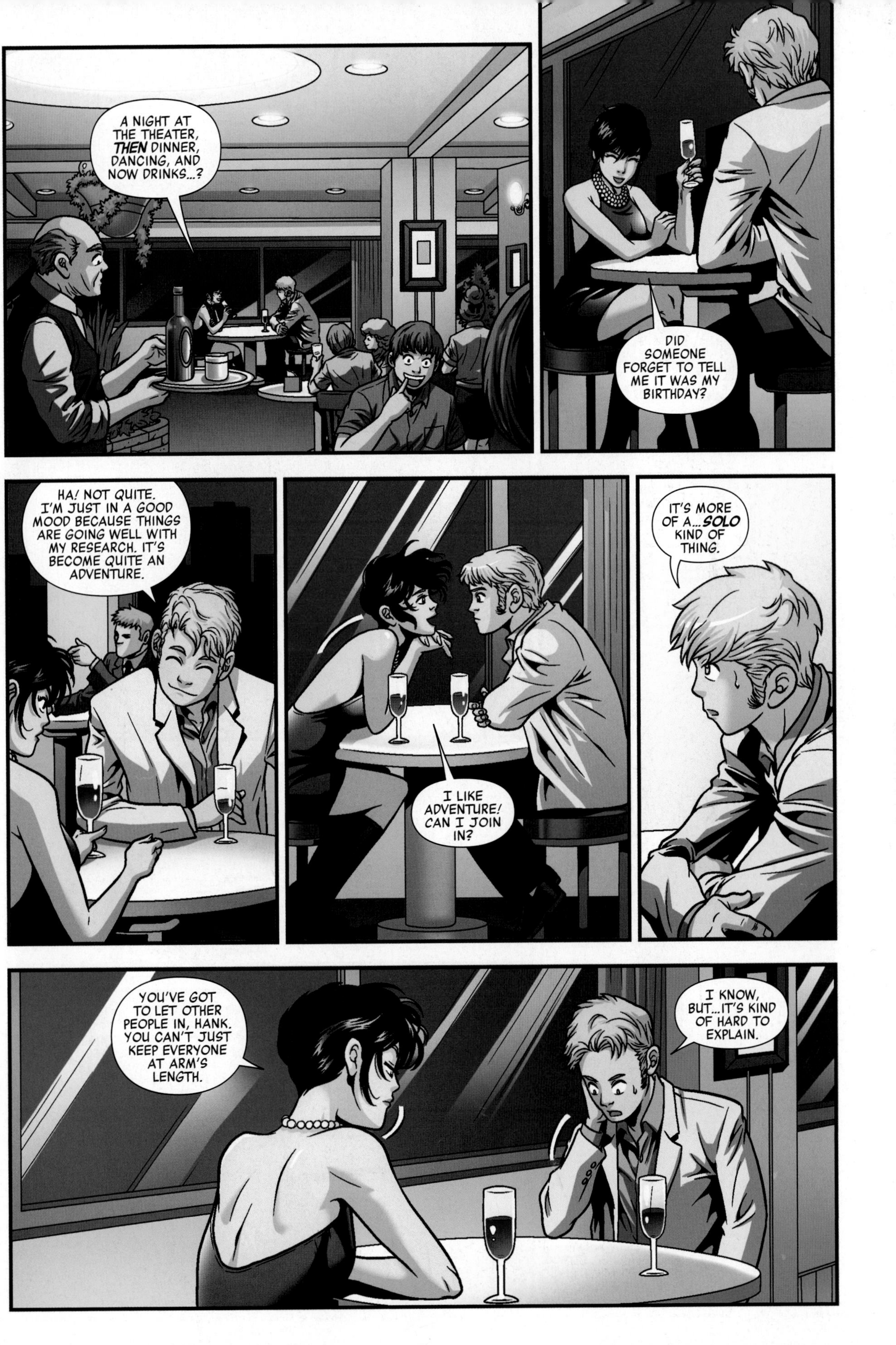
A NIGHT AT THE THEATER, THEN DINNER, DANCING, AND NOW DRINKS...?
DID SOMEONE FORGET TO TELL ME IT WAS MY BIRTHDAY?
HA! NOT QUITE. I'M JUST IN A GOOD MOOD BECAUSE THINGS ARE GOING WELL WITH MY RESEARCH. IT'S BECOME QUITE AN ADVENTURE.
I LIKE ADVENTURE! CAN I JOIN IN?
IT'S MORE OF A...SOLO KIND OF THING.
YOU'VE GOT TO LET OTHER PEOPLE IN, HANK. YOU CAN'T JUST KEEP EVERYONE AT ARM'S LENGTH.
I KNOW, BUT...IT'S KIND OF HARD TO EXPLAIN.

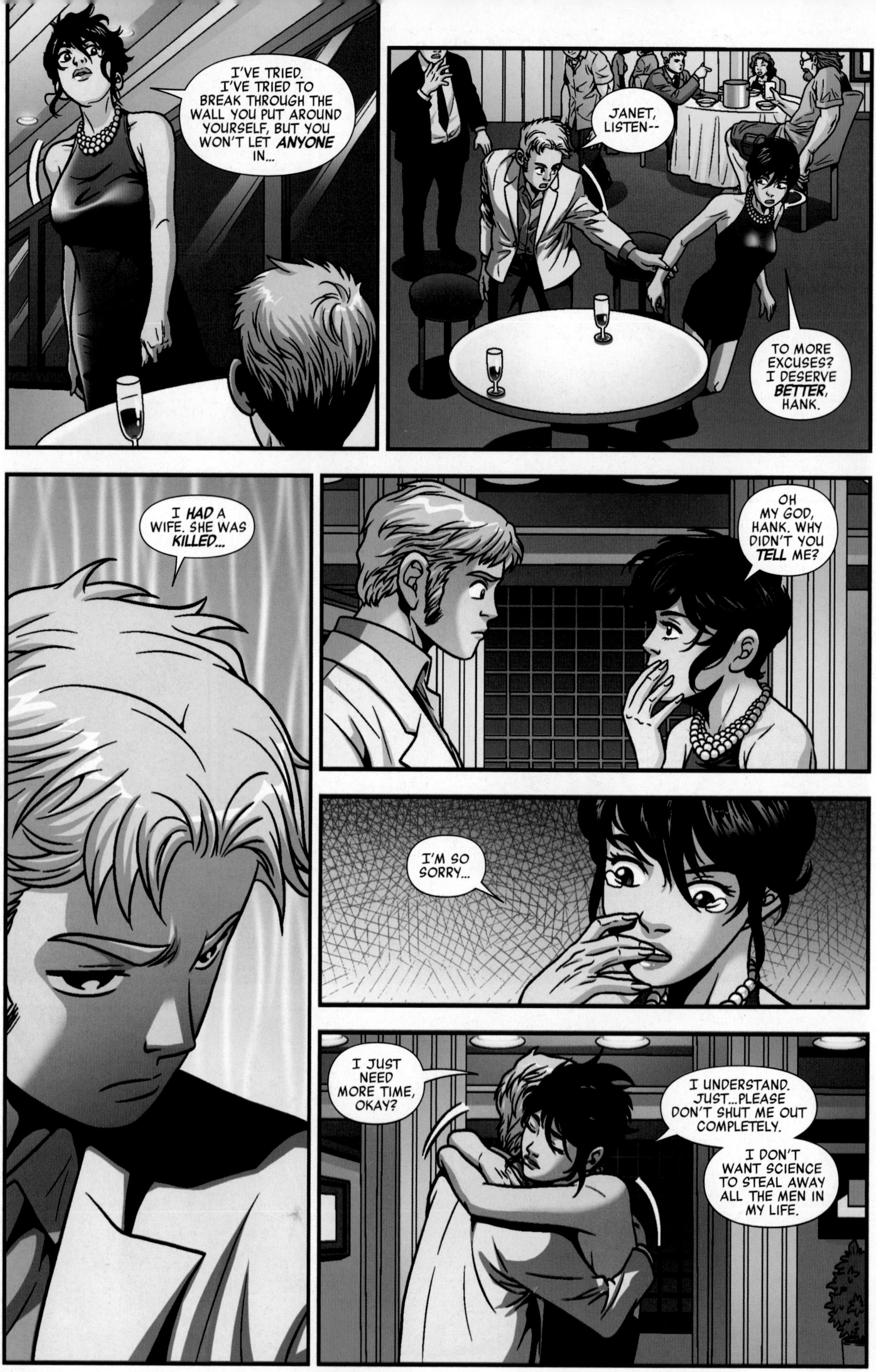

I'VE TRIED. I'VE TRIED TO BREAK THROUGH THE WALL YOU PUT AROUND YOURSELF, BUT YOU WON'T LET ANYONE IN...
JANET, LISTEN--
TO MORE EXCUSES? I DESERVE BETTER, HANK.
I HAD A WIFE. SHE WAS KILLED...
OH MY GOD, HANK. WHY DIDN'T YOU TELL ME?
I'M SO SORRY...
I JUST NEED MORE TIME, OKAY?
I UNDERSTAND. JUST...PLEASE DON'T SHUT ME OUT COMPLETELY.
I DON'T WANT SCIENCE TO STEAL AWAY ALL THE MEN IN MY LIFE.

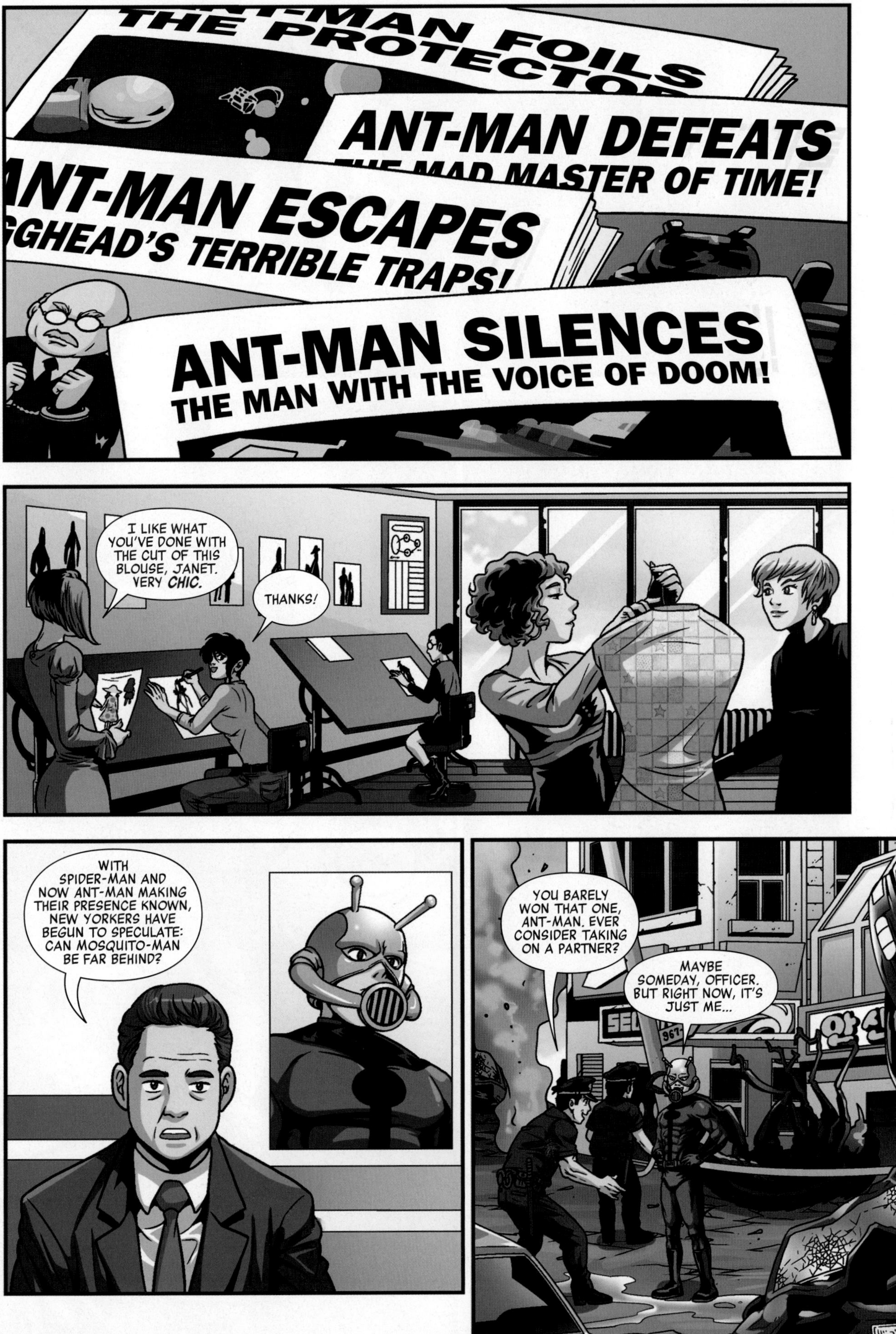
NT-MAN FOILS
THE PROTECTO
ANT-MAN DEFEATS
MAD MASTER OF TIME!
NT-MAN ESCAPES
GGHEAD'S TERRIBLE TRAPS!
ANT-MAN SILENCES
THE MAN WITH THE VOICE OF DOOM!
I LIKE WHAT YOU'VE DONE WITH THE CUT OF THIS BLOUSE, JANET. VERY CHIC.
THANKS!
WITH SPIDER-MAN AND NOW ANT-MAN MAKING THEIR PRESENCE KNOWN, NEW YORKERS HAVE BEGUN TO SPECULATE: CAN MOSQUITO-MAN BE FAR BEHIND?
YOU BARELY WON THAT ONE, ANT-MAN. EVER CONSIDER TAKING ON A PARTNER?
MAYBE SOMEDAY, OFFICER. BUT RIGHT NOW, IT'S JUST ME...

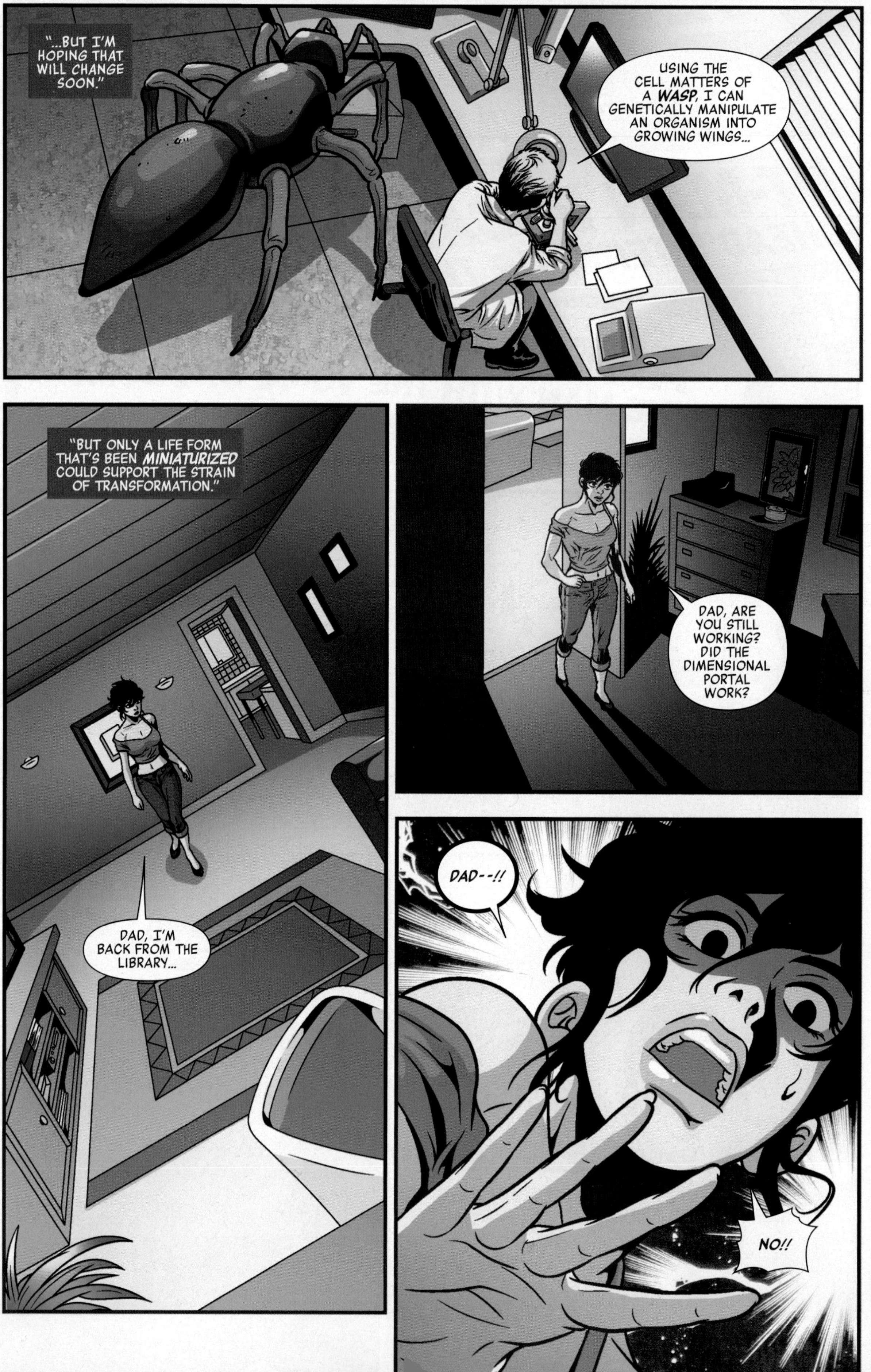
"...BUT I'M HOPING THAT WILL CHANGE SOON."
USING THE CELL MATTERS OF A *WASP*, I CAN GENETICALLY MANIPULATE AN ORGANISM INTO GROWING WINGS...
"BUT ONLY A LIFE FORM THAT'S BEEN *MINIATURIZED* COULD SUPPORT THE STRAIN OF TRANSFORMATION."
DAD, I'M BACK FROM THE LIBRARY...
DAD, ARE YOU STILL WORKING? DID THE DIMENSIONAL PORTAL WORK?
DAD--!!
NO!!

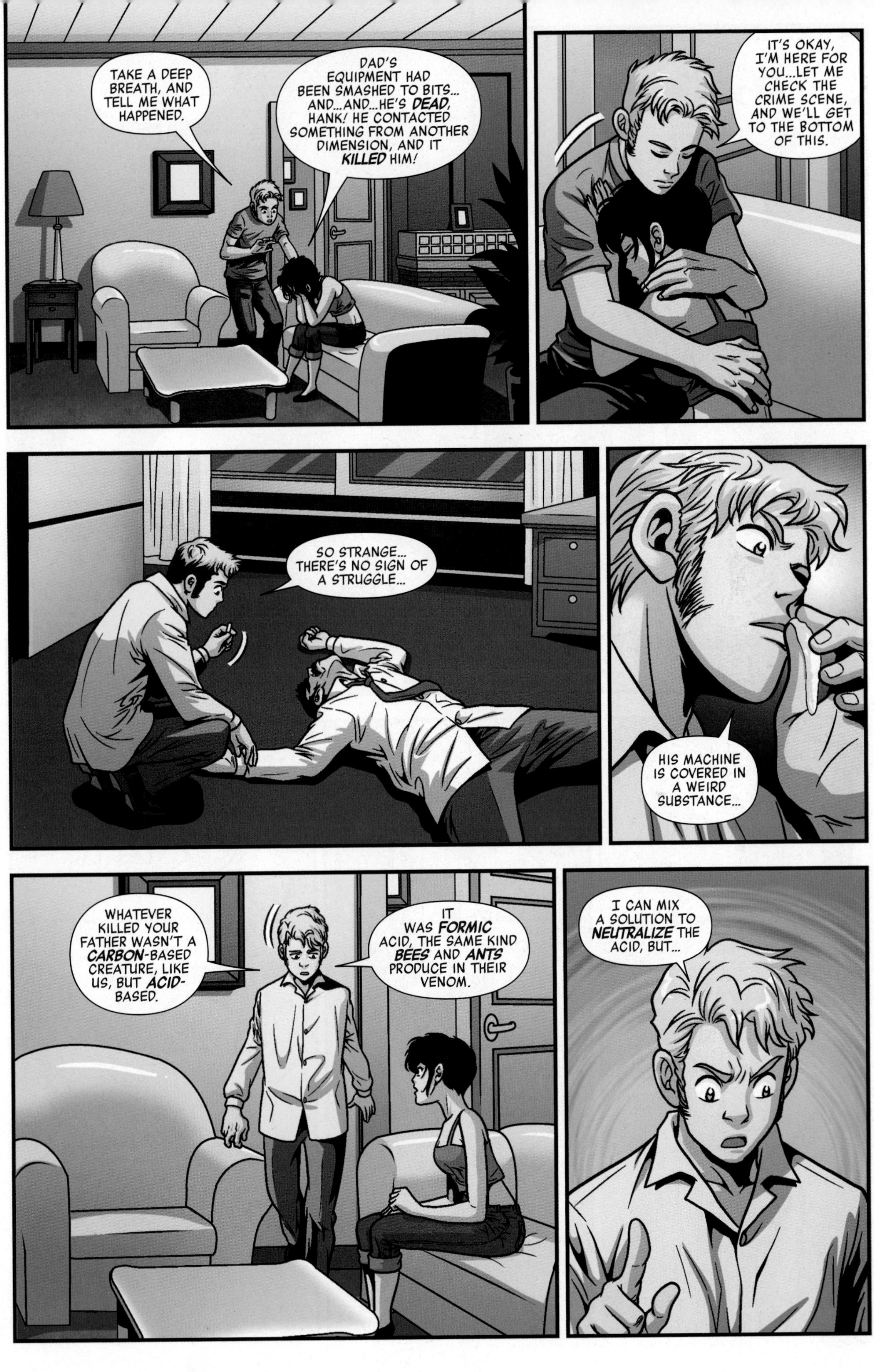

TAKE A DEEP BREATH, AND TELL ME WHAT HAPPENED.
DAD'S EQUIPMENT HAD BEEN SMASHED TO BITS... AND...AND...HE'S DEAD, HANK! HE CONTACTED SOMETHING FROM ANOTHER DIMENSION, AND IT KILLED HIM!
IT'S OKAY, I'M HERE FOR YOU...LET ME CHECK THE CRIME SCENE, AND WE'LL GET TO THE BOTTOM OF THIS.
SO STRANGE... THERE'S NO SIGN OF A STRUGGLE...
HIS MACHINE IS COVERED IN A WEIRD SUBSTANCE...
WHATEVER KILLED YOUR FATHER WASN'T A CARBON-BASED CREATURE, LIKE US, BUT ACID-BASED.
IT WAS FORMIC ACID, THE SAME KIND BEES AND ANTS PRODUCE IN THEIR VENOM.
I CAN MIX A SOLUTION TO NEUTRALIZE THE ACID, BUT...

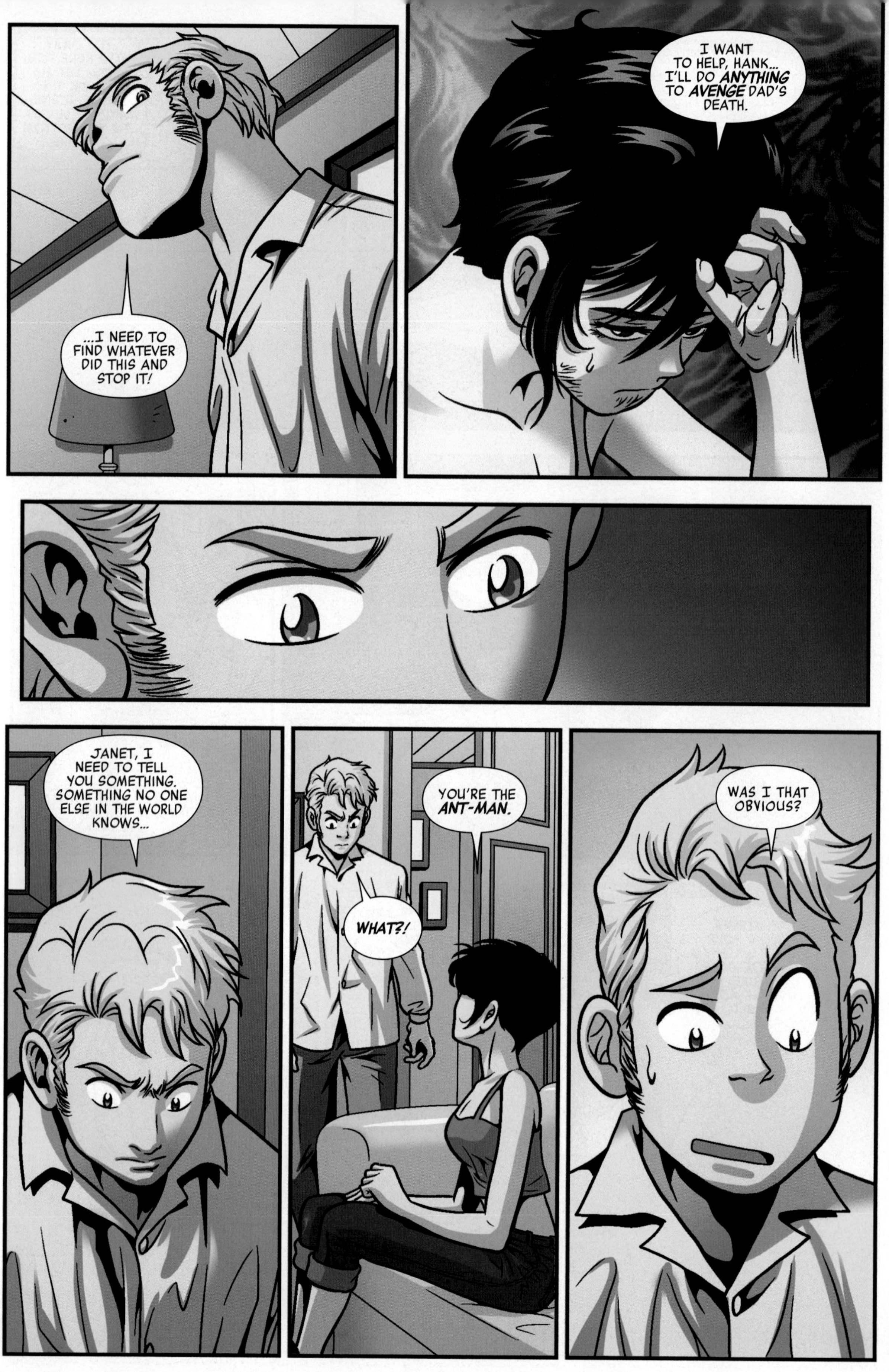
...I NEED TO FIND WHATEVER DID THIS AND STOP IT!
I WANT TO HELP, HANK... I'LL DO **ANYTHING** TO **AVENGE** DAD'S DEATH.
JANET, I NEED TO TELL YOU SOMETHING. SOMETHING NO ONE ELSE IN THE WORLD KNOWS...
YOU'RE THE **ANT-MAN.**
WHAT?!
WAS I THAT OBVIOUS?

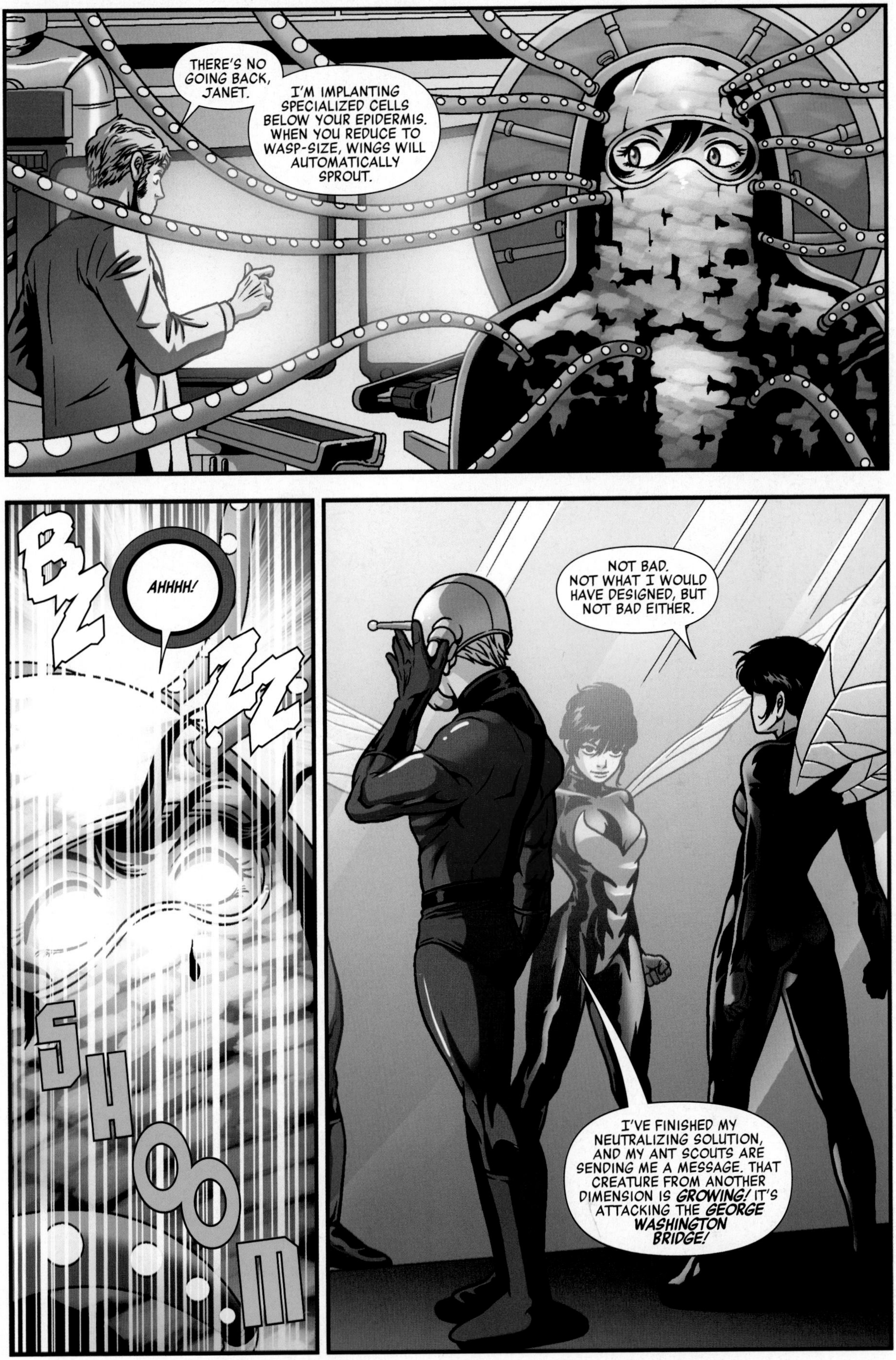
THERE'S NO GOING BACK, JANET.
I'M IMPLANTING SPECIALIZED CELLS BELOW YOUR EPIDERMIS. WHEN YOU REDUCE TO WASP-SIZE, WINGS WILL AUTOMATICALLY SPROUT.
BZZZ
AHHHH!
SHOOOM
NOT BAD. NOT WHAT I WOULD HAVE DESIGNED, BUT NOT BAD EITHER.
I'VE FINISHED MY NEUTRALIZING SOLUTION, AND MY ANT SCOUTS ARE SENDING ME A MESSAGE. THAT CREATURE FROM ANOTHER DIMENSION IS GROWING! IT'S ATTACKING THE GEORGE WASHINGTON BRIDGE!

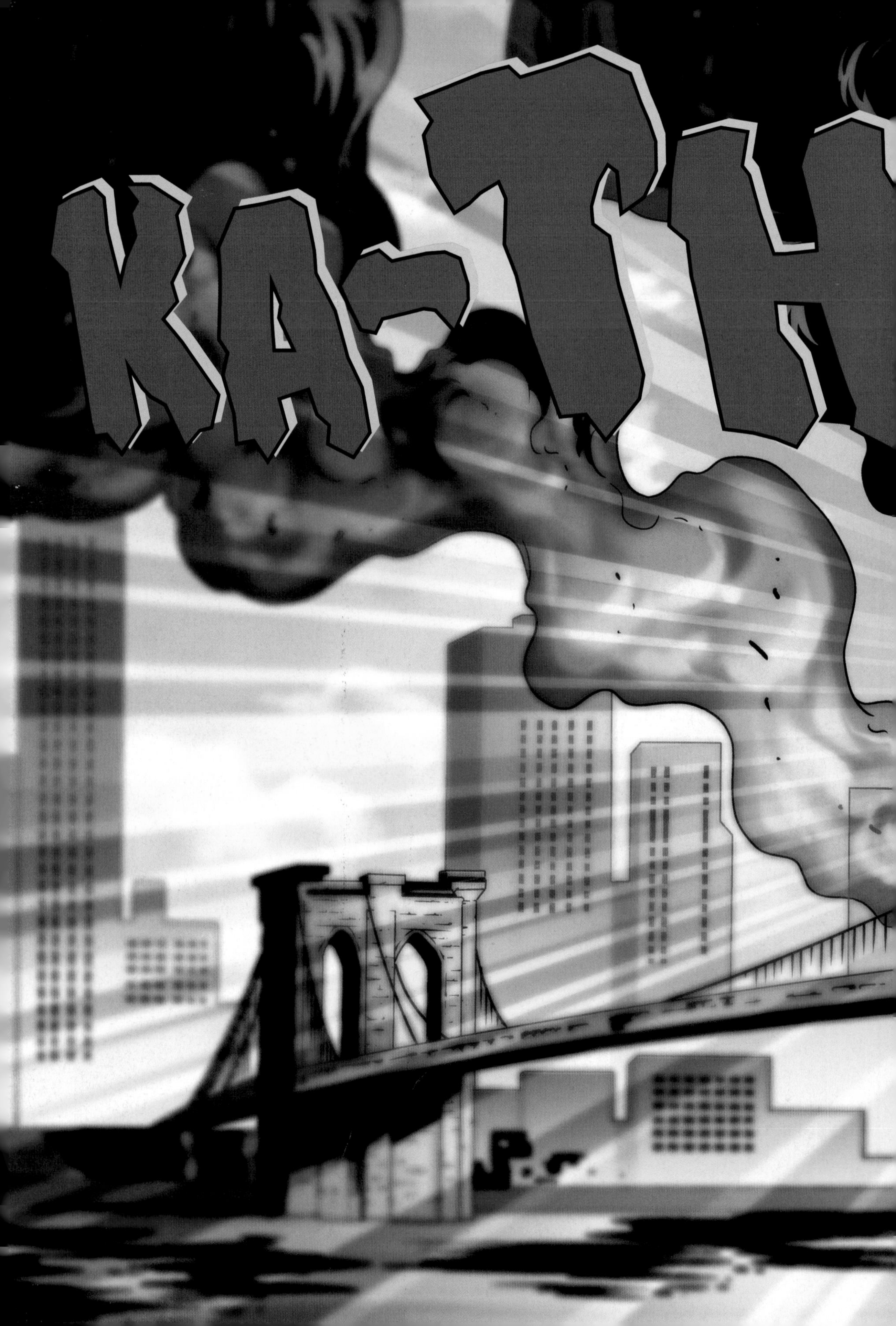
KA-TH

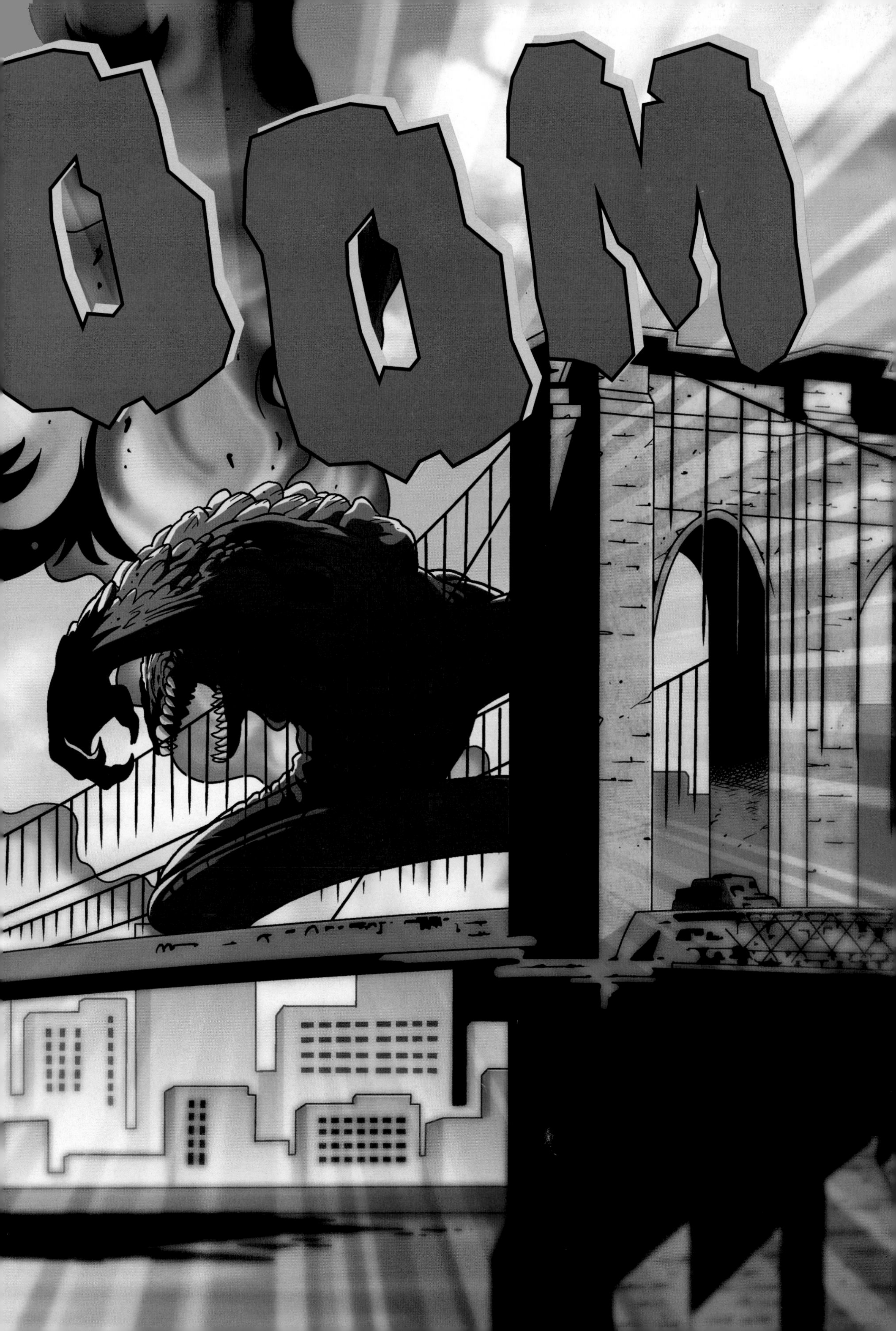
OOM

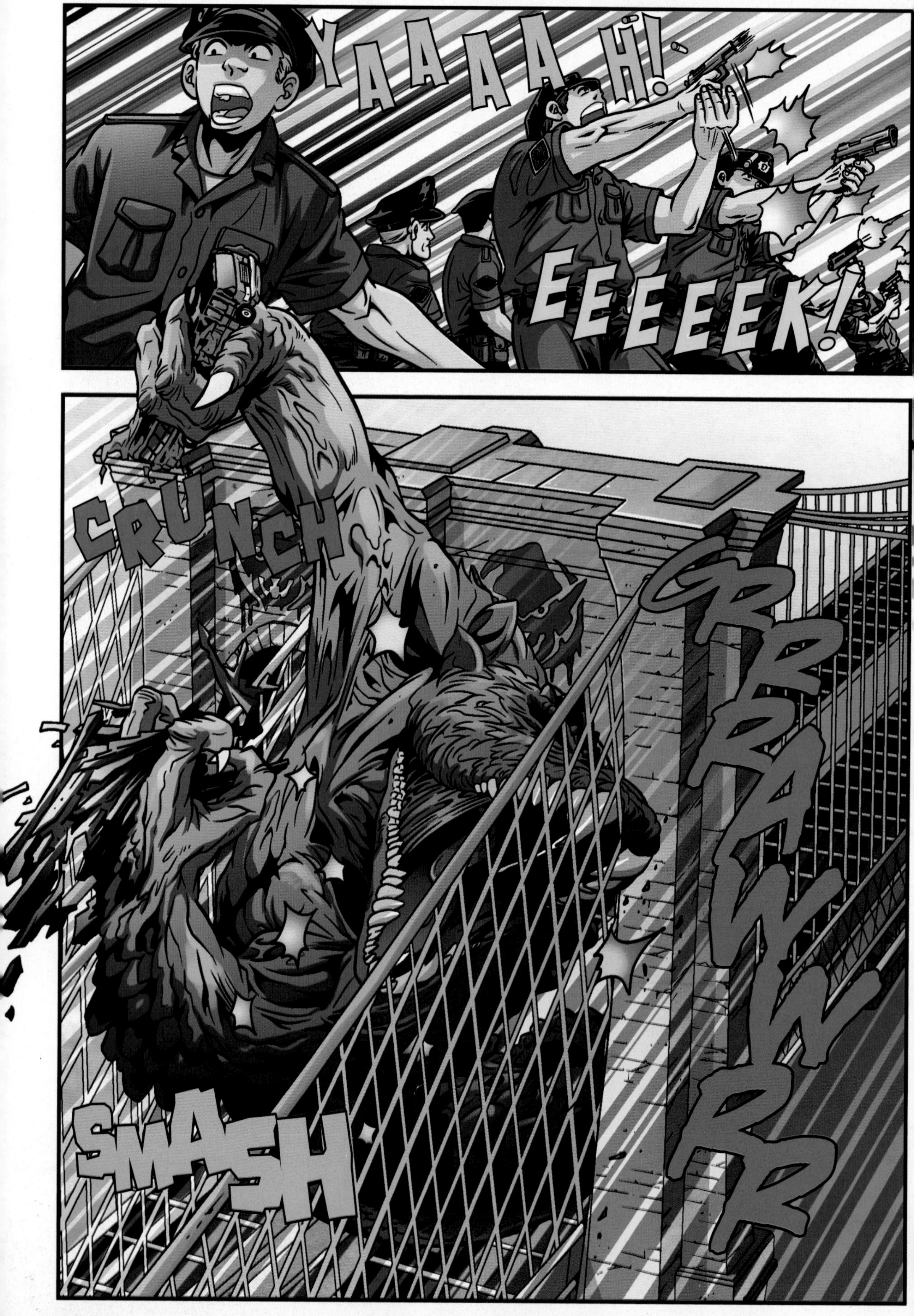
YAAAAH!
EEEEEK!
CRUNCH
GRRAWWRR
SMASH

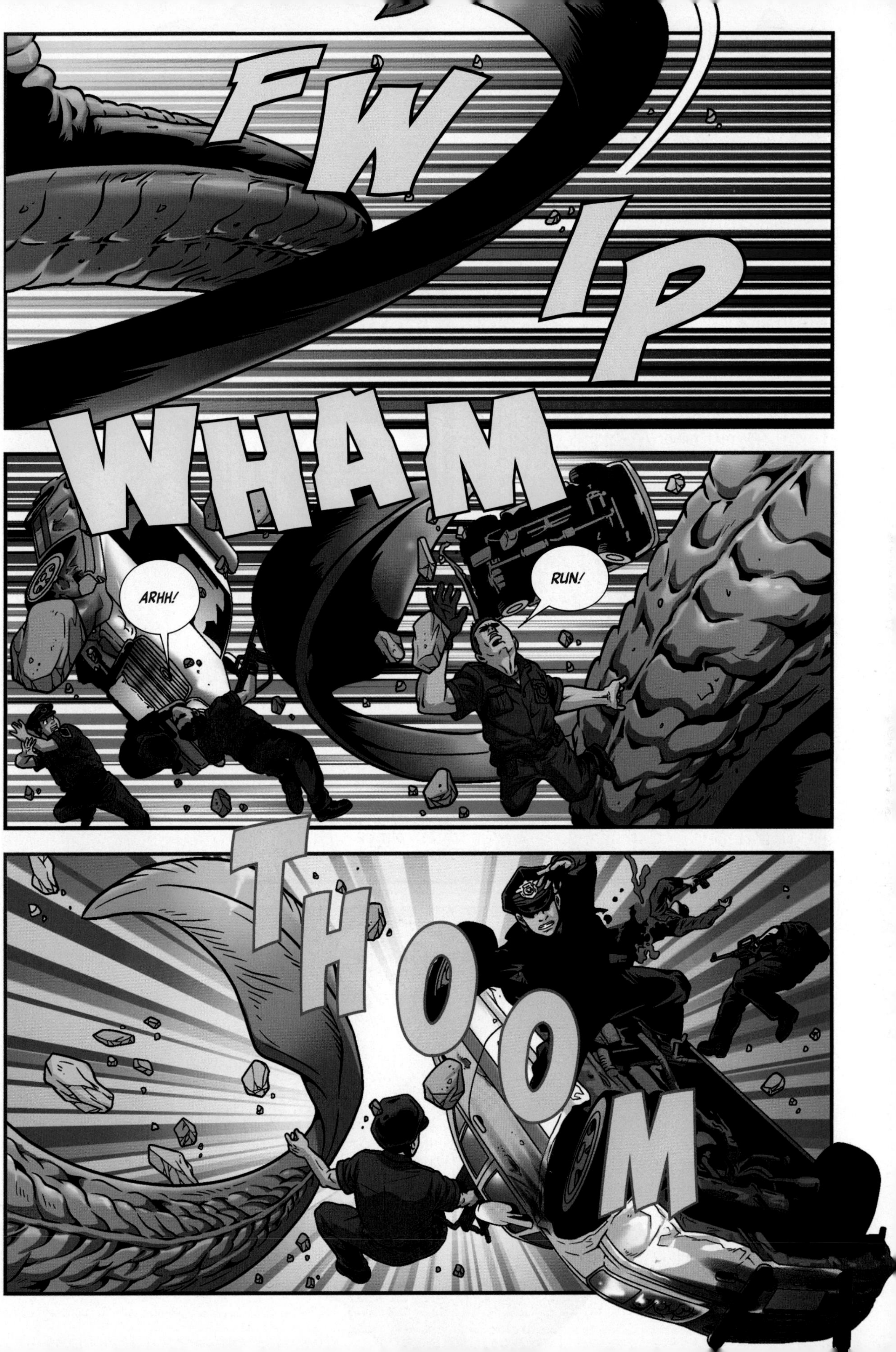
FWIP
WHAM
ARHH!
RUN!
THOOOM

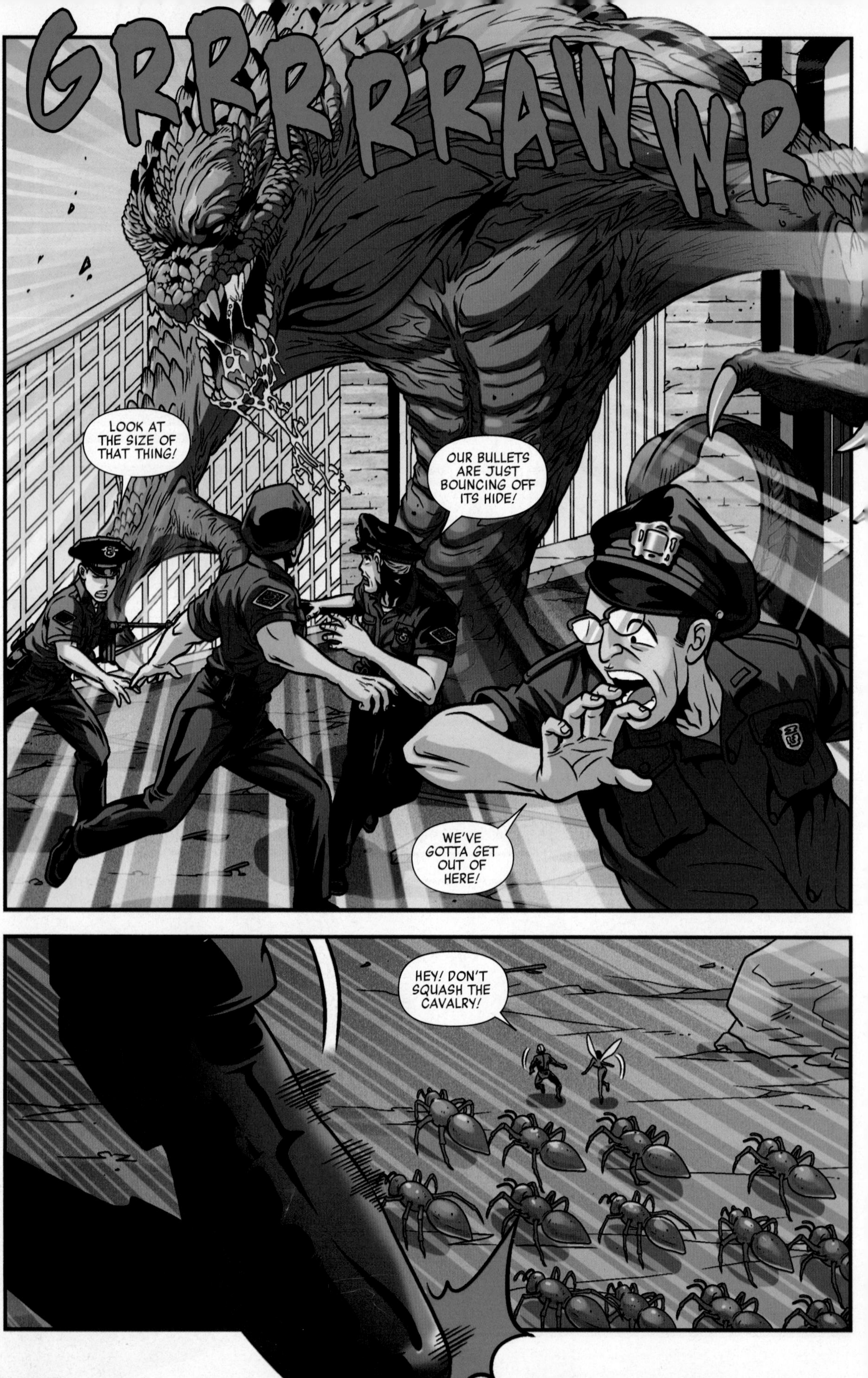
GRRRRRAWWR
LOOK AT THE SIZE OF THAT THING!
OUR BULLETS ARE JUST BOUNCING OFF ITS HIDE!
WE'VE GOTTA GET OUT OF HERE!
HEY! DON'T SQUASH THE CAVALRY!

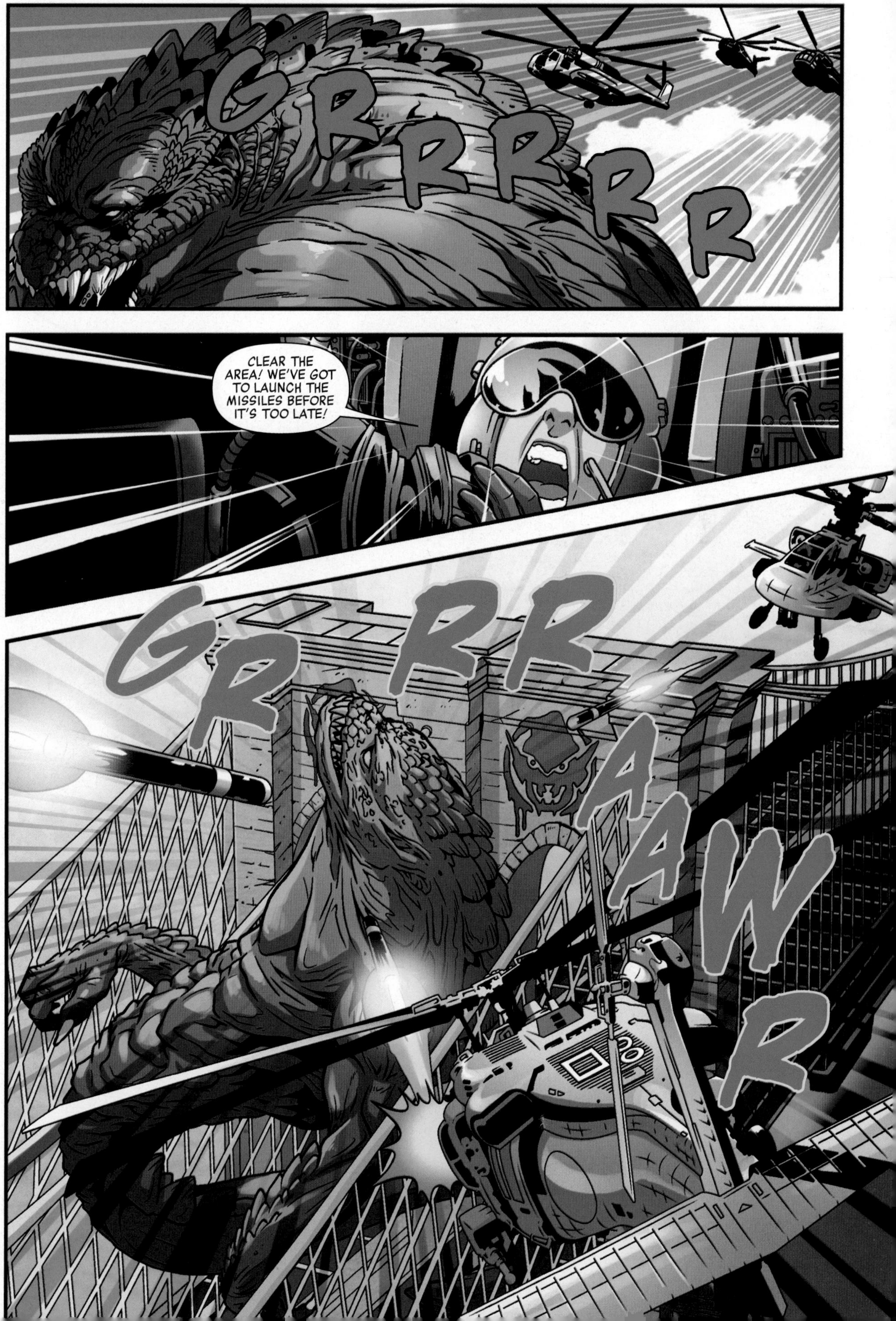
GRRRRRR
CLEAR THE AREA! WE'VE GOT TO LAUNCH THE MISSILES BEFORE IT'S TOO LATE!
GRRRAAWR

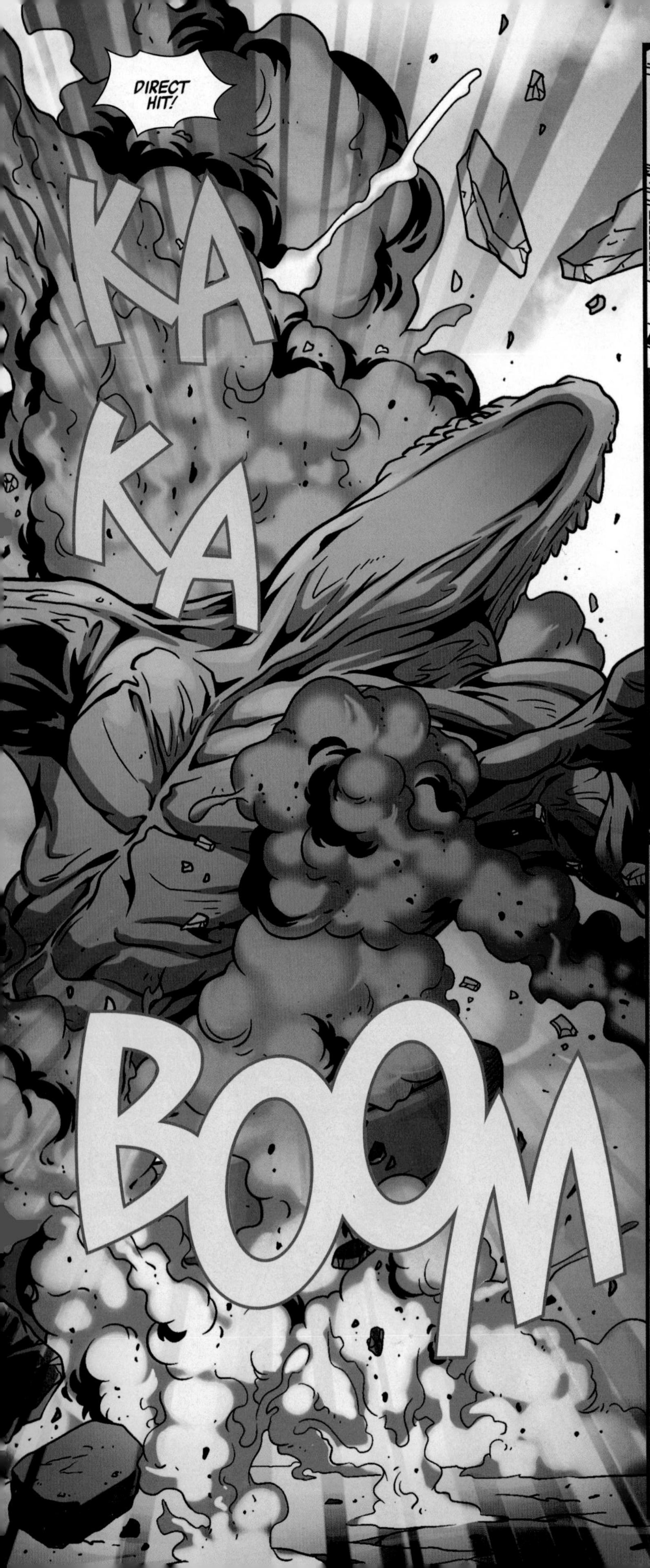
DIRECT HIT!
KA KA KA
BOOM

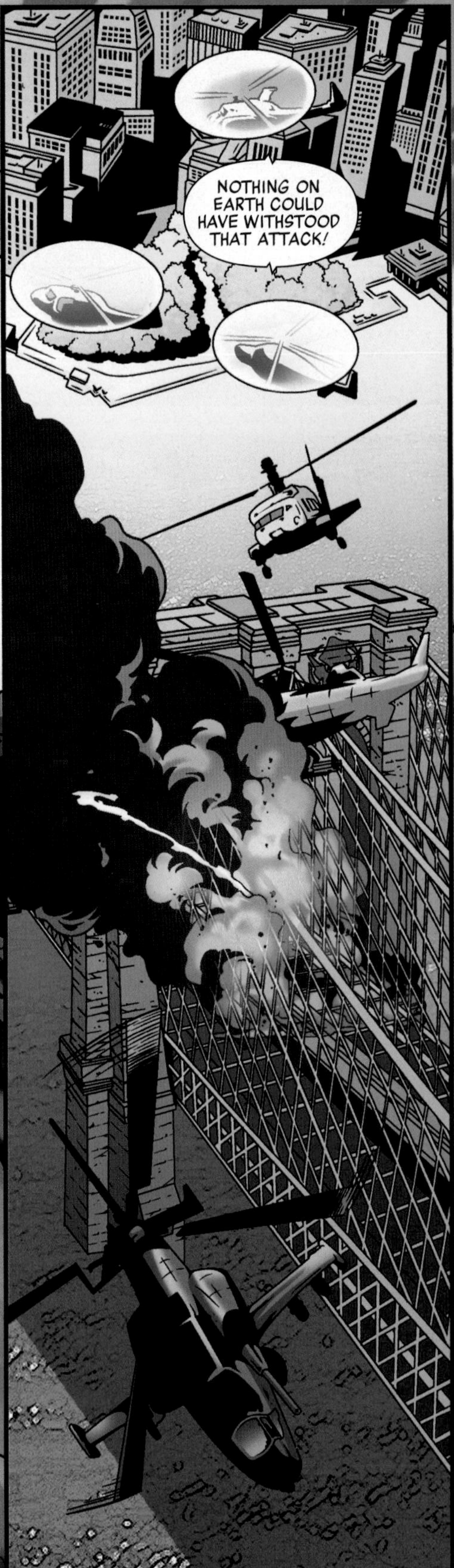
NOTHING ON EARTH COULD HAVE WITHSTOOD THAT ATTACK!

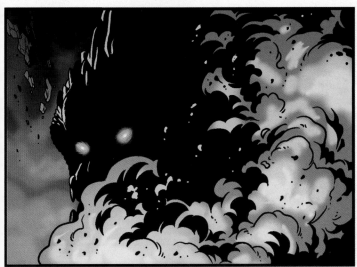

IMPOSSIBLE!

NO... IT CAN'T BE!

GRRRAWNR

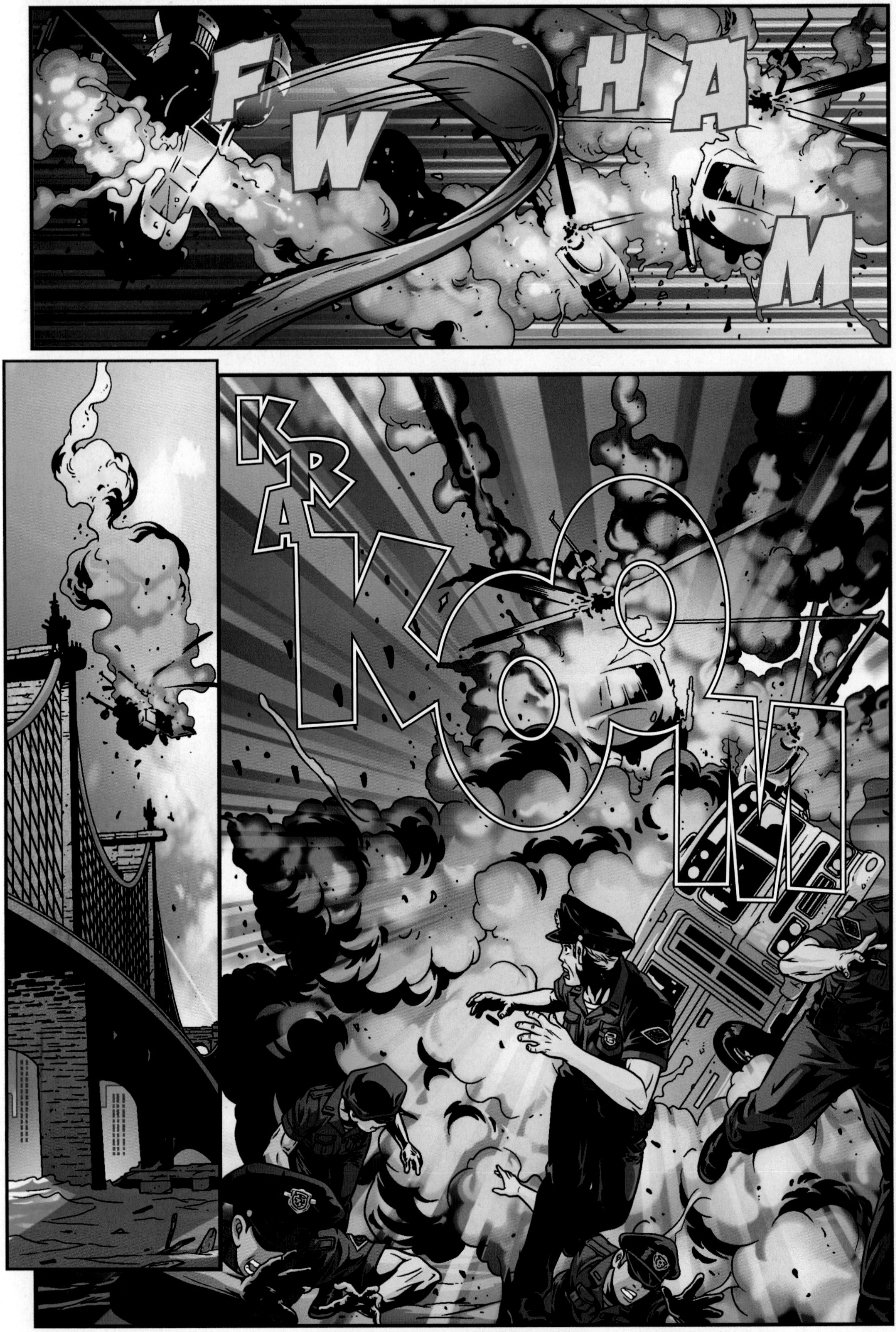
FWHAM
KRAKOOM

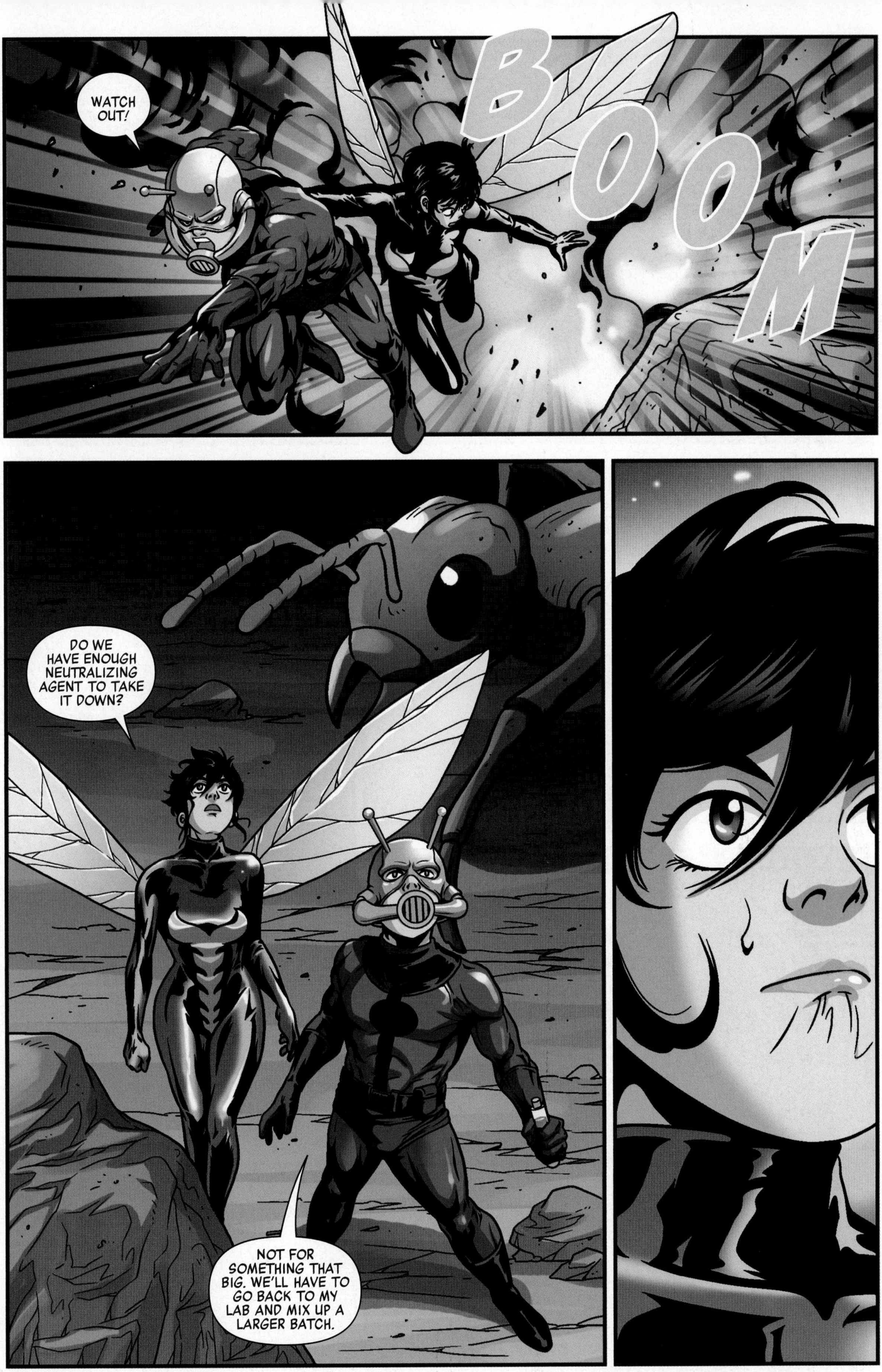
WATCH OUT!
BOOOM
DO WE HAVE ENOUGH NEUTRALIZING AGENT TO TAKE IT DOWN?
NOT FOR SOMETHING THAT BIG. WE'LL HAVE TO GO BACK TO MY LAB AND MIX UP A LARGER BATCH.

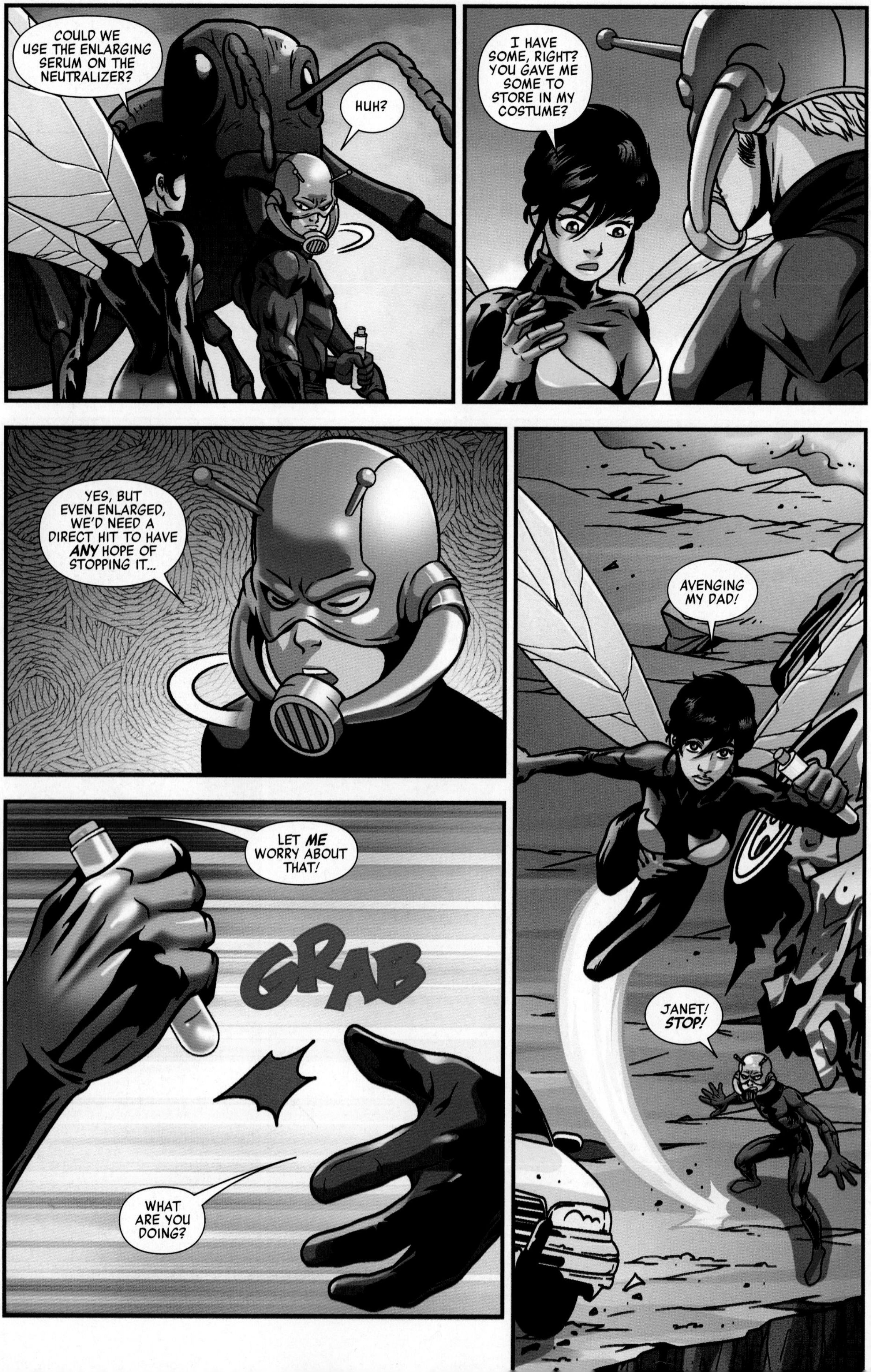
COULD WE USE THE ENLARGING SERUM ON THE NEUTRALIZER?
HUH?
I HAVE SOME, RIGHT? YOU GAVE ME SOME TO STORE IN MY COSTUME?
YES, BUT EVEN ENLARGED, WE'D NEED A DIRECT HIT TO HAVE ANY HOPE OF STOPPING IT...
LET ME WORRY ABOUT THAT!
GRAB
WHAT ARE YOU DOING?
AVENGING MY DAD!
JANET! STOP!

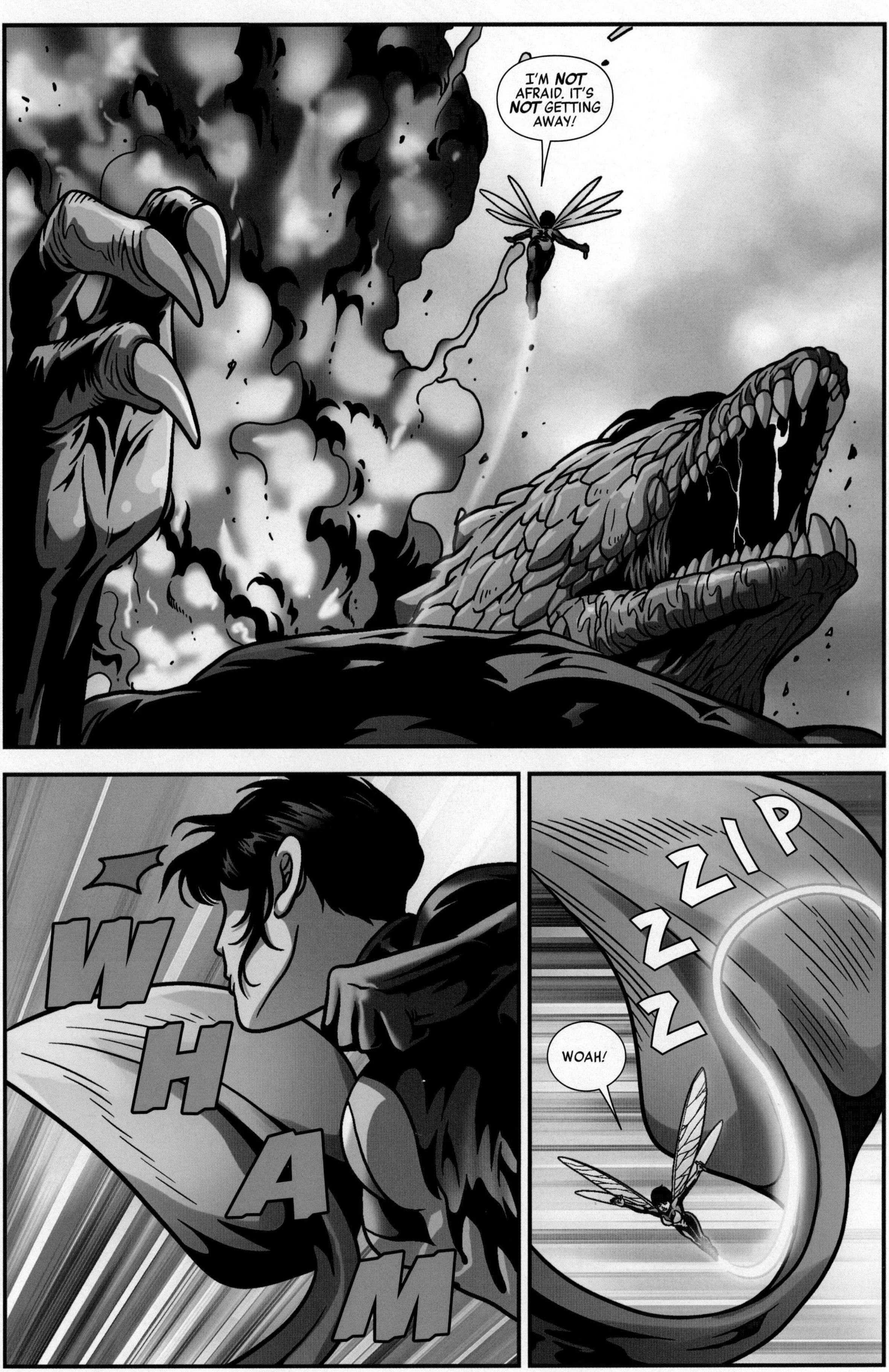
I'M NOT AFRAID. IT'S NOT GETTING AWAY!
WHAM
ZZZIP
WOAH!

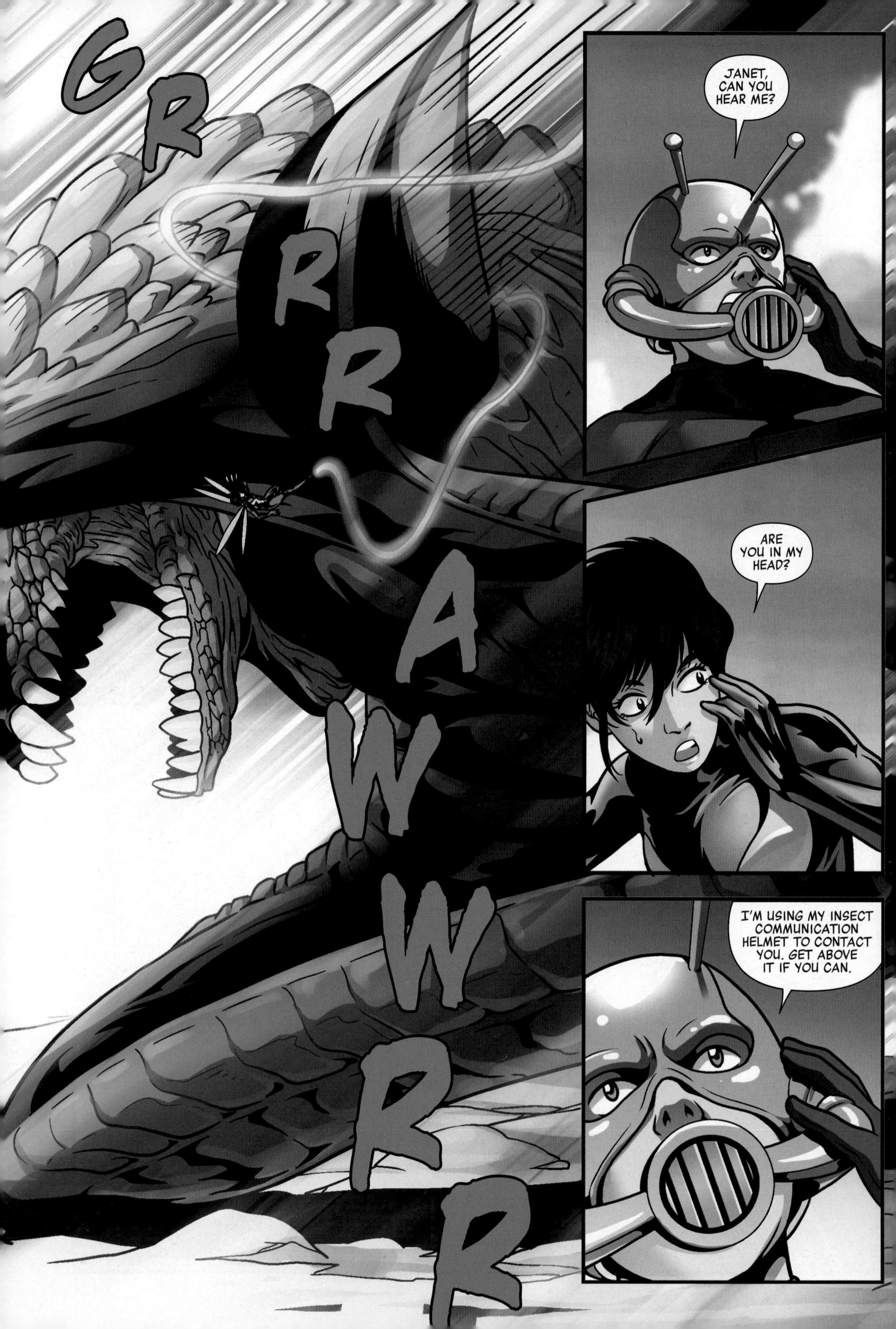
GRRRAWWRR
JANET, CAN YOU HEAR ME?
ARE YOU IN MY HEAD?
I'M USING MY INSECT COMMUNICATION HELMET TO CONTACT YOU. GET ABOVE IT IF YOU CAN.

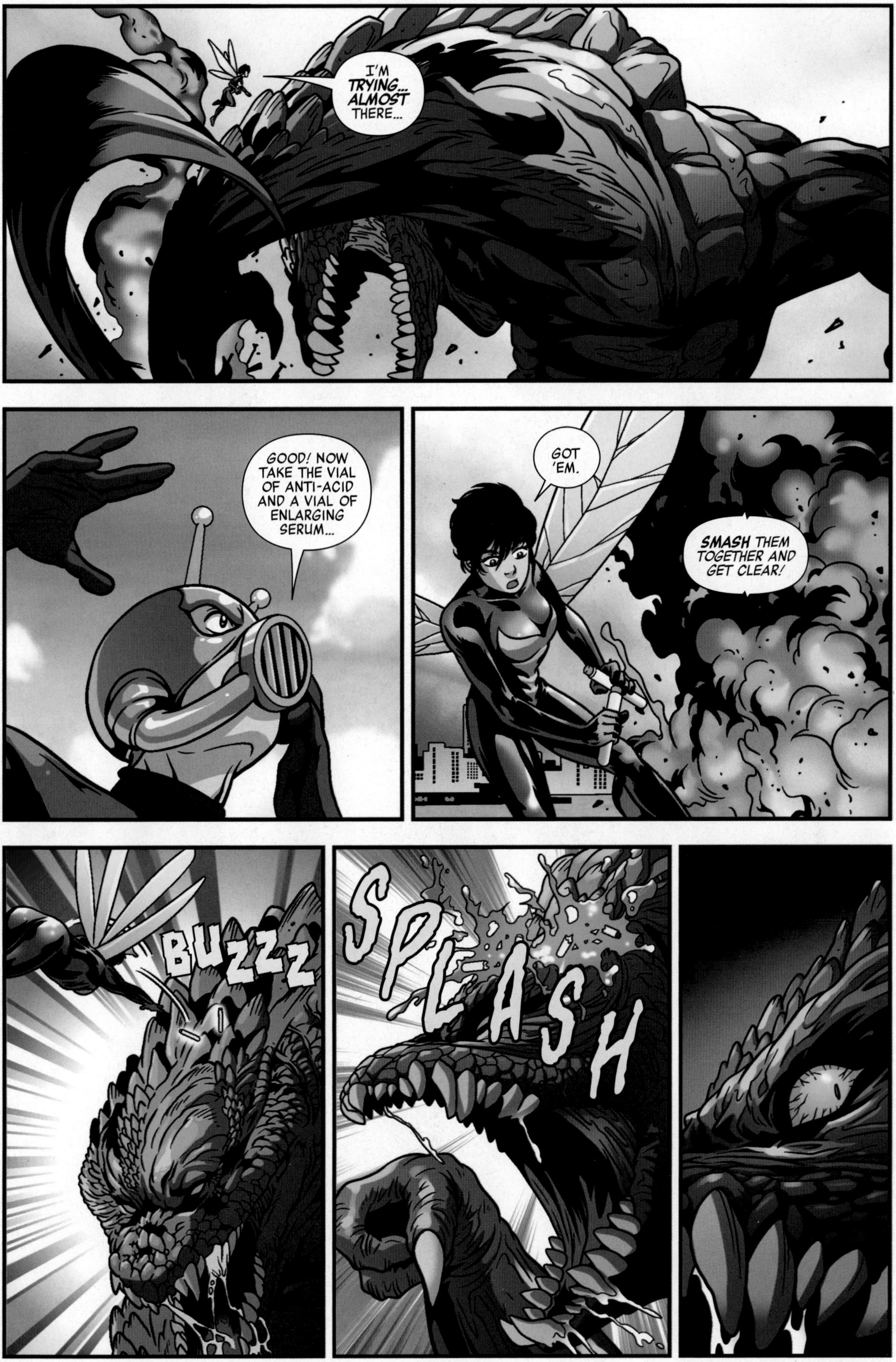
I'M TRYING... ALMOST THERE...
GOOD! NOW TAKE THE VIAL OF ANTI-ACID AND A VIAL OF ENLARGING SERUM...
GOT 'EM.
SMASH THEM TOGETHER AND GET CLEAR!
BUZZZ
SPLASH

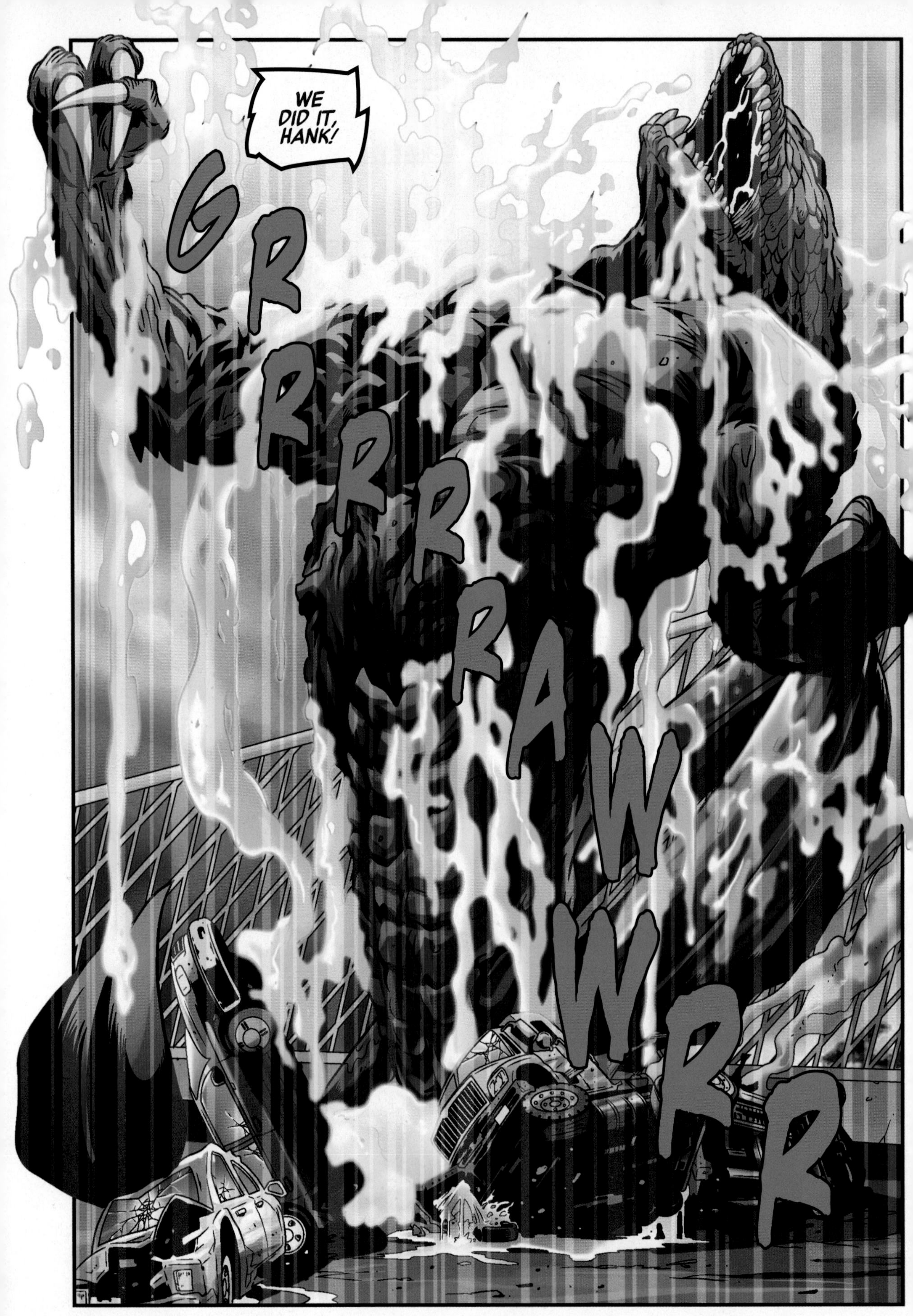
WE DID IT, HANK!
GRRRRRAWWRR

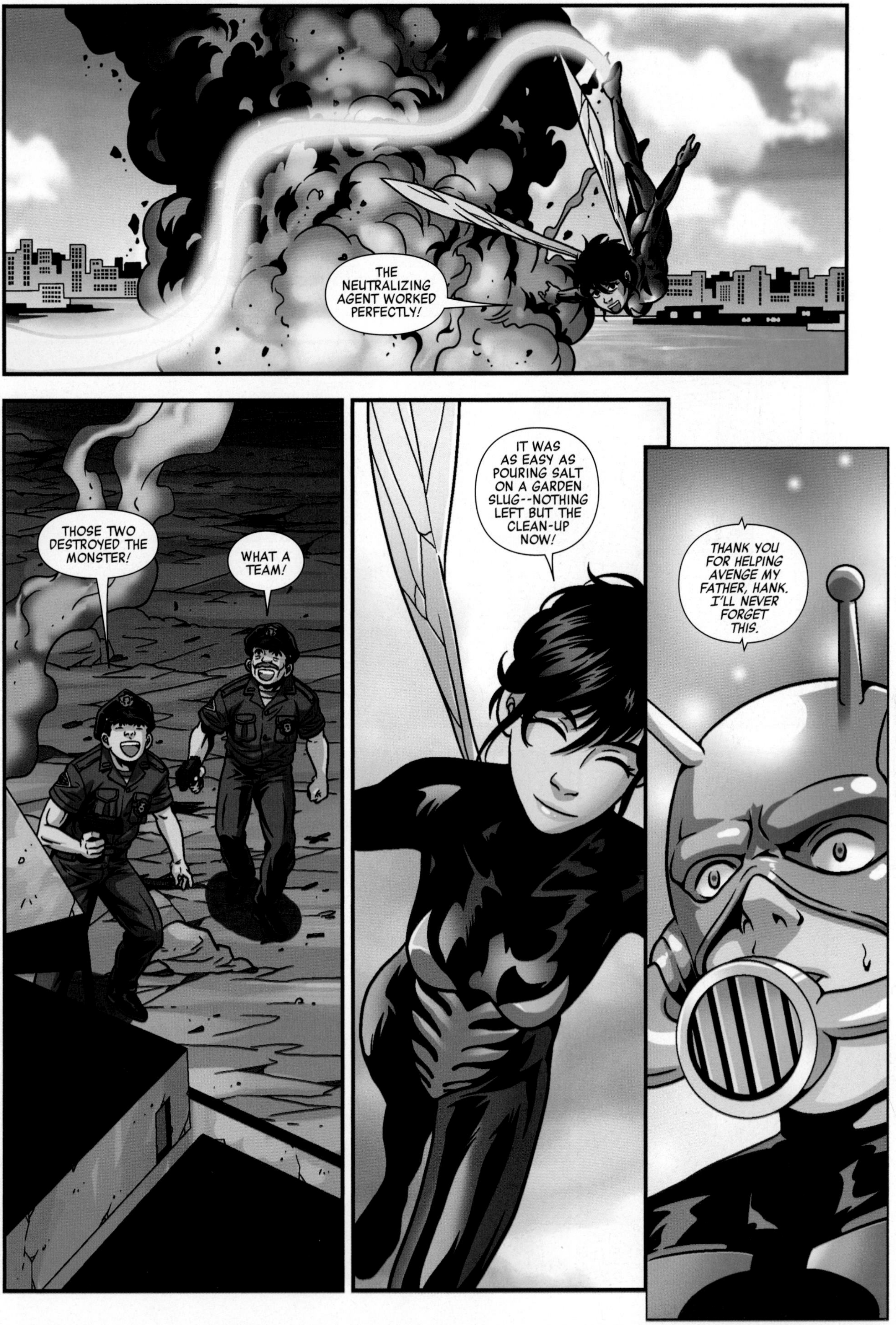
THE NEUTRALIZING AGENT WORKED PERFECTLY!
THOSE TWO DESTROYED THE MONSTER!
WHAT A TEAM!
IT WAS AS EASY AS POURING SALT ON A GARDEN SLUG--NOTHING LEFT BUT THE CLEAN-UP NOW!
THANK YOU FOR HELPING AVENGE MY FATHER, HANK. I'LL NEVER FORGET THIS.

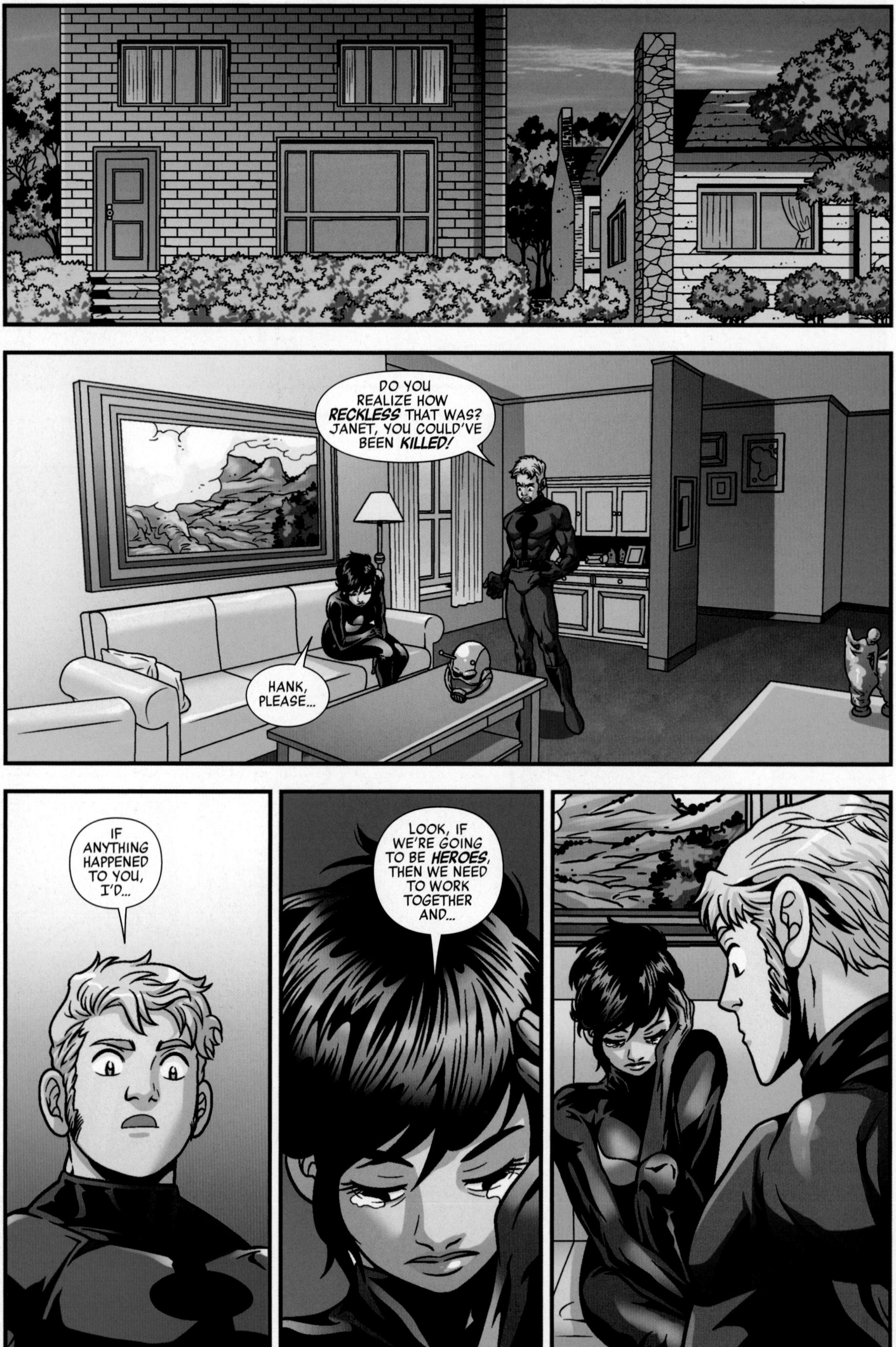
DO YOU REALIZE HOW RECKLESS THAT WAS? JANET, YOU COULD'VE BEEN KILLED!
HANK, PLEASE...
IF ANYTHING HAPPENED TO YOU, I'D...
LOOK, IF WE'RE GOING TO BE HEROES, THEN WE NEED TO WORK TOGETHER AND...

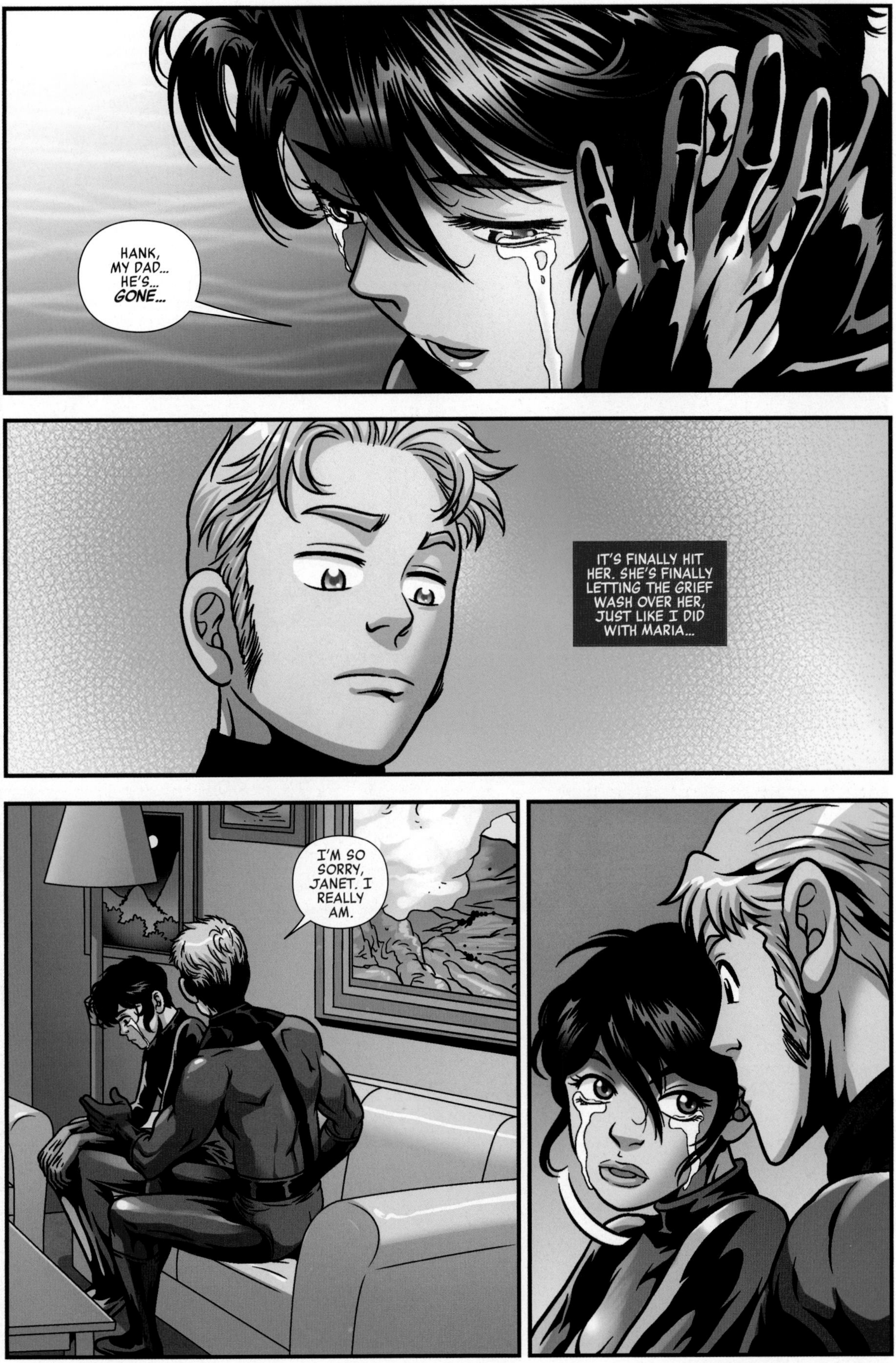
HANK, MY DAD... HE'S... GONE...
IT'S FINALLY HIT HER. SHE'S FINALLY LETTING THE GRIEF WASH OVER HER, JUST LIKE I DID WITH MARIA...
I'M SO SORRY, JANET. I REALLY AM.

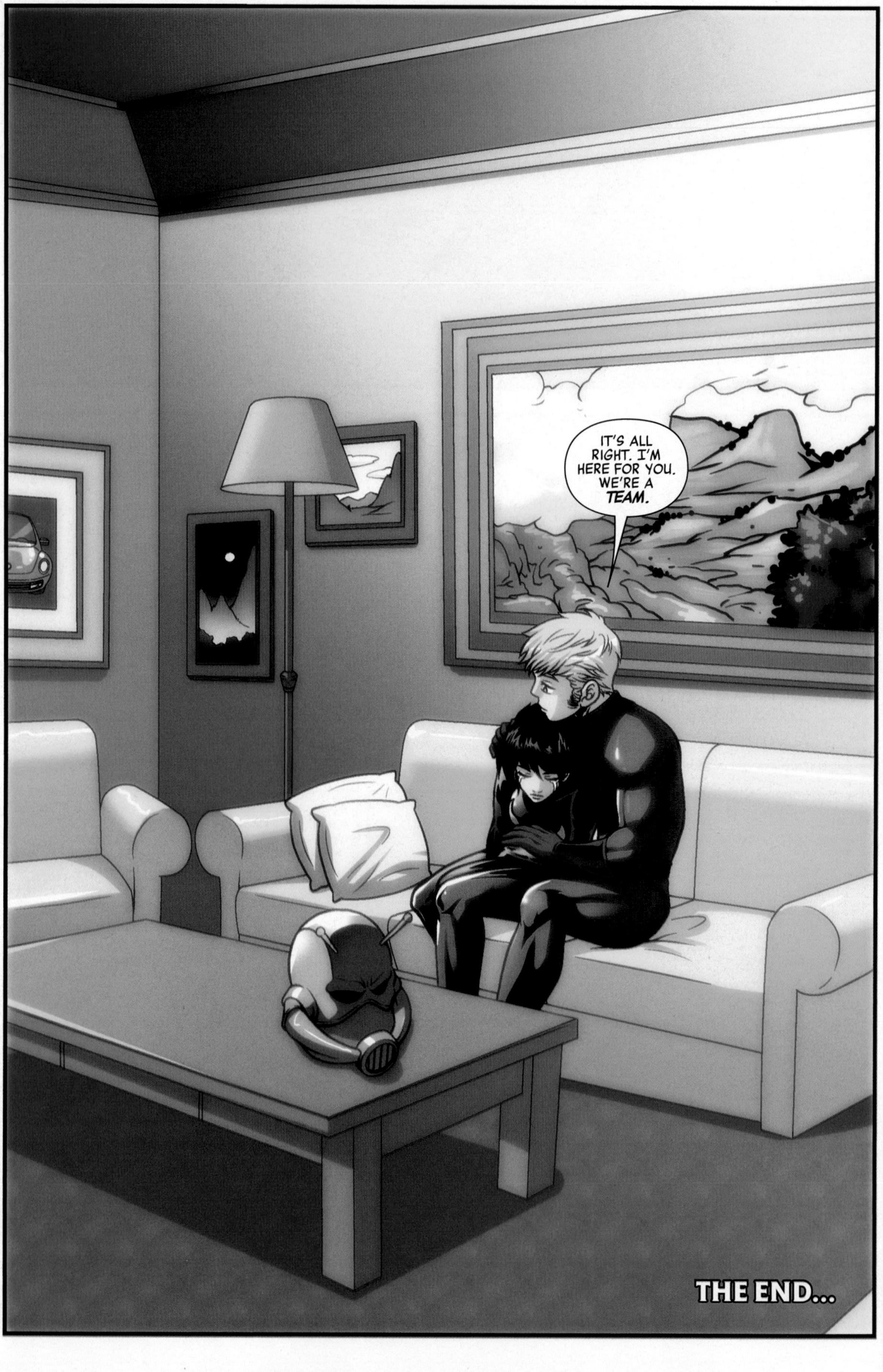
IT'S ALL RIGHT. I'M HERE FOR YOU. WE'RE A TEAM.
THE END...

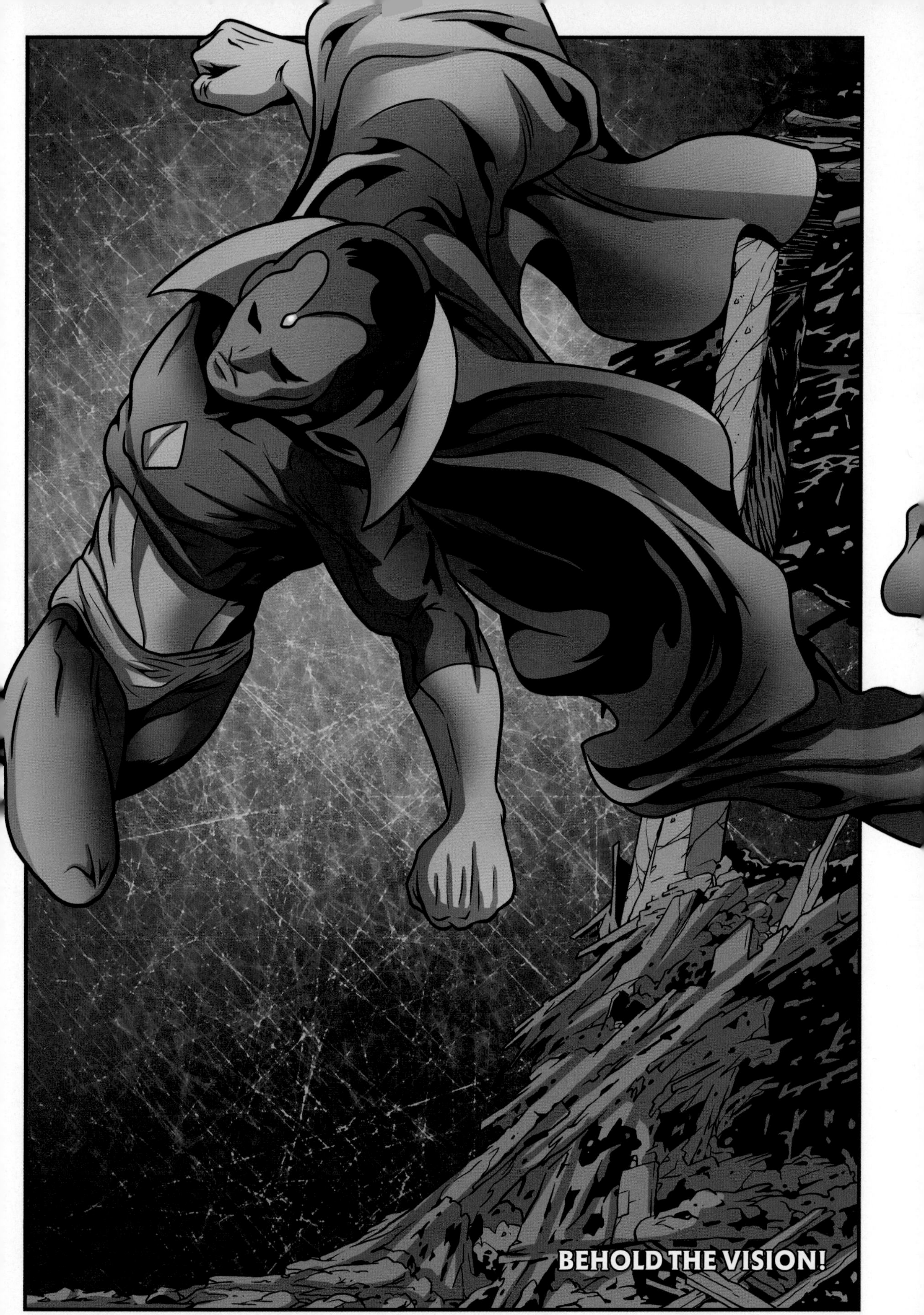
BEHOLD THE VISION!

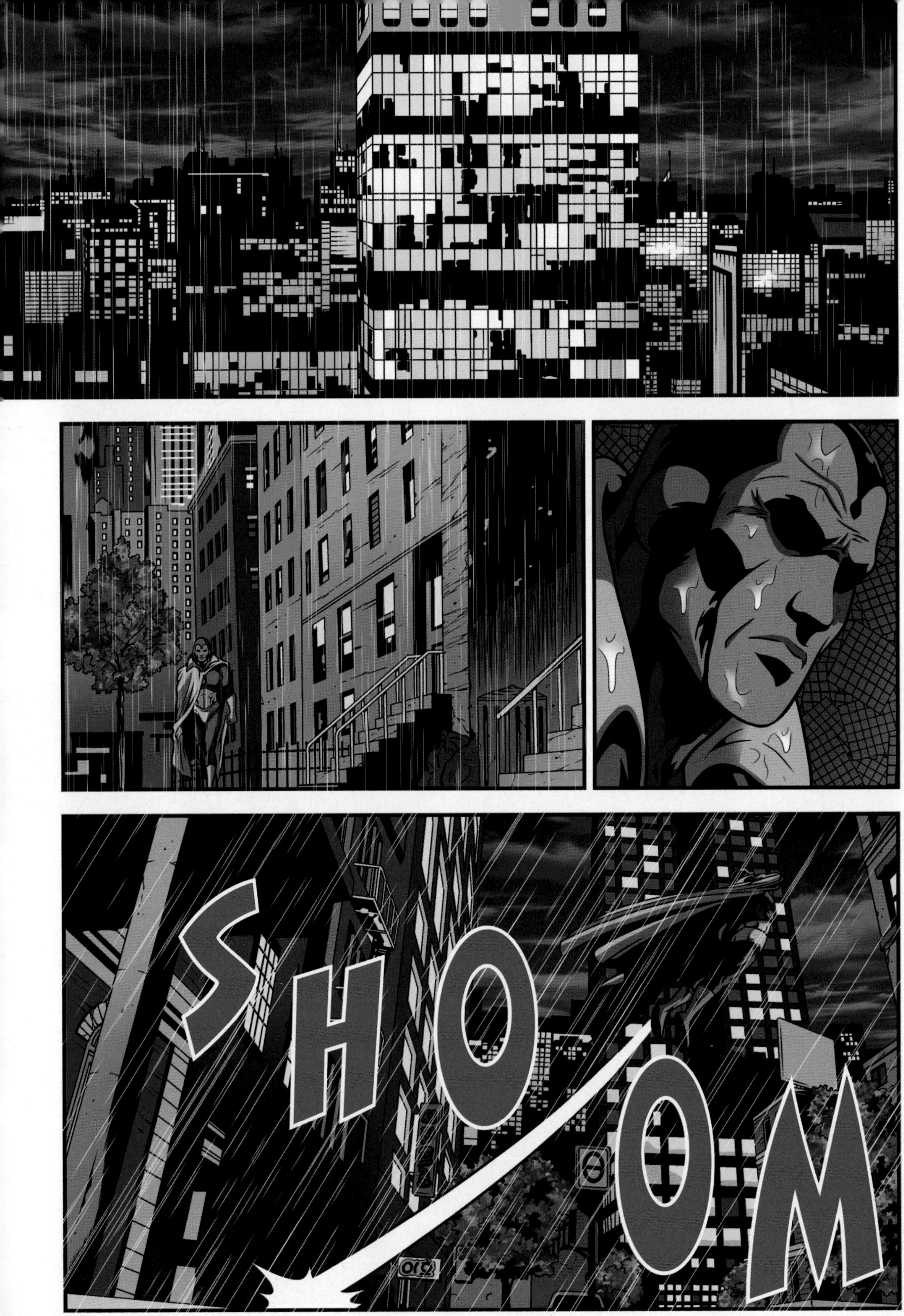
SHOOM

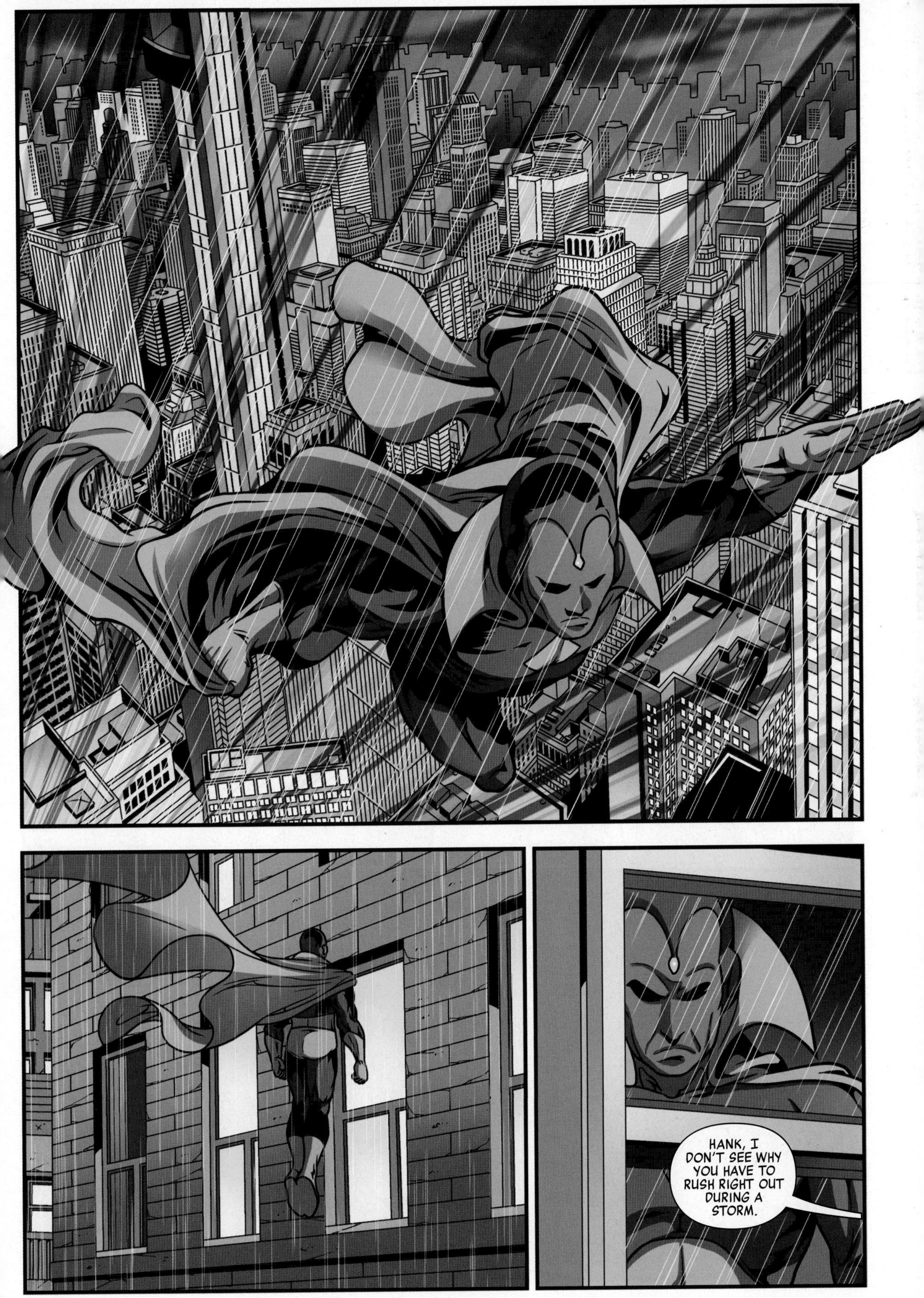
HANK, I DON'T SEE WHY YOU HAVE TO RUSH RIGHT OUT DURING A STORM.

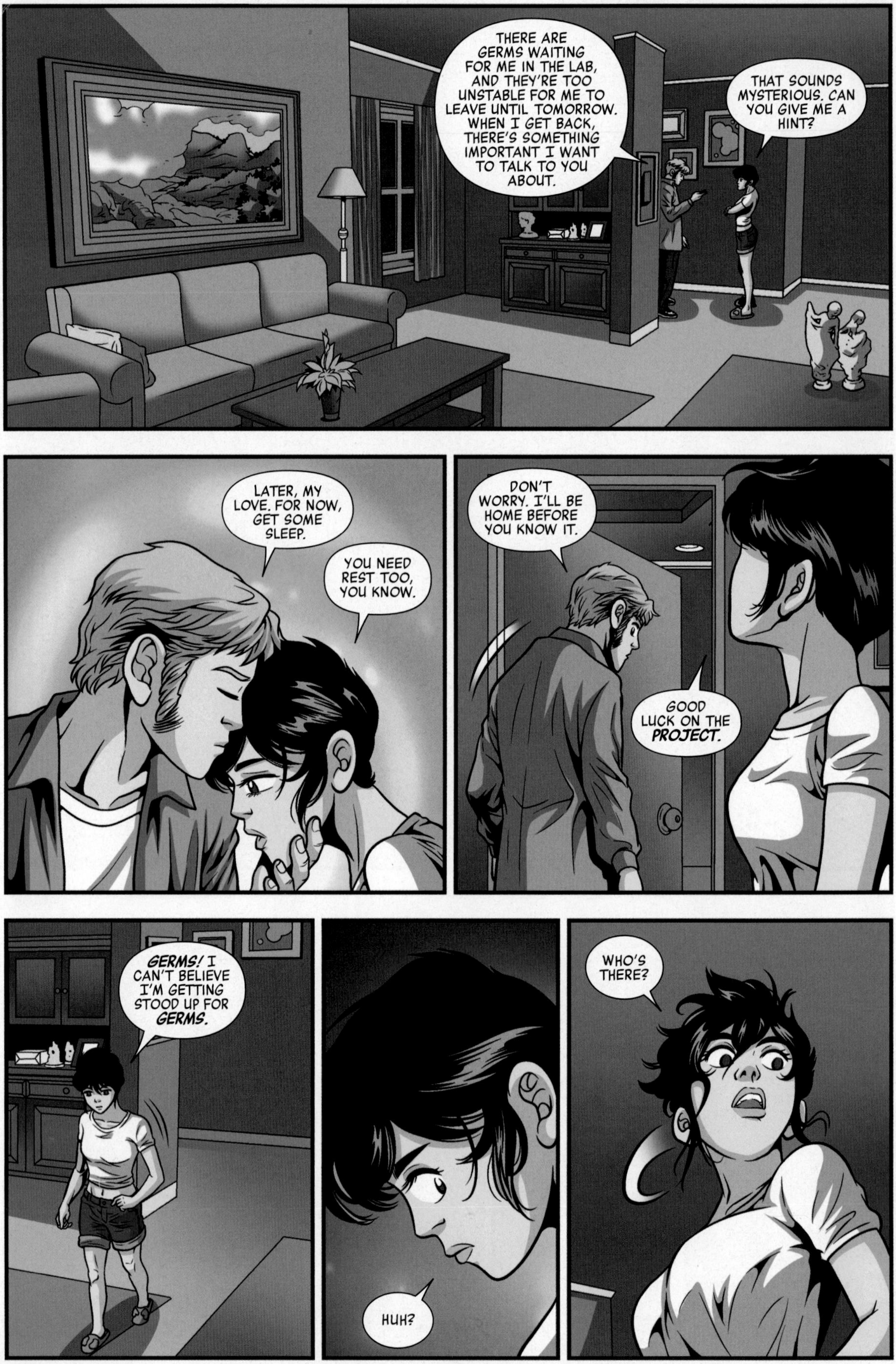
THERE ARE GERMS WAITING FOR ME IN THE LAB, AND THEY'RE TOO UNSTABLE FOR ME TO LEAVE UNTIL TOMORROW. WHEN I GET BACK, THERE'S SOMETHING IMPORTANT I WANT TO TALK TO YOU ABOUT.
THAT SOUNDS MYSTERIOUS. CAN YOU GIVE ME A HINT?
LATER, MY LOVE. FOR NOW, GET SOME SLEEP.
YOU NEED REST TOO, YOU KNOW.
DON'T WORRY. I'LL BE HOME BEFORE YOU KNOW IT.
GOOD LUCK ON THE *PROJECT.*
GERMS! I CAN'T BELIEVE I'M GETTING STOOD UP FOR *GERMS.*
HUH?
WHO'S THERE?

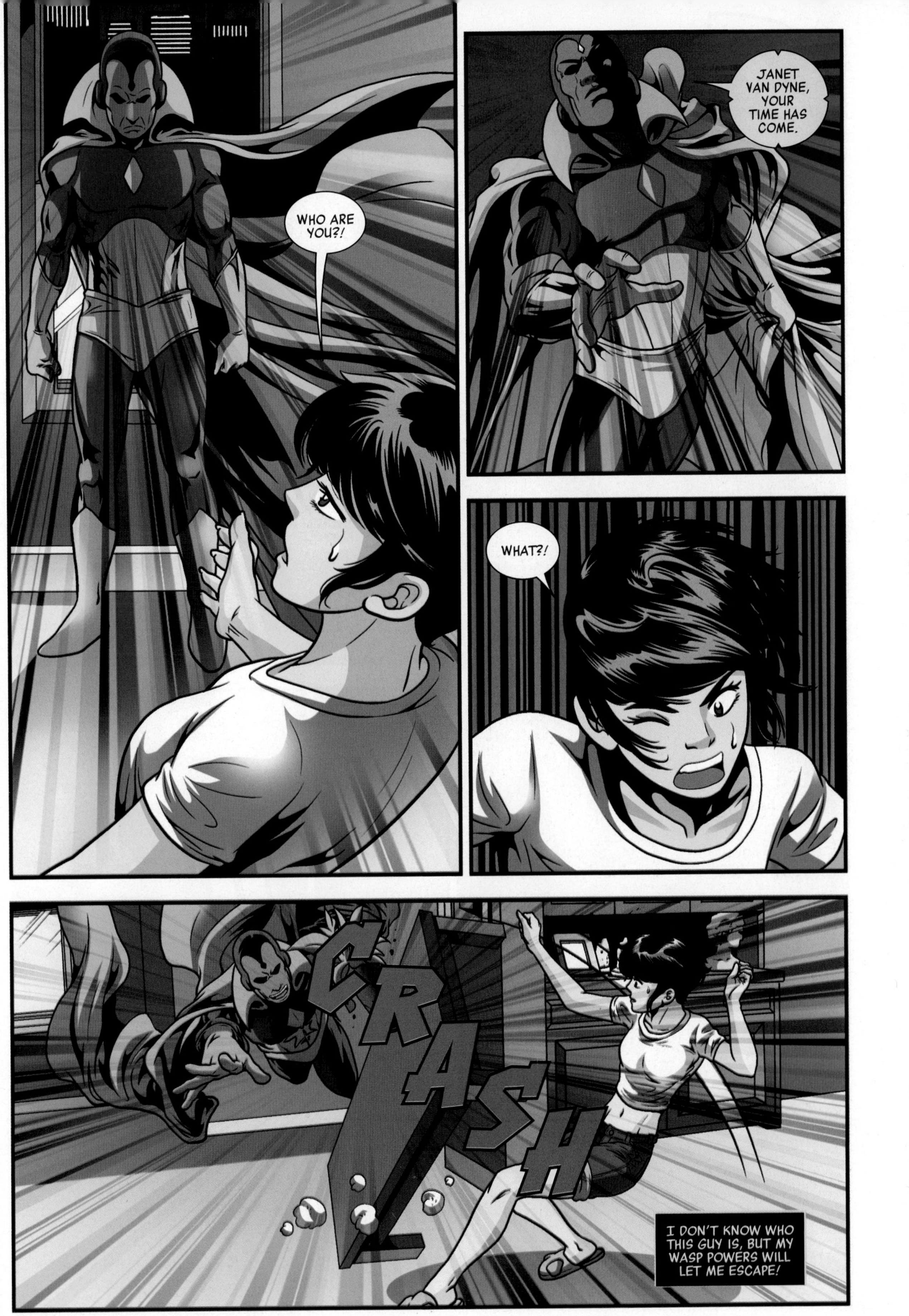
WHO ARE YOU?!
JANET VAN DYNE, YOUR TIME HAS COME.
WHAT?!
CRASH
I DON'T KNOW WHO THIS GUY IS, BUT MY WASP POWERS WILL LET ME ESCAPE!

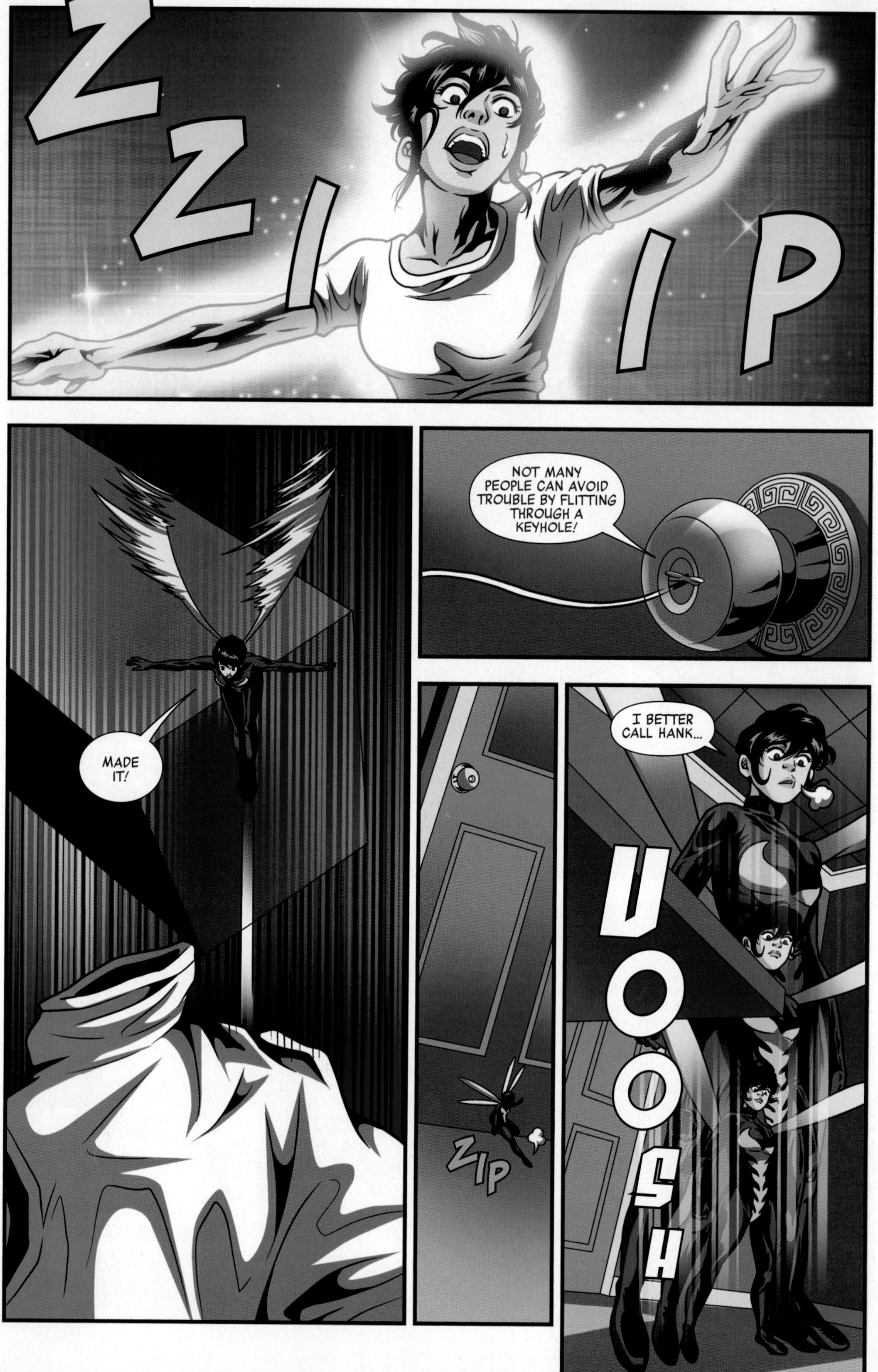
ZZIIP
MADE IT!
NOT MANY PEOPLE CAN AVOID TROUBLE BY FLITTING THROUGH A KEYHOLE!
ZIP
I BETTER CALL HANK...
VOOOSH

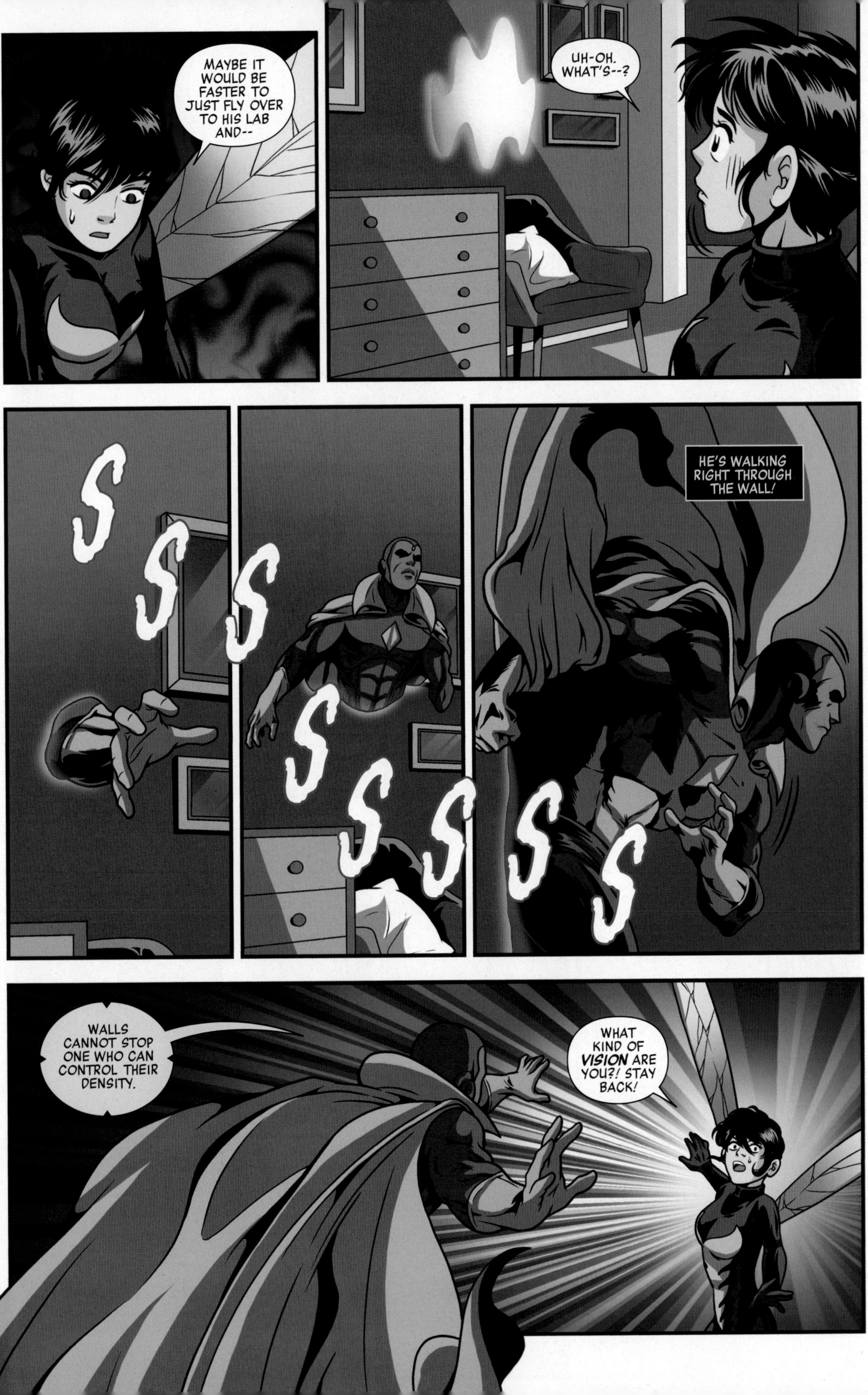
MAYBE IT WOULD BE FASTER TO JUST FLY OVER TO HIS LAB AND--
UH-OH. WHAT'S--?
S S S S S S S S S
HE'S WALKING RIGHT THROUGH THE WALL!
WALLS CANNOT STOP ONE WHO CAN CONTROL THEIR DENSITY.
WHAT KIND OF VISION ARE YOU?! STAY BACK!

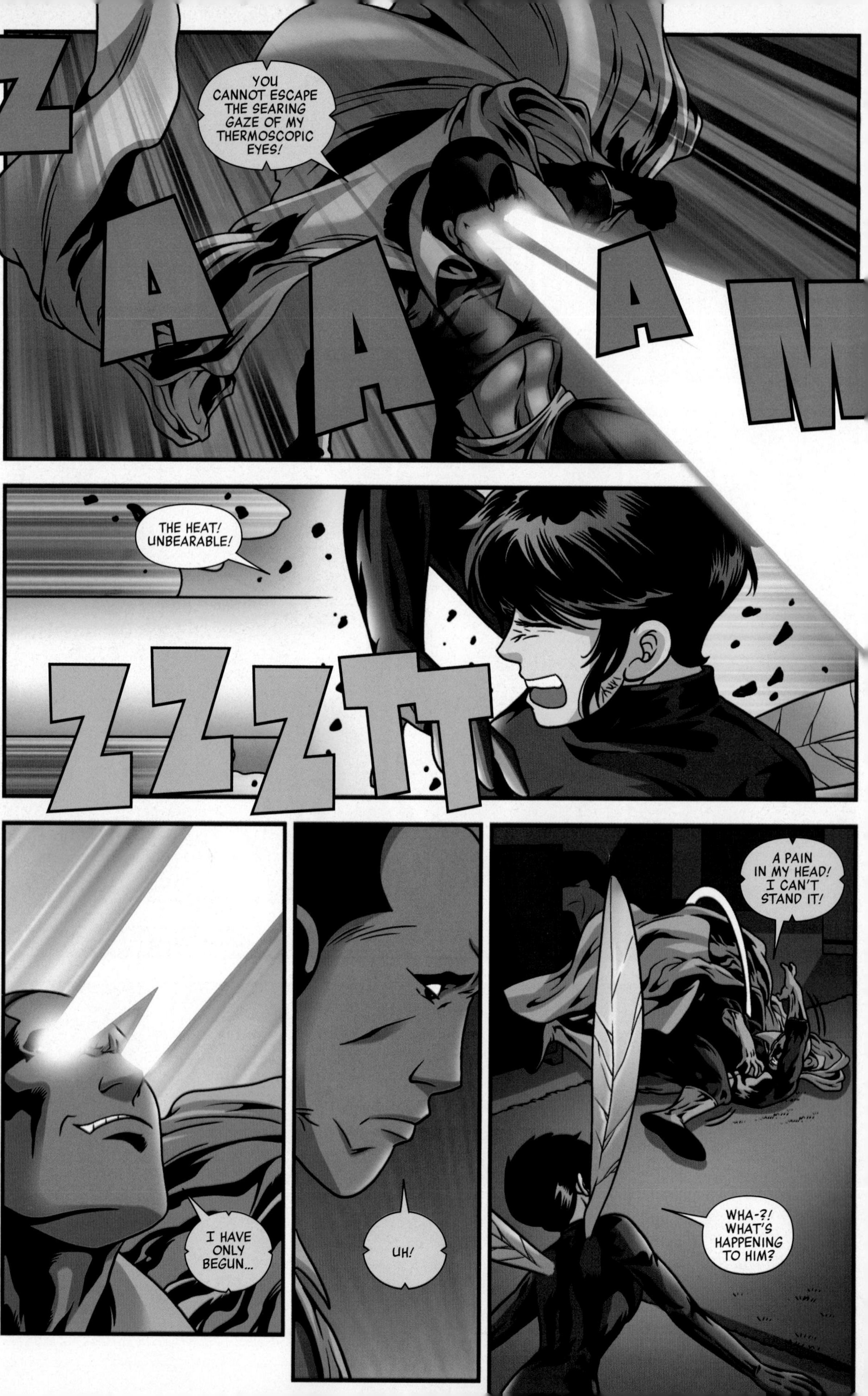
ZAAAM
YOU CANNOT ESCAPE THE SEARING GAZE OF MY THERMOSCOPIC EYES!
THE HEAT! UNBEARABLE!
ZZZTT
I HAVE ONLY BEGUN...
UH!
A PAIN IN MY HEAD! I CAN'T STAND IT!
WHA-?! WHAT'S HAPPENING TO HIM?

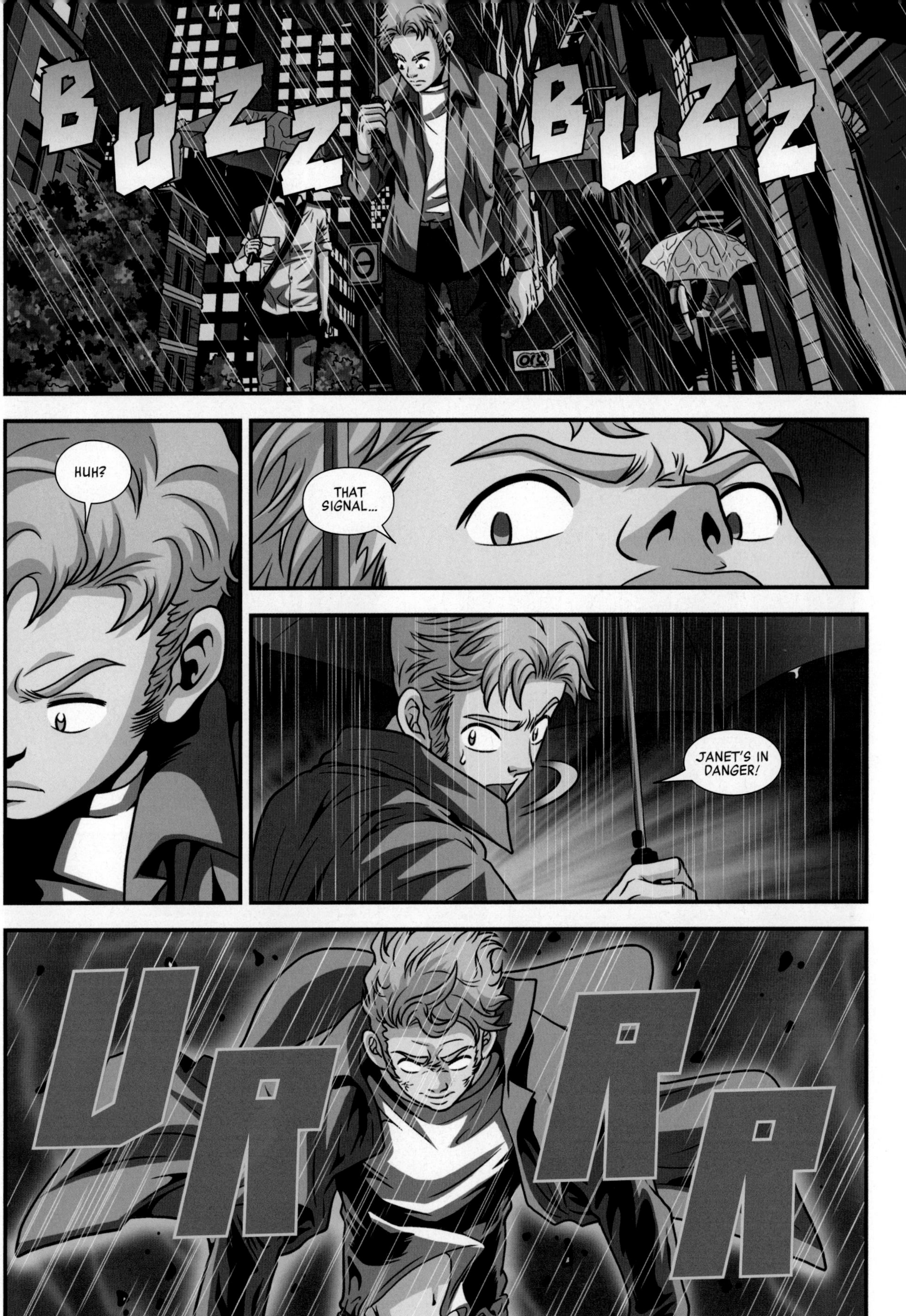
BUZZ BUZZ
HUH?
THAT SIGNAL...
JANET'S IN DANGER!
URRR

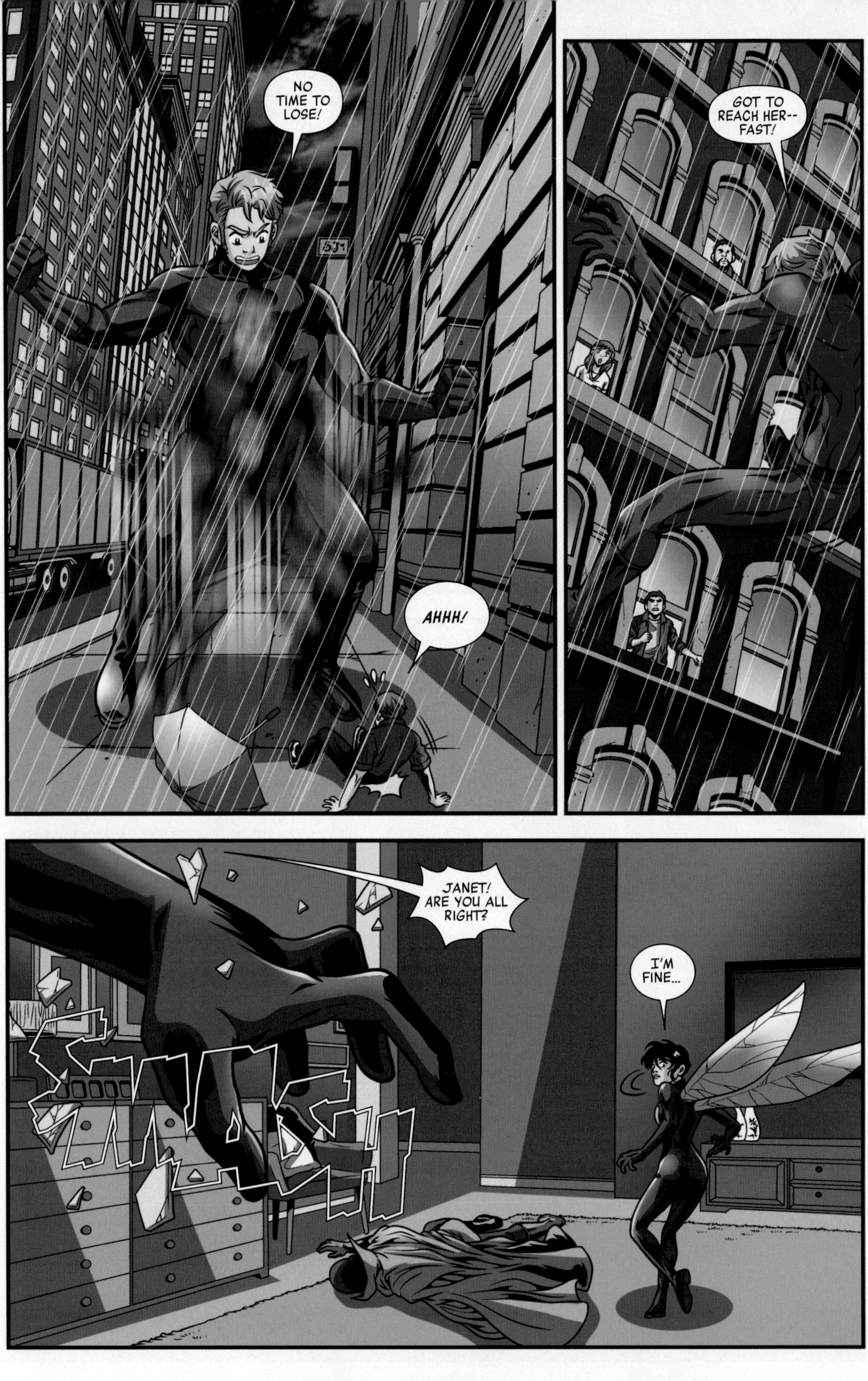
NO TIME TO LOSE!
AHHH!
GOT TO REACH HER-- FAST!
JANET! ARE YOU ALL RIGHT?
I'M FINE...

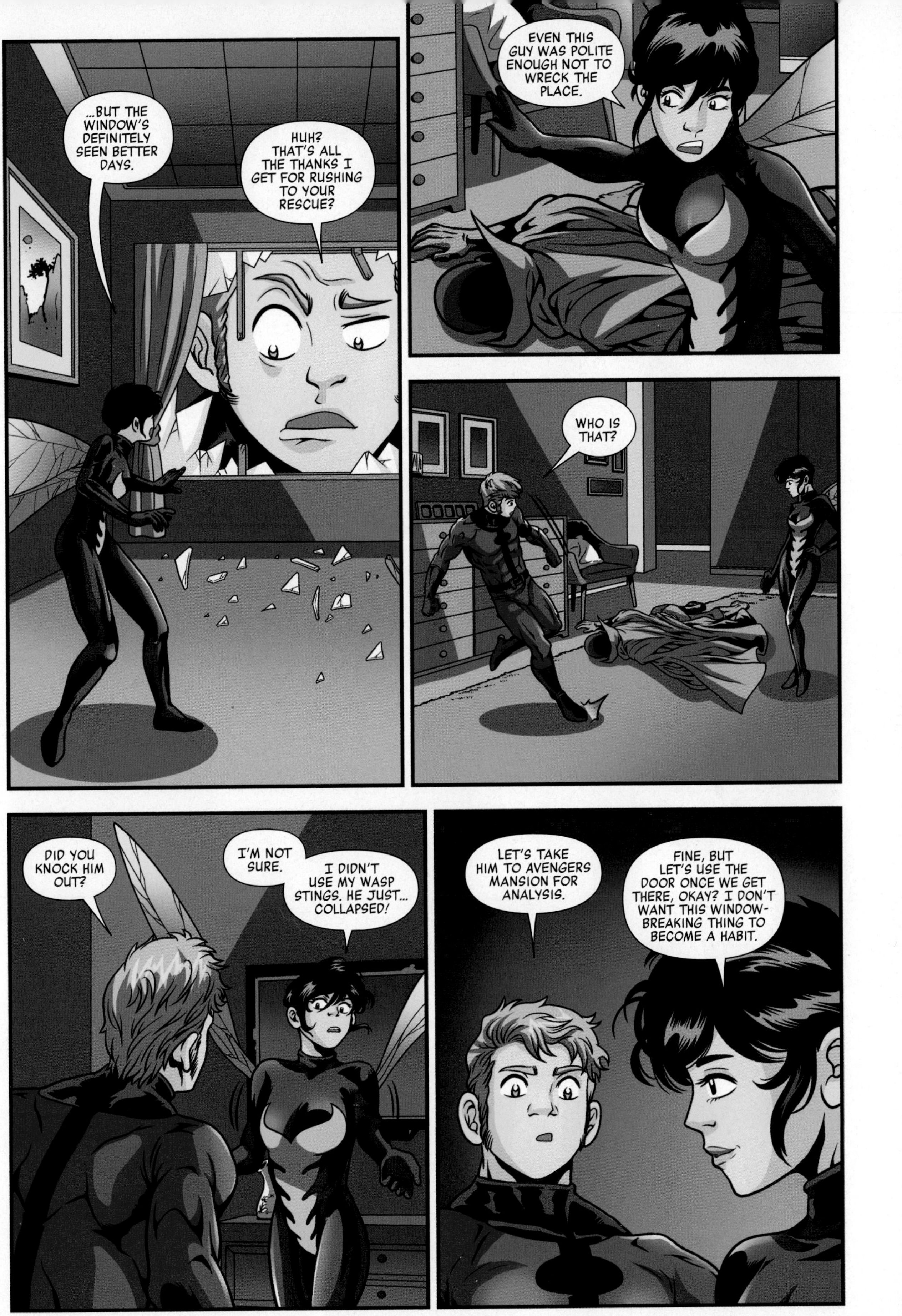
...BUT THE WINDOW'S DEFINITELY SEEN BETTER DAYS.
HUH? THAT'S ALL THE THANKS I GET FOR RUSHING TO YOUR RESCUE?
EVEN THIS GUY WAS POLITE ENOUGH NOT TO WRECK THE PLACE.
WHO IS THAT?
DID YOU KNOCK HIM OUT?
I'M NOT SURE.
I DIDN'T USE MY WASP STINGS. HE JUST... COLLAPSED!
LET'S TAKE HIM TO AVENGERS MANSION FOR ANALYSIS.
FINE, BUT LET'S USE THE DOOR ONCE WE GET THERE, OKAY? I DON'T WANT THIS WINDOW-BREAKING THING TO BECOME A HABIT.

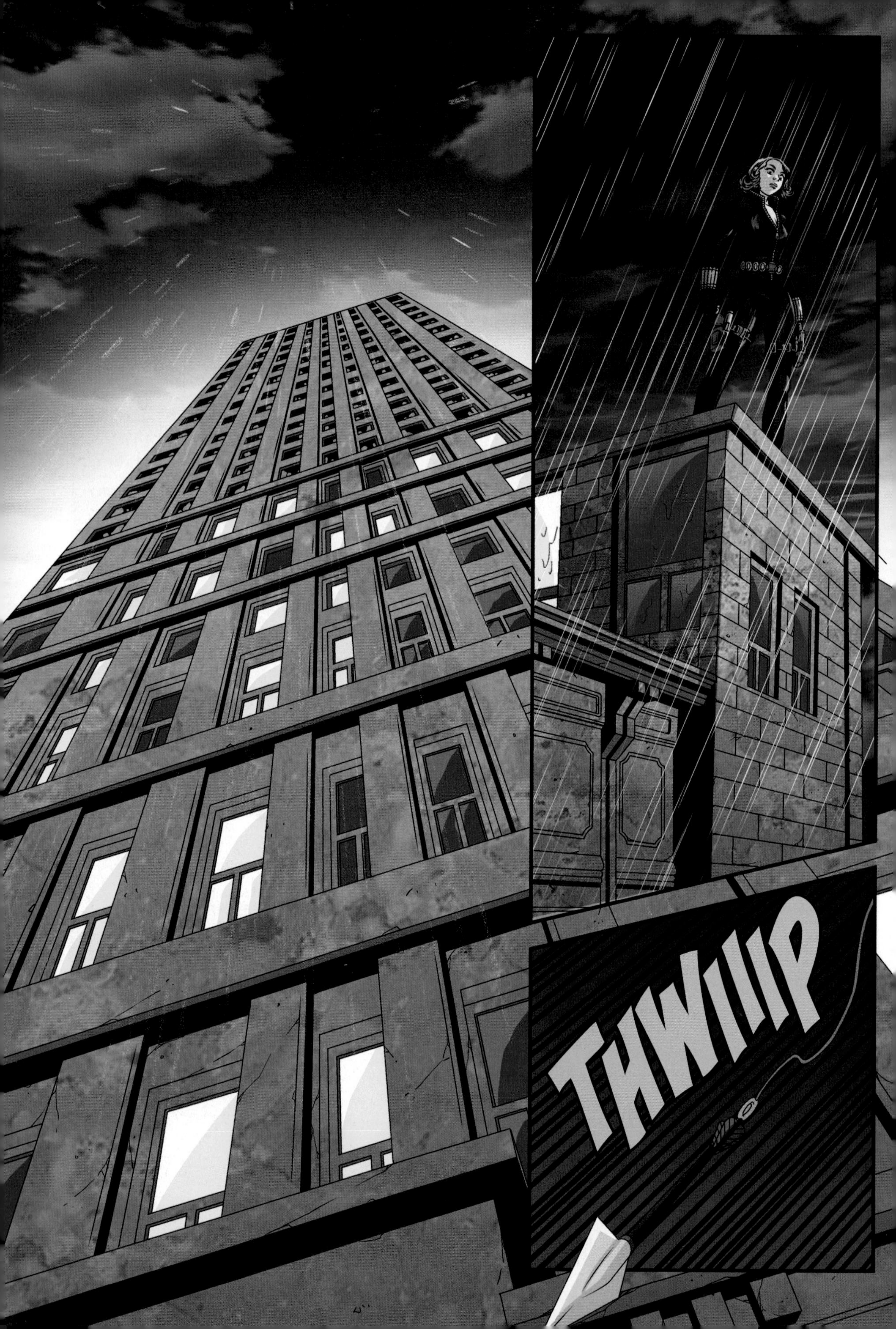
THWIIIP

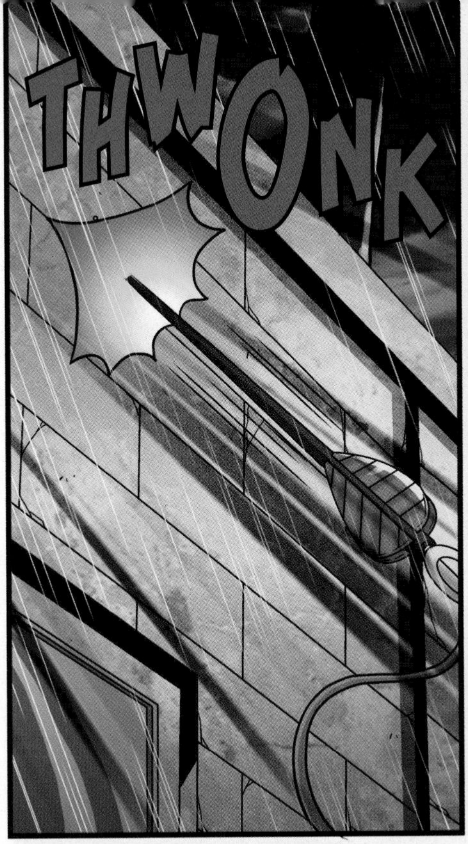
THWONK

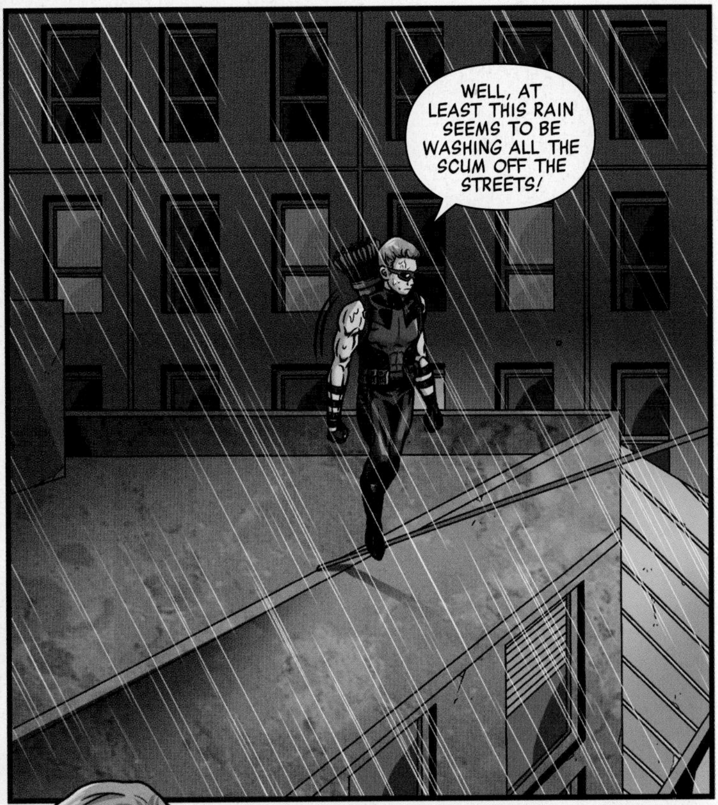
WELL, AT LEAST THIS RAIN SEEMS TO BE WASHING ALL THE SCUM OFF THE STREETS!

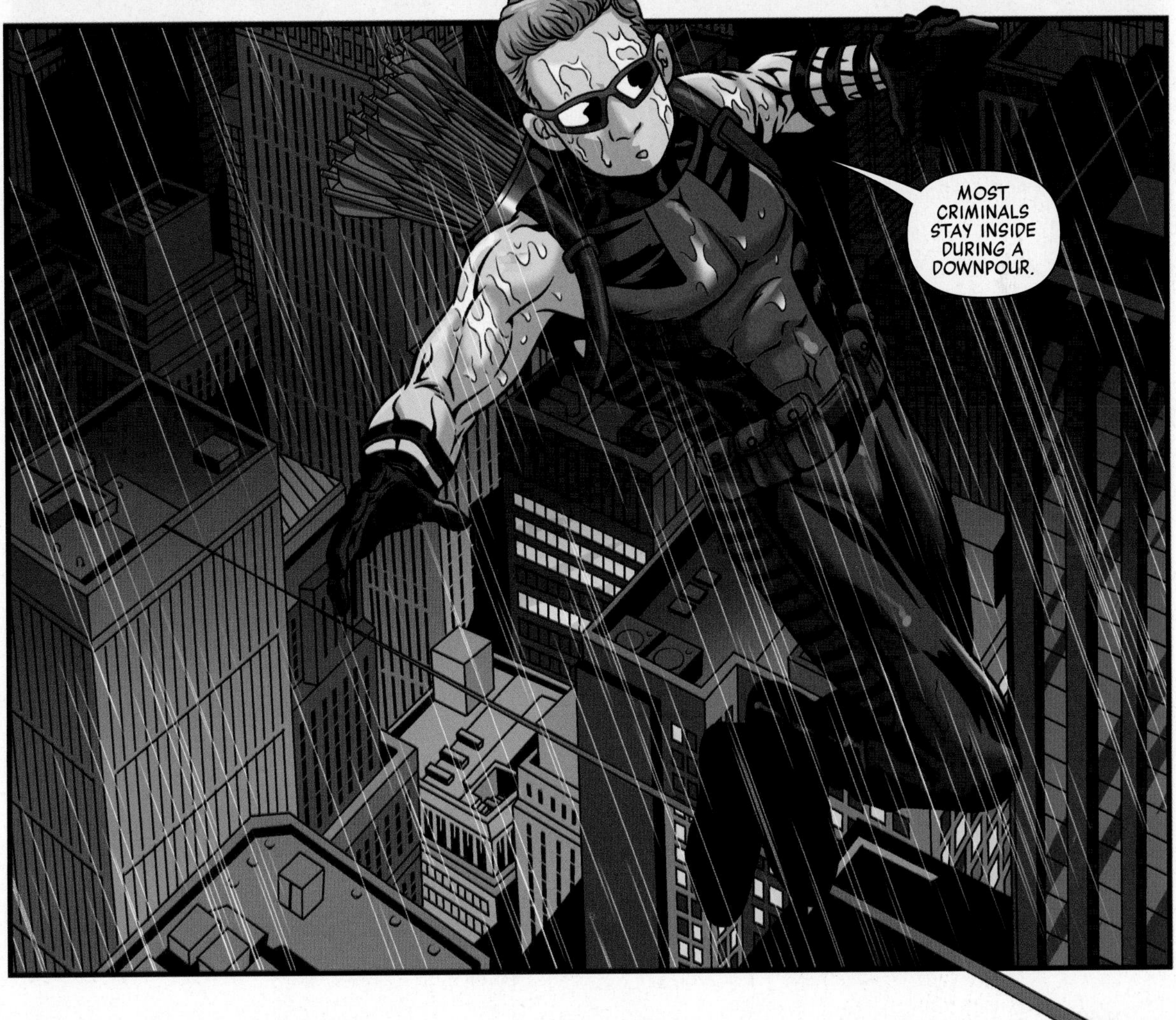
MOST CRIMINALS STAY INSIDE DURING A DOWNPOUR.

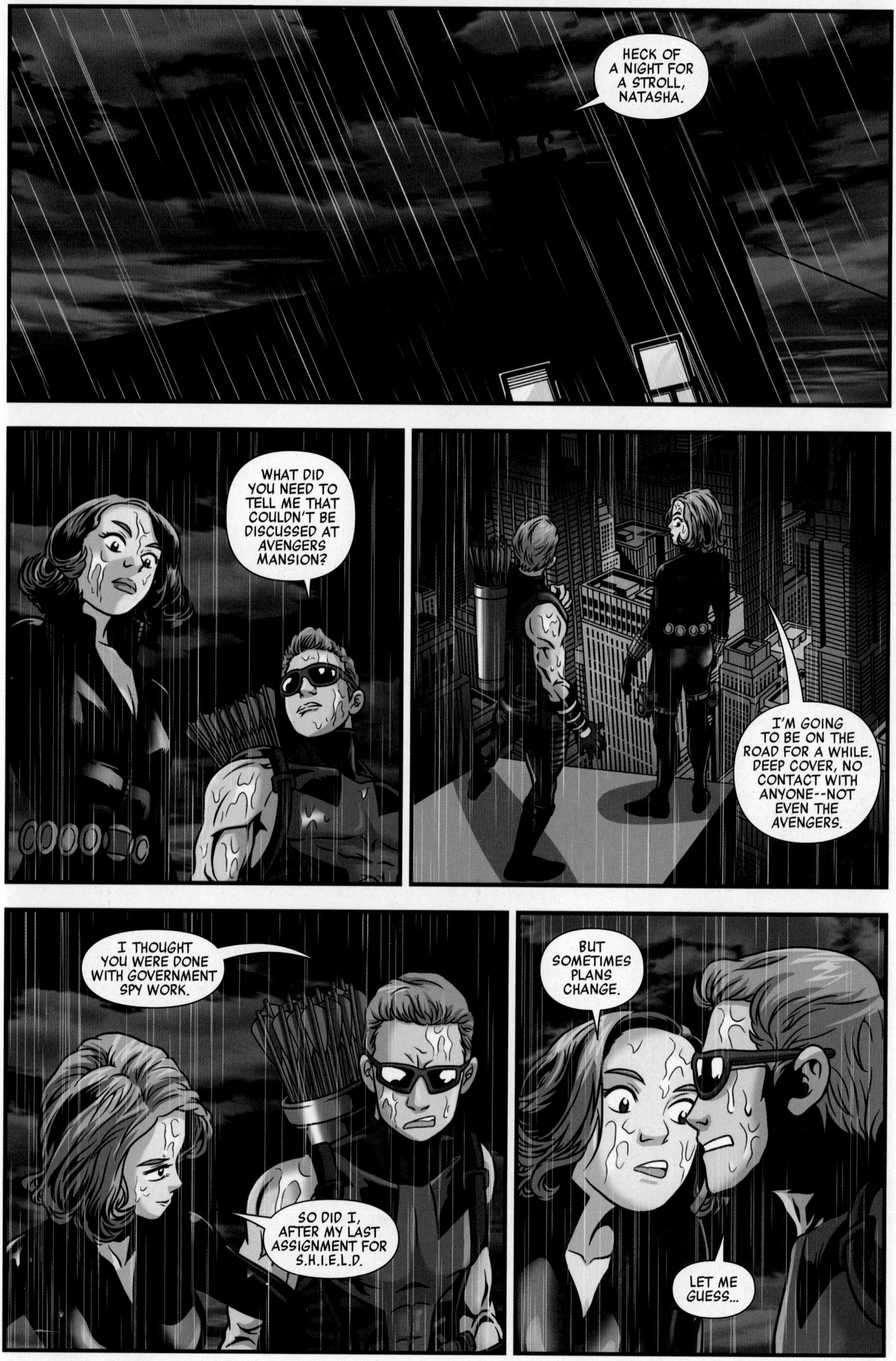
HECK OF A NIGHT FOR A STROLL, NATASHA.
WHAT DID YOU NEED TO TELL ME THAT COULDN'T BE DISCUSSED AT AVENGERS MANSION?
I'M GOING TO BE ON THE ROAD FOR A WHILE. DEEP COVER, NO CONTACT WITH ANYONE--NOT EVEN THE AVENGERS.
I THOUGHT YOU WERE DONE WITH GOVERNMENT SPY WORK.
SO DID I, AFTER MY LAST ASSIGNMENT FOR S.H.I.E.L.D.
BUT SOMETIMES PLANS CHANGE.
LET ME GUESS...

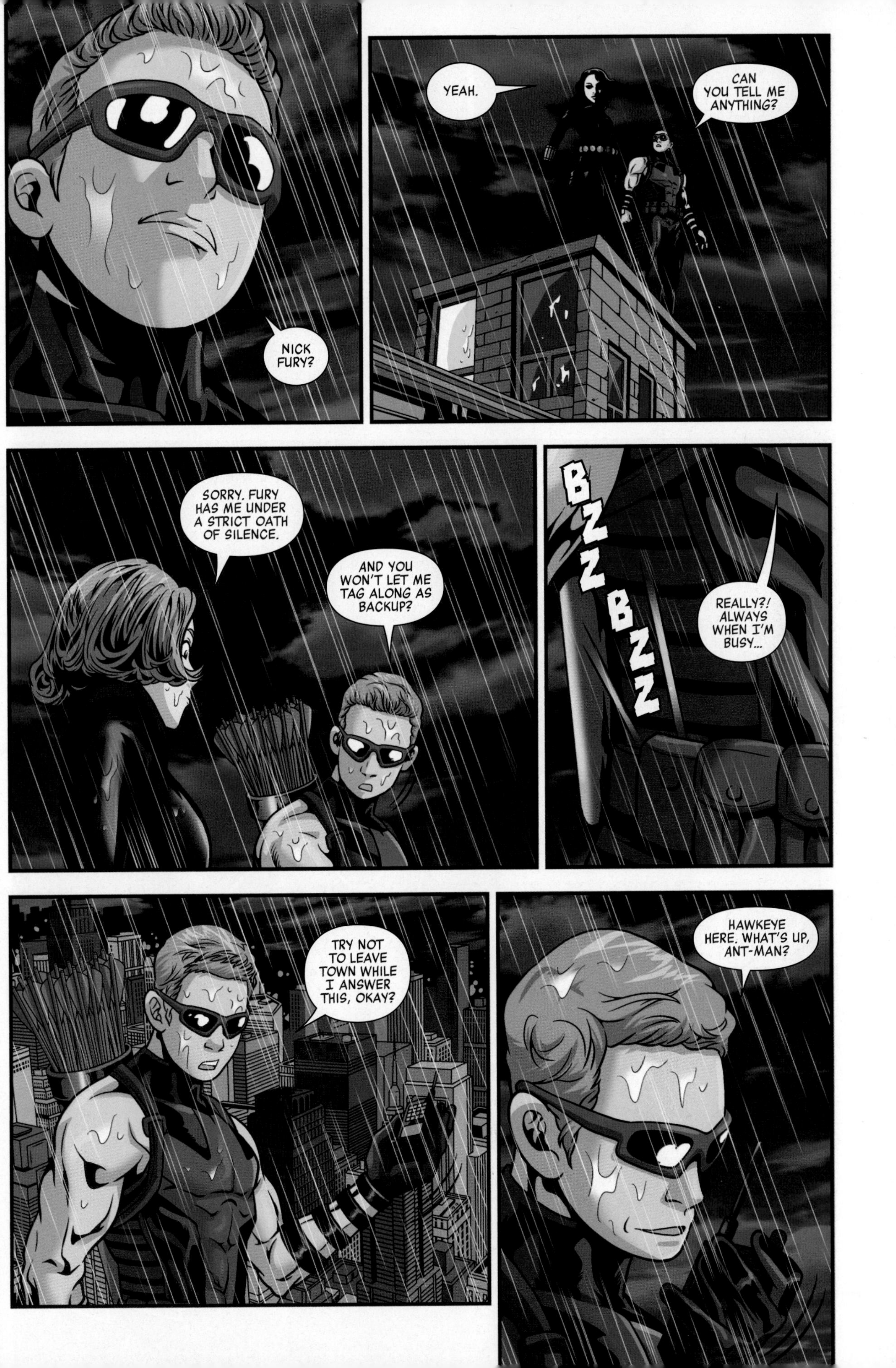
NICK FURY?
YEAH.
CAN YOU TELL ME ANYTHING?
SORRY. FURY HAS ME UNDER A STRICT OATH OF SILENCE.
AND YOU WON'T LET ME TAG ALONG AS BACKUP?
BZZ BZZ
REALLY?! ALWAYS WHEN I'M BUSY...
TRY NOT TO LEAVE TOWN WHILE I ANSWER THIS, OKAY?
HAWKEYE HERE. WHAT'S UP, ANT-MAN?

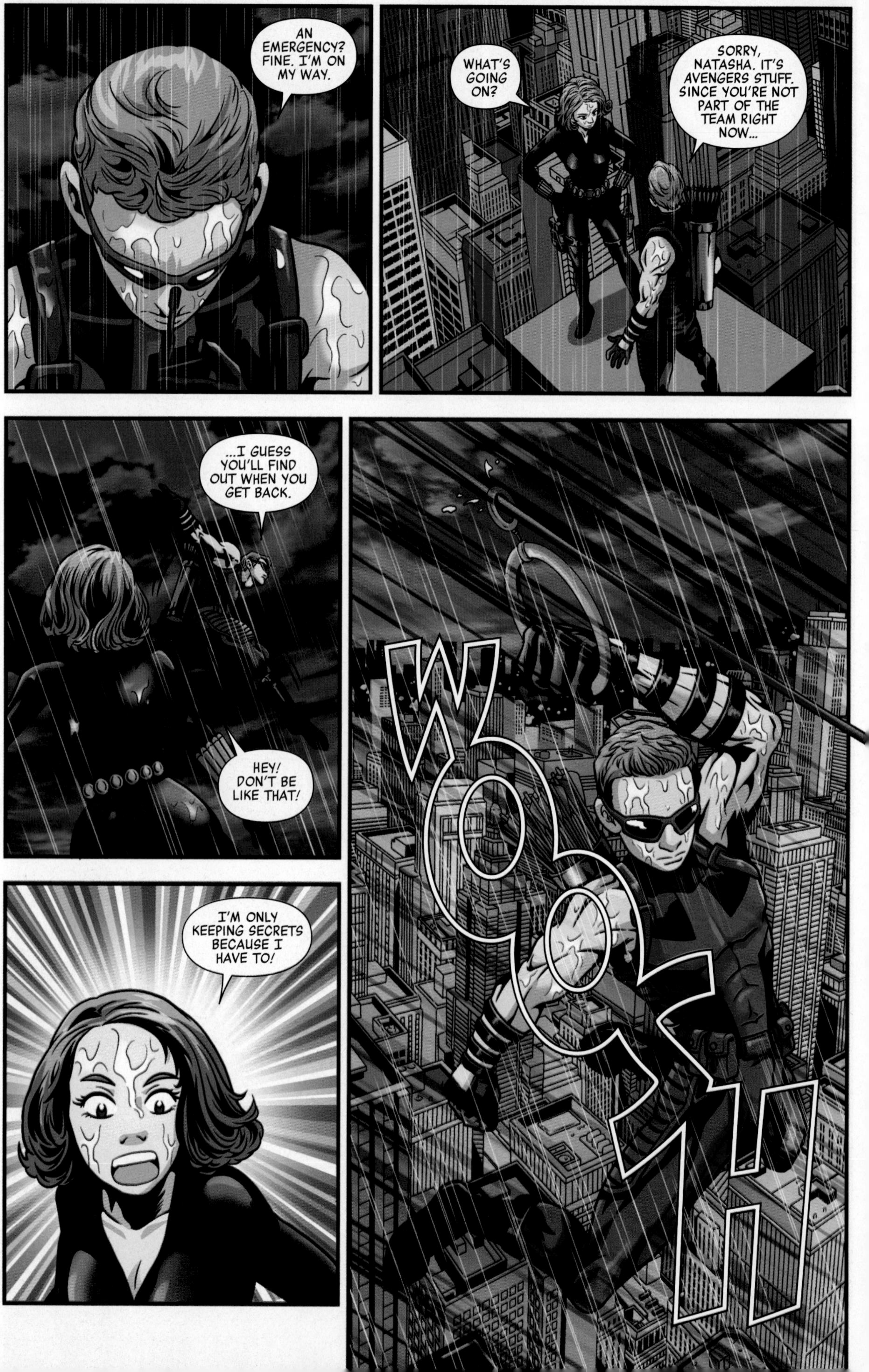
AN EMERGENCY? FINE. I'M ON MY WAY.
WHAT'S GOING ON?
SORRY, NATASHA. IT'S AVENGERS STUFF. SINCE YOU'RE NOT PART OF THE TEAM RIGHT NOW...
...I GUESS YOU'LL FIND OUT WHEN YOU GET BACK.
HEY! DON'T BE LIKE THAT!
I'M ONLY KEEPING SECRETS BECAUSE I HAVE TO!
WOOOOSH

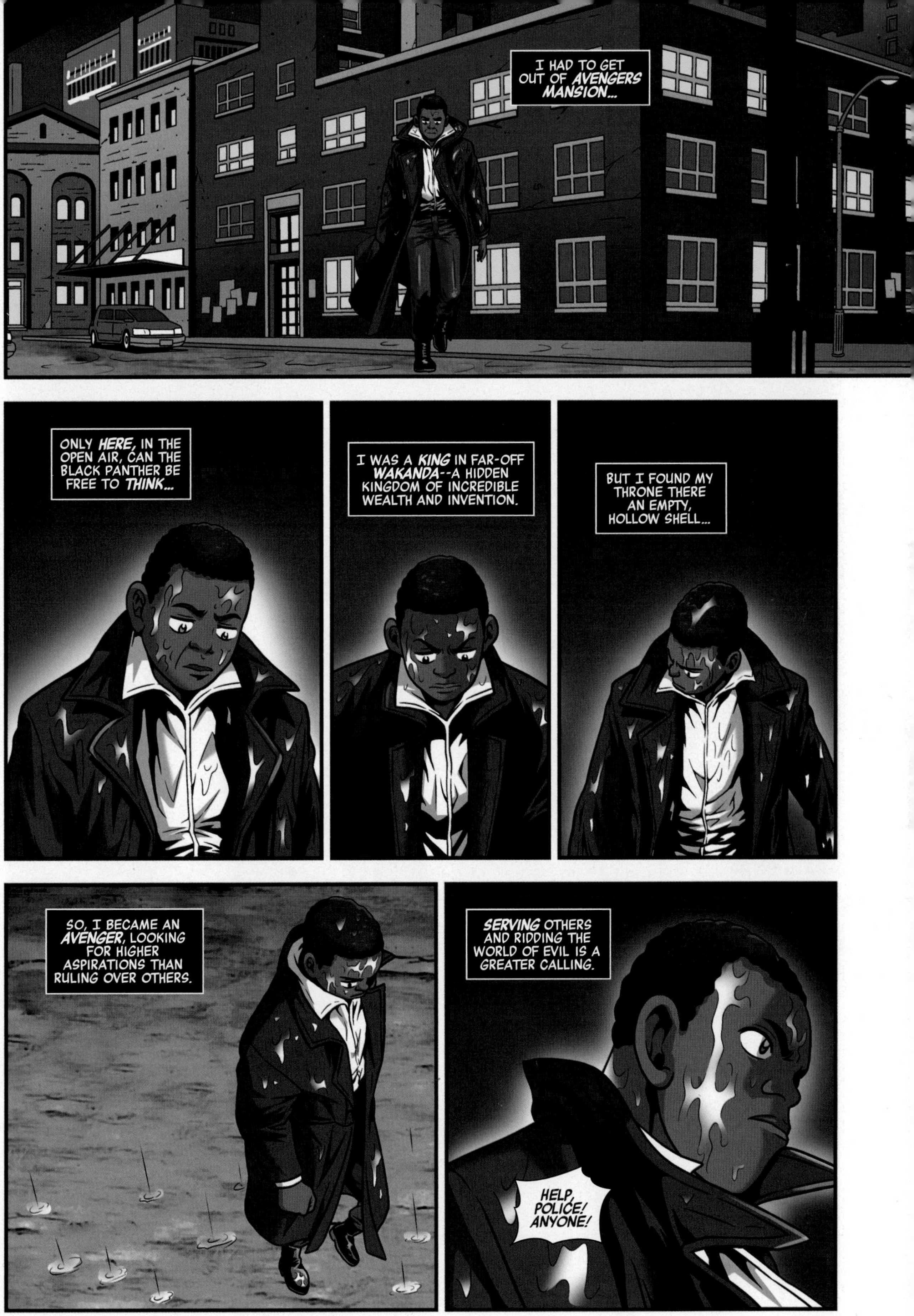
I HAD TO GET OUT OF AVENGERS MANSION...
ONLY HERE, IN THE OPEN AIR, CAN THE BLACK PANTHER BE FREE TO THINK...
I WAS A KING IN FAR-OFF WAKANDA--A HIDDEN KINGDOM OF INCREDIBLE WEALTH AND INVENTION.
BUT I FOUND MY THRONE THERE AN EMPTY, HOLLOW SHELL...
SO, I BECAME AN AVENGER, LOOKING FOR HIGHER ASPIRATIONS THAN RULING OVER OTHERS.
SERVING OTHERS AND RIDDING THE WORLD OF EVIL IS A GREATER CALLING.
HELP, POLICE! ANYONE!

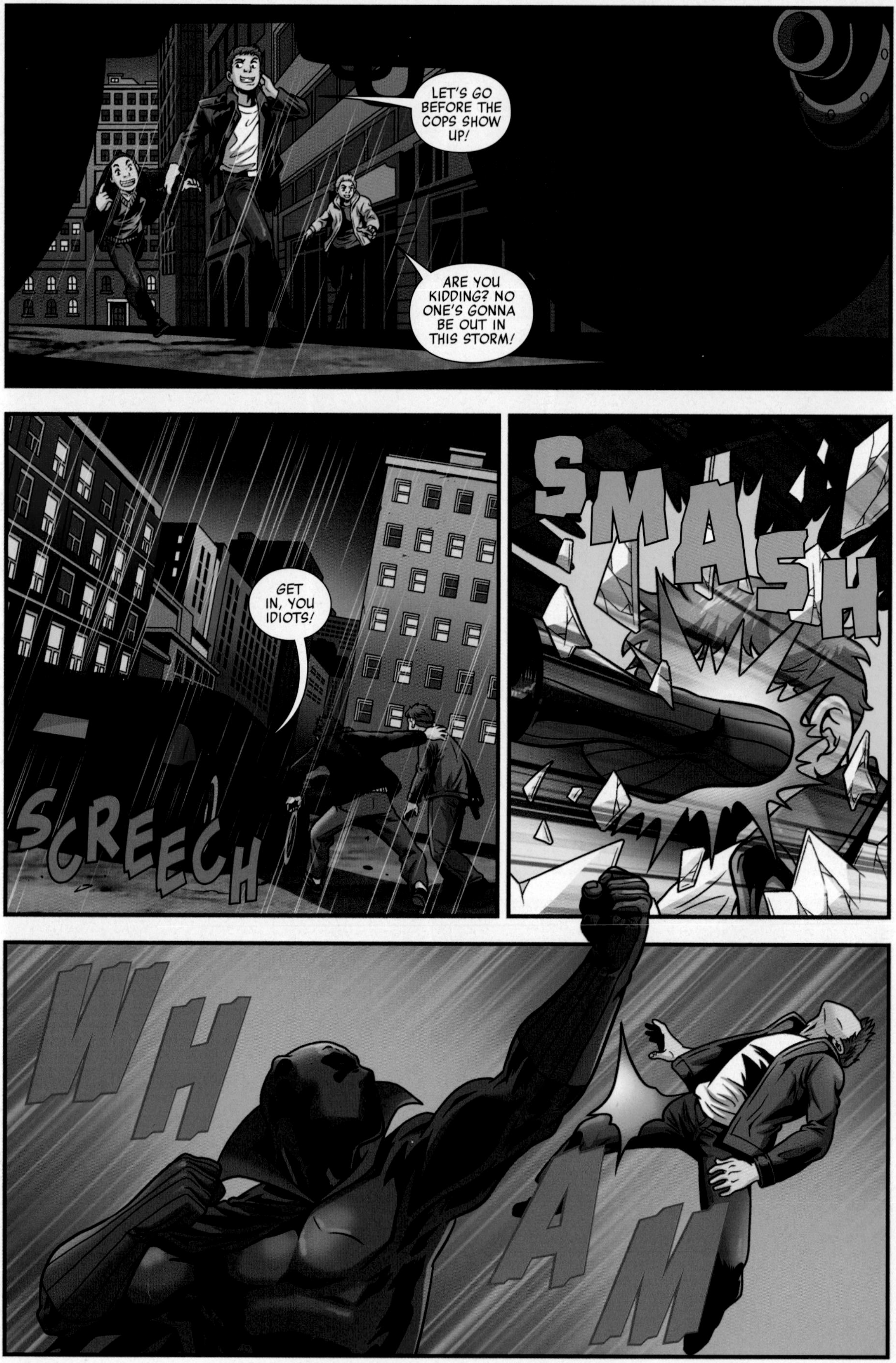
LET'S GO BEFORE THE COPS SHOW UP!
ARE YOU KIDDING? NO ONE'S GONNA BE OUT IN THIS STORM!
GET IN, YOU IDIOTS!
SCREECH
SMASH
WHAM

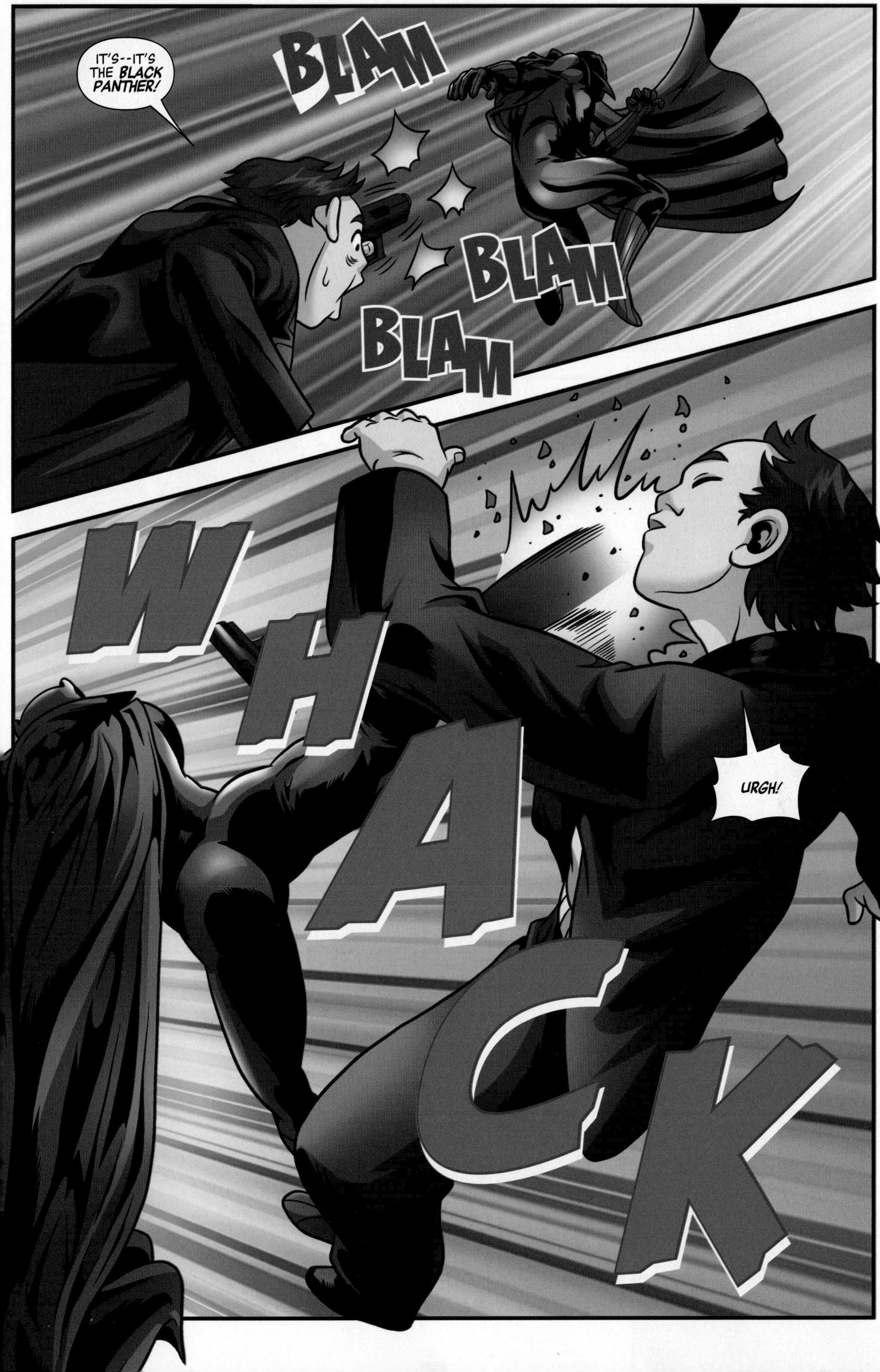
IT'S--IT'S THE BLACK PANTHER!
BLAM
BLAM
BLAM
WHACK
URGH!

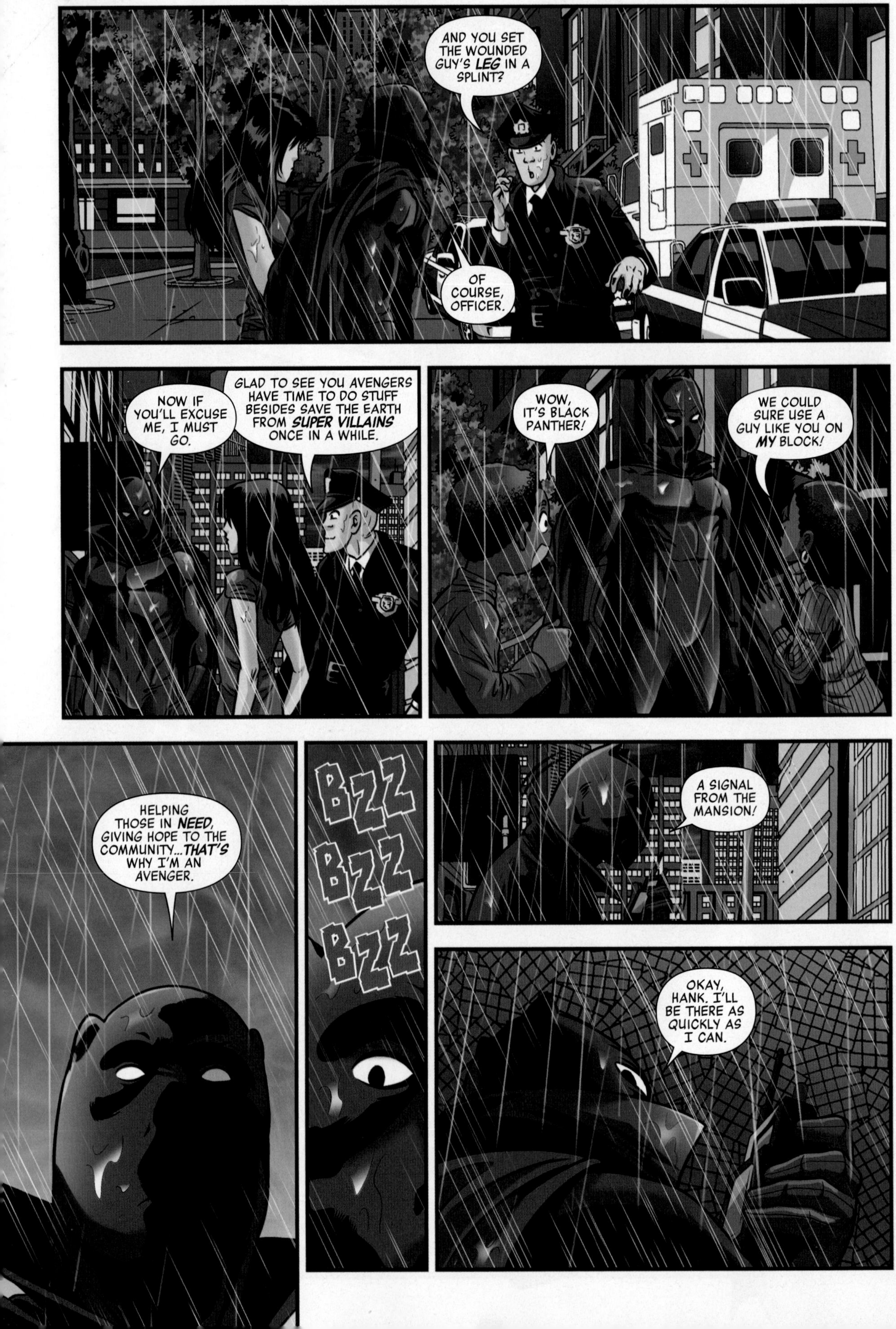
AND YOU SET THE WOUNDED GUY'S LEG IN A SPLINT?
OF COURSE, OFFICER.
GLAD TO SEE YOU AVENGERS HAVE TIME TO DO STUFF BESIDES SAVE THE EARTH FROM SUPER VILLAINS ONCE IN A WHILE.
NOW IF YOU'LL EXCUSE ME, I MUST GO.
WOW, IT'S BLACK PANTHER!
WE COULD SURE USE A GUY LIKE YOU ON MY BLOCK!
HELPING THOSE IN NEED, GIVING HOPE TO THE COMMUNITY...THAT'S WHY I'M AN AVENGER.
BZZ
BZZ
BZZ
A SIGNAL FROM THE MANSION!
OKAY, HANK. I'LL BE THERE AS QUICKLY AS I CAN.

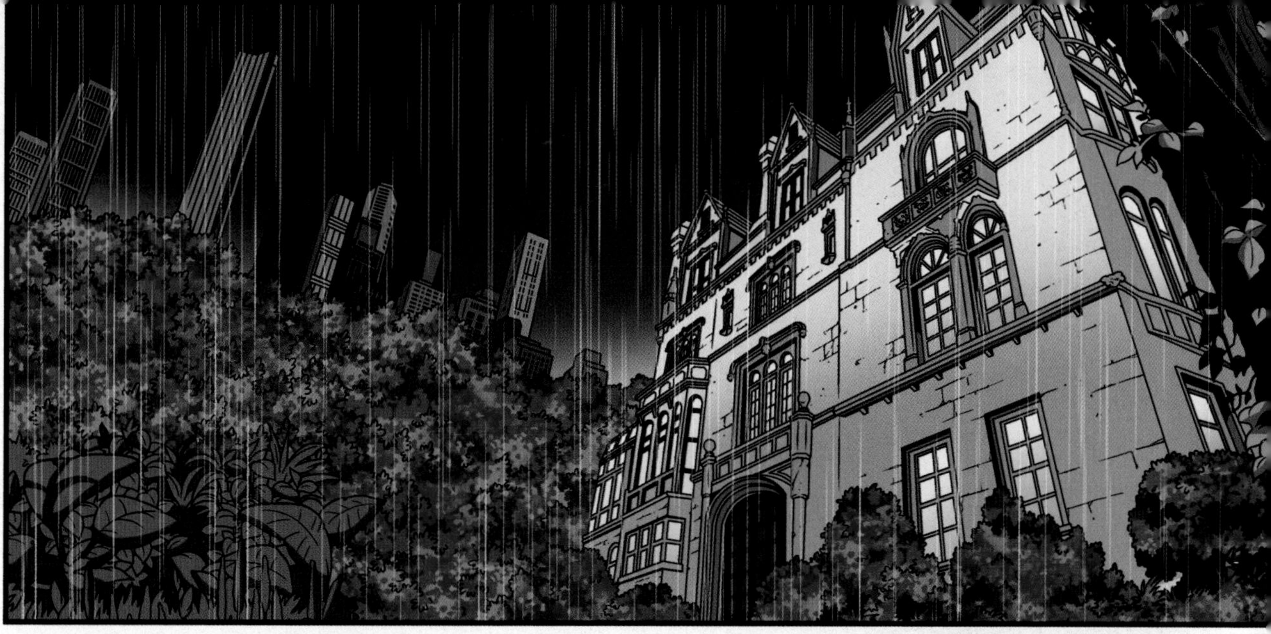

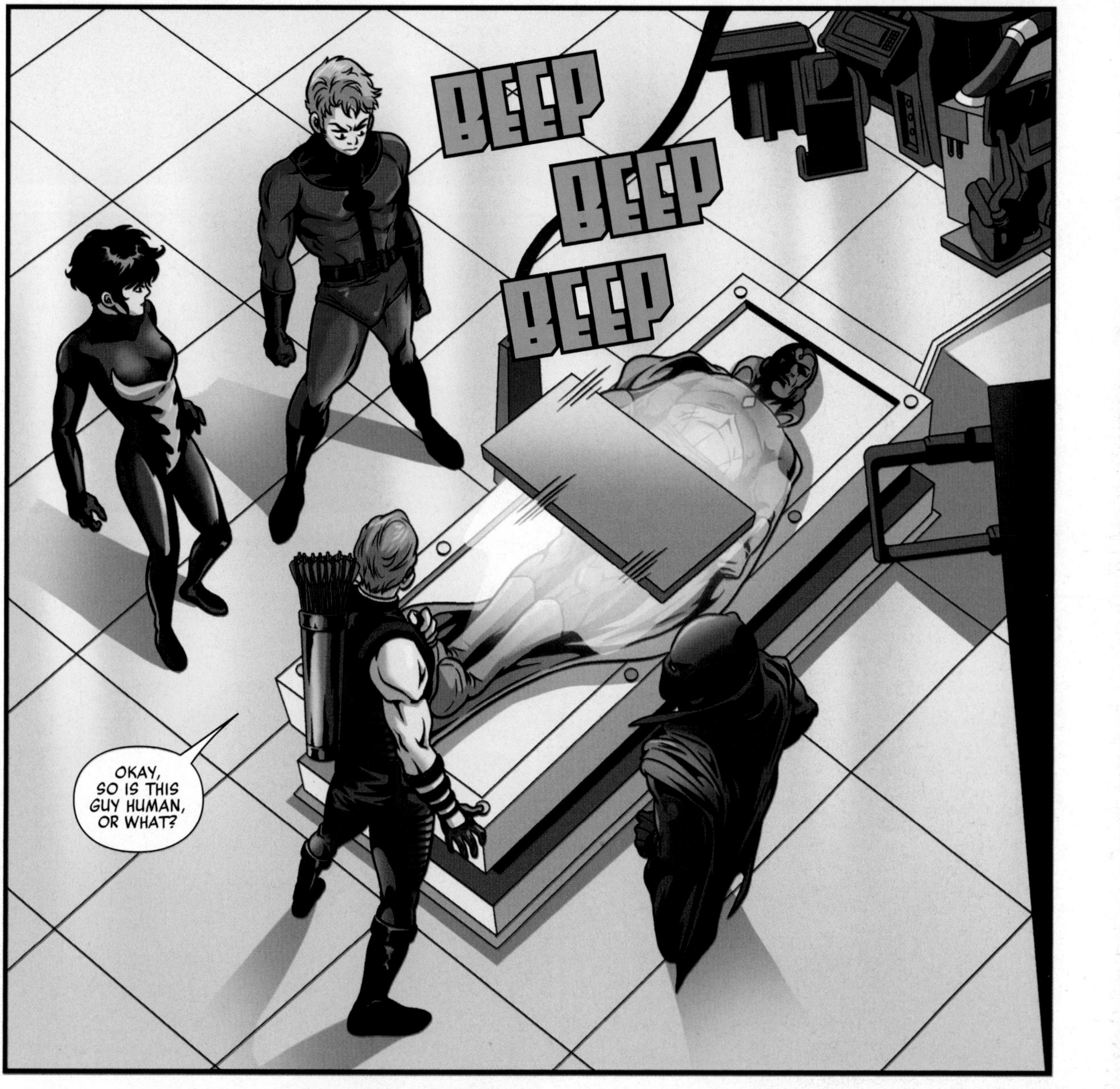
BEEP
BEEP
BEEP
OKAY, SO IS THIS GUY HUMAN, OR WHAT?

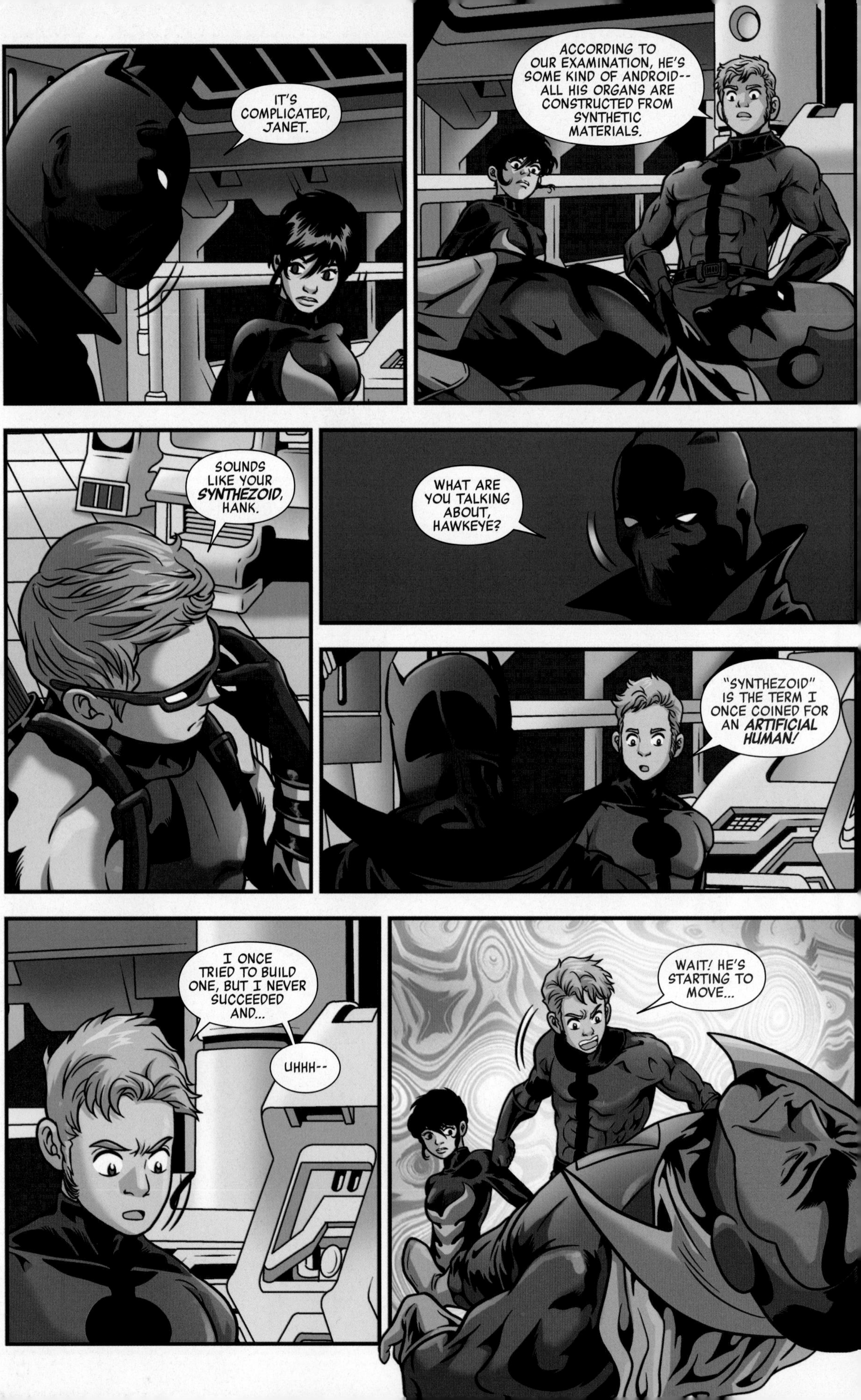
IT'S COMPLICATED, JANET.
ACCORDING TO OUR EXAMINATION, HE'S SOME KIND OF ANDROID-- ALL HIS ORGANS ARE CONSTRUCTED FROM SYNTHETIC MATERIALS.
SOUNDS LIKE YOUR SYNTHEZOID, HANK.
WHAT ARE YOU TALKING ABOUT, HAWKEYE?
"SYNTHEZOID" IS THE TERM I ONCE COINED FOR AN ARTIFICIAL HUMAN!
I ONCE TRIED TO BUILD ONE, BUT I NEVER SUCCEEDED AND...
UHHH--
WAIT! HE'S STARTING TO MOVE...

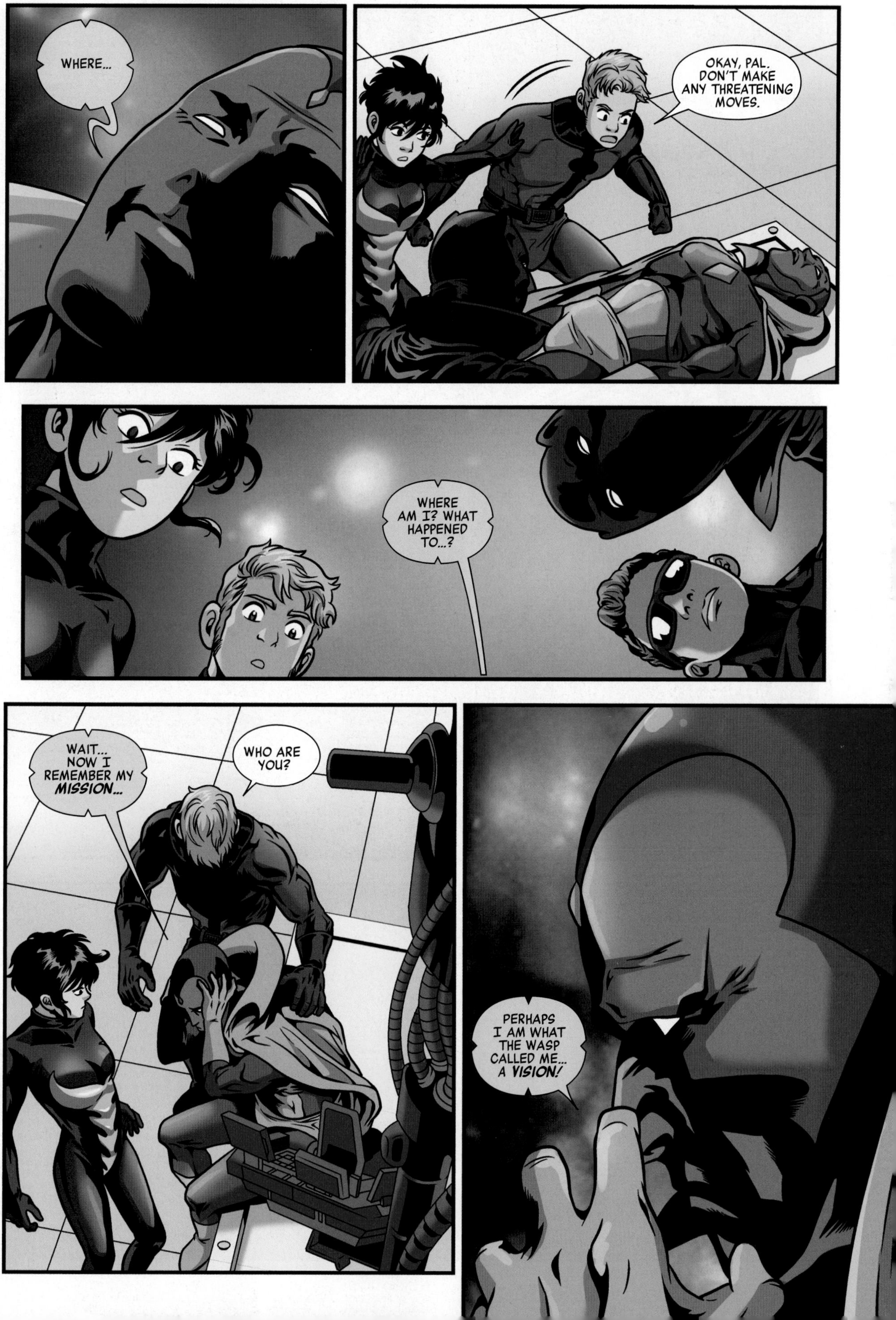
WHERE...
OKAY, PAL. DON'T MAKE ANY THREATENING MOVES.
WHERE AM I? WHAT HAPPENED TO...?
WAIT... NOW I REMEMBER MY MISSION...
WHO ARE YOU?
PERHAPS I AM WHAT THE WASP CALLED ME... A VISION!

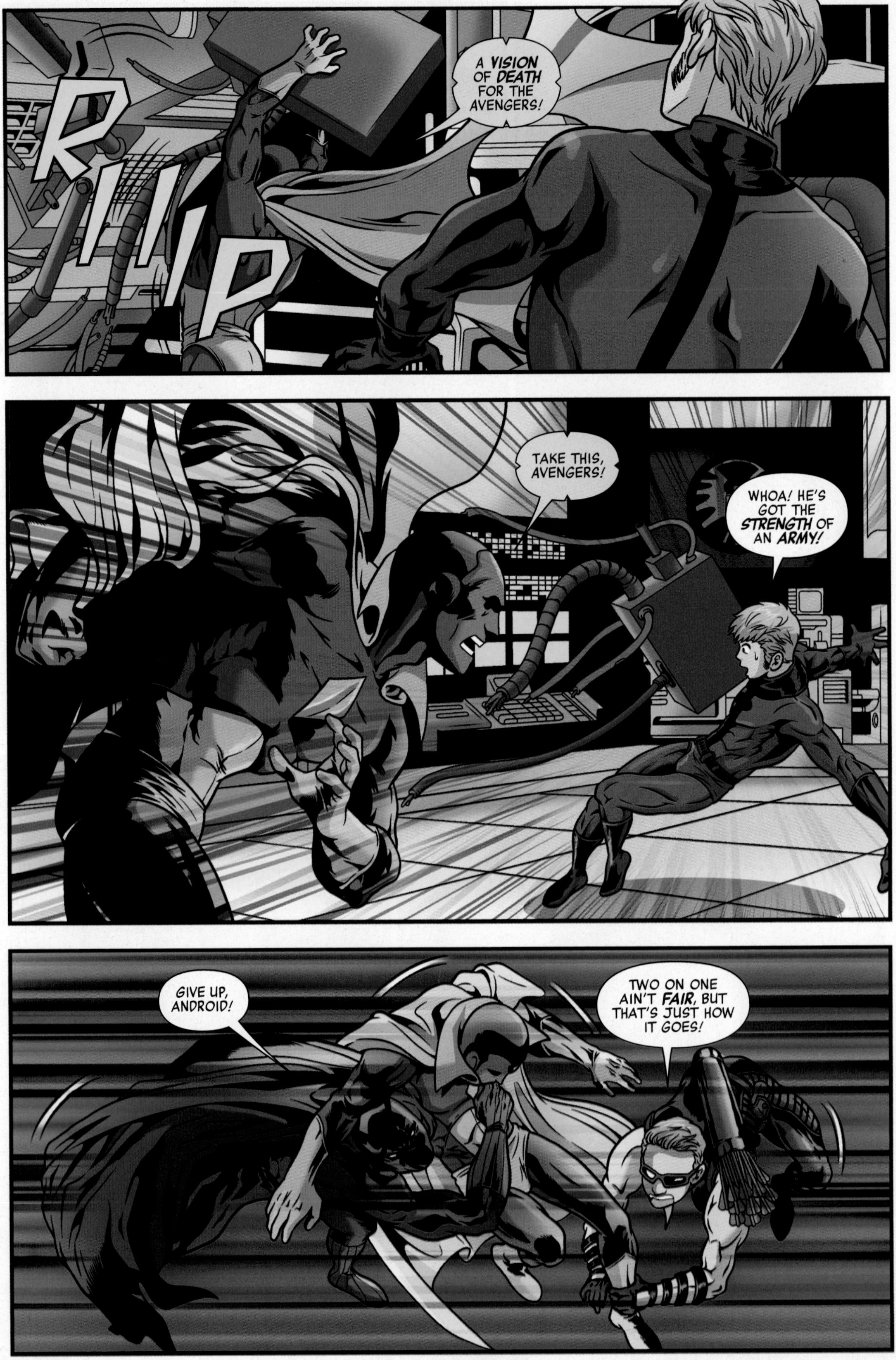
RIIIP
A VISION OF DEATH FOR THE AVENGERS!
TAKE THIS, AVENGERS!
WHOA! HE'S GOT THE STRENGTH OF AN ARMY!
GIVE UP, ANDROID!
TWO ON ONE AIN'T FAIR, BUT THAT'S JUST HOW IT GOES!

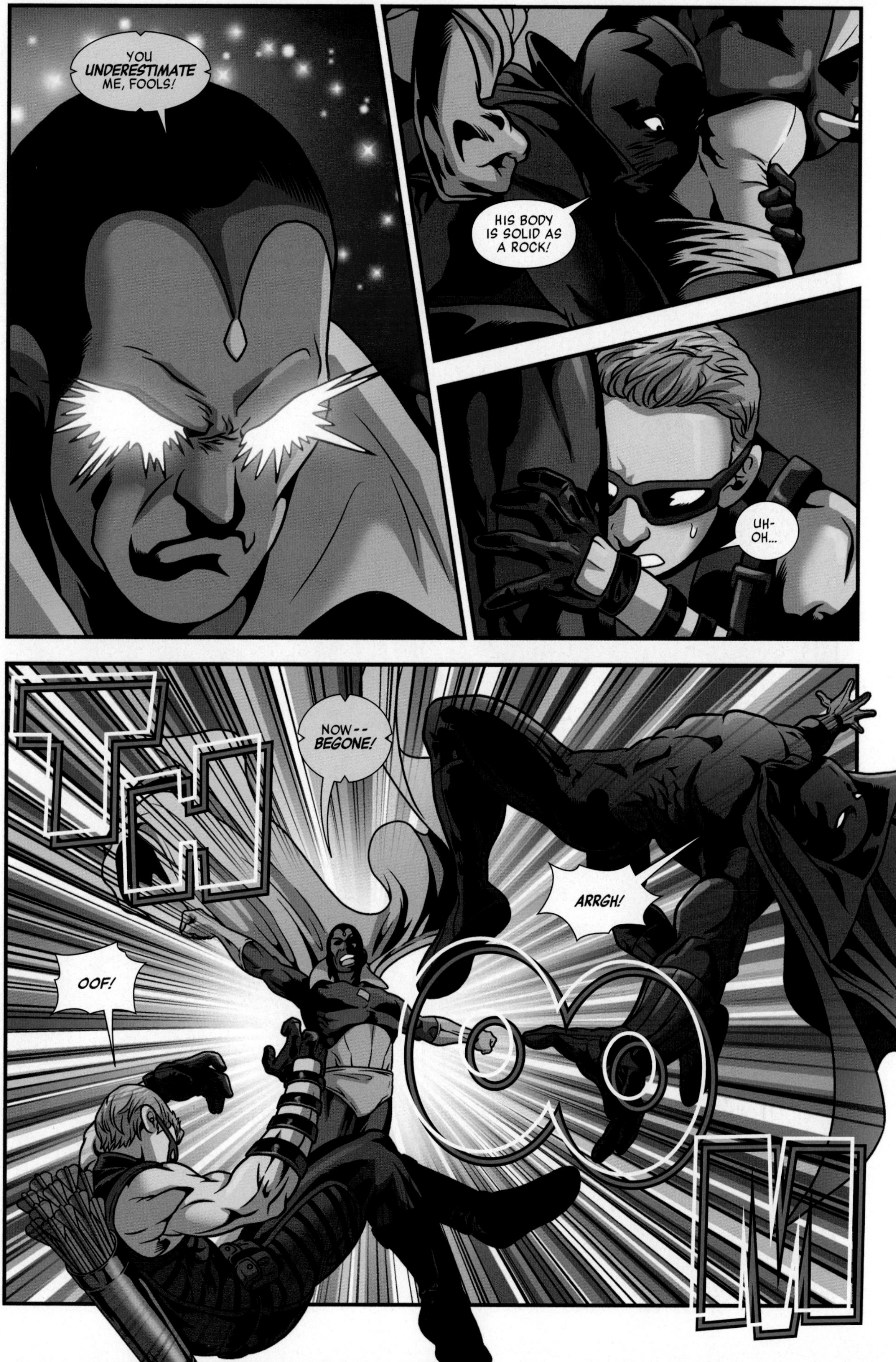
YOU UNDERESTIMATE ME, FOOLS!
HIS BODY IS SOLID AS A ROCK!
UH-OH...
NOW-- BEGONE!
THOOM
ARRGH!
OOF!

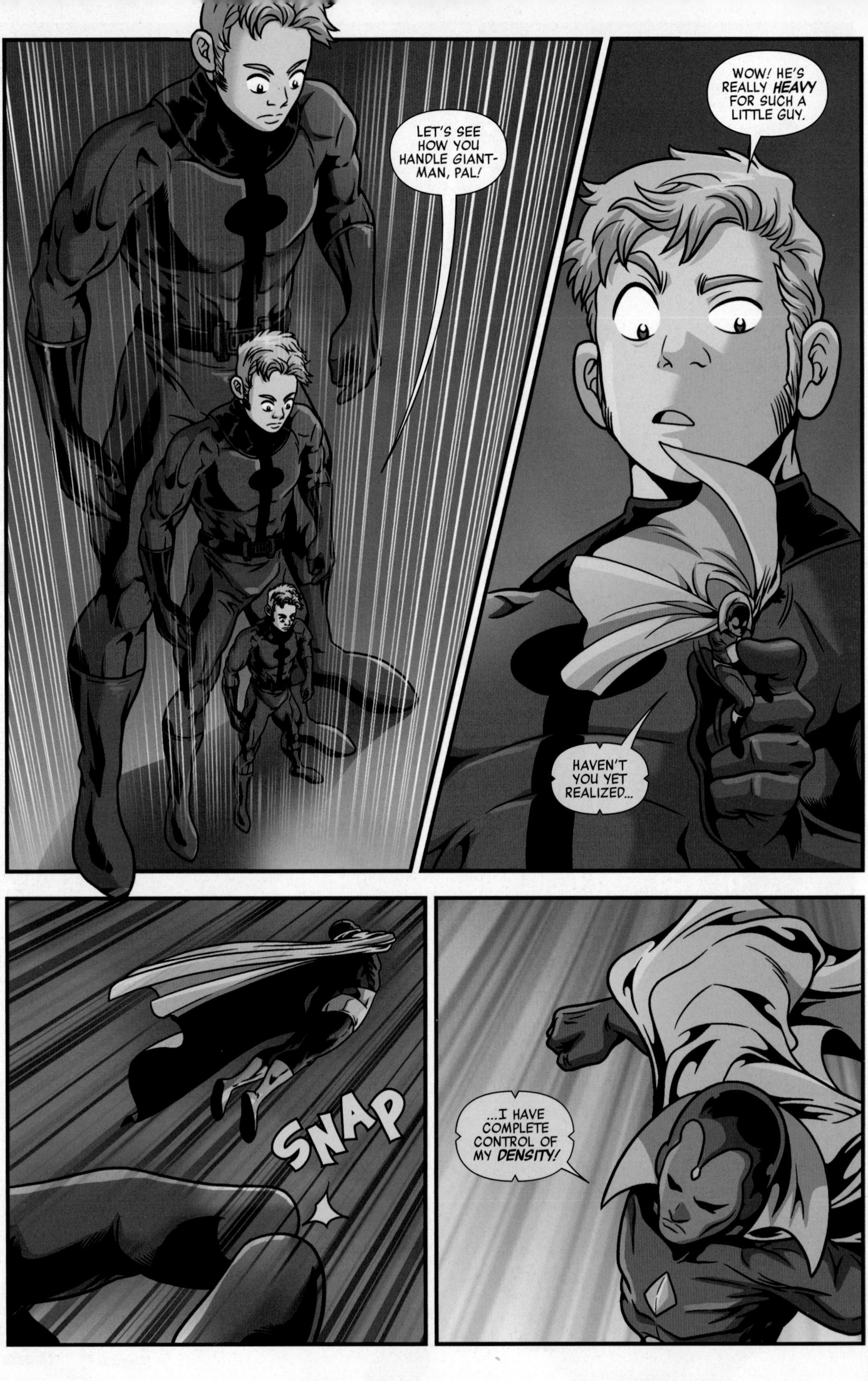
LET'S SEE HOW YOU HANDLE GIANT-MAN, PAL!
WOW! HE'S REALLY HEAVY FOR SUCH A LITTLE GUY.
HAVEN'T YOU YET REALIZED...
SNAP
...I HAVE COMPLETE CONTROL OF MY DENSITY!

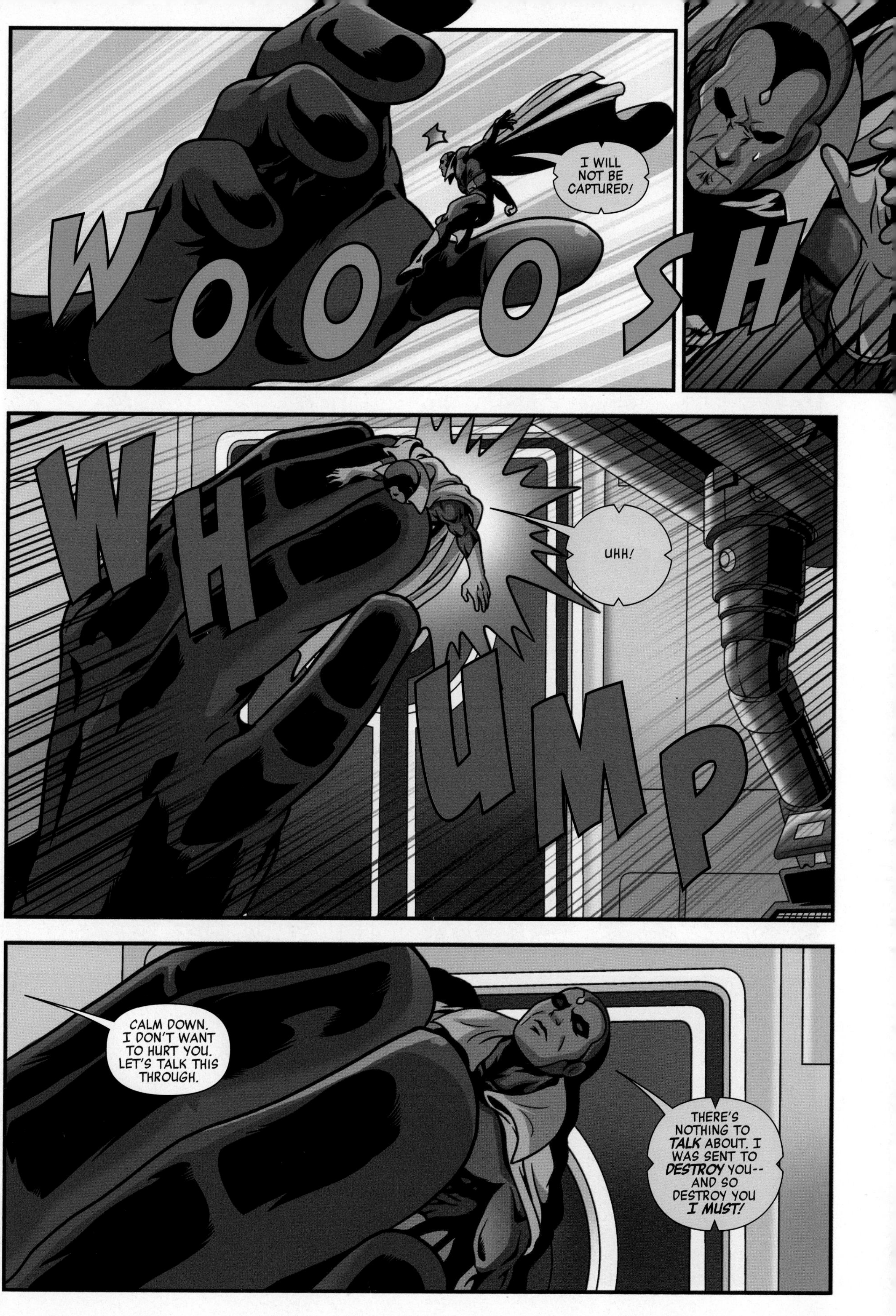
I WILL NOT BE CAPTURED!
WOOOSH
WHUMP
UHH!
CALM DOWN. I DON'T WANT TO HURT YOU. LET'S TALK THIS THROUGH.
THERE'S NOTHING TO **TALK** ABOUT. I WAS SENT TO **DESTROY** YOU-- AND SO DESTROY YOU **I MUST!**

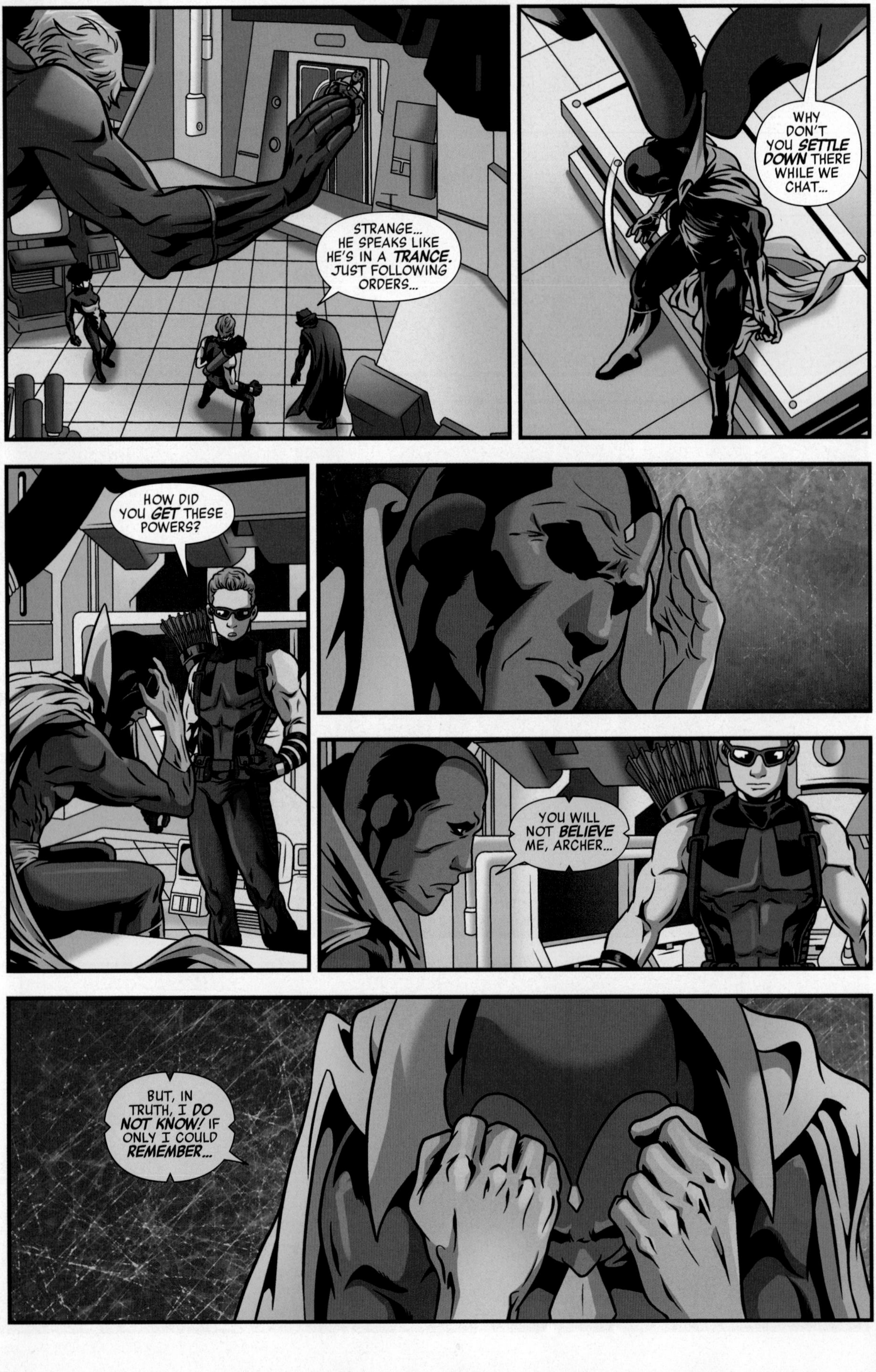
STRANGE... HE SPEAKS LIKE HE'S IN A TRANCE. JUST FOLLOWING ORDERS...
WHY DON'T YOU SETTLE DOWN THERE WHILE WE CHAT...
HOW DID YOU GET THESE POWERS?
YOU WILL NOT BELIEVE ME, ARCHER...
BUT, IN TRUTH, I DO NOT KNOW! IF ONLY I COULD REMEMBER...

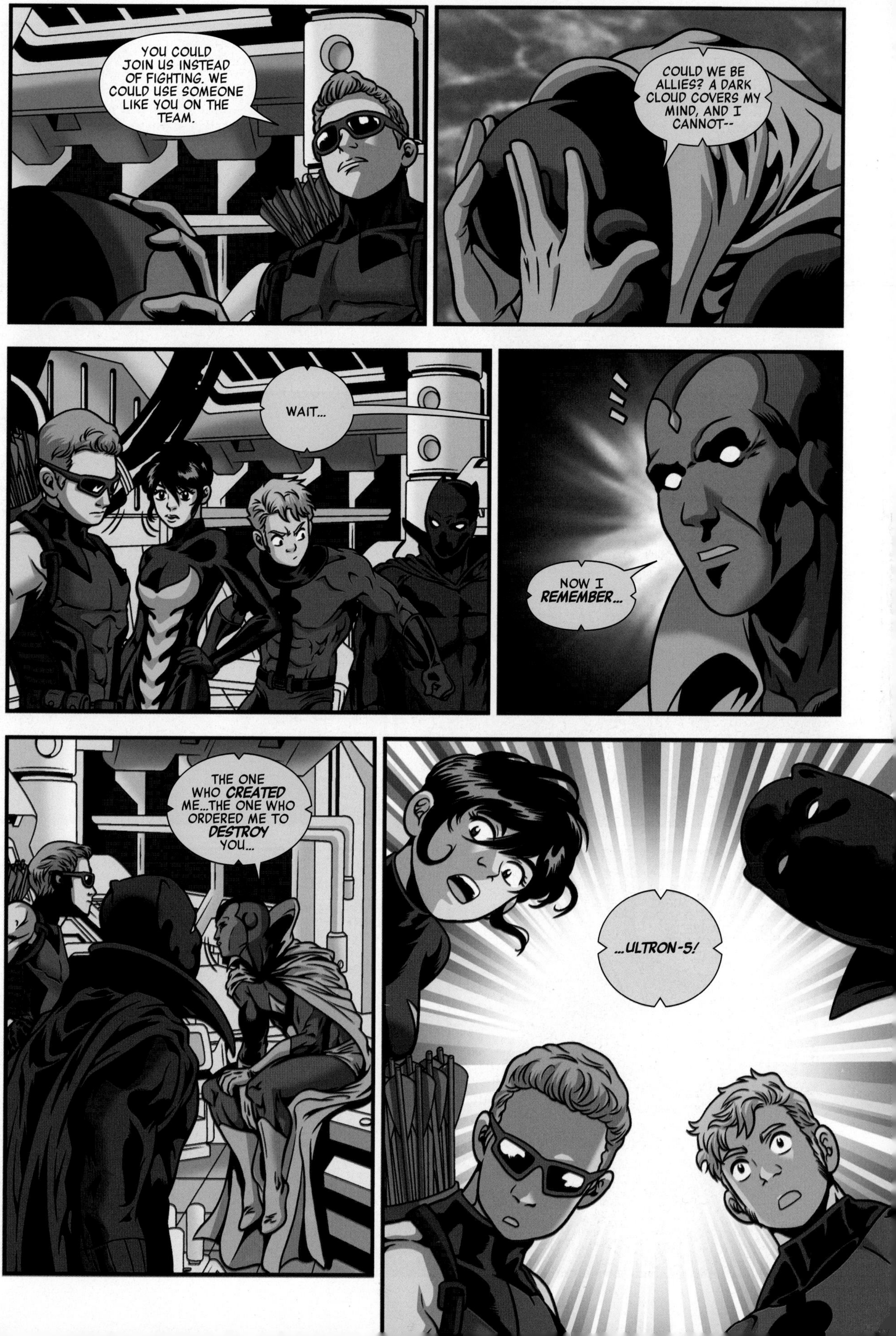
YOU COULD JOIN US INSTEAD OF FIGHTING. WE COULD USE SOMEONE LIKE YOU ON THE TEAM.
COULD WE BE ALLIES? A DARK CLOUD COVERS MY MIND, AND I CANNOT--
WAIT...
NOW I REMEMBER...
THE ONE WHO CREATED ME...THE ONE WHO ORDERED ME TO DESTROY YOU...
...ULTRON-5!

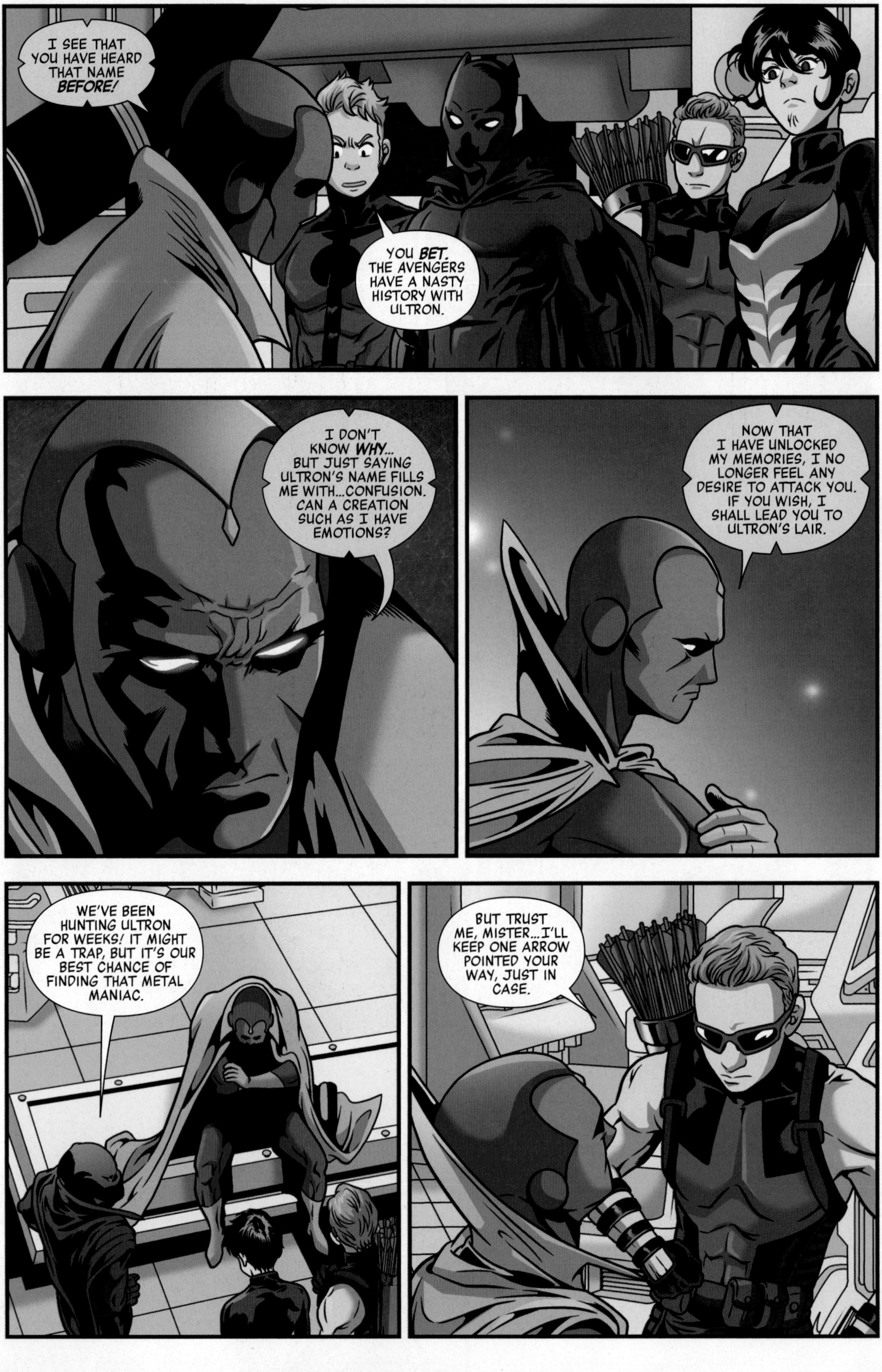
I SEE THAT YOU HAVE HEARD THAT NAME BEFORE!
YOU BET. THE AVENGERS HAVE A NASTY HISTORY WITH ULTRON.
I DON'T KNOW WHY... BUT JUST SAYING ULTRON'S NAME FILLS ME WITH...CONFUSION. CAN A CREATION SUCH AS I HAVE EMOTIONS?
NOW THAT I HAVE UNLOCKED MY MEMORIES, I NO LONGER FEEL ANY DESIRE TO ATTACK YOU. IF YOU WISH, I SHALL LEAD YOU TO ULTRON'S LAIR.
WE'VE BEEN HUNTING ULTRON FOR WEEKS! IT MIGHT BE A TRAP, BUT IT'S OUR BEST CHANCE OF FINDING THAT METAL MANIAC.
BUT TRUST ME, MISTER...I'LL KEEP ONE ARROW POINTED YOUR WAY, JUST IN CASE.

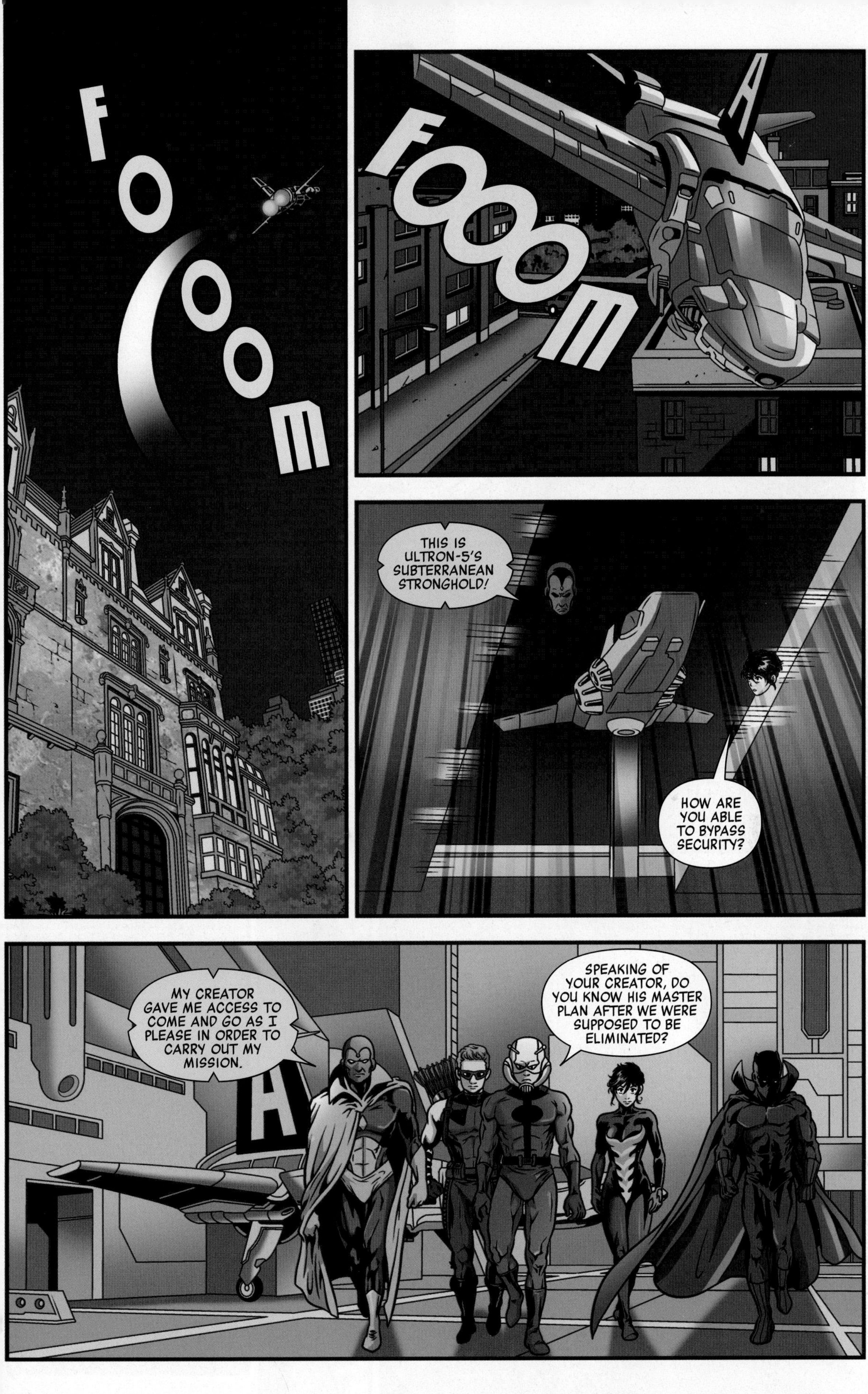
FOOOOM
FOOOOM
THIS IS ULTRON-5'S SUBTERRANEAN STRONGHOLD!
HOW ARE YOU ABLE TO BYPASS SECURITY?
MY CREATOR GAVE ME ACCESS TO COME AND GO AS I PLEASE IN ORDER TO CARRY OUT MY MISSION.
SPEAKING OF YOUR CREATOR, DO YOU KNOW HIS MASTER PLAN AFTER WE WERE SUPPOSED TO BE ELIMINATED?

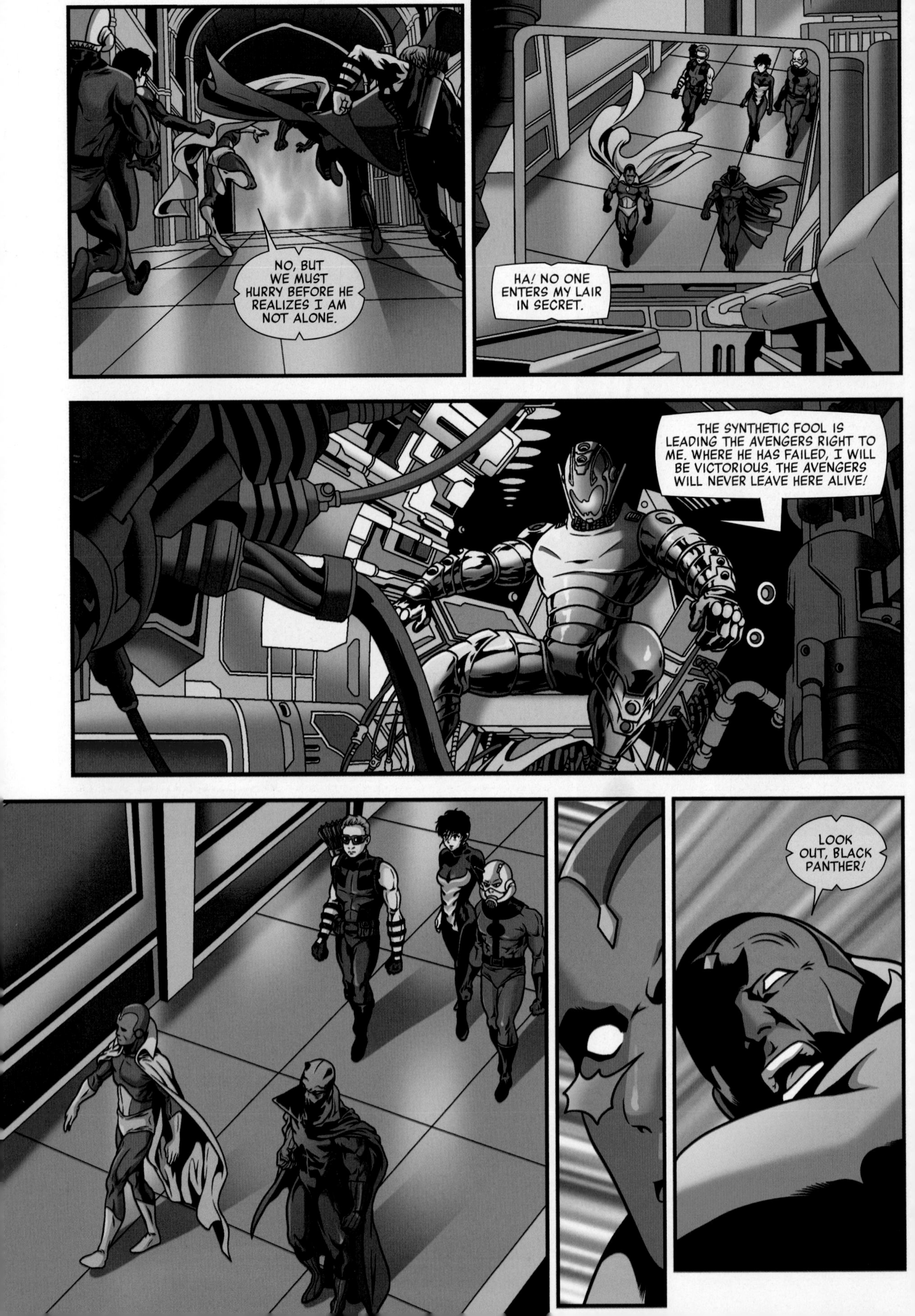
NO, BUT WE MUST HURRY BEFORE HE REALIZES I AM NOT ALONE.
HA! NO ONE ENTERS MY LAIR IN SECRET.
THE SYNTHETIC FOOL IS LEADING THE AVENGERS RIGHT TO ME. WHERE HE HAS FAILED, I WILL BE VICTORIOUS. THE AVENGERS WILL NEVER LEAVE HERE ALIVE!
LOOK OUT, BLACK PANTHER!

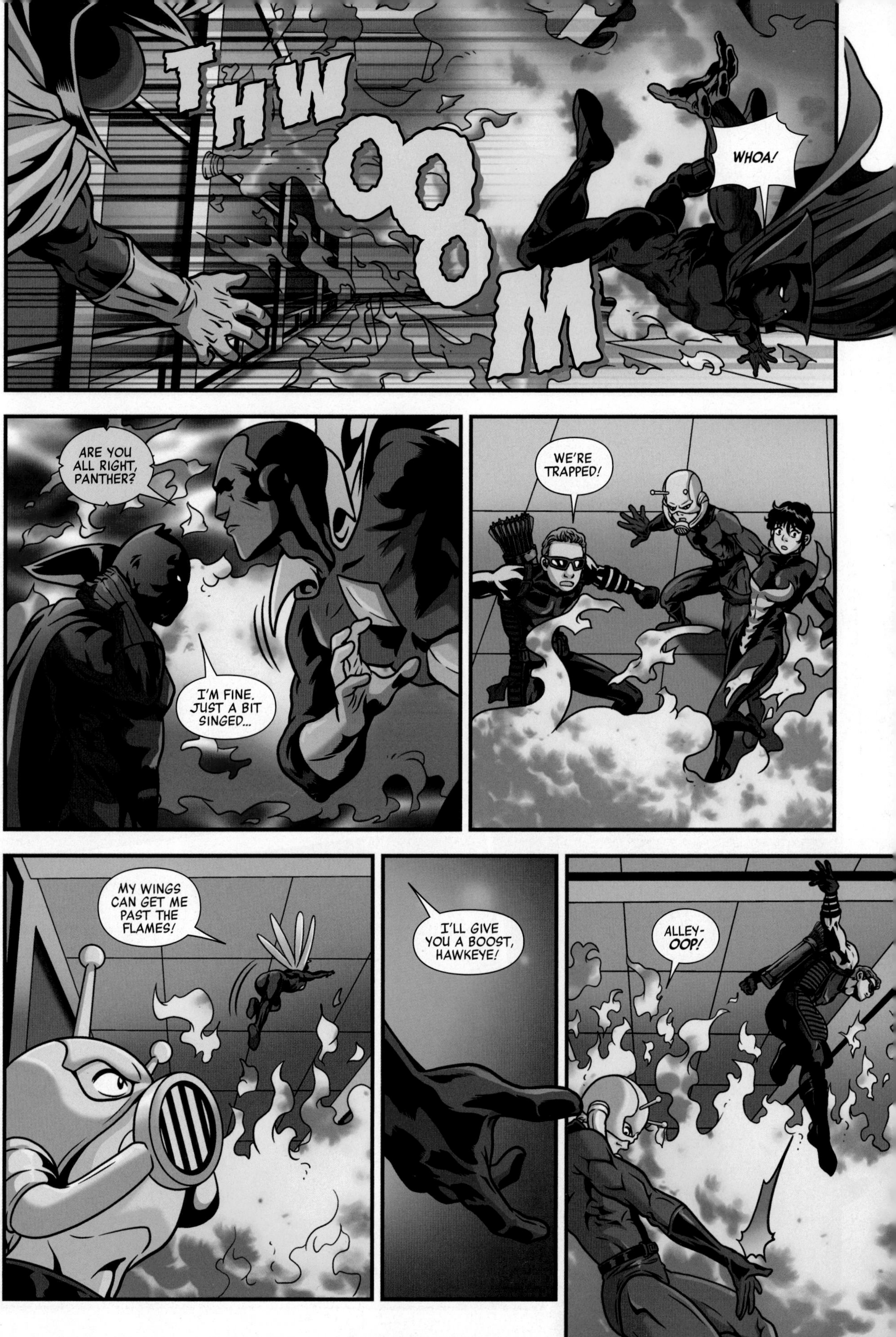
THWOOOM
WHOA!
ARE YOU ALL RIGHT, PANTHER?
I'M FINE. JUST A BIT SINGED...
WE'RE TRAPPED!
MY WINGS CAN GET ME PAST THE FLAMES!
I'LL GIVE YOU A BOOST, HAWKEYE!
ALLEY-OOP!

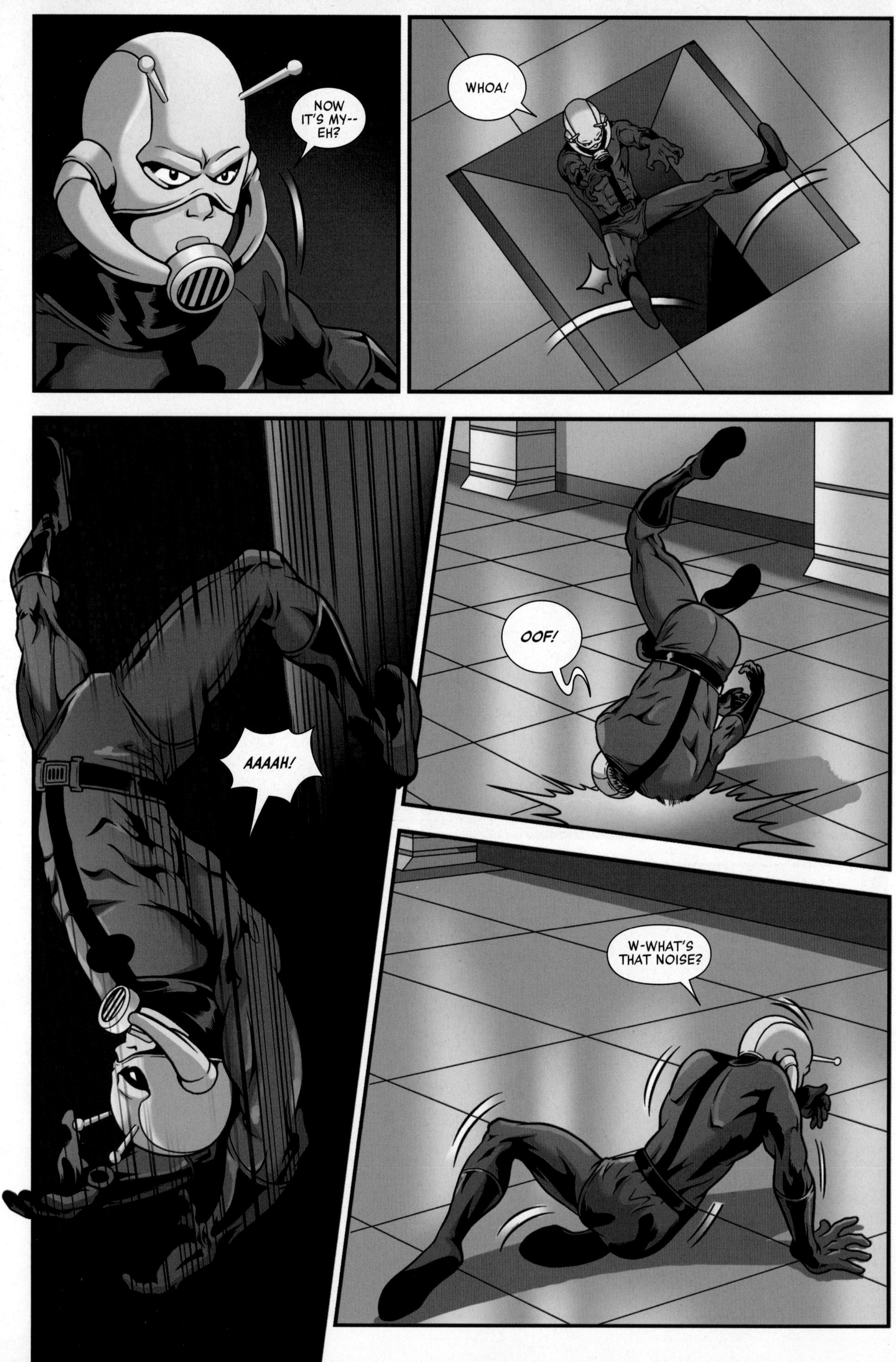
NOW IT'S MY-- EH?
WHOA!
AAAAH!
OOF!
W-WHAT'S THAT NOISE?

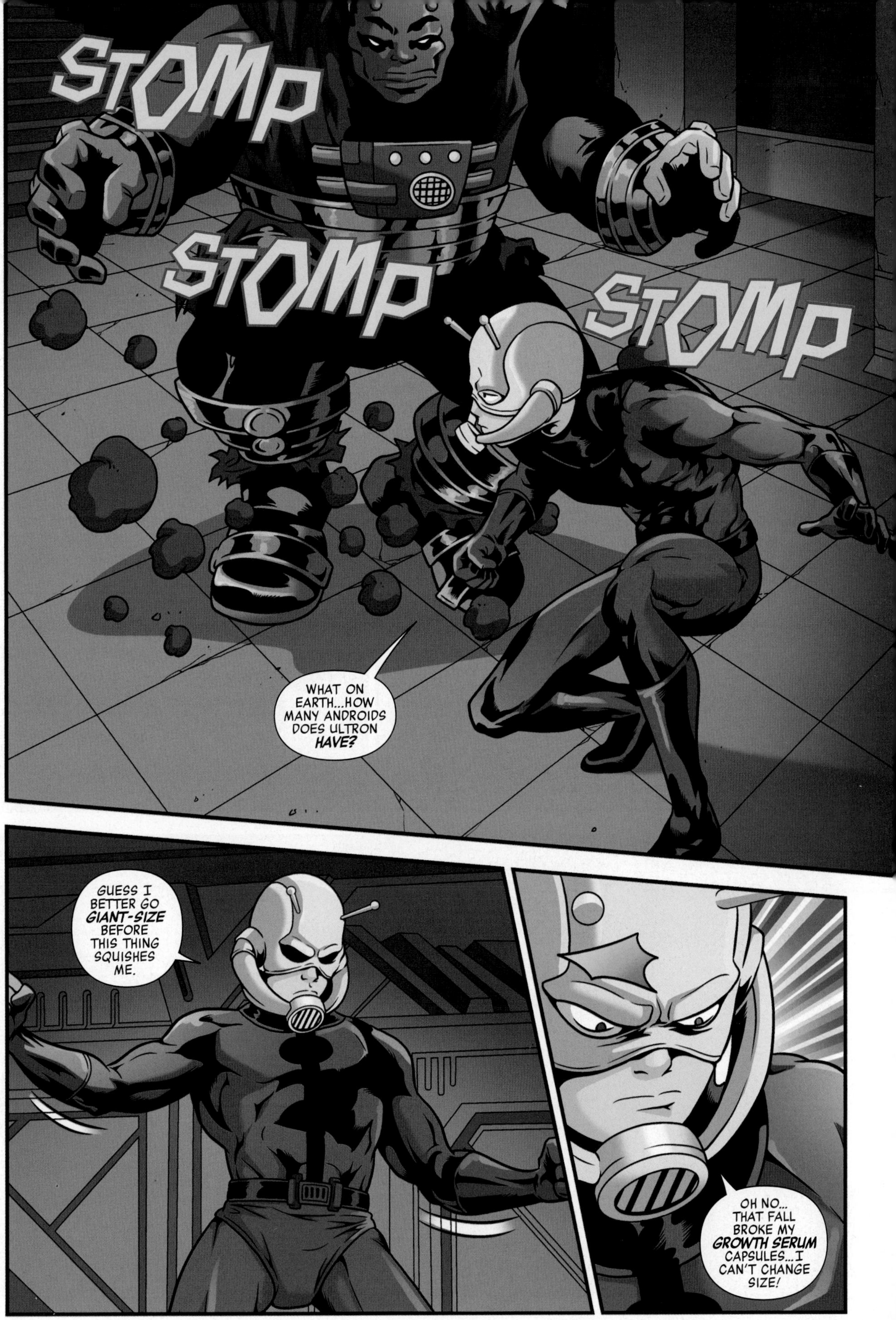
STOMP
STOMP
STOMP
WHAT ON EARTH...HOW MANY ANDROIDS DOES ULTRON HAVE?
GUESS I BETTER GO GIANT-SIZE BEFORE THIS THING SQUISHES ME.
OH NO... THAT FALL BROKE MY GROWTH SERUM CAPSULES... I CAN'T CHANGE SIZE!

ROAR!

WHAM

EVEN AT REGULAR SIZE, I'M NO SLOUCH, PAL!

CRACK

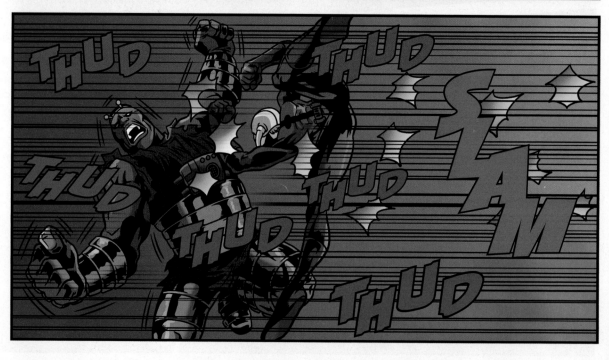

THUD THUD THUD THUD THUD THUD SLAM

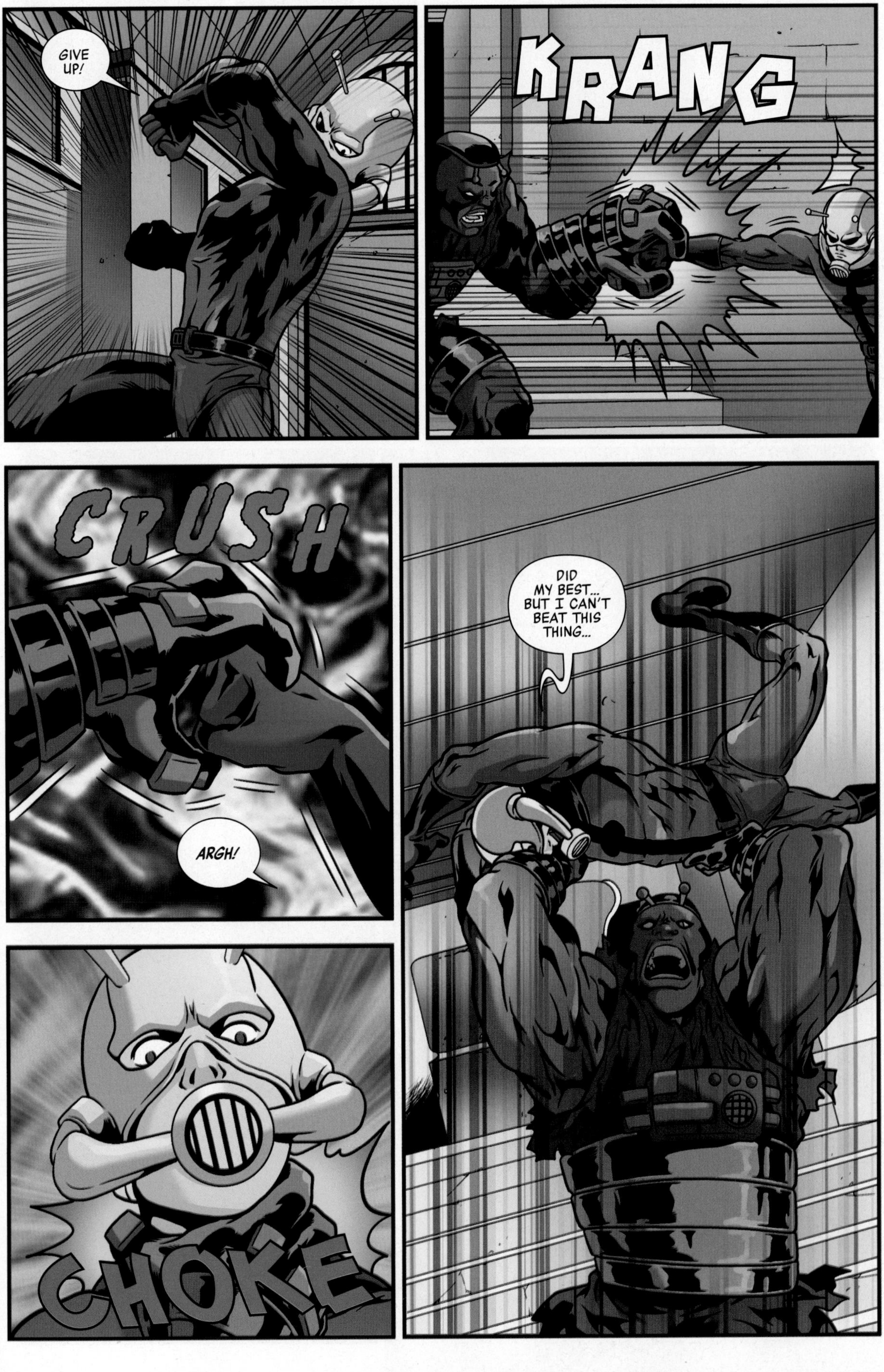
GIVE UP!
KRANG
CRUSH
ARGH!
CHOKE
DID MY BEST... BUT I CAN'T BEAT THIS THING...

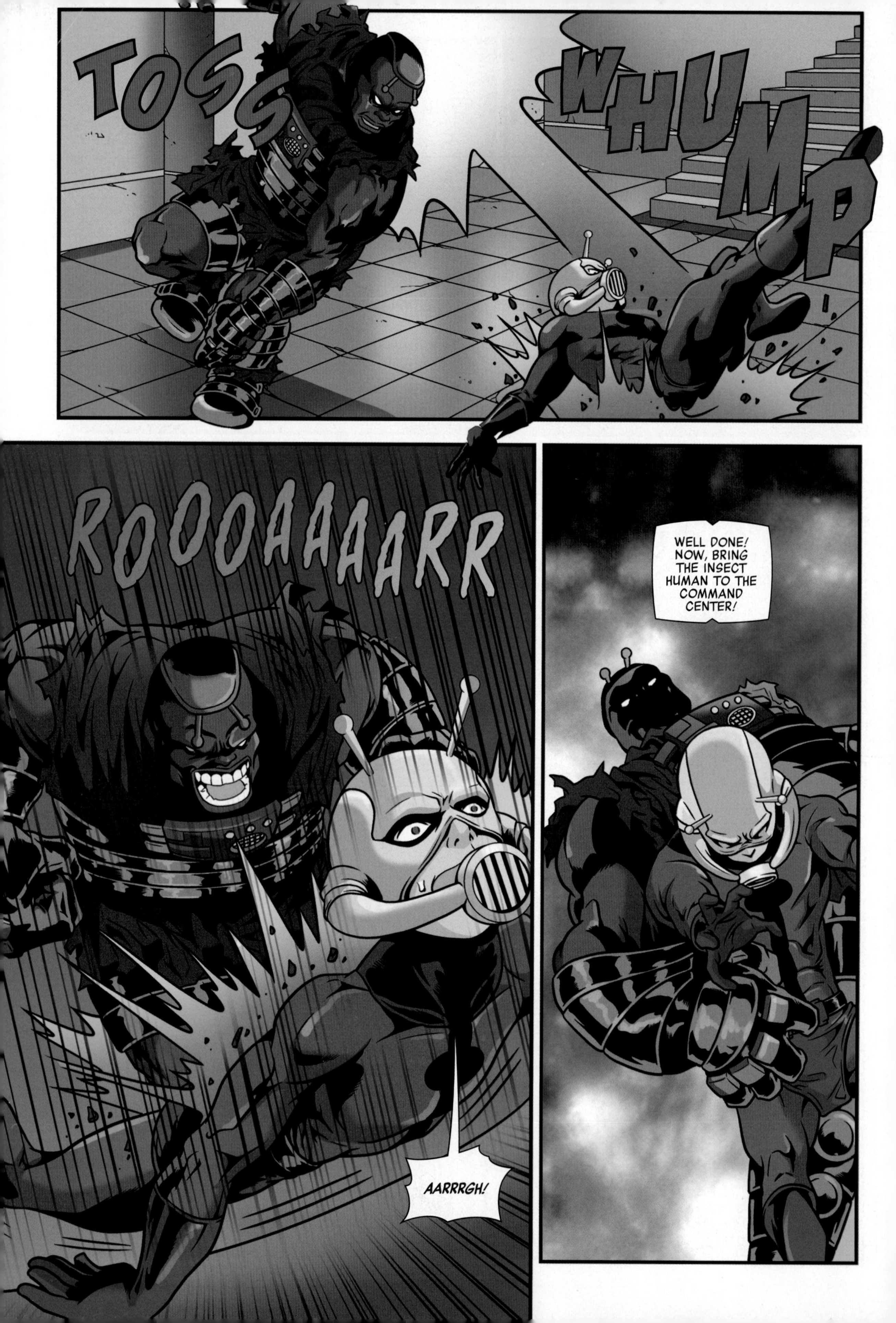
TOSS
WHUMP
ROOOAAAAARR
AARRRGH!
WELL DONE! NOW, BRING THE INSECT HUMAN TO THE COMMAND CENTER!

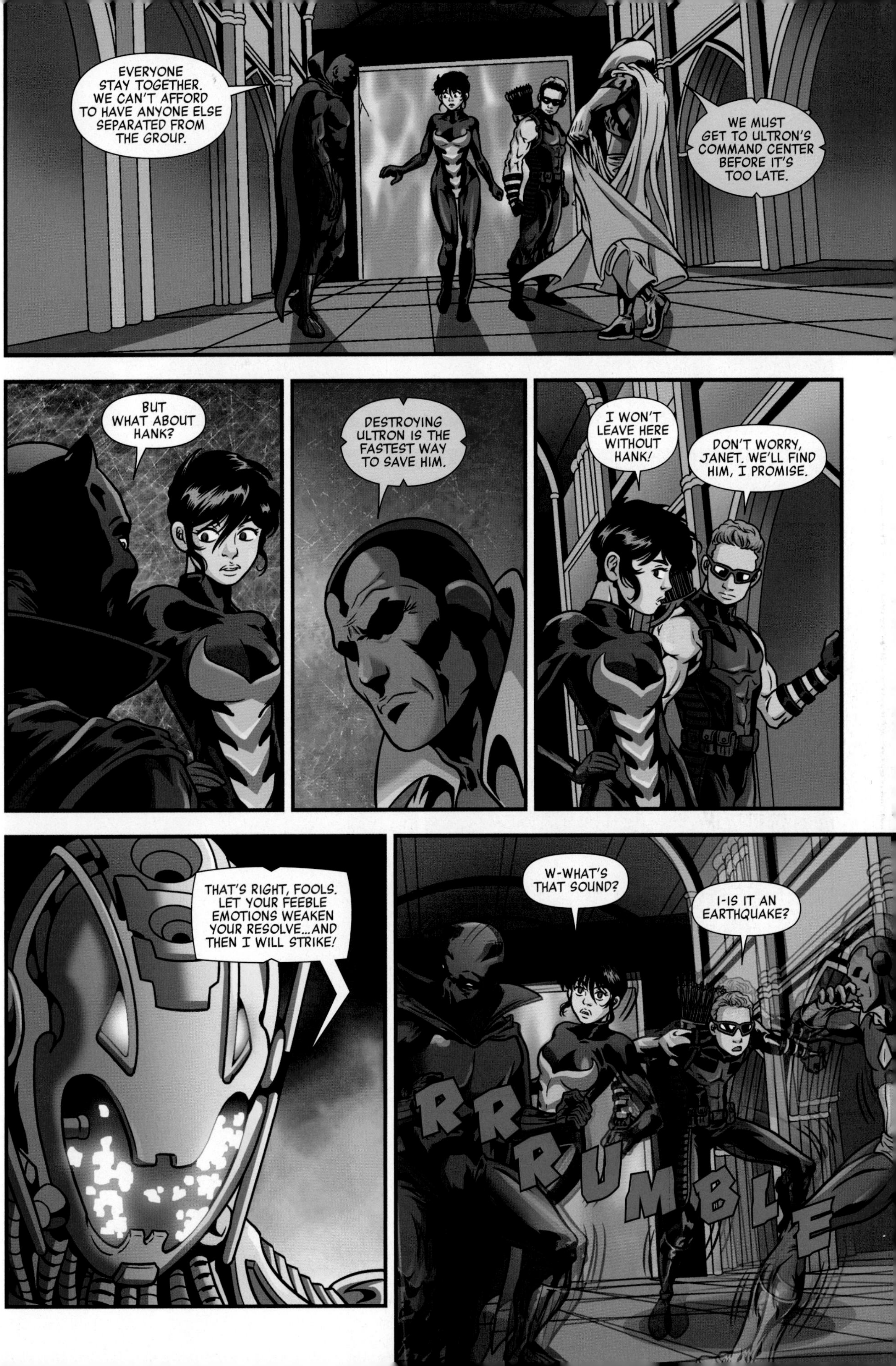
EVERYONE STAY TOGETHER. WE CAN'T AFFORD TO HAVE ANYONE ELSE SEPARATED FROM THE GROUP.
WE MUST GET TO ULTRON'S COMMAND CENTER BEFORE IT'S TOO LATE.
BUT WHAT ABOUT HANK?
DESTROYING ULTRON IS THE FASTEST WAY TO SAVE HIM.
I WON'T LEAVE HERE WITHOUT HANK!
DON'T WORRY, JANET. WE'LL FIND HIM, I PROMISE.
THAT'S RIGHT, FOOLS. LET YOUR FEEBLE EMOTIONS WEAKEN YOUR RESOLVE...AND THEN I WILL STRIKE!
W-WHAT'S THAT SOUND?
I-IS IT AN EARTHQUAKE?
RRRUMBLE

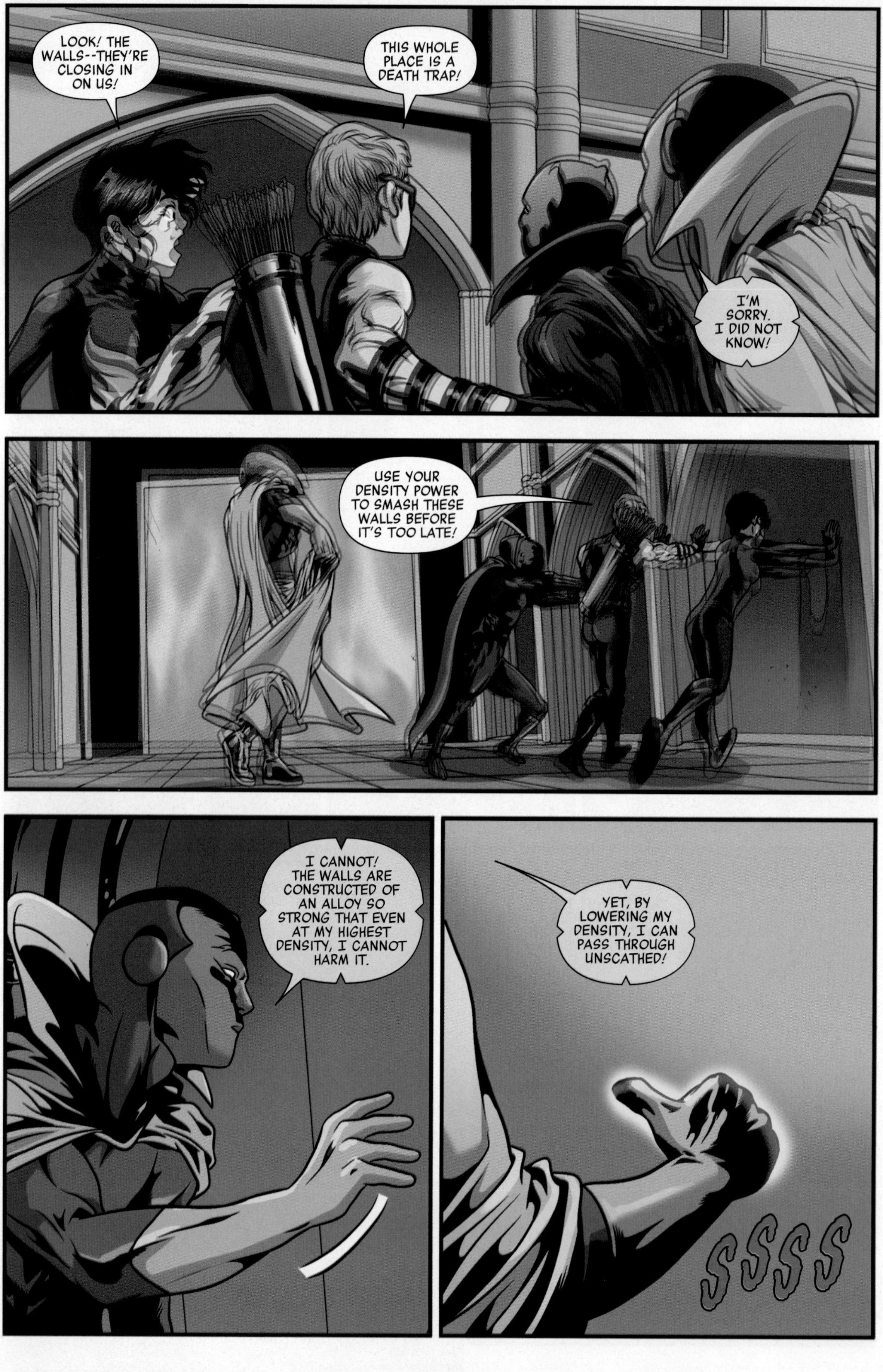
LOOK! THE WALLS--THEY'RE CLOSING IN ON US!
THIS WHOLE PLACE IS A DEATH TRAP!
I'M SORRY. I DID NOT KNOW!
USE YOUR DENSITY POWER TO SMASH THESE WALLS BEFORE IT'S TOO LATE!
I CANNOT! THE WALLS ARE CONSTRUCTED OF AN ALLOY SO STRONG THAT EVEN AT MY HIGHEST DENSITY, I CANNOT HARM IT.
YET, BY LOWERING MY DENSITY, I CAN PASS THROUGH UNSCATHED!
SSSS

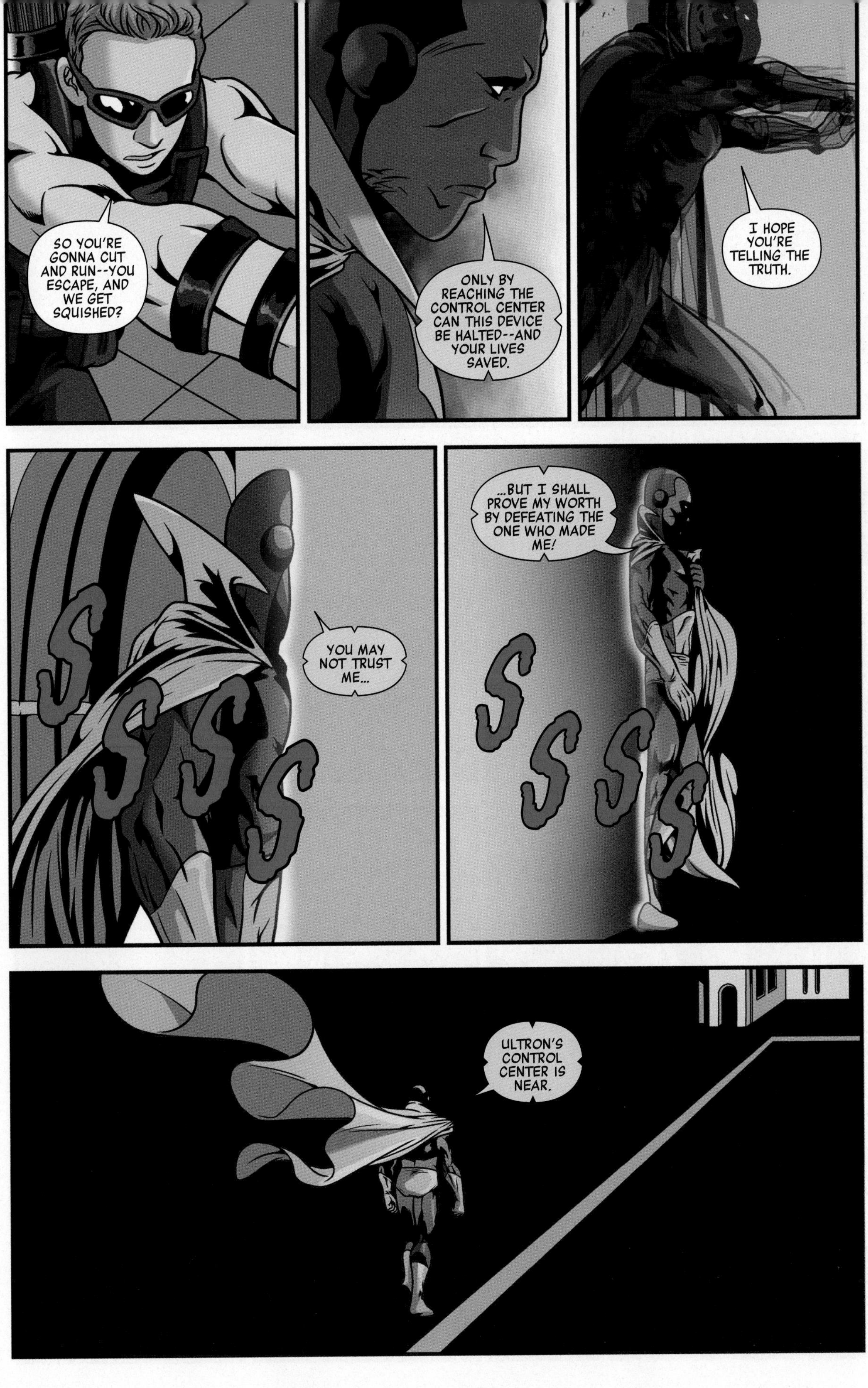
SO YOU'RE GONNA CUT AND RUN--YOU ESCAPE, AND WE GET SQUISHED?
ONLY BY REACHING THE CONTROL CENTER CAN THIS DEVICE BE HALTED--AND YOUR LIVES SAVED.
I HOPE YOU'RE TELLING THE TRUTH.
SSSS
YOU MAY NOT TRUST ME...
...BUT I SHALL PROVE MY WORTH BY DEFEATING THE ONE WHO MADE ME!
SSSS
ULTRON'S CONTROL CENTER IS NEAR.

MY CREATION...
YOU'VE RETURNED
TO YOUR SENSES,
AT LAST.

YOU WERE WISE
TO DESERT THOSE
DOOMED MORTALS!

I...

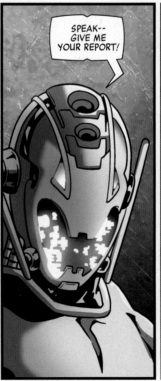

SPEAK--
GIVE ME
YOUR REPORT!

YOU
CREATED
ME--YOU
GAVE ME
LIFE...

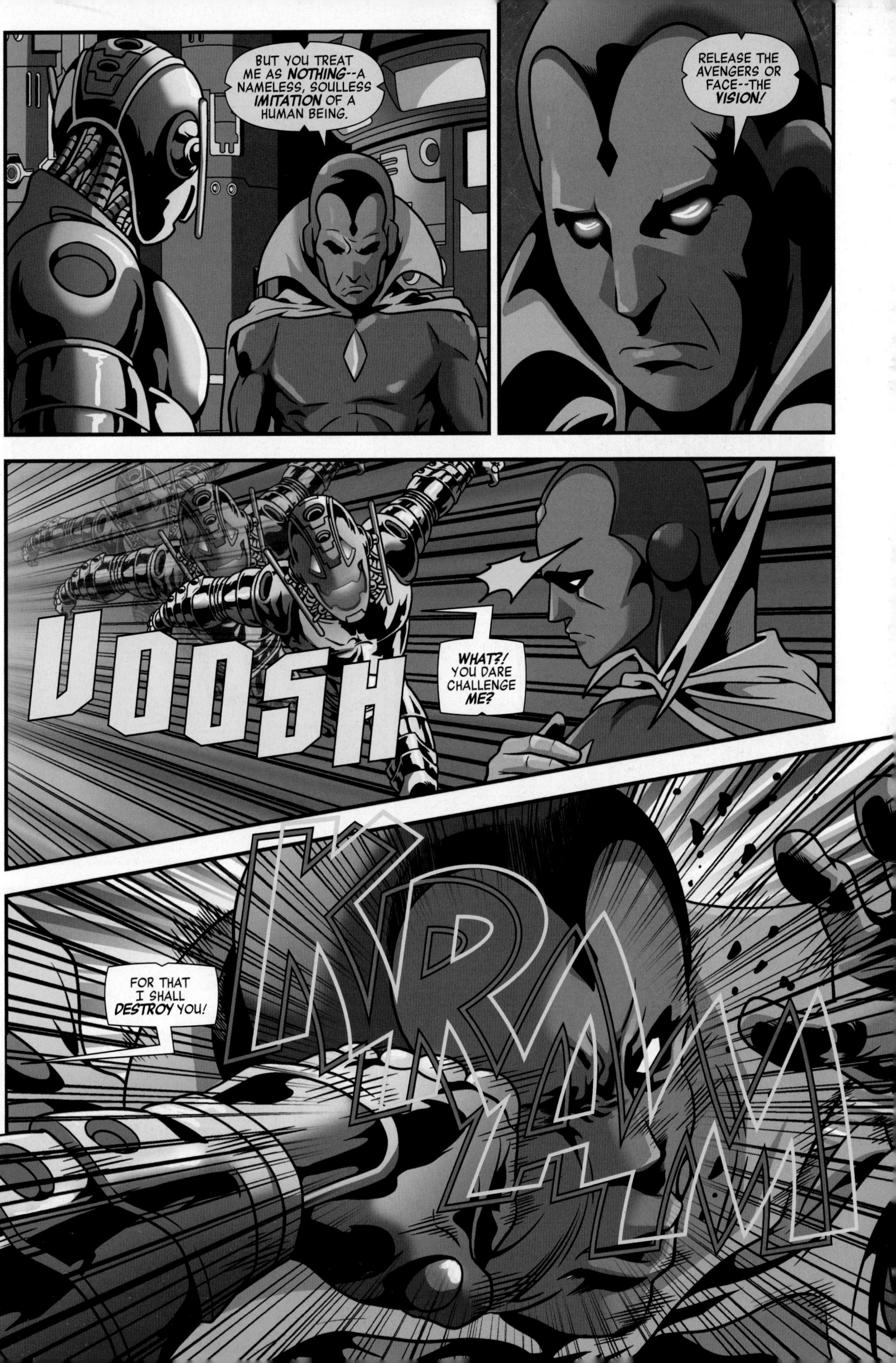

BUT YOU TREAT ME AS NOTHING--A NAMELESS, SOULLESS IMITATION OF A HUMAN BEING.
RELEASE THE AVENGERS OR FACE--THE VISION!
VOOSH
WHAT?! YOU DARE CHALLENGE ME?
KRAM
FOR THAT I SHALL DESTROY YOU!

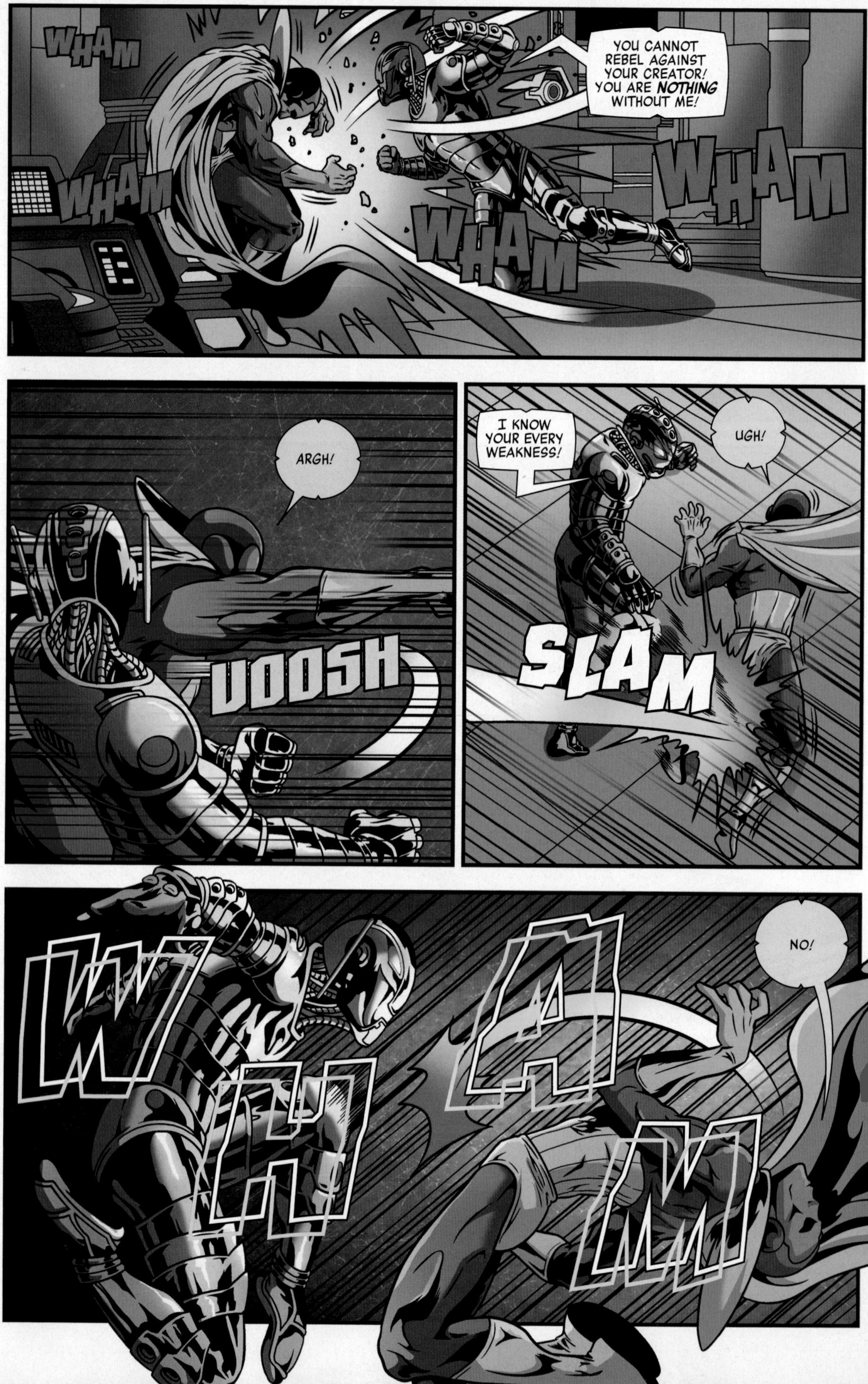
WHAM
YOU CANNOT REBEL AGAINST YOUR CREATOR! YOU ARE NOTHING WITHOUT ME!
WHAM
WHAM
WHAM
ARGH!
VOOSH
I KNOW YOUR EVERY WEAKNESS!
UGH!
SLAM
NO!
WHAM

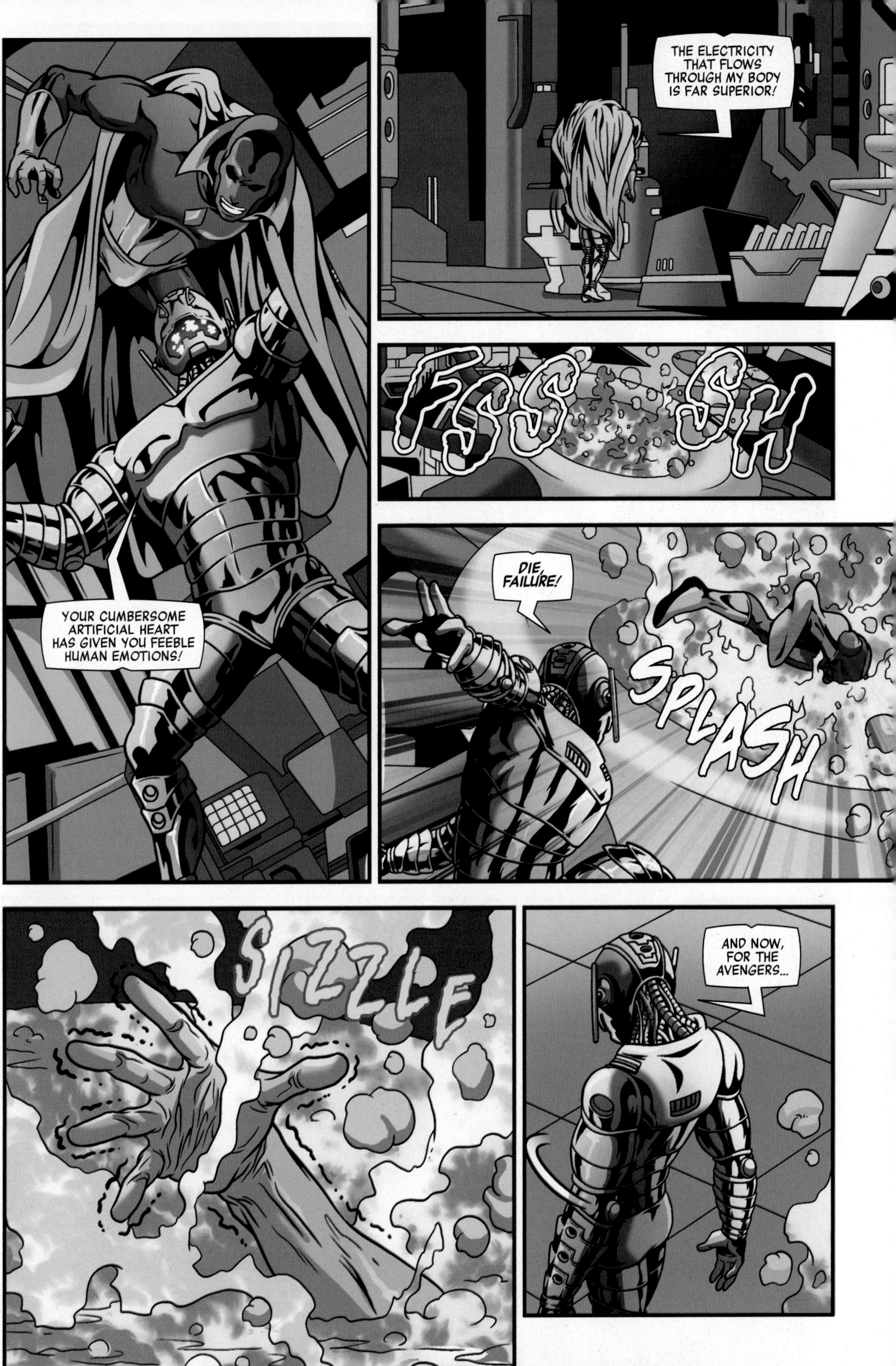
THE ELECTRICITY THAT FLOWS THROUGH MY BODY IS FAR SUPERIOR!
YOUR CUMBERSOME ARTIFICIAL HEART HAS GIVEN YOU FEEBLE HUMAN EMOTIONS!
FSSSH
DIE, FAILURE!
SPLASH
SIZZLE
AND NOW, FOR THE AVENGERS...

EH?
IT CANNOT BE!
YOU LIVE! BUT HOW...?!

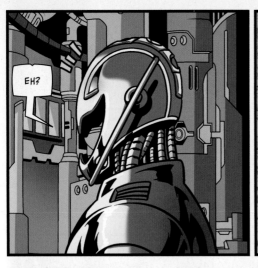

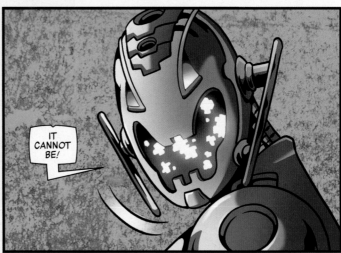

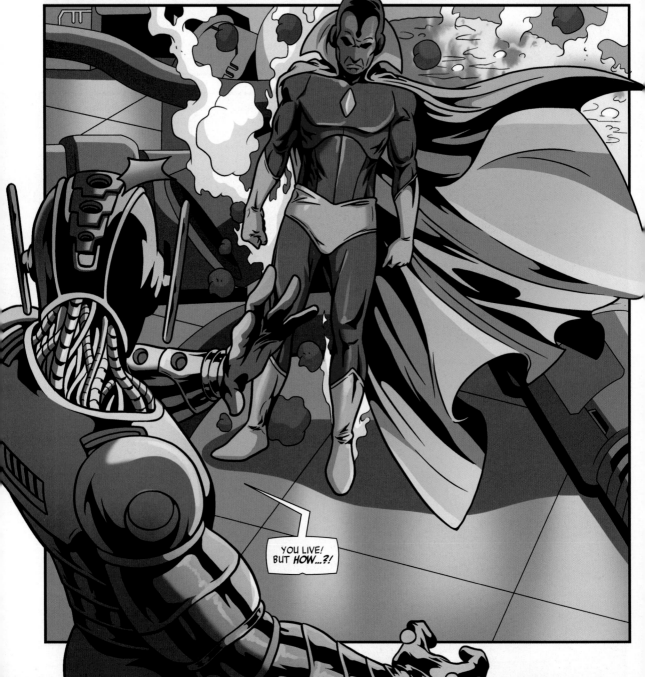

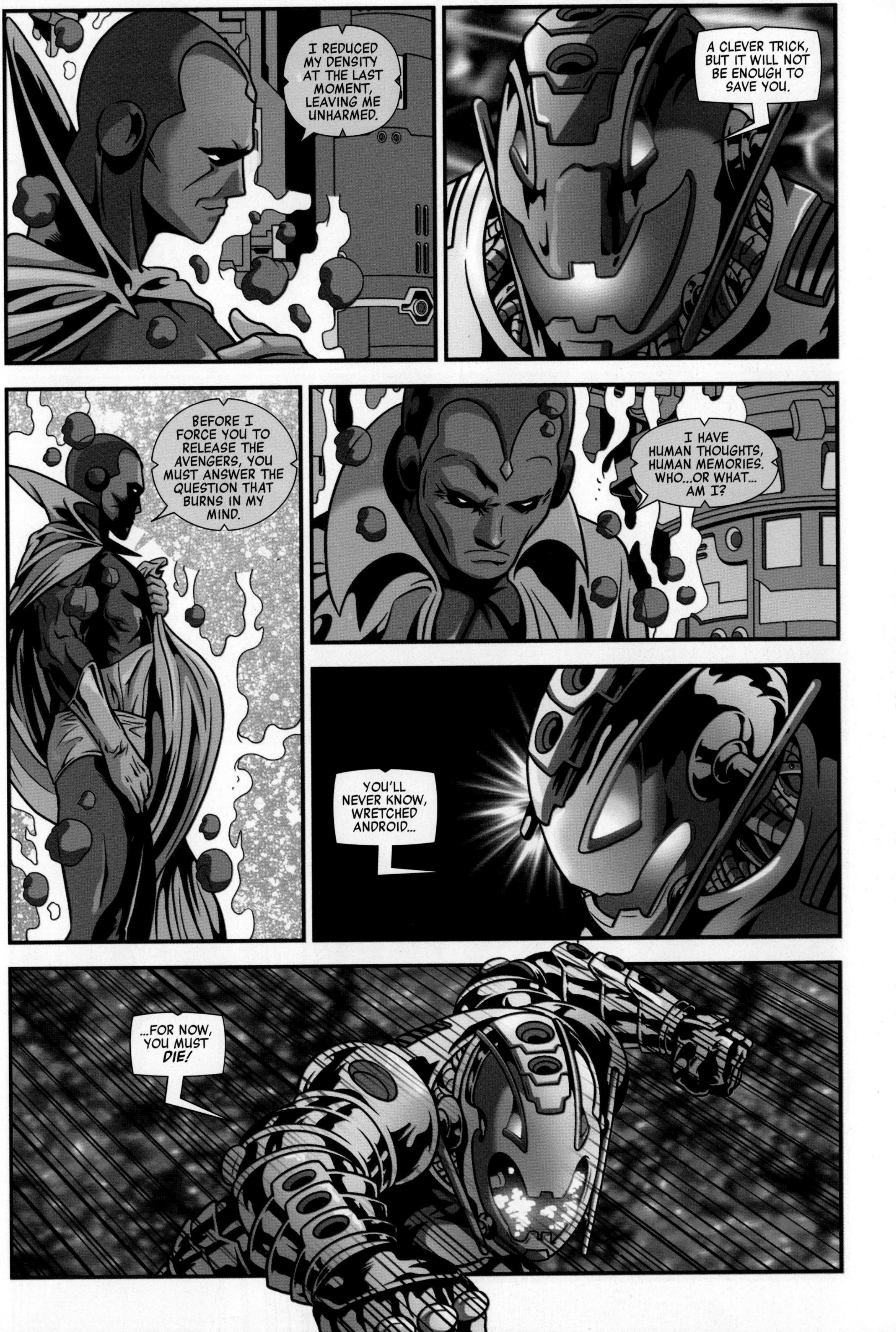
I REDUCED MY DENSITY AT THE LAST MOMENT, LEAVING ME UNHARMED.
A CLEVER TRICK, BUT IT WILL NOT BE ENOUGH TO SAVE YOU.
BEFORE I FORCE YOU TO RELEASE THE AVENGERS, YOU MUST ANSWER THE QUESTION THAT BURNS IN MY MIND.
I HAVE HUMAN THOUGHTS, HUMAN MEMORIES. WHO...OR WHAT... AM I?
YOU'LL NEVER KNOW, WRETCHED ANDROID...
...FOR NOW, YOU MUST DIE!

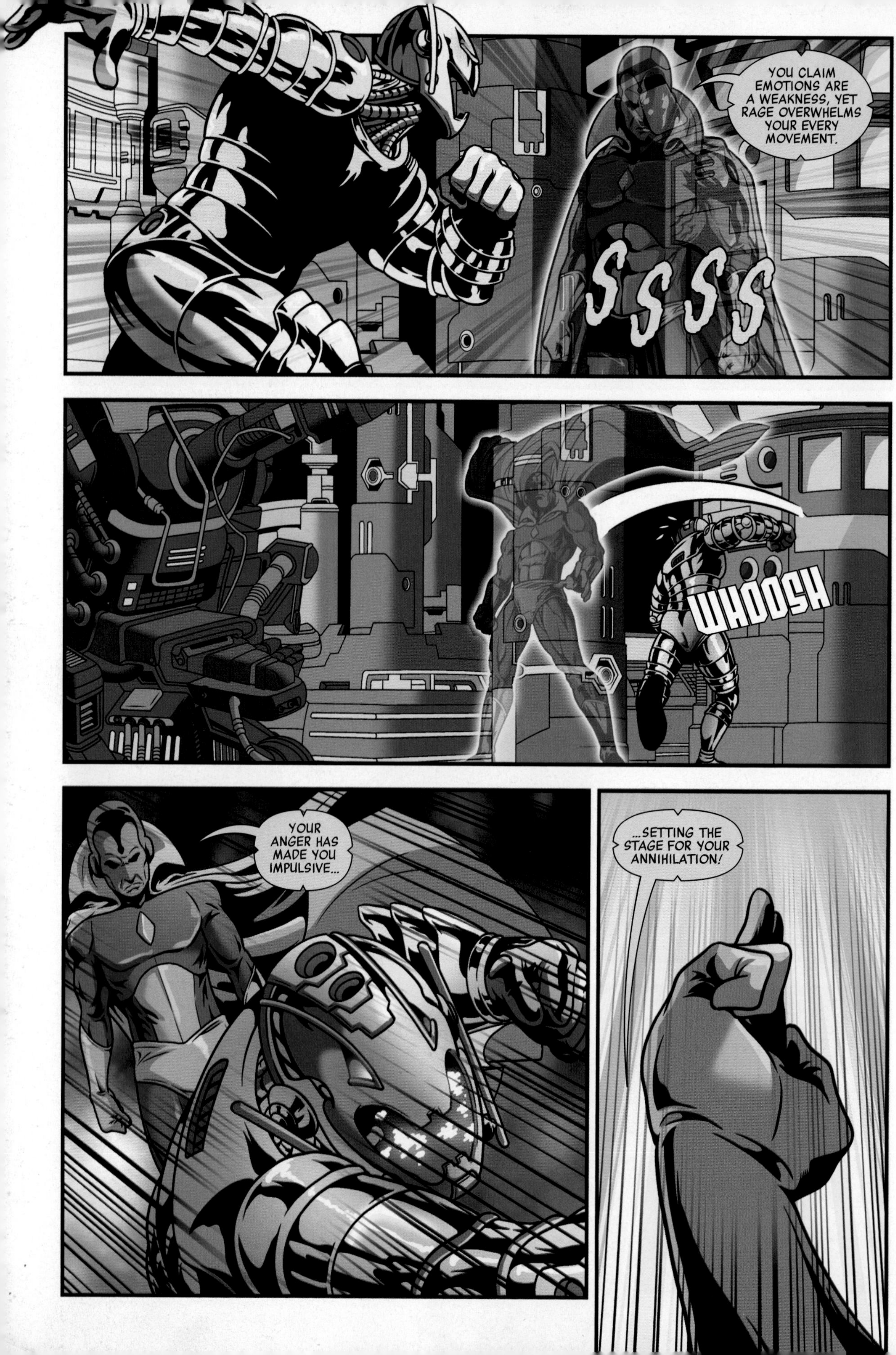
YOU CLAIM EMOTIONS ARE A WEAKNESS, YET RAGE OVERWHELMS YOUR EVERY MOVEMENT.
SSSS
WHOOSH
YOUR ANGER HAS MADE YOU IMPULSIVE...
...SETTING THE STAGE FOR YOUR ANNIHILATION!

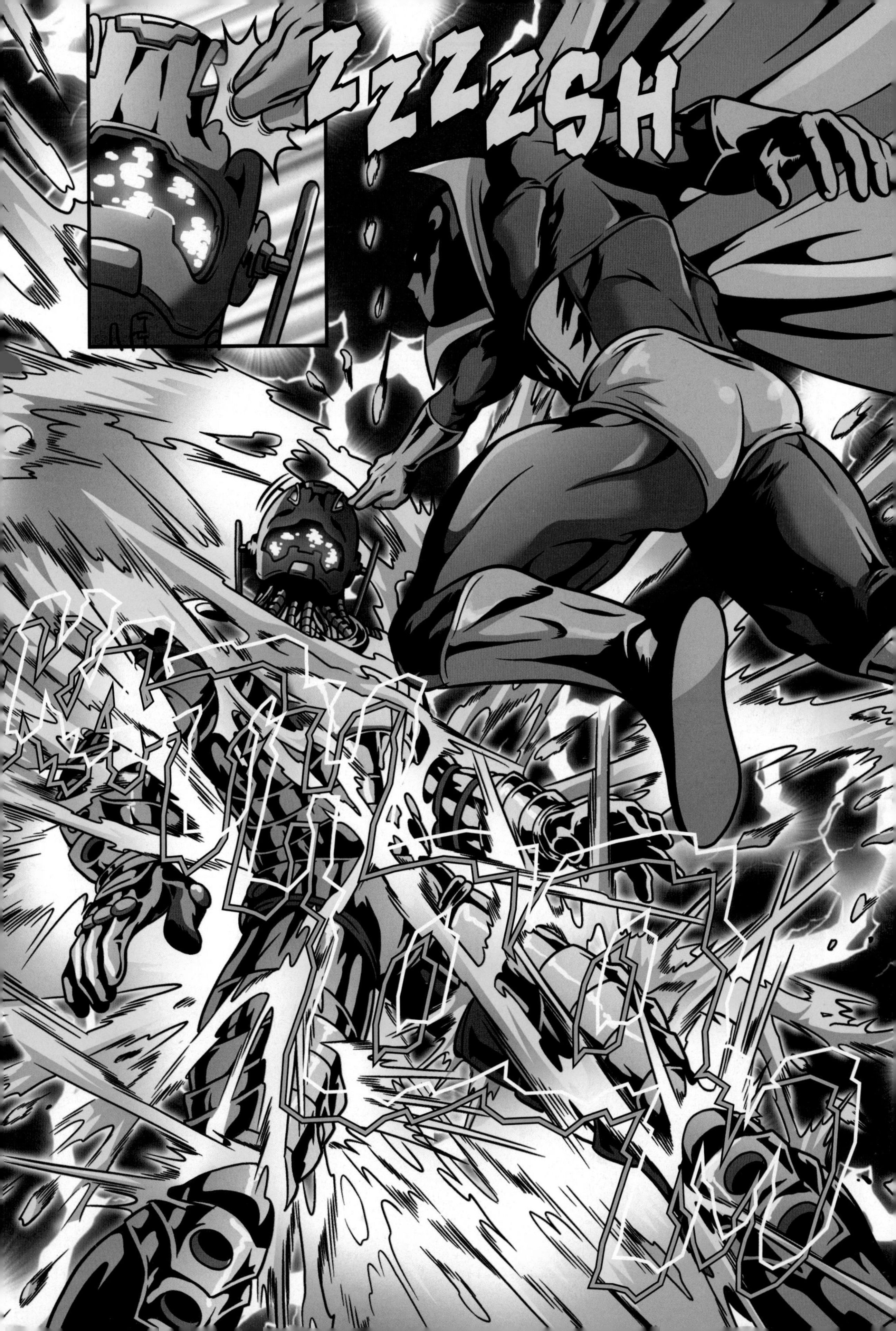
ZZZZSH

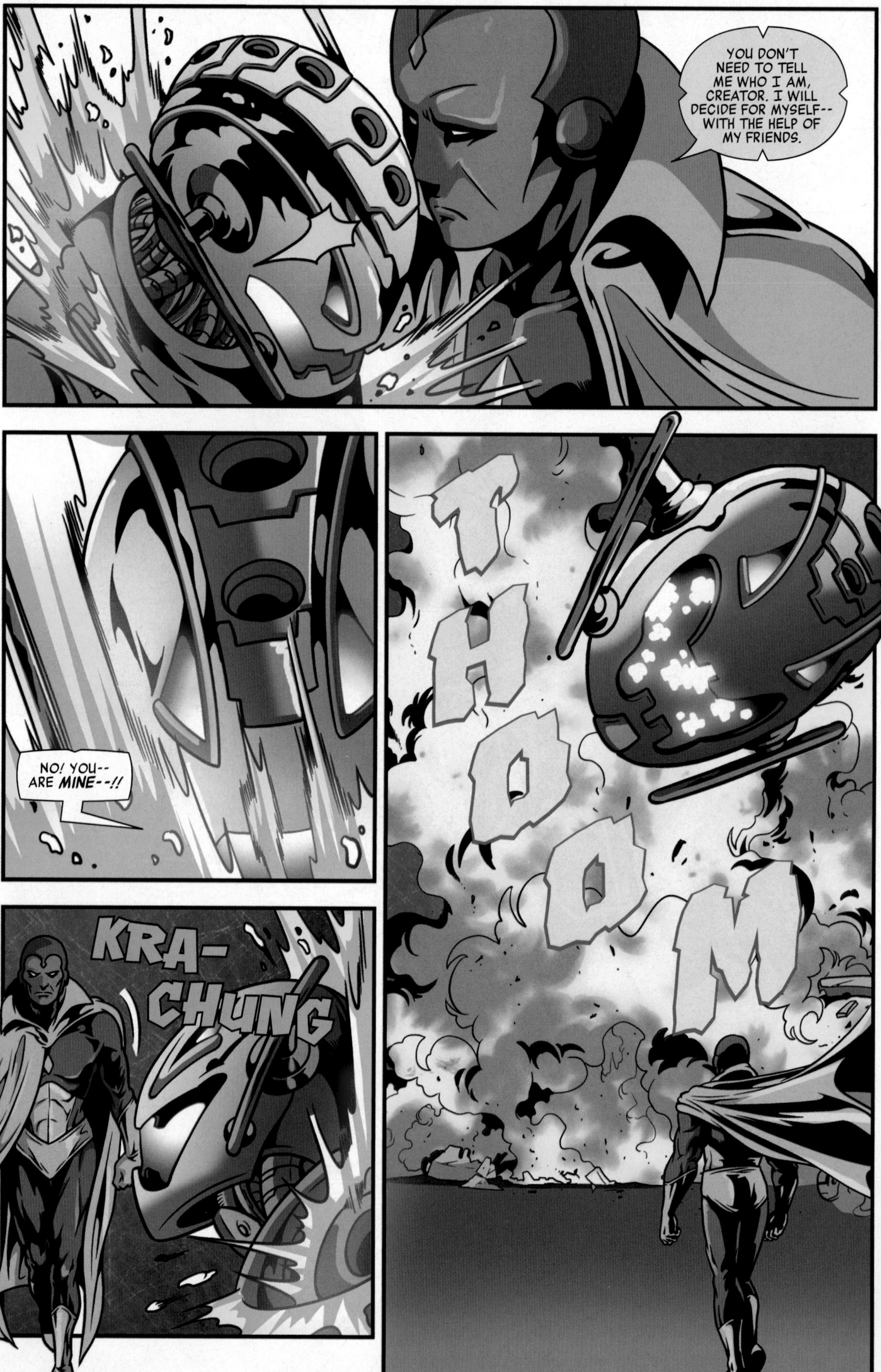

YOU DON'T NEED TO TELL ME WHO I AM, CREATOR. I WILL DECIDE FOR MYSELF-- WITH THE HELP OF MY FRIENDS.
NO! YOU-- ARE MINE--!!
THOOOM
KRA-CHUNG

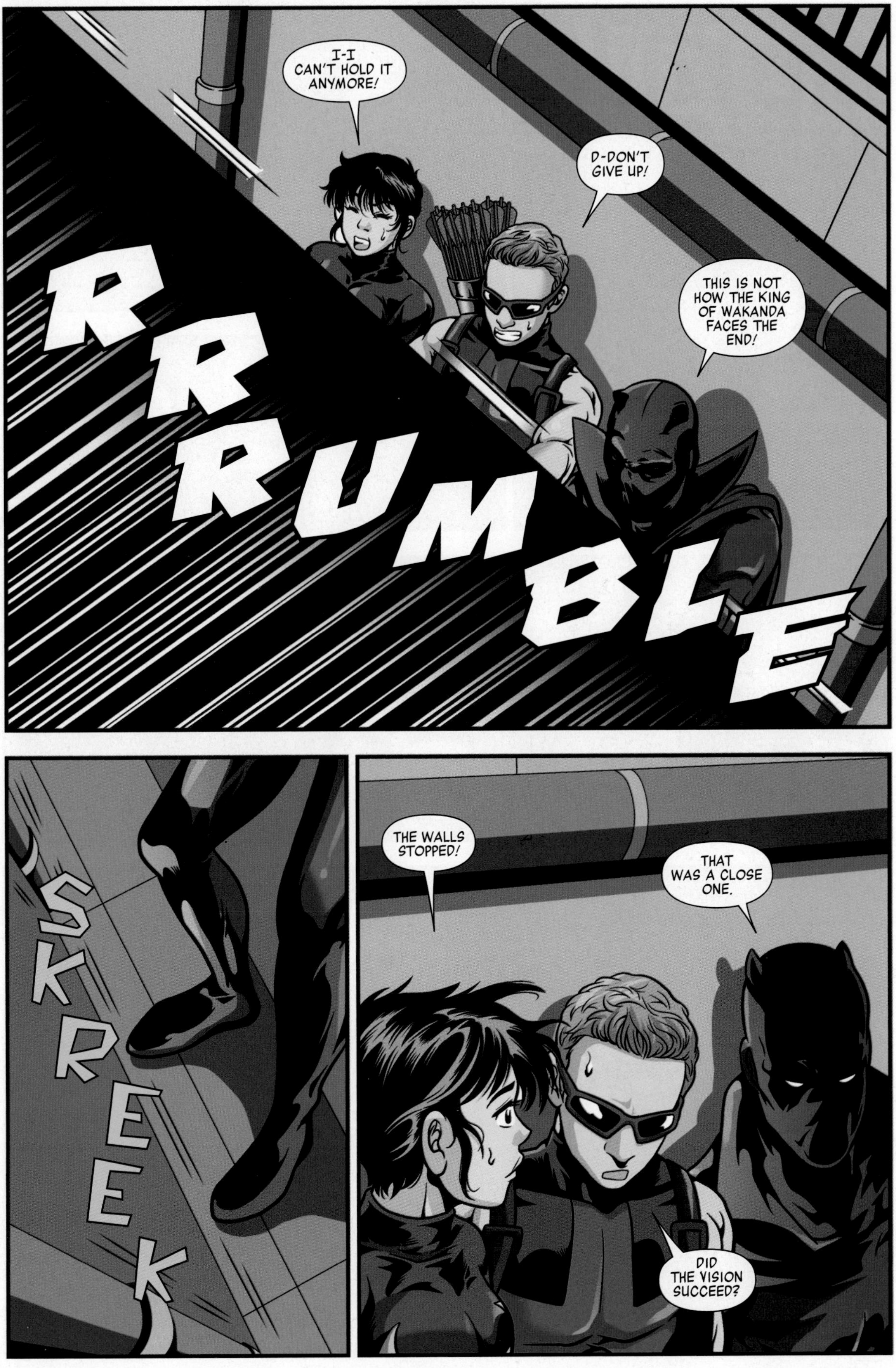
I-I CAN'T HOLD IT ANYMORE!
D-DON'T GIVE UP!
THIS IS NOT HOW THE KING OF WAKANDA FACES THE END!
RRRUMBLE
SKREEK
THE WALLS STOPPED!
THAT WAS A CLOSE ONE.
DID THE VISION SUCCEED?

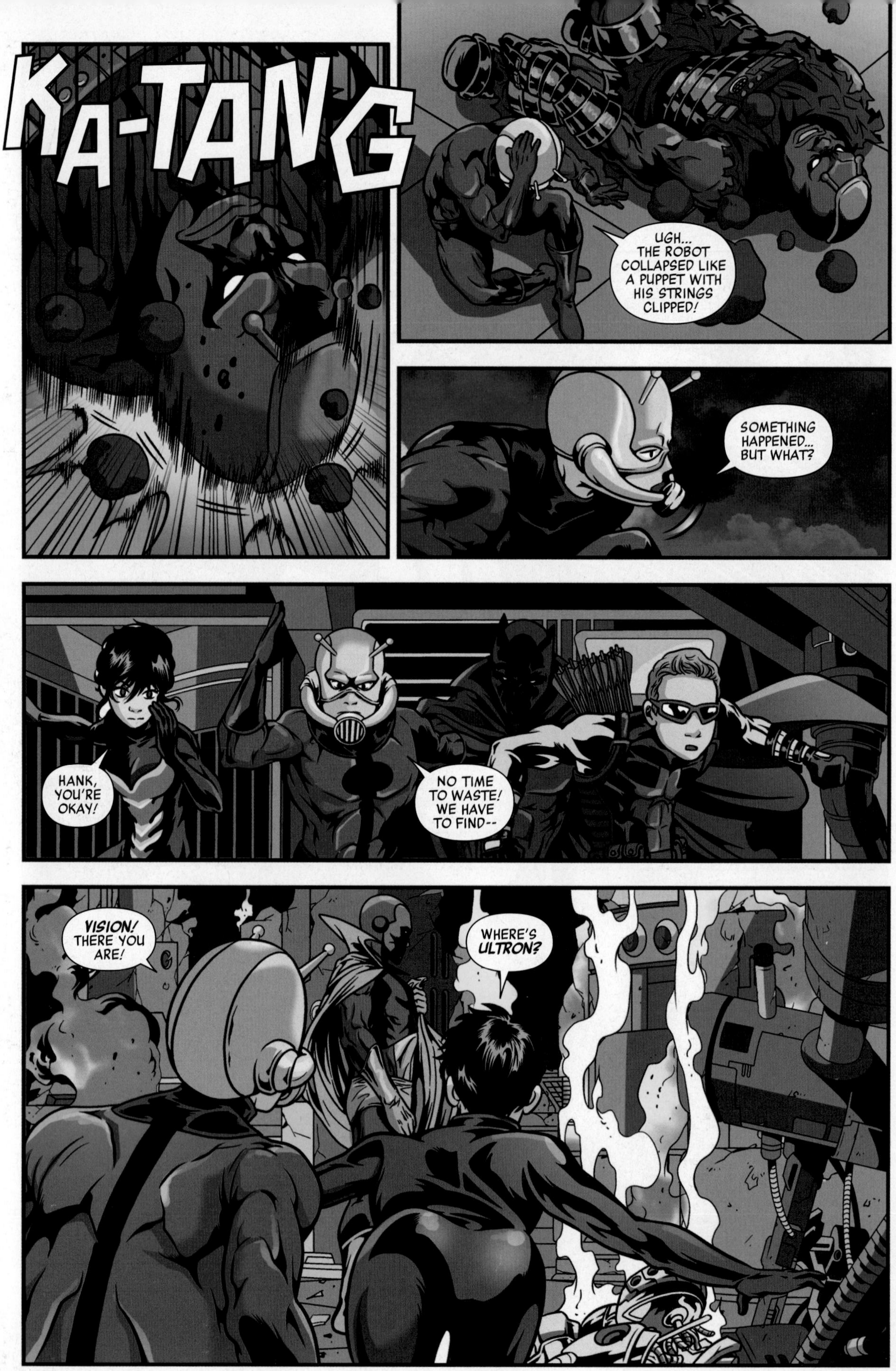
KA-TANG
UGH... THE ROBOT COLLAPSED LIKE A PUPPET WITH HIS STRINGS CLIPPED!
SOMETHING HAPPENED... BUT WHAT?
HANK, YOU'RE OKAY!
NO TIME TO WASTE! WE HAVE TO FIND--
VISION! THERE YOU ARE!
WHERE'S ULTRON?

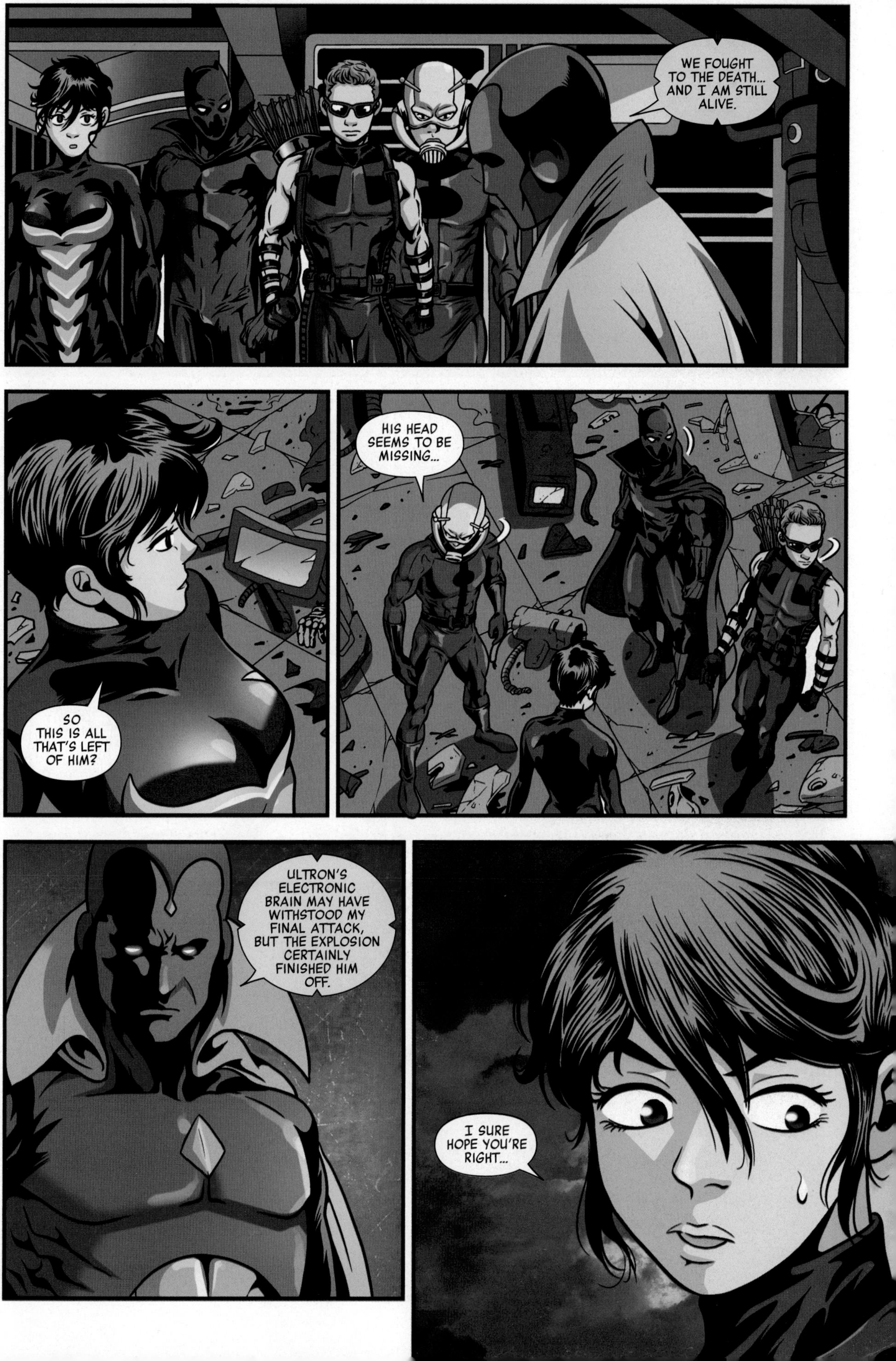
WE FOUGHT TO THE DEATH... AND I AM STILL ALIVE.
SO THIS IS ALL THAT'S LEFT OF HIM?
HIS HEAD SEEMS TO BE MISSING...
ULTRON'S ELECTRONIC BRAIN MAY HAVE WITHSTOOD MY FINAL ATTACK, BUT THE EXPLOSION CERTAINLY FINISHED HIM OFF.
I SURE HOPE YOU'RE RIGHT...

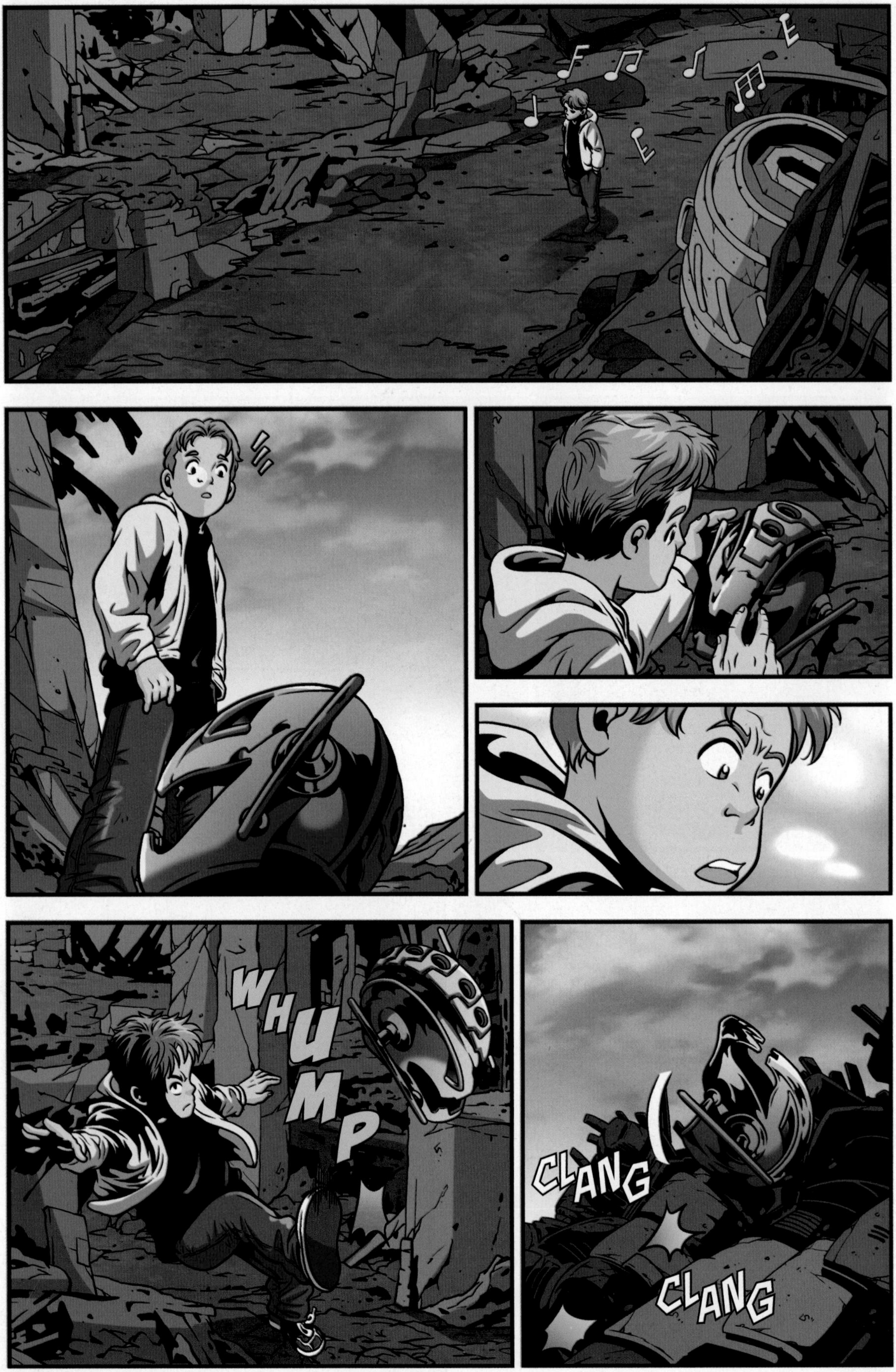
WHUMP
CLANG
CLANG

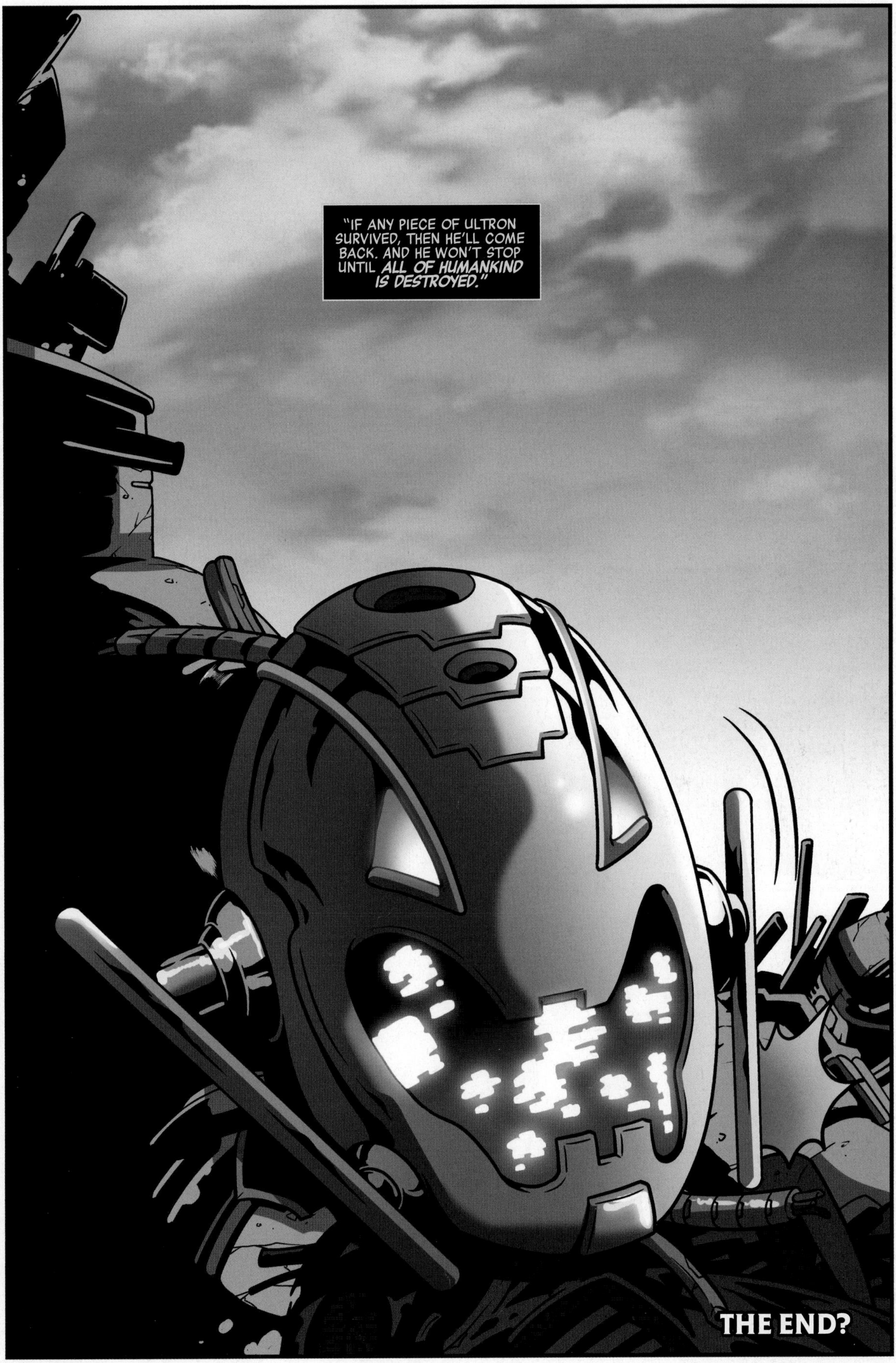
"IF ANY PIECE OF ULTRON SURVIVED, THEN HE'LL COME BACK. AND HE WON'T STOP UNTIL ALL OF HUMANKIND IS DESTROYED."
THE END?

CREATOR PROCESS

TRANSLATOR JI EUN PARK

I am pleased with the publication of the Korean adaptation of the Avengers comics, which are loved throughout the world. Though I had difficulties with some of the older expressions in the original work that aren't used much nowadays, I did my best to show the characteristics of the distinctive characters and the delicate emotional lines as much as possible. It was a wonderful experience for me to read the new English script based on my translation.

WRITER SI YEON PARK

I was happy to join this project, as I myself am a long-time fan of the Avengers, and I have worked with the artist (Woo Bin Choi) several times. I wanted to preserve Marvel's original sentiments, while making the story fun and accessible for Korean readers. The Avengers comics are exciting stories about heroes, and I hope this is the start of a new kind of comic series.

ARTIST WOO BIN CHOI

You wouldn't think so, but it can actually be a more difficult and laborious process to adapt a comic than it is to create an original, especially when you're working with foreign characters. But I was proud to work with Marvel, especially to bring these classic issues to a worldwide audience. This book was my chance to become a different kind of fan of Marvel super heroes. I hope readers have fun!

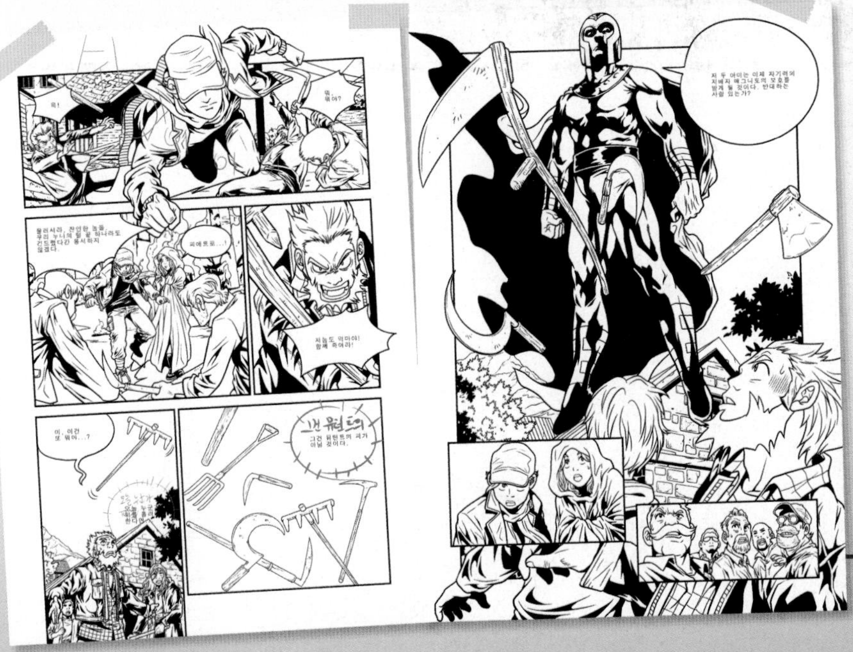

INKER MIN JU LEE

To ink my colleagues' work, I draw distinct black lines around the sketched figures and shape the backgrounds. I wanted to pay particular attention to the characters' appearance and personalities, and the backgrounds. I'm delighted to be part of the group creating this new Avengers comic, and hope to make better and better work.

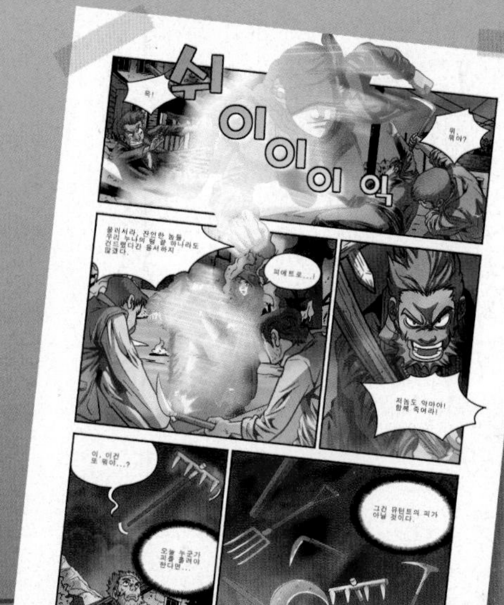

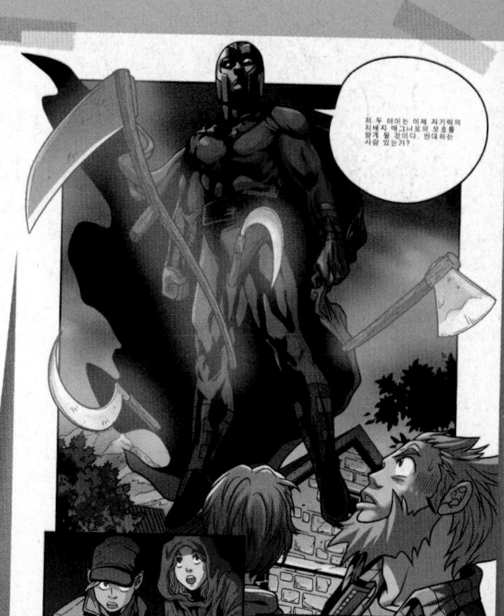

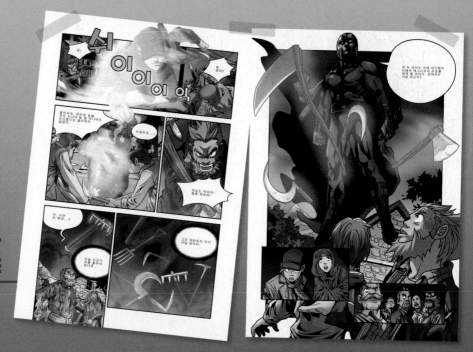

COLORIST JAE WOONG LEE

For the Avengers, color is very important. The original comics used darker, denser colors, so to adapt them for our younger audience, we made the colors brighter and more cheerful. At the same time, each character is symbolized by a specific color, so we tried to respect the original intentions, as well. I was proud to participate in the re-creation of these classic issues.